CURRICULUM: QUEST FOR RELEVANCE

edited by
William Van Til
Indiana State University

HOUGHTON MIFFLIN COMPANY · BOSTON
New York · Atlanta · Geneva, Ill. · Dallas · Palo Alto

FOR A PERSON AND A GROUP—
BEE, MY WIFE, AND THE MEMBERS OF THE ASSOCIATION FOR SUPERVISION AND CURRICULUM DEVELOPMENT, MY CURRICULUM ORGANIZATION. THEY BELIEVE IN THE IMPORTANCE OF PEOPLE.

Preface

Curriculum: Quest for Relevance is, I believe, a curriculum book with a difference: its contents focus on today and tomorrow, rather than on yesterday. The book is divided into three parts which focus on current criticisms of the curriculum, curriculum for the 1970s and curriculum for the future. Part One reports the trenchant views of today's compassionate critics, the critics of compulsory education, the high school radical critics and the advocates of affective education. Part Two presents the views of contemporary educational leaders on curriculum for the 1970s; this section first appeared as the special March 1970 curriculum issue of *Kappan*, the Phi Delta Kappa journal. Part Three is tomorrow-oriented, and offers some of the most promising educational futurist thinking yet available in article and pamphlet form.

Curriculum: Quest for Relevance is designed for use in a variety of curriculum courses, such as curriculum development, curriculum theory and practice, elementary curriculum and secondary curriculum. Because of its present–future orientation, some educators may use it as the basic text for a course; others may find it a useful supplement to books oriented more toward past events. *Curriculum: Quest for Relevance* should be especially helpful in new teacher orientation and in-service programs for experienced teachers.

My thanks go, above all, to those whose writings appear in this volume and to their publishers.

My thanks, too, to the students in my doctoral seminars on curriculum at Indiana State University. Theodore Kowalski, John S. Burd, Martha K. Hedley, O. Pierre Lee, Vera Channels, James C. Campbell, Sister Joanne Golding and Betty Jean Searcy proposed alternative outlines for the book; they read and appraised many articles and books on curriculum—past, present and future—and recommended the best for consideration. Rita Schrenker, Ronald M. Leathers, Edwin A. Gray and David N. Kelsey proposed alternative outlines, read widely on topics selected, identified major issues and recommended authors for consideration as possible contributors to the issue of *Kappan* which became Part Two of this anthology. I am, of course, responsible for all decisions concerning the organization and selection of contributors; I wrote all the part introductions and selection headnotes.

My thanks to my research assistant at Indiana State University, Marvin Kelly, who is now Assistant Professor of Education at the University of South Florida, and to my secretaries and additional typist, Gail Rudd, Judy Braden and Mitzi Williams.

Thanks to William MacDonald, my editor at Houghton Mifflin. Thanks to Ann Lebowitz for copy editing.

Thanks to the Association for Supervision and Curriculum Development, the John Dewey Society and the National Society of College Teachers of Education for entrusting their presidencies to me during the 1960s and teaching me much in the process.

And always thanks for being granted Bee.

WILLIAM VAN TIL

Contents

Preface   v

Part One: Current Criticisms of the Curriculum   1

A. The Compassionate Critics   9

1. Prologue: Is Progressive Education Obsolete?
   William Van Til   9
2. How Children Fail
   John Holt   17
3. The Way It Spozed to Be
   James Herndon   23
4. 36 Children
   Herbert Kohl   29
5. Death at an Early Age
   Jonathan Kozol   40
6. Our Children Are Dying
   Nat Hentoff   49
7. The Lives of Children
   George Dennison   53
8. Epilogue: The Key Word Is Relevance
   William Van Til   62
9. Epilogue: Crisis in the Classroom
   Charles E. Silberman   66

B. The Critics of Compulsory Education   73

10. Freedom and Learning: The Need for Choice
    Paul Goodman   73
11. Educating **Contra Naturam**
    Theodore Roszak   79

C. Criticism by the High School Radicals   93

12. The High School Revolutionaries
    Marc Libarle and Tom Seligson   93
13. Our Time Is Now
    John Birmingham   101

D. Advocates of Affective Education 107

14. The Invisible Curriculum
    Hanne Lane Hicks 107
15. Teaching the Young to Love
    Jack R. Frymier 109
16. Reach, Touch, and Teach
    Terry Borton 113

Part Two: Curriculum for the 1970s 123

A. An Approach to Curriculum 129

17. A Cross-Cutting Approach to the Curriculum: The Moving Wheel
    Theodore Brameld 129
18. How Fare the Disciplines?
    Arthur W. Foshay 134
19. The Science Curriculum: Unfinished Business for an Unfinished Country
    R. Thomas Tanner 141
20. Relevance and the Curriculum
    Lawrence E. Metcalf and Maurice P. Hunt 148

B. Black Studies 156

21. The Question of Black Studies
    Charles V. Hamilton 156
22. Black Studies and Sound Scholarship
    Stephen J. Wright 162

C. The Work of the Schools 169

23. Priorities in Change Efforts
    Fred T. Wilhelms 169
24. Curriculum for the Disadvantaged
    Robert J. Havighurst 175
25. 'Alternative Schools': Challenge to Traditional Education?
    Donald W. Robinson 181

D. Humanism and Instructional Technology 185

26. A Humanist's Approach
    Joseph Wood Krutch 185
27. Instructional Technology and the Curriculum
    David Engler 190

E. Changing the Curriculum 195

28. The Multiple Forces Affecting Curriculum Change
    Ronald C. Doll 195
29. Who Changes the Curriculum and How?
    Muriel Crosby 201

Contents

F. Looking to the Future   211

30. A Curriculum Continuum: Possible Trends in the 70's   211
   Harold G. Shane

Part Three: Curriculum for the Future   219

A. Alternative Futures   225

31. Prologue: The Temper of the Times   225
   William Van Til
32. Learning and Teaching in the Future   229
   John I. Goodlad
33. Youth Revolt: The Future Is Now   234
   Margaret Mead
34. Interpersonal Relationships: U.S.A. 2000   242
   Carl R. Rogers
35. Future Shock and the Curriculum   249
   Harold G. Shane
36. Future-Planning and the Curriculum   258
   Harold G. Shane and June Grant Shane

B. The Technological Revolution and the Future   270

37. Computer Technology and the Future of Education   270
   Patrick Suppes
38. The IMPENDING Instruction Revolution   277
   Harold E. Mitzel
39. The Knowledge Machine   288
   Elizabeth C. Wilson
40. Educational Technology and Professional Practice   298
   William Van Til

C. Aspects of the Curriculum of the Future   306

41. Science Education in 1991   306
   Leopold E. Klopfer
42. Teaching and Learning Mathematics: 1991   320
   Max S. Bell
43. Teaching of Social Sciences, 1991   330
   Mark M. Krug
44. Foreign Language Teaching in 1975: How Will It Be Different?   338
   Howard Lee Nostrand
45. Cultural Change and the Curriculum: 1970–2000 A.D.   344
   June Grant Shane and Harold G. Shane
46. Epilogue: The Year 2000: Teacher Education   358
   William Van Til

PART ONE

Contemporary Criticisms
of the Curriculum

The tides of dissatisfaction run high in America today. For some, "the way it is" means war, overpopulation, environmental pollution, racial discrimination, slums, inadequate schools, and unresponsive government. For others, "the way things are today" means the breakdown of law and order, crime in the streets, riots and burnings, dirty movies and obscene books, urban congestion, and governmental neglect of whites with European backgrounds. To many Americans of varying backgrounds, it seems that something has gone wrong with the quality of life for too many people in contemporary America. Spectacular manifestations of dissatisfaction include the hippy culture, black-white confrontations, revolutionary bombings, widespread responsiveness to patriotic appeals, and hardhat flag-waving. The halls of government ring with angry words. No one seems able to "bring us together."

Today the major criticisms of the American school curriculum stem from those dissatisfied with "the way it is." They regard the standard curriculum as sterile, lifeless, coercive, indifferent to the actual lives of children and youth, and blind to the problems of the times. The failure of American education is reported under such titles as The Way It Spozed To Be, How Children Fail, Compulsory Mis-Education, Educating Contra Naturam, The Underachieving School, The Vanishing Adolescent, The High School Revolutionaries, and Growing Up Absurd. The smell of death pervades some titles: Our Children Are Dying, Murder in the Classroom, Death at an Early Age.

1

Part One of this anthology is primarily devoted to the views of authors dissatisfied with the American school curriculum today. (We must leave to some future anthologist the task of reporting conservative counter-criticisms of the curriculum, should such a movement develop among the current critics of, for instance, sex education programs and sensitivity training.)

The history of American education demonstrates that waves of criticism of the school curriculum invariably accompany tides of dissatisfaction with the existing social order. For instance, historian R. Freeman Butts has cogently demonstrated that during the eighteenth and nineteenth centuries, as Americans rejected aristocracy in favor of an emerging democracy, the curriculum of American schools moved from elitist programs toward universal public education. In the late nineteenth and early twentieth centuries, as social problems again changed, the traditional curriculum was challenged by the progressive critics, as historian Lawrence A. Cremin has demonstrated in The Transformation of the School (New York: Alfred A. Knopf, 1961).

The same relationship has prevailed in recent decades. In the early 1950s the public school curriculum was repeatedly assailed as socialistic, communistic, atheistic, and unpatriotic by right-wing individuals and reactionary forces. This assault took place while Senator Joseph McCarthy was charging subversion in governmental, intellectual, and even military circles, a period termed the "era of McCarthyism." Many educators remained silent but some responded at substantial risk to their own careers. Defenses of American education were difficult to mount in the climate of our times. (Should an honor roll of the defenders of education against the unwarranted criticism of the early 1950s ever be compiled, it should include such names as Harold Benjamin, Willard Goslin, Virgil Rogers, Richard Barnes Kennan, Ernest Melby, Robert A. Skaife, William H. Burton, and others.)

In the middle and later 1950s the major criticisms of the school curriculum came from supporters of academic education. Carefully distinguishing themselves from the right-wing reactionaries and reiterating that they were not "enemies of the schools," the spokesmen for academic programs assailed progressive education. They opposed the progressive educators' emphasis upon the importance of the individual learner, interdisciplinary education, problem-centered instruction, and curricular content related to the individual's life experiences. (Ironically, the viewpoint of yesterday's academic critics is precisely the opposite of that expressed by today's critics of "the way it is." The educational views of historian Arthur E. Bestor and Admiral Hyman G. Rickover are antithetical to the opinions of John Holt, Herbert Kohl, Jonathan Kozol, George Dennison, and others among today's critics of the schools.)

The academic critics reflected a dissatisfaction with the schools which grew out of attitudes widespread in the America of the mid-Fifties. The cold war with the Soviet Union was at its most frigid. American fears were

2

mounting as to the ability of American science and technology to compete with the Russians. Calls for manpower trained in science and mathematics were sounded. With the launching of the Russian Sputnik in 1957, American social hysteria increased, and the schools proved to be a handy scapegoat. Magazines called for the closing of the "carnival" in the schools; intellectual leaders who had not been in an elementary or secondary school since their own graduations loftily condemned the schools for lack of academic rigor. The appropriately-titled National Defense Education Act followed swiftly in 1958. Projects in the separate academic disciplines proliferated; heavy emphasis was placed on the fields singled out for favor in the National Defense Education Act: science, mathematics, modern languages, and guidance. The schools struggled to adapt to the new dispensation. Once again, dissatisfaction with the social order created and sanctioned criticisms of the curriculum of American schools.

In the early 1960s, a proposal fostered by Jerome Bruner's The Process of Education (Cambridge, Mass.: Harvard University Press, 1960) relating to the structure of the disciplines was the talk of educational circles. The "disciplines proposal" stressed that each of the scholarly disciplines has an innate structure or logic, which can provide a means of teaching that subject on any level in a meaningful and rigorous way; the function of instruction, according to Bruner, was to introduce the student to the several modes of inquiry used in the disciplines. Concepts, relationships, and principles were stressed in curriculum development. By the 1960s, substantial government and foundation funds were invested in various projects conceived along these lines. The disciplines proposal supplied an ideology which unified and solidified the otherwise disparate and even competitive approaches of projects in the various subject fields.

By the late 1960s some grim social realities had taken precedence in the public mind over the cold war, competition with the Russians, scientific expertise, and the like. America was engaged in a frustrating hot war in Vietnam. The nation was confronted by racial antagonism at home. People were worried about disadvantaged Americans who could find no place in the economy, and alienated young people who repudiated American society. Social priorities changed. In an era of black dissent which affected all institutions in American society, of student dissent which began in the colleges and spread into the high schools, of alienation and disillusion, and of real and palpable survival-threatening problems, dissatisfaction permeated the social order. And with it came new criticisms and new demands upon the curriculum of American schools.

Part One focuses on this current criticism. The interrelationships among the ideas of the new critics will be discussed in the remainder of this introduction. Excerpts from the writings of the current critics will follow, constituting Part One of this anthology.

Part One is prefaced by an article by the editor, written in the early 1960s to express a conviction that the issues raised by progressive educators were not obsolete, though the attention of curriculum workers seemed to have turned elsewhere. The editor concluded:

> The central questions posed and the relevant contributions toward workable answers for our times made by such interpreters of the progressive movement in education are not obsolete. They must and will persist. In time, they will be embodied in the form of new proposals for modern education, new syntheses which build upon predecessors, as is common in the world of ideas. The overanxious gravediggers, and those who currently give them comfort, will discover as this twentieth century rolls along that what they have mistaken for a corpse is indeed very much alive.

This contention was supported during the later Sixties by the emergence of a school of thought still so new that no satisfactory name has yet been coined for it. The young teachers who are its spokesmen have been called "the romantic critics," "the radical critics," and other names which similarly miss the mark. In this book they will be called "the compassionate critics," for their common characteristic seems to be a sympathetic concern for the welfare of children and youth. Many of them began as formal teachers, but soon recognized the inanity and inappropriateness of the traditional curriculum for the situations in which they found themselves, and began instead to focus upon children and youth.

The first of the compassionate critics to be heard (and the first from whom we present a selection) was John Holt. In How Children Fail, Holt repeatedly illustrates from his own private-school teaching experience how children's fears of failing contribute to actual failure. The notion of the curriculum as an essential body of knowledge seems to Holt to contribute to this self-fulfilling prophecy of expected failure and actual failure. He calls for schools in which each child would satisfy his curiosity, develop his abilities, and pursue his interests in his own way. Thus, Holt aligns himself with a child-centered approach to education.

Meanwhile James Herndon (from whom we next excerpt) was reporting, first in Harper's magazine in 1965 and later in The Way It Spozed to Be, his experiences teaching in a ghetto school in an unnamed West Coast metropolis. In his account of his defeats, Herndon writes with sympathy and wry "black humor" of the lives of teachers and students in a 98% Negro urban school. For both, nothing is ever "the way it spozed to be." The curriculum is not merely ineffectual, it is positively harmful. He ends his book on a note of despair: "But frankly, I have almost no hope that there will be any significant change in the way we educate our children — for that, after all, would involve liberty, the last thing we may soon expect — and so I have thought mainly to describe one time for you, parents, kids, readers, the way it is."

Herbert Kohl is a vital, sensitive, and amazingly ingenious teacher. Faced with 36 sixth-grade black children in East Harlem, Kohl first tried to retain the standard curriculum. But the burden of irrelevance was too heavy; he could not communicate with his children. So, a bit at a time, he abandoned the formal curriculum in favor of another kind of education, which first took place in ten-minute "breaks." An analysis of words the children actually used developed into a study of language and myths, and the children began writing about their own lives. Kohl's Thirty-Six Children is an exciting story of success in creating a curriculum out of the teacher's imagination and the children's experience. Yet it has bitter overtones, such as Kohl's description of his attempt to learn what had happened to his children years later: "I stopped searching, don't want to know the full extent of misery and tragedy of the children's present lives. Recently one of the kids told me: 'Mr. Kohl, one good year isn't enough. . . .' "

In New York City, Herbert Kohl and his 36 children successfully created a curriculum and got away with it. In Boston, Jonathan Kozol, a substitute teacher with a year-long assignment in a fourth-grade class for black children, tried to develop a curriculum related to students' lives and to establish some genuine contacts with children — and was fired by school officials for deviation from the established fourth-grade course of study. Of all of the compassionate critics, Kozol is the most politically sensitive, probably because of his extensive encounters with the school authorities. He deals not only with the inadequacies of the curriculum for black children but also with the broader school and societal situation which prompted the title of his book: Death at an Early Age: The Destruction of the Hearts and Minds of Negro Children in the Boston Public Schools. Kozol is an earnest and angry young man, and after reading his description of his experiences, the reader will understand why.

If the authorities who represent a bungling and bigoted society are the villains of Death at an Early Age, a school administrator is the hero of Our Children Are Dying. Nat Hentoff, a journalist, reports on a sensitive and tough-minded school principal, Elliott Shapiro of P.S. 119 in New York City. Though best known for his struggle to call to official attention the fact that rats were rife throughout his decrepit building, Shapiro is also a curriculum innovator. He emphasizes both better approaches to teaching basic skills and such new content as American and African black history and culture. Hentoff's account of Shapiro's sensitivity in dealing with children and staff demonstrate that compassion need not be the monopoly of young teachers.

George Dennison in The Lives of Children tells of his experiences with 23 children and three full-time teachers at the First Street School, a "mini-school" in New York City. Dennison is a man of patience, courage, and integrity. He held to his convictions about freedom and learning under adverse conditions, including physical attacks. His ruthlessly realistic depiction of the obscenity and violence which marked the children's relationships to their environment is unsurpassed in the literature of the compassionate critics. The quoted excerpts can only partially convey the depth of the problems which characterize the lives of his children. Unlike most of the compassionate criticis, Dennison recognizes his intellectual debt to precedent. Some of his fellow critics, overly impressed with the novelty of their approaches, misinterpret or deprecate their heritage from the child-centered wing of the progressive education movement. In general, the compassionate critics are long on wisdom about children and short on knowledge of the educational leaders who preceded their own generation. Dennison, however, draws from Dewey and Tolstoy, in addition to A. S. Neill and Paul Goodman.

As an epilogue to the compassionate critics, the editor of this volume, who believes that current critics, like the child-centered progressives, have some but not all of the answers, appends a comment. In "The Key Word Is Relevance," which appeared in Today's Education, the NEA journal, the editor again reiterates his conviction that, if educators are to achieve relevance, there can be no substitute for knowing the learner as an individual. But neither is there a substitute for illuminating the social realities which characterize the total environment, or for a philosophy which gives direction to the educational enterprise by clarifying values through the use of the method of intelligence. Some of the compassionate critics and their supporters may scorn these additional concerns as pretentious, unattainable, or even unnecessary, but the editor regards them as essential to meaningful education.

An additional epilogue to the writings of the compassionate critics comes from the most-discussed book of 1970, Charles E. Silberman's Crisis in the Classroom, the report of a 3½-year study by the Carnegie Corporation. In the excerpts selected from his insightful and extremely provocative book, Silberman stresses the importance of purposes and accounts for the failure of the recent movement to reform the curriculum through reconstructing separate subject disciplines. More than eight years after the editor asked "Is Progressive Education Obsolete?" and answered that it is not, Silberman too stresses the importance of the questions raised by the leaders of the progressive movement.

Another kind of probing criticism of education comes from those who challenge the social and educational axiom of the desirability of compulsory education, terming it, in Paul Goodman's ringing phrase, "compulsory miseducation." They call for "free choice, with no processing whatever," and attempt to refute the assumptions upon which the American system of free universal public education is based. To them, compulsory education is a tool used by the Establishment to manipulate children into conformity and acceptance of a sick society.

The first of the critics of compulsory education quoted is Paul Goodman, a persistent and provocative controversialist in American social thought. Goodman has been an effective gadfly since the publication of *Growing Up Absurd* (New York: Random House, 1947) and is an educational hero to the younger generation. He is frequently invited by students to lecture on college campuses. He combines his "conservative anarchism" with the compassionate critics' deep concern for the lives of children. Our sample of his dissenting views, entitled "Freedom and Learning: The Need For Choice," is reprinted from Saturday Review.

Another opponent of required schooling, as yet less well known to professional educators, is the historian Theodore Roszak. Roszak is a spokesman for the "counter-culture," a view of the world which is sharply critical of Establishment ways and strongly supportive of their repudiation by a variety of dissenting forces. Taking as his point of departure Leo Tolstoy's views on education, he inveighs against an educational system which seems to him contrary to the nature of man. Roszak has come to the attention of contemporary educators particularly through his television address to the Association for Supervision and Curriculum Development in 1970, an expanded version of which is reproduced here.

To some, the critics of compulsory education have put their fingers on the tragic flaw in the educational process. To others, critics of compulsory education seem to be burning down the railroad station rather than rebuilding it while the trains keep running or, in the lighter words of the folk saying, throwing out the baby with the bath.

From still another quarter comes vigorous and unsparing criticism of elementary and secondary school education. The high school radicals have experienced and observed contemporary American education as a ghastly failure verging on farce. Representatives of junior and senior high school radical students speak out in The High School Revolutionaries, a collection edited by Marc Libarle and Tom Seligson, two young men who have taught in New York City public schools. The abuses and grievances which the high school students allege are various — and they include the curriculum. Representative excerpts from the writings of two white students in Eastern suburban schools, a black student from a metropolitan ghetto, and a white girl from a small city, are reprinted here. They stress boredom, irrelevance, and evasion of social realities as characteristic of the school curriculums they know best.

A surprisingly mature and insightful piece of writing and editing comes from then seventeen-year-old John Birmingham, one of the founders of the high school underground press, in Our Time Is Now (New York: Frederick A. Praeger, 1970). His book is essentially a compilation of material from underground newspapers of varying degrees of quality and penetration. Birmingham is just as earnest and intent as his contemporaries who contribute to The High School Revolutionaries. But he apparently differs from them in believing that wisdom does not necessarily reside exclusively in those under thirty. He sees promise not only in reforms fostered by the students themselves, such as independent study, but even in changes instigated by school administrations. Young Birmingham may be heard from again in American life.

Another form of criticism comes from educators working within the existing system. The supporters of education of the emotions are not revolutionaries; they call attention to an aspect of learning which they think has been grossly undervalued. They believe that affective education is needed in American schools and that cognitive learning should not be granted the dominance called for by most of the advocates of study of the disciplines (with the notable exception of the psychologically-oriented Jerome Bruner).

Hanne Lane Hicks in a brief, well-written plea supports "an invisible curriculum" of concern, respect, enjoyment, and care.

Jack R. Frymier devotes an issue of the magazine he edits to the need for teaching young people to love and editorializes on the need for affective education. Frymier is himself a capable worker in fields related to cognition. Yet it seems to him that the failure of the schools basically involves love and hate.

Terry Borton draws upon his experience in the Philadelphia public schools, one of the few large school systems concerned with affective education, for illustrations of his ideas on emotion-related education in "Reach, Touch, and Teach." His illustrations help the teacher to see possible tangible approaches to this neglected area in the American curriculum.

What follows, then, is representative of the latest criticism of the American school curriculum. The critics vary in the degree of their penetration and analytic power; they range, as well, from moderate to revolutionary. They may be more powerful in their analysis of what is wrong than persuasive in their proposals of what to do about it. But they are all vigorous, forceful, and sometimes eloquent. The contemporary critics are well worth reading in full; excerpts alone cannot do full justice to them and their ideas. They have much to say and they are in dead earnest.

A. The Compassionate Critics

1

Prologue: Is Progressive Education Obsolete?

William Van Til

In 1962, the editor of this anthology contended in a Saturday Review *article that the questions raised by such progressive educators as John Dewey, William Heard Kilpatrick, George Counts and Boyd H. Bode were inescapable and that their contributions to workable answers must be taken into account by American education. Consequently, he held, progressive education is not obsolete.*

The article appeared during a period when curriculum leaders seemed absorbed with technology, organizational innovation, and the structure of the disciplines proposal. However, since publication, this article has been reprinted in more than a dozen anthologies on contemporary education. Apparently it struck a sensitive nerve.

Is progressive education outmoded? One's first impulse is to say "yes." Who today, among the voices being heard on education, is talking about the concerns which characterized many leaders of education during the first half of the twentieth century? Specifically, who today is talking about the ideas which occupied John Dewey, George Counts, Boyd H. Bode, and William Heard Kilpatrick, those symbols of the intellectual leadership of the "new education," symbols of the varied versions of the progressive movement in education? Practically nobody, at least nobody who is being heard widely.

Instead, American education in the early 1960s is engrossed with the application of technology to education, with competing new proposals for organization of the school program, and with stress on reconstruction of academic disciplines. The mass media foster the interest in technology, organization, and disciplines. If an educator tries to be heard on more fundamental aspects, he often encounters the silent treatment.

The Industrial Revolution has finally reached education. As a result,

William Van Til, "Is Progressive Education Obsolete?", *Saturday Review*, February 17, 1962, 56–57, 82–84. Copyright 1962 Saturday Review, Inc.

matters of technology have virtually become table talk in education today. In professional discussions and in the mass media reporting we hear constantly about educational television, language laboratories, courses on film, and programmed learning through teaching machines.

A second stress in today's education emphasizes organization of the school program. Proposals are varied and often conflicting. They include such organizational proposals as team teaching, the dual progress plan, the nongraded school, and increasing the course requirements within the existing Carnegie unit structure.

Currently, a third stress is the new interest in the academic disciplines. In part, the emphasis is upon updating knowledge through efforts by specialists in the disciplines. The work of such groups as the Physical Science Study Committee and the varied mathematics programs at Yale, Maryland, and Illinois are watched intently. Science, mathematics, and foreign languages ride high as the favored fields of the national government, which has become a significant curriculum maker on the elementary and high school levels. The fields of English and physical education make frantic and failing attempts to latch onto the benefits of the National Defense Education Act; leadership in reconstruction of the curriculum in these fields has been assumed by the College Entrance Examination Board and by a football coach, respectively. There are indications that Commissioner McMurrin intends to attempt to do for the arts as well as for English what post-Sputnik apprehension did for the sciences. Rumors, alarms, and confusions surround the status of the social studies. The phrase "structures of the disciplines" is being bandied about, with none too clear a definition emerging as yet.

Technology, organization, and the disciplines seem a far cry from the philosophical, social, and psychological ideas that engaged the leaders of the progressive movement in education in the first half of the twentieth century. There appears to have been a change in "fashions in ideas," to use the chilling and accurate phrase Irwin Edman coined for a phenomenon of our times. Consequently, progressive education seems outmoded. Lawrence A. Cremin even consigned it to history in his "The Transformation of the School: Progressivism in American Education, 1876–1957." He began his preface as follows: "The death of the Progressive Education Association in 1955 and the passing of its journal, *Progressive Education*, two years later marked the end of an era in American pedagogy. Yet one would scarcely have known it from the pitifully small group of mourners at both funerals." Martin Mayer recapitulated the Cremin position in his widely read book, "The Schools."

One might readily conclude that progressive education is outmoded save for a stubborn fact. The fact is that the questions raised by the progressive movement in education are not obsolete. They will not die. They cannot be killed. They cannot be exorcised by any voodooism yet known to technology, organization, or the reconstruction of disciplines which remains aloof from these questions.

The basic questions which men like John Dewey, William Heard Kilpatrick, George Counts, and Boyd H. Bode raised are inescapable questions:

What are the aims of education? Upon what foundations should the school program be built? Given such aims and foundations, what should the schools teach? To these probing and fundamental questions, matters of organization and technique, while important, are necessarily subordinate.

The progressive education movement of the first half of the twentieth century, symbolized by Dewey, Kilpatrick, Counts, and Bode, was essentially a quest for workable answers for our times to questions such as these. No one claims that the Holy Grail was found; no one claims that the questioners came up with final, definitive, eternal answers. The "new educators" did not completely agree among themselves on workable answers for our times. But at least the "new educators" asked the right questions.

One wing of the progressive movement sought the answers primarily in the potential of the individual learner. A pioneer in this respect was the man whose ninetieth birthday was celebrated on November 20, 1961 — William Heard Kilpatrick. Many of today's schoolmen will remember Kilpatrick's classes in the Horace Mann Auditorium of Teachers College, Columbia University. Hundreds attended each session, yet the quiet man with the mane of white hair used committees and reports so skillfully that each student found opportunities to speak out and battle over ideas.

The heart of Kilpatrick's first major contribution to education, "The Project Method," was founded on his faith in the potential of the individual learner. In back of the recurrent Kilpatrickian phrases which valued "purposeful activity," "intrinsic motivation," "planning," in back of his opposition to "extrinsic subject matter" which disregarded individuals, in back of his opposition to meaningless rote learning, lay Kilpatrick's belief that clues to significant content can be found within the learner and can be developed fully in collaboration with a mature adult who fosters self-direction and independent thought. The later Kilpatrick increased his stress on the importance of social orientation and the urgency of meeting social problems. But the mark Kilpatrick lastingly left on the progressive movement still derives largely from his faith in the potentiality of the learner when that potentiality is cultivated by skillful and sensitive teachers. To many educators, probably to most, insight into the relationship between the individual and his education was the major contribution of the progressive education which Kilpatrick espoused, though he was concerned for philosophical and social, as well as psychological, foundations. And — mistake it not — the insight derived from Kilpatrick made a massive contribution to education in an era that had lost sight of the importance of the learner and his purposes and potential.

A second wing of the progressive movement set forth answers to the perennial questions of aims, foundations, and content largely in terms of the society which surrounded the schools. George Counts, a battler for socially oriented schools in a democracy, serves as a symbol of this emphasis. To George Counts, for instance, the times cried out for an education realistically geared to the new social order which was emerging. He threw his eloquent challenge to the Progressive Education Association assembled in convention in 1932. He amplified his ideas in the pamphlet "Dare the Schools Build A New Social Order?" and for years educators found themselves forced to face the issues Counts raised. Whether one condemned aspects of his viewpoint as indoctrination and a potential abuse of the method of intelligence, thus classifying it as a new liberal's version of authoritarianism, or whether one hailed it as a realistic recognition of the overpowering importance of social problems, as an indication that the social sciences had come of age, an educator who heard Counts had to take into account stress on society. The role of education with respect to social change and to reform was an imperative and recurrent theme with Counts and his fellow social reconstructionists. The pivotal place of social realities in education could not be forgotten after Counts was heard, even though indoctrination might be repudiated.

George Counts lived his faith. He helped turn back Communist infiltration of teachers' unions. He was a tower of strength in the Liberal Party; he was a candidate for public office and in the vanguard of social movements of his time. He is still active in his retirement.

To others equally immersed in the progressive movement, democratic values were central to all considerations. For instance, to Boyd H. Bode, the Lincoln-like man from Illinois who made his major contribution through Ohio State University, the crucial need was for the clarification of differences between the democratic way of life and the way of its authoritarian competitors. As he saw it, the road out of value confusion led through a remorseless and unremitting use of the method of intelligence in human affairs. To Bode, progressive education was at the crossroads and a child-centered view would never suffice. Nor was indoctrination the road to a better world. He conducted his classes in philosophy of education through the Socratic method and he fostered thought with every heckling, humorous, or trenchant exchange of ideas into day-by-day learning experiences.

I venture for your consideration the bold hypothesis that each of these men touched on part of the whole, that each perceived and particularly stressed an aspect of education which we neglect at our peril, that each succeeded nobly, and, where he failed, failed gallantly in building the "new education." Each asked the right questions; each responded with relevant contributions toward workable answers for our times.

The thinker who came closest to the reconciliation of the individual, society, and philosophical foundations — was the extraordinary John Dewey, whose centennial was celebrated by the John Dewey Society three years ago through meetings in scores of universities across the nation. The word "extraordinary" is used advisedly. During his long lifetime, this incredible man lived a full life as a person, participated in social and civic action, conducted the most famous laboratory school in history, became the father figure of the progressive education movement (and, to shift the analogy, sometimes served as mother hen by reconciling conflicts and even smoothing ruffled feathers in the flock), became a towering figure in philosophy, and, in the process, managed to leave for posterity a legacy of 5,000 pages of articles and 18,000 pages in book form.

Yet even Dewey, prodigious though his endeavors were, never achieved extensive translation of his ideas into a new curriculum. Underbrush in philosophy needed to be cleared. After his Laboratory School experimentation, and after setting forth his pedagogical creed in such books as "The School and Society" and "Democracy and Education," Dewey gave himself to this Herculean labor as he built his philosophy of experimentalism. He constantly reacted to trends and tendencies in progressive education, as he did in his critique "Experience and Education." He made only occasional critical forays into program building. He would be the first to admit, were he alive, that much remained to be done to implement his ideas on what he preferred to term simply "education," rather than "progressive education."

So we turn back to the thinking of representative intellectual leaders of the progressive movement in education, not in any spirit of ancestor worship, but for the inescapable questions they raised and for the insights they contributed toward workable solutions for our times. Cremin says it well in his final paragraphs: "There remained a timelessness about many of the problems the progressives raised and the solutions they proposed. . . . And for all the talk about pedagogical breakthroughs and crash programs, the authentic progressive vision remained strangely pertinent to the problems of mid-century America. Perhaps it only awaited the reformulation and resuscitation that would ultimately derive from a larger research and reform in American life and thought." With these words Cremin partially redeems the strange inconsistency of pointing out brilliantly in early chapters that social currents created progressive education well before the official establishment of a Progressive Education Association, yet conveying the impression in his final chapter that the demise of an organization and a magazine meant the death of progressive education. The fact that ideas live beyond organizations apparently escaped the overanxious gravediggers who gleefully greeted Cremin's book as the definitive obituary for progressive education as a force in American ideas.

The questions raised and many of the tentative answers ventured by the early leaders of progressive education are not dead nor will they die. In time, the sponsors of new educational technology, the advocates of varied forms of educational organization, the proponents of study of the structure of separate disciplines, must face the inescapable questions and consider the possible solutions proposed.

The problem for sponsors and users of programmed learning through teaching machines does not lie in the capacity of the machine to produce positive reinforcement, whether it takes the form of a kind word, a pat on the head, or, indeed, a bottle of Coca-Cola. Given technical ingenuity, a reinforcing reward will be forthcoming. The harder problem for sponsors and users of the teaching machine is whether positive reinforcement will be used to bring nearer George Orwell's "1984" and Aldous Huxley's "Brave New World," or whether programmed learning, using positive reinforcement selectivity and with discrimination, will reduce the skill-drudgery of education and free teachers and students for more humane aspects of learning and human development, such as creativity, the use of reflective thought, and experiences in freedom. Consider, for instance, this quotation from "Walden Two," a Utopia envisioned by the pioneer of teaching machines, B. F. Skinner of Harvard, a Utopia which appears to some of us an authoritarian nightmare world of behavioristic conditioning. T. E. Frazier, spokesman for "Walden Two," says approvingly, "Now that we *know* how positive reinforcement works and why negative doesn't . . . we can be more deliberate, and hence more successful, in our cultural design. We can achieve a sort of control under which the controlled, even though they are following a code much more scrupulously than was ever the case under the old system, nevertheless *feel free*. They are doing what they want to do, not what they are forced to do. That's the source of the tremendous power of positive reinforcement — there's no restraint and no revolt. By a careful cultural design, we control not the final behavior, but the *inclination* to behave — the motives, the desires, the wishes.

"The curious thing is that in that case *the question of freedom never arises.*"

In the light of this quotation we can understand why Aldous Huxley recently reminded us in "Brave New World Revisited" that it may be later than we think. He wrote as his conclusion, "The older dictators fell because they never could supply their subjects with enough bread, enough circuses, enough miracles and mysteries. Nor did they possess a really effective system of mind-manipulation. . . . Under a scientific dictator, education will really work — with the result that most men and women will grow up to love their servitude and will never dream of revolution. There seems to be no good reason why a thoroughly scientific dictatorship should ever be overthrown."

The problem before the sponsors of educational television is not how wide a circle over six states, or indeed a nation, can be reached by a plane flying for Midwest Airborne Television. Nor is it bouncing beams off satellites for global television. Technology will solve those problems. The real problem is whether the device will realize the gloomy prophecy of an old Vanderbilt University professor who once said at a meeting of the American Association of University Professors, "Gentlemen, the time is coming when one Harvard University professor will determine through his history course on television what history is taught in the United States — and even if it's Arthur Schlesinger, Jr., I say the hell with it!" — or whether imaginative educational TV will provide learners with a magic carpet to a wider world of experience made at once more expansive and more closely detailed.

The problem before the sponsors and users of team teaching is not precisely how many students to instruct at any given time in any given space. It is not whether a new magical number combination, proposed for better staff utilization, or some flexible magic of numbers out of Lexington, Massachusetts, will take the place of the former magic number — 25 or 30 in each classroom. Experience and, we hope, genuine controlled experimentation, will supply the answer here. The real problem is whether team teaching actually will improve learning, whether it will evolve toward emphasis on the *interrelationships* of subject matter, whether it can provide sufficient personalized contacts with teachers and sufficient firsthand experiences by students to enable young people to deal with significant problems.

The problem before the sponsors and users of the dual progress plan is not the technical difficulty of introducing specialized science, mathematics, and arts teachers into elementary school organization through the demonstrations at Ossining and Long Beach in New York. The real problem for the sponsors and users of the dual progress plan is recognized by the originator of the plan as whether the dual progress plan will or will not better answer some of Dewey's persistent queries; George Stoddard poses the issue in his new book, "The Dual Progress Plan," which should be read along with the Association for Supervision and Curriculum Development pamphlet, "The Self-Contained Classroom," for differing organizational approaches to possibly compatible goals.

The problem before the liberal arts professors currently reconstructing and updating knowledge in such disciplines as physics, biology, and mathematics is not whether they can cram all of man's new knowledge into separate watertight compartments, which will then be siphoned off during the elementary and high school years. They can't. Even if they could, they would endlessly face true obsolescence, for knowledge swiftly dates and, like fish, won't keep. The real problem, of which some of the reconstructors of disciplines are aware and of which others appear quite unaware, is whether the scholars can identify concepts in their new knowledge which can be made meaningful to children and youth, appropriate to both the general and specialized education needed for living in today's society, crucial in the process of critical thinking and problem solving — or whether their reconstructed and amplified knowledge, however new, will prove to be inert subject matter in Alfred North Whitehead's sense.

The problem for those who are studying the structures of the disciplines may be first to make clear what they mean. Granted that they can and do, the question will face them as to whether their studies of structures of disciplines are to be achieved as culminations built upon the experience of learners, as Dewey recommended. Or will their studies of structures of disciplines be evasions of problems central to general education, formal orientations to content which bear little relationship to how young people live and learn?

One can derive little encouragement for the future of study of the structure of the disciplines from the views of Charles B. Keller, director of the John Hay Fellows Program, who believes "too many social studies teachers have emphasized the creation of good citizens rather than the content and discipline of their subjects." He says, "Attitudes cannot be taught in formal classroom situations. We weaken education — and schools — when we try to do so. What students should do in school is to study subjects and become acquainted with facts and ideas. Subjects as such have disciplines that will help to develop students' minds." Is this the conception of educational aims and psychology of learning which is to characterize the new advocacy of studying the structure of disciplines? Surely this was not the conception of Arthur W. Foshay when, in his presidential address to the Association for Supervision and Curriculum Development in 1961, he advised "that we educators take directly into account the nature of the organized bodies of knowledge, in addition to the nature of the growing child and the nature of our society, as we try to make curriculum decisions."

If their work is to have meaning, rather than to be innovation for unclear purposes, the sponsors and users of the new technology, organization, and approaches to disciplines must come to terms with the questions that engaged the intellectual leadership of the progressive movement in education. Questions of "why" and "what" have necessary precedence over questions of "how" and "when." The inescapable questions relate to the aims of education, the foundations of the program, and what the schools should teach as appropriate content based on such aims and foundations.

Is, then, the progressive movement in education obsolete? I think not. The questions raised by the "new education" are remorseless, inevitable, demanding. The answers provided by the intellectual leaders of the progressive movement were promising beginnings, useful leads, valid foreshadowings.

When considerations of "why" are dodged, we get prescriptions which simply cannot be appraised. One cannot truly evaluate the proposals made in widely read books which are characterized by indifference to aims and purposes in the early chapters and which then constantly smuggle in unanalyzed value assumptions through the remainder of the pages. Two knights entered in the educational jousting show this tendency: both the great and good James B. Conant and the provocative and prancing Martin Mayer.

Conant, for instance, does not set forth aims for education in "The American High School Today." Yet he steadily makes assumptions as to what knowledge is of most worth.

In "Slums and Suburbs," Conant says, "It is after visits to schools like these that I grow impatient with both critics and defenders of public education who ignore the realities of school situations to engage in fruitless debate about educational philosophy, purposes, and the like. These situations call for action, not hair-splitting arguments." Yet "Slums and Suburbs" is permeated with proposals for action which must be based on philosophic assumptions.

In "The Schools," Martin Mayer colorfully rejects all possible formulations of aims. He says, "It is well to rid oneself immediately of this business of 'the aims of education.' Discussions on this subject are among the dullest and most fruitless of human pursuits. Whatever the ideal general 'aims of education' may be, they certainly cannot be accomplished in schools." He then proceeds to lace through his book individualistic approbations and denunciations based on his acceptance of undefined aims.

One of the myths of our times is that the several tendencies which characterized what is broadly termed progressive education prevailed, were fully achieved, and are now being repudiated. This sedulously cultivated myth is incomprehensible. The reality is that progressive education has never been tried on any significant scale.

As the inescapable queries reassert themselves and the tentative proposals of the varied interpretations of progressive education are reconsidered, educators will find it necessary to utilize the insights of Dewey, Bode, Counts, and Kilpatrick. An education which takes into account the individual, his society, and his values — an education which builds upon the soundest possible scholarship derivative from psychological, social, and philosophical foundations — is imperative in developing a curriculum appropriate for twentieth-century man.

The central questions posed and the relevant contributions toward workable answers for our times made by such interpreters of the progressive movement in education are not obsolete. They must and will persist. In time, they will be embodied in the form of new proposals for modern education, new syntheses which build upon our predecessors, as is common in the world of ideas. The overanxious gravediggers, and those who currently give them comfort, will discover as this twentieth century moves along that what they have mistaken for a corpse is indeed very much alive.

2

How Children Fail

John Holt

John Holt, who has taught at both the high school and elementary levels, describes in his summary from How Children Fail *the deadly connection between fear of failing and actual failure by children. An eloquent and compassionate critic, Holt implored educators to focus on children rather than on the promulgation of the formal curriculum. His call was heard by kindred spirits and his influential first book went into several printings.*

John Holt now writes articles and reviews for major magazines and acts as a consultant to experimentally-oriented schools. His most recent book, What Do I Do Monday?, *was published in 1970.*

Nobody starts off stupid. You have only to watch babies and infants, and think seriously about what all of them learn and do, to see that, except for the most grossly retarded, they show a style of life, and a desire and ability to learn that in an older person we might well call genius. Hardly an adult in a thousand, or ten thousand, could in any three years of his life learn as much, grow as much in his understanding of the world around him, as every infant learns and grows in his first three years. But what happens, as we get older, to this extraordinary capacity for learning and intellectual growth?

What happens is that it is destroyed, and more than by any other one thing, by the process that we misname education — a process that goes on in most homes and schools. We adults destroy most of the intellectual and creative capacity of children by the things we do to them or make them do. We destroy this capacity above all by making them afraid, afraid of not doing what other people want, of not pleasing, of making mistakes, of failing, of being *wrong*. Thus we make them afraid to gamble, afraid to experiment, afraid to try the difficult and the unknown. Even when we do not create children's fears, when they come to us with fears ready-made and built-in, we use these fears as handles to manipulate them and get them to do what we want. Instead of trying to whittle down their fears, we build them up, often to monstrous size. For we like children who are a little afraid of us, docile, deferential children, though not, of course, if they are so obviously afraid that they threaten our image of ourselves as kind, lovable people whom there is no reason to fear. We find ideal the kind of "good" children who are just enough afraid of us to do everything we want, without making us feel that fear of us is what is making them do it.

We destroy the disinterested (I do *not* mean *un*interested) love of learning in children, which is so strong when they are small, by encouraging and compelling them to work for petty and contemptible rewards — gold stars, or papers marked 100 and tacked to the wall, or A's on report cards, or honor rolls, or dean's lists, or Phi Beta Kappa keys — in short, for the ignoble satisfaction of feeling that they are better than someone else. We encourage them to feel that the end and aim of all they do in school is nothing more than to get a good mark on a test, or to impress someone with what they seem to know. We kill, not only their curiosity, but their feeling that it is a good and admirable thing to be curious, so that by the age of ten most of them will not ask questions, and will show a good deal of scorn for the few who do.

In many ways, we break down children's convictions that things make sense, or their hope that things may prove to make sense. We do it, first of all, by breaking up life into arbitrary and disconnected hunks of subject matter, which we then try to "integrate" by such artificial and irrelevant devices as having children sing Swiss folk songs while they are studying the geography of Switzerland, or do arithmetic problems about rail-splitting while they are studying the boyhood of Lincoln. Furthermore, we continually confront them with what is senseless, ambiguous, and contradictory; worse, we do it without knowing that we are doing it, so that, hearing nonsense shoved at them as if it were sense, they come to feel that the source of their confusion lies not in the material but in their own stupidity. Still further, we cut children off from their own common sense and the world of reality by requiring them to play with and shove around words and symbols that have little or no meaning to them. Thus we turn the vast majority of our students into the kind of people for whom all symbols are meaningless; who cannot use symbols as a way of learning about and dealing with reality; who cannot understand written instructions; who, even if they read books, come out knowing no more than when they went in; who may have a few new words rattling around in their heads, but whose mental models of the world remain unchanged and, indeed, impervious to change. The minority, the able and successful students, we are very likely to turn into something different but just as dangerous: the kind of people who can manipulate words and symbols fluently while keeping themselves largely divorced from the reality for which they stand; the kind of people who like to speak in large generalities but grow silent or indignant if someone asks for an example of what they are talking about; the kind of people who, in their discussions of world affairs, coin and use such words as megadeaths and megacorpses, with scarcely a thought to the blood and suffering these words imply.

We encourage children to act stupidly, not only by scaring and confusing them, but by boring them, by filling up their days with dull, repetitive tasks that make little or no claim on their attention or demands on their intelligence. Our hearts leap for joy at the sight of a roomful of children all slogging away at some imposed task, and we are all the more pleased and satisfied if someone tells us that the children don't really like what they are doing. We tell ourselves that this drudgery, this endless busywork, is good preparation for life, and we fear that without it children would be hard to "control." But why must this busywork be so dull? Why not give tasks that are interesting and demanding? Because, in schools where every task must be completed and every answer must be right, if we give children more demanding tasks they will be fearful and will instantly insist that we show them how to do the job. When you have acres of paper to fill up with pencil marks, you have no time to waste on the luxury of thinking. By such means children are firmly established in the habit of using only a small part of their thinking capacity. They feel that school is a place where they must spend most of their time doing dull tasks in a dull way. Before long they are deeply settled in a rut of unintelligent behavior from which most of them could not escape even if they wanted to. . . .

Behind much of what we do in school lie some ideas, that could be expressed roughly as follows: (1) Of the vast body of human knowledge, there are certain bits and pieces that can be called essential, that everyone should know; (2) the extent to which a person can be considered educated, qualified to live intelligently in today's world and be a useful member of society, depends on the amount of this essential knowledge that he carries about with him; (3) it is the duty of schools, therefore, to get as much of this essential knowledge as possible into the minds of children. Thus we find ourselves trying to poke certain facts, recipes, and ideas down the gullets of every child in school, whether the morsel interests him or not, even if it frightens him or sickens him, and even if there are other things that he is much more interested in learning.

These ideas are absurd and harmful nonsense. We will not begin to have true education or real learning in our schools until we sweep this nonsense out of the way. Schools should be a place where children learn what they most want to know, instead of what we think they ought to know. The child who wants to know something remembers it and uses it once he has it; the child who learns something to please or appease someone else forgets it when the need for pleasing or the danger of not appeasing is past. This is why children quickly forget all but a small part of what they learn in school. It is of no use or interest to them; they do not want, or expect, or even intend to remember it. The only difference between bad and good students in this respect is that the bad students forget right away, while the good students are careful to wait until after the exam. If for no other reason, we could well afford to throw out most of what we teach in school because the children throw out almost all of it anyway.

The notion of a curriculum, an essential body of knowledge, would be absurd even if children remembered everything we "taught" them. We don't and can't agree on what knowledge is essential. The man who has trained himself in some special field of knowledge or competence thinks, naturally, that his specialty should be in the curriculum. The classical scholars want Greek and Latin taught; the historians shout for more history; the mathematicians urge more math and the scientists more science; the modern language experts want all children taught French, or Spanish, or Russian; and so on. Everyone wants to get his specialty into the act, knowing that as the demand for his special knowledge rises, so will the price that he can charge for it. Who wins this struggle and who loses depends not on the real needs of children or even of society, but on who is most skillful in public relations, who has the best educational lobbyists, who best can capitalize on events that have nothing to do with education, like the appearance of Sputnik in the night skies.

The idea of the curriculum would not be valid even if we could agree what ought to be in it. For knowledge itself changes. Much of what a child learns in school will be found, or thought, before many years, to be untrue. I studied physics at school from a fairly up-to-date text that proclaimed that the fundamental law of physics was the law of conservation of matter — matter is not created or destroyed. I had to scratch that out before I left school. In economics at college I was taught many things that were not true of our economy then, and many more that are not true now. Not for many years after I left college did I learn that the Greeks, far from being a detached and judicious people surrounded by chaste white temples, were hot-tempered, noisy, quarrelsome, and liked to cover their temples with gold leaf and bright paint; or that most of the citizens of Imperial Rome, far from living in houses in which the rooms surrounded an atrium, or central court, lived in multi-story tenements, one of which was perhaps the largest building in the ancient world. The child who really remembered everything he heard in school would live his life believing many things that were not so.

Moreover, we cannot possibly judge what knowledge will be most needed forty, or twenty, or even ten years from now. At school, I studied Latin and French. Few of the teachers who claimed then that Latin was essential would make as strong a case for it now; and the French might better have been Spanish, or better yet, Russian. Today the schools are busy teaching Russian; but perhaps they should be teaching Chinese, or Hindi, or who-knows-what? Besides physics, I studied chemistry, then perhaps the most popular of all science courses; but I would probably have done better to study biology, or ecology, if such a course had been offered (it wasn't). We always find out, too late, that we don't have the experts we need, that in the past we studied the wrong things; but this is bound to remain so. Since we can't know what knowledge will be most needed in the future, it is senseless to try to teach it in advance. Instead, we should try to turn out people who love learning so much and learn so well that they will be able to learn whatever needs to be learned.

How can we say, in any case, that one piece of knowledge is more important than another, or indeed, what we really say, that some knowledge is essential and the rest, as far as school is concerned, worthless? A child who wants to learn something that the school can't and doesn't want to teach him will be told not to waste his time. But how can we say that what he wants to know is less important than what we want him to know? We must ask how much of the sum of human knowledge anyone can know at the end of his schooling. Perhaps a millionth. Are we then to believe that one of these millionths is so much more important than another? Or that our social and national problems will be solved if we can just figure out a way to turn children out of schools knowing two millionths of the total, instead of one? Our problems don't arise from the fact that we lack experts enough to tell us what needs to be done, but out of the fact that we do not and will not do what we know needs to be done now.

Learning is not everything, and certainly one piece of learning is as good as another. One of my brightest and boldest fifth graders was deeply interested in snakes. He knew more about snakes than anyone I've ever known. The school did not offer herpetology; snakes were not in the curriculum; but as far as I was concerned, any time he spent learning about snakes was better spent than in ways I could think of to spend it; not least of all because, in the process of learning about snakes, he learned a great deal more about many other things than I was ever able to "teach" those unfortunates in my class who were not interested in anything at all. In another fifth-grade class, studying Romans in Britain, I saw a boy trying to read a science book behind the cover of his desk. He was spotted, and made to put the book away, and listen to the teacher; with a heavy sigh he did so. What was gained here? She traded a chance for an hour's real learning about science for, at best, an hour's temporary learning about history — much more probably no learning at all, just an hour's worth of daydreaming and resentful thoughts about school.

It is not subject matter that makes some learning more valuable than others, but the spirit in which the work is done. If a child is doing the kind of learning that most children do in school, when they learn at all — swallowing words, to spit back at the teacher on demand — he is wasting his time, or rather, we are wasting it for him. This learning will not be permanent, or relevant, or useful. But a child who is learning naturally, following his curiosity where it leads him, adding to his mental model of reality whatever he needs and can find a place for, and rejecting without fear or guilt what he does not need, is growing — in knowledge, in the love of learning, and in the ability to learn. He is on his way to becoming the kind of person we need in our society, and that our "best" schools and colleges are *not* turning out, the kind of person who, in Whitney Griswold's words, seeks and finds meaning, truth, and enjoyment in everything he does. All his life he will go on learning. Every experience will make his mental model of reality more complete and more true to life, and thus make him more able to deal realistically, imaginatively, and constructively with whatever new experience life throws his way.

We cannot have real learning in school if we think it is our duty and our right to tell children what they must learn. We cannot know, at any moment, what particular bit of knowledge or understanding a child needs most, will most strengthen and best fit his model of reality. Only he can do this. He may not do it very well, but he can do it a hundred times better than we can. The most we can do is try to help, by letting him know roughly what is available and where he can look for it. Choosing what he wants to learn and what he does not is something he must do for himself.

There is one more reason, and the most important one, why we must reject the idea of school and classroom as places where, most of the time, children are doing what some adult tells them to do. The reason is that there is no way to coerce children without making them afraid, or more afraid. We must not try to fool ourselves into thinking that this is not so. The would-be progressives, who until recently had great influence over most American public school education, did not recognize this — and still do not. They thought, or at least talked and wrote as if they thought, that there were good ways and bad ways to coerce children (the bad ones mean, harsh, cruel, the good ones gentle, persuasive, subtle, kindly), and that if they avoided the bad and stuck to the good they would do no harm. This was one of their greatest mistakes, and the main reason why the revolution they hoped to accomplish never took hold.

The idea of painless, non-threatening coercion is an illusion. Fear is the inseparable companion of coercion, and its inescapable consequence. If you think it your duty to make children do what you want, whether they will or not, then it follows inexorably that you must make them afraid of what will happen to them if they don't do what you want. You can do this in the old-fashioned way, openly and avowedly, with the threat of harsh words, infringement of liberty, or physical punishment. Or you can do it in the modern way, subtly, smoothly, quietly, by withholding the acceptance and approval which you and others have trained the children to depend on; or by making them feel that some retribution awaits them in the future, too vague to imagine but too implacable to escape. You can, as many skilled teachers do, learn to tap with a word, a gesture, a look, even a smile, the great reservoir of fear, shame, and guilt that today's children carry around inside them. Or you can simply let your own fears, about what will happen to you if the children don't do what you want, reach out and infect them. Thus the children will feel more and more that life is full of dangers from which only the goodwill of adults like you can protect them, and that this goodwill is perishable and must be earned anew each day.

The alternative — I can see no other — is to have schools and classrooms in which each child in his own way can satisfy his curiosity, develop his abilities and talents, pursue his interests, and from the adults and older children around him get a glimpse of the great variety and richness of life. In short, the school should be a great smörgåsbord of intellectual, artistic, creative, and athletic activities, from which each child could take whatever he wanted, and as much as he wanted, or as little. When Anna was in the sixth grade, the year after she was in my class, I mentioned this idea to her. After describing very sketchily how such a school might be run, and what the children might do, I said, "Tell me, what do you think of it? Do you think it would work? Do you think the kids would learn anything?" She said, with utmost conviction, "Oh, yes, it would be wonderful!" She was silent for a minute or two, perhaps remembering her own generally unhappy schooling. Then she said thoughtfully, "You know, kids really like to learn; we just don't like being pushed around."

No, they don't; and we should be grateful for that. So let's stop pushing them around, and give them a chance.

3

The Way It Spozed to Be

James Herndon

James Herndon writes of his experiences in the late 1950s as a new white teacher in a school he identifies only as George Washington Junior High School, located in a Negro district of a West Coast city. The Way It Spozed to Be is an honest and often rueful account of how most things turned out wrong. Herndon has a keen eye for both the pathetic and the ludicrous in the school in general and the curriculum in particular; he can report dispassionately on the foibles of students, fellow educators, and himself. The selected excerpts describe some of his encounters with his colleagues and their conceptions of curriculum.

After avoiding being fired by resigning, Herndon worked as a substitute teacher, and finally obtained a post in a suburban school where he wrote The Way It Spozed to Be.

COLLEAGUES

Teachers are always willing to give advice to new (or old) teachers, and I talked to them all during those first six or seven weeks. The advice was of two kinds. The first kind was useful enough and was about methods and equipment you could use to do certain things — sets of flash cards, how to group students, controlled readers, recorders, easily corrected tests, good films — but after a short time I was already using most of these. My problem was not what to use but how to get the kids to respond in such a way that they learned something. That brought up the other kind of advice, which was also the most common and which was useless to me. This advice was a conglomeration of dodges, tricks, gimmicks to get the kids to do what they were spozed to do, that is, whatever the teacher had in mind for them to do. It really involved a kind of gerrymandering of the group — promises, favors, warnings, threats, letting you pass out or not pass out paper, sit in a certain place or not, A's, plusses, stars, and also various methods for getting the class working before they knew it. The purpose of all these methods was to get and keep an aspect of order, which was reasonable enough, I suppose. But the purpose of this order was supposed to be so that "learning could take place." So everyone said — not wanting to be guilty of the authoritarian predilection for order for its own sake — while at the same time admitting that most of the kids weren't learning anything this way. Everyone agreed that our students were on the average a couple of years below grade level, everyone agreed that was because they were "deprived" kids, but no one agreed that simply because nothing was going on the way they were doing it, they ought to try something else.

It's not my purpose or even desire to criticize these teachers — they were as good or better than most and they had a difficult job — but frankly I could never come to terms with their attitude. They knew a certain way, or ways, to teach. They knew how to get control of the class and, that established, some ways to present the material they thought important. The control didn't work consistently because the kids were not easily threatened, having little to lose. Promises were fairly successful at the beginning of the year, but their power steadily declined as the kids saw through them or were disillusioned about their value. The material which was so important, which had to be "covered," was supposed to lead toward understanding, broader knowledge, scientific method, good citizenship or, more specifically, toward better writing, speech, figuring, grammar, geography, whatever it was. But actually what was happening was that they were presenting the students, every day, with something for them either to do or not-do, while keeping them through order from any other alternative. If a kid couldn't or wouldn't do his assignment, he had only the choice of not-doing it, of doing nothing. Almost every teacher admitted that this last was the choice of half the class on any given day.

The kids who chose to do the assignment seemed rarely to benefit from it; even if they did the speller conscientiously, their written work remained badly spelled. The A's promised as prize for hard work didn't materialize. The result was that these teachers faced, every year, the certain knowledge that the first day of school was the best they could hope for, since the progress and morale of the class could only be downhill. The only question left was whether or not they could hold out.

Following this point in our talks, such as they were, would flow generalities of analysis and interpretation. Since their teaching methods were right in other schools, they argued, it must be the fact of "deprivation" which was at fault here. Deprivation was identified as a problem now, and problems were supposed to be dealt with in such a way that they ceased to exist. If deprivation was hindering learning, then someone should do something about that deprivation.

What to do? The first and best thing, they all knew, was education. With education would come better skills, with skills would come better jobs, with better jobs would come middle-class incomes and the attendant middle-class mores, values and ideas of order. After that the school program, curriculum and methods, being essentially right, would work since the reason they didn't work now was that the students were of the wrong kind; i.e., they were deprived.

But how were they to get educated, The Tribe, if the education they were getting right here and now wasn't working? How get these skills (values, ideas of order) if the methods used to teach them weren't producing any skills by and large? I hate to keep saying this, but the inescapable fact is that they weren't working and that therefore the rest was simply nonsense. . . .

Mrs. A's Advice

In my free period that first day back I conferred with Mrs. A, who was sticking around to let me know what she'd been doing. She was an extremely attractive woman, perhaps thirty, well-dressed, light-colored, her hair nicely waved and under control; everything else was pretty well under control too, as I discovered. She told me, although not in so many words, that my classes had been a mess when she took over, that she considered them well on their way to straightening up after a month with her, and that it was now up to me to keep them that way. She got this across to me very nicely in the kind but firm manner some people have with training animals.

She advised me to figure out a regular and consistent plan of work, or simply to accept the one she had devised, and see to it that the students did this, or if not that they at least did nothing else during the period. I should grade all papers immediately and hand them back so that students who did the work could see their rewards promptly.

It was important, she said, to get them into the proper mood for school-work as soon as they entered the room. In particular, avoid beginning the period by talking to them, explaining, or lecturing, which they would not listen to and which only encouraged them to start talking themselves. She believed that I talked to the class too much anyway — there was no point in their expressing opinions about things they knew nothing about. Let them learn something first, she said, and then they might have something to say.

The best method for getting them in order was to have a paragraph writ-ten out on the board when they entered, and get them in the habit of copying this paragraph in their notebooks immediately they sat down, giving a time limit for its completion, erasing the paragraph when the time was up, and grading the notebooks frequently. Copying was something they could all do without further explanation from me; it got them in the mood for schoolwork, quiet, their materials ready, all set for the day's lesson, whatever it was.

I didn't have a lot to say to this advice. In the face of the nonexistent notebooks and the unused or all-wrong spellers, the list of those trooping down to the office for misbehavior, I couldn't see that the regimen had been a great success. In any case, the advice wasn't new. I'd been getting the same advice since September, especially the part about the paragraph. Perhaps after a year or so of this it might work; I didn't think so, but it didn't matter either. I knew damn well that they'd been getting this treat-ment for the past six years, that during this time they'd learned practically nothing about the "skills" this type of order was spozed to produce — no adverbs, not how to spell, no punctuation, not adding, subtracting, multi-plying or dividing; many hadn't even learned how to read. I couldn't see my way had been a great success either — in fact, I didn't know what my way was — but the other was a failure and was going to be a failure. I couldn't see any reason to keep on doing it. I really couldn't.

I didn't say any of this to her. After all, she began to tell me about her own life; how she'd taught for five years, then had kids, stayed at home until the kids were in school, and was now coming back into the profession. She had a job for next year, full-time, for the district. She thought that what these kids needed was to learn to conform to the ordinary standards of American society, morals, and language. She also thought that too many teachers, faced with these children — we ignored The Word — just gave up on them, con-sidered them hopeless, wouldn't give them a chance.

It wasn't surprising that we had so little to say to each other. She believed my classes were a mess because I was white and they were Negro kids and so I thought they weren't worth making an effort for. I thought she was working hard to help them in a way that hadn't ever helped them, wouldn't help them in the future, and was in fact cementing them into failure, rebellion or apathy. She thought I couldn't imagine them ever being tolerable students or responsible citizens. I thought that she, a middle-class Negro woman in a lamb's-wool sweater, had less contact with these students than I, knew less about them, mistrusted them more, thought less of their capabilities, and disliked them, as they were now, utterly. . . .

CARROTS — MRS. X'S ADVICE

Two days after vacation I received a note from the secretary that Mrs. X (another name I don't remember) was coming down to talk to me. Mrs. X was the District Language and Social Studies consultant for GW.

Mrs. X didn't visit my classes. She met me in the teachers' room during my free period and opened the conversation by telling me that she came, as she did with all the new teachers, to offer any help or advice she could.

This Mrs. X was white, elderly, tall, stringy, wore a print dress — the very picture, I must say, of the old-lady school-teacher. She asked me if I had any problems I cared to mention. Did I? I began to outline them — 9D's apathy, 7H's conglomeration of inabilities. I raced enthusiastically into a point-by-point description of the problems of 7H for a starter; I considered myself something of an expert on the subject. I spoke as if we two were going to reform the entire system, then and there.

Before I'd gotten fairly started, she interrupted. Now, we all have our problems, she said, and sometimes we're tempted to consider our own problems as being unique. But with *these* children (leaving out The Word, as usual) I've found that a simpler, more direct approach works best. I feel already that you may be making it all too complicated for yourself. In my experience, the best advice I can give you beginning teachers is, hold out a carrot.

A carrot? I didn't get it.

You know, she said brightly, the carrot, or perhaps we should say a sugar cube. If you want the goat to pull the cart, but he doesn't want to, you hold a carrot out in front of him. He tries to reach the carrot because he does want it. In doing so he pulls the cart. *If*, she said with a kind of wink, *if* you've attached the carrot to the cart.

I must have seemed a little stupid to her. Seeing that I just sat there, she tried to explain. Teaching these children is like training animals. For each task you want them to do, you must offer them a carrot.

You mean, I finally said, you try to get the goat to pull the cart without his realizing it. That is, the goat actually does what you want him to do, but all the time he thinks he's just trying to get that carrot. He doesn't realize he's pulling the cart. Not only that, but pulling the cart isn't something that any goat, any normal goat, ever wants to do, but . . .

I think you're trying to make it complicated again, she said, frowning.

You mean, I tried again, to get the student to do the assignment because of some reward he's going to get, not because he realizes that the assignment is valuable or interesting to him. You mean, the assignment itself can't be the carrot . . .

She felt happier. That's it, she said. Of course the reward must vary. There are individual differences as we know. A carrot for one, a sugar cube for another.

Mercifully the bell rang. Mrs. X went back to her desk in the district office, downtown. I sneaked a quick smoke, my mind filled with carrots and outrage, and arrived upstairs a bit late to greet 9D. . . .

. . . If virtually all the kids from "lower-income" and "minority" groups are in our own low-ability groups, we turn to the counselors, the social workers, the clinics. Them is deprived kids, goes the cry, and someone ought to do something about it.

Deprived of what? Of intelligence? Do we claim that lower-class kids are just naturally dumber than middle-class kids, and that why they all in that dumb class? Naturally not. We have a list. They are deprived of ego strength, of realistic goal-orientation, of family stability, of secure peer relationships; they lack the serene middle-class faith in the future. Because of all that, they also lack self-control, cannot risk failure, won't accept criticism, can't take two steps back to go one forward, have no study habits, no basic skills, don't respect school property, and didn't read "Cowboy Small."

You can add to this list, or you can find another. But what such a list adds up to is something simple: some kids can't take it as well as others.

Some kids can't stand there calmly while they talk to the flag in Spanish. Or they can in kindergarten, like Jay, but can't keep it up in the fourth or seventh grade. If the kids went along with us in the old days, it was for two reasons: first, there were fewer of them and we were able to allow them enough leeway to live; and second, they were white, middle-class kids in America. Not that the system in general was right for them — only that they fit the ideal of America in 1960 without much worry about it, had a richer life-diet outside of school, and so were tough enough to take it.

All right. Some can take it, and some can't. Those who cannot expose the point — it's not any good for anyone. My wife's father was once bitten by a cottonmouth, and survived. Another man from the same community was bitten and died. No one argued that the experience was good for either one of them. Sitting in a classroom or at home pretending to "study" a badly written text full of false information, adding up twenty sums when they're all the same and one would do, being bottled up for seven hours a day in a place where you decide nothing, having your success or failure depend, a hundred times a day, on the plan, invention and whim of someone else, being put in a position where most of your real desires are not only ignored but actively penalized, undertaking nothing for its own sake but only for that illusory carrot of the future — maybe you can do it, and maybe you can't, but either way, it's probably done you some harm.

It's difficult to stop. One always doubts the message is clear enough. I took a ride over by GW the other day, just to take a look. It hadn't changed, that I could see. Now, of course, it won't change for me at all. As far as I'm concerned, Roy and Harvey, Alexandra and Ruth still go there. If I were to work there again, I guess I'd try to do about the same thing, in about the same way, and as often have little idea about how it was going to turn out.

The only thing is, I now know they aren't unique — that GW is not unique. More colorful, no doubt, more vehement in showing us the error of our ways, less cooperative while we talk to the flag, but, as Sullivan said, rather more like the rest of us than less.

What to do? You can read suggestions for change in a lot of recent books by serious and intelligent men. I suppose I could add mine. But frankly, I have almost no hope that there will be any significant change in the way we educate our children — for that, after all, would involve liberty, the last thing we may soon expect — and so I have thought merely to describe one time for you, parents, kids, readers, the way it is.

4

Thirty-Six Children

Herbert Kohl

If a "born teacher" exists it is Herbert Kohl. 36 Children (New York: New American Library, 1967), his account of learning to teach the hard way, is a contemporary classic. The irrelevant curriculum accounted for his initial difficulties. Yet he rallied, won the children over, and developed a curriculum for sixth-graders which combined creativity with academic accomplishment.

After three years in the New York City schools, Kohl directed a teachers' and writers' group and worked with parent groups in Harlem for community participation in education. Recently he wrote The Open Classroom *(New York: The New York Review, 1969), "a handbook for teachers who want to work in an open environment."*

The books arrived the next morning before class. There were twenty-five arithmetic books from one publisher and twelve from another, but in the entire school there was no complete set of sixth-grade arithmetic books. A few minutes spent checking the first day's arithmetic assignment showed me that it wouldn't have mattered if a full set had existed, since half the class had barely mastered multiplication, and only one child, Grace, who had turned in a perfect paper, was actually ready for sixth-grade arithmetic. It was as though, encouraged to believe that the children couldn't do arithmetic by judging from the school's poor results in teaching it, the administration decided not to waste money on arithmetic books, thereby creating a vicious circle that made it even more impossible for the children to learn.

The situation was almost as dismal in reading — the top class of the sixth grade had more than half its members reading on fourth-grade level and only five or six children actually able to read through a sixth-grade book. There were two full sets of sixth-grade readers available, however, and after the arithmetic situation I was grateful for anything. Yet accepting these readers put me as a teacher in an awkward position. The books were flat and uninteresting. They only presented what was pleasant in life, and even then limited the pleasant to what was publicly accepted as such. The people in the stories were all middle-class and their simplicity, goodness, and self-confidence were unreal. I couldn't believe in this foolish ideal and knew that anyone who had ever bothered to observe human life couldn't believe it. Yet I had to teach it, and through it make reading important and necessary. Remembering the children, their anxiety and hostility, the alternate indifference, suspicion, and curiosity they approached me with, knowing how essential it is to be honest with children, I felt betrayed by the books into hypocrisy. No hypocrite can win the respect of children, and without respect one cannot teach.

One of the readers was a companion to the social studies unit on the growth of the United States and was full of stories about family fun in a Model T Ford, the first wireless radio in town, and the joys of wealth and progress. The closest the book touched upon human emotion or the real life of real children was in a story in which children accepted a new invention before their parents did, even though the adults laughed at the children. Naturally, everything turned out happily.

The other reader was a miscellany of adventure stories (no human violence or antagonists allowed, just treasure hunts, animal battles, close escapes), healthy poems (no love except for mother, father, and nature), and a few harmless myths (no Oedipus, Electra, or Prometheus). I also managed to get twenty dictionaries in such bad condition that the probability of finding any word still intact was close to zero.

The social studies texts (I could choose from four or five) praised industrial America in terms that ranged from the enthusiastic to the exorbitant. Yet the growth of modern industrial society is fascinating, and it was certainly possible to supplement the text with some truth. I decided to work with what was given me and attempt to teach the sixth-grade curriculum as written in the New York City syllabus, ignoring as long as possible the contradictions inherent in such a task.

The class confronted me, surrounded by my motley library, at nine that second morning and groaned.

"Those phoney books?"

"We read them already, Mr. Kohl."

"It's a cheap, dirty, bean school."

My resolve weakened, and I responded out of despair.

"Let me put it straight to you. These are the only books here. I have no more choice than you do and I don't like it any better. Let's get through them and maybe by then I'll figure out how to get better ones."

The class understood and accepted the terms. As soon as the books were distributed the first oral reading lesson began. Some children volunteered eagerly, but most of the class tried not to be seen. The children who read called out the words, but the story was lost. I made the lesson as easy as possible by helping children who stumbled, encouraging irrelevant discussion, and not letting any child humiliate himself. It was bad enough that more than half the class had to be forced to use books they couldn't read.

The lesson ended, and a light-skinned boy raised his hand.

"Mr. Kohl, remember that ten minutes you gave us yesterday? Couldn't we talk again now? We're tired after all this reading."

I wasn't sure how to take Robert's request. My initial feeling was that he was taking advantage of me and trying to waste time. I felt, along with the official dogma, that no moment in school should be wasted — it must all be pre-planned and structured. Yet why shouldn't it be "wasted"? Hadn't most of the class wasted years in school, not merely moments? . . .

I tried for the next six weeks to use the books assigned and teach the official curriculum. It was hopeless. The class went through the readers perfunctorily, refused to hear about modern America, and were relieved to do arithmetic — mechanical, uncharged — as long as nothing new was introduced. For most of the day the atmosphere in the room was stifling. The children were bored and restless, and I felt burdened by the inappropriateness of what I tried to teach. It was so dull that I thought as little as the children and began to despair. Listening to myself on the growth of urban society, realizing that no one else was listening, that though words were pronounced the book was going unread, I found myself vaguely wondering about the children.

But there were moments. The ten-minute breaks between lessons grew until, in my eyes, the lessons were secondary. Everything important happening in the classroom happened between lessons.

First it was the piano, Leverne wanting to play, picking up a few tunes, teaching them to other children, to Charisse and Desiree, to Grace, Pamela, and Maurice. Then it was the six of them asking me to teach them to read music and their learning how in one afternoon.

There was Robert Jackson. I took time to look at his art, observe him working. He was good, accurate; he thought in terms of form and composition. Seeing I was interested, other children told me of Robert's reputation and the neighborhood legend about him — when he was four, his mother gave him a pencil as a pacifier, and he began to draw. They told of the money he made drawing, of his ability to draw "anything."

I watched the girls gossiping, talking about records, parties, boys. After a few days, talk of the summer was exhausted. The children began wandering about the room looking for things to do. They seemed relaxed and eager to work then, though bored and restless during lessons. Unwilling to lose this will and energy I brought checkers and chess to school as well as magazines and books. I developed the habit of taking five minutes in the morning to describe what I had brought in. I sketched the history of chess and told the class about the wise man who asked a king, as reward for a favor, for the number of grains of wheat that resulted from placing one on the first square of a checkerboard and then progressively doubling the amount until the whole board was occupied. I commented that the king went broke, and that afternoon, to my surprise, three children told me I was right and showed me how far they'd gotten trying to figure out how much wheat the king owed the wise man.

The checkers provided quite a lesson for me. Only four of the boys in the class knew how to play. Two of them grabbed one set while another set was grabbed by Sam, a tall, respected boy who nevertheless could not play checkers. He sat down with one boy who could play and managed a game with the help of the fourth boy who could play. Within a few days all of the boys knew how to play. The boys also learned that the laws of physical dominance in the class didn't coincide with the laws of checker dominance, and learned to accept this. Over a period of a few weeks the rights of winners and losers were established and respected. During the first few days there were fights, the board was frequently knocked to the floor, and the game was called "cheap" and "phoney." But nothing very serious or extended could develop in a ten- or fifteen-minute period, and whenever things seemed a bit tight I quickly ended the break and the class returned to "work." After a week six or seven boys retained their interest in checkers while three began to explore chess. They grabbed the game, asked me to show them how to set up the men and make the moves, and then they took over. Within a week, two more boys had joined them in developing an idiosyncratic version of chess (when they forgot the moves they were too proud to ask me) which satisfied them very well.

Leverne stuck to the piano and Robert drew while several other boys kept searching the room for something to do. One of them, Ralph, showed me a copy of the *New York Enquirer* one day and asked me what I thought about it. I facetiously remarked that he could probably do better and stick closer to the truth. Two days later he asked me what I'd meant, and struggling to remember what I'd said, I came up with the idea that he report what went on in his neighborhood. He looked at me strangely and asked me if I meant it. I said, "Sure," and he sat down and wrote, though it took him nearly a month to show me what he was doing. The girls were more interested in magazines that I had brought in, and some of them asked me for books. . . .

September 25 was the day of the first Patterson-Liston fight. I had been reading Patterson's *Victory Over Myself* and brought it to school with me. I asked the class if they knew of the fight and they laughed. Sides had been drawn for days, bets made; several of the boys were going to see the televised fight at the RKO, and others defensively claimed relatives and friends who would be in attendance. I read from Patterson's book and talked of the family photograph he tried to remove his face from. We talked of self-hatred and confidence, of the fighters' personalities, of good and bad, winners and losers. Many of the kids wanted Patterson to win, but they were too cynical to believe that he would just because he was a good person. He had to win with his fists.

Some girls felt the whole thing was brutal though they reluctantly admitted that the fight fascinated them too. An argument broke out about the fighters' size and the money involved. I remembered seeing some facts about the fight in *The New York Times* that morning, found two charts, and put them on the board.

The class studied them intently, the first thing they had all looked at so closely all year. They checked off the characteristics and their implications: Patterson younger, maybe faster; Liston older but bigger, heavier, longer reach, stronger . . . Then one boy rebelled and said facts weren't everything, personality counted and Patterson had to be more confident. A girl countered by saying Liston was too confident and a big head who thought too much of himself.

Facts on Title Fight

Place—Comiskey Park, Chicago, capacity 49,000.

Promoter — Championship Sports, Inc.

Time—10:30 P.M., Eastern daylight time.

Television—Closed circuit with Chicago and approximate 100-mile radius blacked out.

Radio—Nationwide by American Broadcasting Company (also foreign broadcasts to eight countries).

Closed circuit TV proceeds — $2,000,000 guaranteed. About 4,000,000 expected.

Radio proceeds (domestic and foreign—about $400,000.

Movie proceeds (Post-Fight showing)—about $550,000.

Estimated gate—$750,000.

Estimated attendance—35,000.

Fighters' shares—Patterson, 55 per cent of ancillary rights (closed circuit TV, radio, movies) and 45 per cent of net gate; Liston, 12½ per cent of net in all revenue phases.

Prices of seats—$100, $50, $30, $20 and $10.

Scoring—Referee and two judges; 5-point maximum a round.

Return bout—If Liston wins, return bout within a year. Percentage, 30 per cent for each fighter and 40 per cent for promoter.

HOW RIVALS COMPARE

PATTERSON		LISTON
27 years	Age	28 years
189 lbs.	Weight	212 lbs.
6 feet	Height	6 ft. 1 in.
71 in.	Reach	84 in.
16½ in.	Neck	17½ in.
40 in.	Chest (Normal)	44 in.
42 in.	Chest (Expanded)	46½ in.
32½ in.	Waist	33 in.
14½ in.	Biceps	16½ in.
12¾ in.	Fist	14 in.
21½ in.	Thigh	25½ in.
6 in.	Wrist	8½ in.
15½ in.	Calf	12 in.
9½ in.	Ankle	12 in.

After a while the discussion turned to the money and trouble arose — what were ancillary rights, how could you tell what 55 percent, 12½ percent, and 45 percent of the money earned was, could the fighters be sure they weren't being cheated? "Domestic" created problems as well as "promoter." The kids wanted to know who made the guarantee to the fighters, whether it was verbal or written, how much the government took. The questions were real and the curiosity genuine. I answered as many as I could without preaching or handing out dictionaries, without pausing for a lesson on percentage or saying, "Don't you wish you could read now?" The children knew what they couldn't do, and were grateful for the fact that one time in school a teacher answered their questions when they needed answering, and didn't make them feel foolish for asking in the first place.

It was eleven thirty when the discussion ended so I gave the class the rest of the morning off. Some of the children immediately set to copying the charts on the blackboard. Someone borrowed *Victory Over Myself* and a group of children sat looking at the photographs in the book. The morning passed effortlessly and well. At noon I noticed that the book had disappeared, and over the next three months it periodically reappeared in someone else's hands until Patterson must have ceased interesting the children and it appeared on my desk one day.

That afternoon I expected the children to come in as excited and enthusiastic about what had occurred that morning as I was. But it was as if nothing had happened at all. The next day was worse. The children came in sleepy and irritable, wanting to hear nothing of the fight, of school, of anything. Money had been lost, people had argued. Things had happened on the streets the night before — the kids looked at me as if to say "You just can't understand." Charisse actually said:

"Mr. Kohl, we're tired. Let's do reading instead of talking."

One day Ralph cursed at Michael and unexpectedly things came together for me. Michael was reading and stumbled several times. Ralph scornfully called out, "What's the matter, psyches, going to pieces again?" The class broke up and I jumped on that word "psyches."

"Ralph, what does *psyches* mean?"

An embarrassed silence.

"Do you know how to spell it?"

Alvin volunteered. "S-i-k-e-s."

"Where do you think the word came from? Why did everybody laugh when you said it, Ralph?"

"You know, Mr. Kohl, it means, like crazy or something."

"Why? How do words get to mean what they do?"

Samuel looked up at me and said: "Mr. Kohl, now you're asking questions like Alvin. There aren't any answers, you know that."

"But there are. Sometimes by asking Alvin's kind of questions you discover the most unexpected things. Look."

I wrote *Psyche*, then *Cupid*, on the blackboard.

"That's how *psyche* is spelled. It looks strange in English, but the word doesn't come from English. It's Greek. There's a letter in the Greek alphabet that comes out *psi* in English. This is the way *psyche* looks in Greek."

Some of the children spontaneously took out their notebooks and copied the Greek.

"The word *psyche* has a long history. *Psyche* means mind or soul for the Greeks, but it was also the name of a lovely woman who had the misfortune to fall in love with Cupid, the son of Venus, the jealous Greek goddess of love. . . ."

The children listened, enchanted by the myth, fascinated by the weaving of the meaning of *psyche* into the fabric of the story, and the character, Mind, playing tricks on itself, almost destroying its most valuable possessions through its perverse curiosity. Grace said in amazement:

"Mr. Kohl, they told the story and said things about the mind at the same time. What do you call that?"

"*Myth* is what the Greeks called it."

Sam was roused.

"Then what happened? What about the history of the word?"

"I don't know too much, but look at the words in English that come from *Cupid* and *Psyche*."

I cited *psychological, psychic, psychotic, psychodrama, psychosomatic, cupidity* — the children copied them unasked, demanded the meanings. They were obviously excited.

Leaping ahead, Alvin shouted: "You mean words change? People didn't always speak this way? Then how come the reader says there's a right way to talk and a wrong way?"

"There's a right way now, and that only means that's how most people would like to talk now, and how people write now."

Charles jumped out of his desk and spoke for the first time during the year.

"You mean one day the way we talk — you know, with words like *cool* and *dig* and *sound* — may be all right?"

"Uh huh. Language is alive, it's always changing, only sometimes it changes so slowly that we can't tell."

Neomia caught on.

"Mr. Kohl, is that why our reader sounds so old-fashioned?"

And Ralph.

"Mr. Kohl, when I called Michael *psyches*, was I creating something new?"

Someone spoke for the class.

"Mr. Kohl, can't we study the language we're talking about instead of spelling and grammar? They won't be any good when language changes anyway."

We could and did. That day we began what had to be called for my conservative plan book "vocabulary," and "an enrichment activity." Actually it was the study of language and myth, of the origins and history of words, of their changing uses and functions in human life. We began simply with the words *language* and *alphabet*, the former from the Latin for tongue and the latter from the first two letters of the Greek alphabet. Seeing the origin of *alphabet* and the relationship of *cupidity* to Cupid and *psychological* to Psyche had a particularly magical effect upon the children. They found it easy to master and acquire words that would have seemed senseless and tedious to memorize. Words like *psychic* and *psychosomatic* didn't seem arbitrary and impenetrable, capable of being learned only painfully by rote. Rather they existed in a context, through a striking tale that easily accrued associations and depth. After a week the children learned the new words, asked to be tested on them, and demanded more.

"Vocabulary" became a fixed point in each week's work as we went from Cupid and Psyche to Tantalus, the Sirens, and the Odyssey and the linguistic riches that it contains. We talked of Venus and Adonis and spent a week on first *Pan* and *panic*, *pan-American*, then *pandemonium*, and finally on *demonic* and *demons* and *devils*. We studied *logos*, *philos*, *anthropos*, *pathos*, and their derivatives. I spun the web of *mythos* about language and its origins. I went to German (*kindergarten*), Polynesian (*taboo*), or Arabic (*assassin*), showing what a motley open-ended fabric English (and for that matter any living language) is. The range of times and peoples that contributed to the growth of today's American English impressed me no less than it did the class. It drove me to research language and its origins; to reexplore myth and the dim origins of man's culture; and to invent ways of sharing my discoveries with the children.

The children took my words seriously and went a step farther. Not content to be fed solely words that grew from sources that I, the teacher, presented, they asked for words that fitted unnamed and partially articulated concepts they had, or situations they couldn't adequately describe.

"Mr. Kohl, what do you call it when a person repeats the same thing over and over again and can't stop?"

"What is it called when something is funny and serious at the same time?"

"What do you call a person who brags and thinks he's big but is really weak inside?"

"Mr. Kohl, is there a word that says that something has more than one meaning?"

The class became word-hungry and concept-hungry, concerned with discovering the "right" word to use at a given time to express a specific thought. I was struck by the difference of this notion of rightness and "the right way" to speak and write from the way children are supposed to be taught in school. They are supposed to acquire correct usage, right grammar and spelling, the right meaning of a word, and the right way to write a sentence. Achievement and I.Q. tests give incomplete sentences and the child is instructed to fill in the "right" word. Many teachers correct children's writing on the basis of a canon of formal rightness without bothering to ask what the children's words mean. I did the same thing myself.

I noticed that the children frequently said that they were bad at their friends, or their parents, or some teacher who angered them. They insisted upon describing a certain type of anger as "being bad at," and I kept telling them that it was wrong because "to be bad at" someone doesn't exist in English. And in a way I was "right"; it didn't exist, nor did the concept it was trying to express exist in English as I spoke and wrote it. But the children did mean "to be bad at," and meant something very specific by it. "To be bad" is a way of defying authority and expressing anger at the same time, as indicating one's own strength and independence. The use of "bad" here is ironical and often admiring. One child explained to me that down South a "bad nigger" was one who was strong enough and brave enough to be defiant of the white man's demands no matter how much everyone else gave in. Only later did I discover Bessie Smith in J. C. Johnson's "Black Mountain Blues," using "bad" in the same way as the kids:

> Back on Black Mountain a child would smack your face
> Back on Black Mountain a child would smack your face
> Babies cry for liquor and all the birds sing bass.
>
> Black Mountain people are bad as they can be
> Black Mountain people are bad as they can be
> They uses gun powder just to sweeten their tea

I think that before we talked about language and myth the children, if they thought about it at all, felt that most words were either arbitrary labels pinned on things and concepts the way names seem to be pinned onto babies, or indicators of connections amongst these labels. These "labels" probably represented the way the adult world capriciously decided to name things. I doubt whether the children ever thought of adults as having received language from yet other adults even more remote in time. My pupils must have found the language of their teachers strange and arbitrary indeed. The "right" language of school texts and middle-class teachers must have seemed threatening and totalitarian, especially since the only living words the children knew and used were the words they used on the streets, words teachers continually told them were "wrong" and "incorrect."

The idea that words were complex phenomena with long and compelling histories was never presented to the children. I doubt many teachers entertained it. The canons of the schools pretend that a small preselected segment of the language of the moment is an eternally correct and all-inclusive form. This form is embodied in basic word lists and controlled vocabulary readers, as if the mastering of language consists of learning a list of fifty or a hundred words by rote. The use of language in human life is continually avoided or ignored, as if it poses too great a threat to "correctness" and "rightness." No wonder then that the children showed so persistently and ingeniously how much they feared and avoided the language of the schools.

Later in the semester I taught the class a lesson on naming, a topic that seems deceptively simple yet minimally encompasses history, psychology, sociology, and anthropology. I put everybody's full name on the blackboard, including my own, and asked the class how people got names. The answer was, naturally, from their parents who made the choice — but not the full choice, it emerged, when Michael remembered that his parents' surnames came from their parents. Then how far back can you go? The children thought and Grace raised a delicate question. If the names go back through the generations how come her name wasn't African since her ancestors must have been? In answer I told the class about my own name — Kohl, changed from Cohen, changed from Okun, changed from something lost in the darkness of history; one change to identify the family as Jewish, one change to deny it. Then I returned to the question of slave names and the destruction of part of the children's African heritage that the withholding of African names implied.

Neomia said that she knew of someone who changed his name because he wanted to start a new life, and Sam told the class that his brother called himself John X because X meant unknown and his original African name was unknown. We talked of people who named their children after famous men and of others who gave exotic names. From there the discussion went on to the naming of animals — pets, wild animals, racehorses; things — boats, houses, dolls; and places. The class knew by that time in the school year that one doesn't talk of words in isolation from human lives and history, and by then I had begun to know what to teach.

The emphasis on language and words opened the children to the whole process of verbal communication. Things that they had been struggling to express, or worse, had felt only they in their isolation thought about, became social, shareable. Speaking of things, of inferiority and ambiguity, or irony and obsession, brought relief, and perhaps for the first time gave the children a sense that there were meaningful human creations that one could discover in a classroom.

Yet not all concepts have been verbalized, and the children frequently talked of having feelings and desires that no words I gave them expressed adequately. They had to create new words, or develop new forms of expression to communicate, and that can neither be taught nor done upon command. We could go to the frontier, however, and speak about the blues, about being bad or hip or cool — about how certain ways of living or historical times created the need for new words. We talked about the nuclear age, the smallness of the modern world, the jargon of democracy and communism, integration and segregation. The children looked in awe at *Finnegans Wake* and Joyce's monumental attempt to forge a new language; they listened to Bob Dylan, recorded the words of soul songs and classical blues, read poetry. We started out talking about words and ended up with life itself. The children opened up and began to display a fearless curiosity about the world.

I sense that I've jumped ahead too quickly, for the whole thing happened slowly, almost imperceptibly. There were days of despair throughout the whole year, and I never learned how to line the class up at three o'clock. There were days when Alvin was a brilliant inspiring pupil at ten and the most unbearable, uncontrollable nuisance at eleven thirty; when after a good lesson some children would turn angry and hostile, or lose interest in everything. There were small fights and hostilities, adjustments and readjustments in the children's relationships to each other and to me. I had to enlarge my vision as a human being, learn that if the complex and contradictory nature of life is allowed to come forth in the classroom there are times when it will do so with a vengeance.

I still stuck to the curriculum as much as possible. The social studies was impossible so I collected the books and returned them to the bookroom. It was too painful to see the children twist their faces into stupid indifference and hear their pained dull answers accompanied by nervous drumming on the desks.

"New York is a large modern country."

"The Hudson is an important ocean."

"The Industrial Revolution was a benefit to all."

Better drop it altogether, try anything so long as it didn't humiliate the children. These answers were not a function of the children's lack of experience, as the hopelessly respectable anti-poverty program believes; rather they were a direct response to the institutionalized hypocrisy that is characteristic of schools in the United States today.

I brought part of my library to school and temporarily substituted it for social studies. The children were curious about those Greeks and Latins who contributed so many words and concepts to our language. I brought in books on Greek and Roman architecture and art, as well as Robert Graves's version of the *Iliad*, a paperback translation of Apuleius' *Cupid and Psyche*, the *Larousse Encyclopedia of Mythology*, and anything else that seemed relevant or interesting. I showed the books to the children and let them disappear into their desks. It was made clear that the books were to be read, the pages to be turned. If someone reads a book so intensely that the book is bruised it is flattering to the book.

For three-quarters of an hour a day the Pantheon circulated along with Floyd Patterson and J. D. Salinger, Partridge's dictionary of word origins made its way through the class with Langston Hughes and the Bobbsey twins. Anything I could get my hands on was brought to class — a great deal remained unread, and some books I hadn't read myself shocked and surprised the class. They were sexy and popular. Later that year my supervisor told me I was running a very effective individualized reading program. That may have been it, but the truth seemed simpler and less structured. I overwhelmed the class with books, many of which I loved, and let them discover for themselves what they liked. There were no reports to be written, no requirements about numbers of pages to be read. Some children hardly read at all, others devoured whatever was in the room. The same is true of my friends.

Robert Jackson grabbed a book on Greek architecture, copied floor plans and perspective drawings, and finally, leaping out of the book, created a reasonably accurate scale model of the Parthenon. Alvin and Michael built a clay volcano, asked for and got a chemistry book which showed them how to simulate an eruption. Sam, Thomas, and Dennis fought their way through war books; through the Navy, the Seabees, the Marines, and the Paratroops. The girls started with the Bobbsey twins and worked through to romantic novels and, in the case of a few, Thurber and O. Henry. I learned that there were no books to fear, and having been divested of my fear of idleness, I also wasn't worried if some children went through periods of being unable to do anything at all. . . .

5

Death at an Early Age

Jonathan Kozol

Jonathan Kozol, author of Death at an Early Age, *taught in Newton, Massachusetts, after being fired in Boston and continued to write.*

The poem which triggered the Jonathan Kozol dismissal in Boston was "Ballad of the Landlord" by Langston Hughes. The poem recounts a social protest by a black tenant against his inadequate housing, the conflict with his landlord which follows, and the resultant jailing of the black tenant. The simple yet eloquent ballad contains no profanity or obscenity whatsoever.

The attitudes of many teachers, I suppose, are derived over the course of years from the kinds of books they use. Many of the books we had at school were very bad for many reasons, and none of them that I recall was very good. I was promised a certain amount of new material during the year, but this material did not appear. The only new material that I had received by the middle of the winter was an expensive boxed edition of *The Bobbsey Twins*. The old books with which we were already saddled confirmed for me almost all of the criticism that I had ever heard about conventional texts, except that perhaps the ones we had outstripped the criticism a little. Of four biographical series that were available in our Fourth Grade classrooms, out of a total of 140 biographies of famous men and women, there was one that had to do with a Negro. That one was George Washington Carver. The geography book given to my pupils and kept within their desks or on their shelves, was about eighteen years old in substance, though it was somewhat newer than that by renewal of copyright. In this book, typical of many others in its title as it was also in approach and manner, a traditional American cross-country journey was traced. During this journey there wasn't one mention, hint, whisper or glimmer of a dark-skinned face. Reading it without any outside source of information, you would have had no reason to suspect either the past history or present existence of a Negro race. The chapter on the South described an idyllic and fantasied landscape in the heart of Dixie: pastoral home of hard-working white citizens, contented white children and untroubled white adults. Cotton production was studied, and a vicarious journey to a Mississippi plantation was undertaken, without ever a reference to, or picture of, a dark-skinned person.

The history book could not get by in the same manner. It had to speak of Negroes because it had to speak of slavery. It did this, however, in a manner that seemed reluctant and half-hearted. "Men treasure freedom above all else," the narrative told us at one point. But it balanced this out by telling us beforehand that "most Southern people treated their slaves kindly. 'Our slaves have good homes and plenty to eat. When they are sick, we take care of them . . .'" In the final event I think that the author came out on the side of emancipation, but he did this in a tone and style which were so lukewarm and insipid as to be without effect. The language used throughout was coy and awkward: "In the dictionary we find that one meaning of the word 'civil' is 'polite.' The Civil War was not a polite one. It was a war between the states of Our America . . ." A final verdict on the War Between the States was the following: "No one can truly say, 'The North was right' or 'The Southern cause was the better.' Remember, each side fought for the ideals it believed in. For in Our America all of us have the right to our beliefs."

The material about the Civil War was not the only disturbing section in this book, but it is the part that seems most relevant. It would always have been simple enough, if I had been obliged to use that section, just to skip over the offensive pages — or, better, not to skip them but rather to read them with the children and then to deal with them critically. Since that time, I have done this in many situations and I do it frequently today. Nonetheless, the fact remained: The book had been printed. The book had been stocked and ordered. The book stood within our bookshelves and it was looked into by dozens of children every day. I wondered for how many years it would continue to misrepresent reality in this manner and to how many future thousands of Negro children it would spread the sad word that their people in bondage did not have the imagination to be free?

There is a school in Boston named for William Lloyd Garrison. It was at this school that the class to which I have referred received twenty-five substitute teachers in the fall of 1964. I once had a chance to work for a few mornings with a group of Fourth, Fifth and Sixth Grade pupils from the Garrison School. I asked them if they would tell me, child by child, the most important facts about the man for whom their school was named. A long silence met my question and then I discovered, by asking some other questions, that not one of these children had the slightest idea either of who he was or what he had done. No principal, no teacher, it appeared, had ever told them. Some of them had been in that school for six or seven years. They had all studied geography. They had all studied history. They had all, I suppose, talked of current events. Their teachers presumably also had some idea of what was going on in the world and could find the affiliation between this, the present day, and the beliefs of the man whose name had been given to their school. The school happened to be one of the most totally segregated (96.8 per cent) in all of Boston. Yet none of these children knew who

William Lloyd Garrison was. So long as a school that is 96.8 per cent Negro can stand in the name of William Lloyd Garrison and so long as teachers and principals are unable to tell the children in whose name their building stands, then I don't think it will be surprising that geography and history books will also resort to evasions about America and it will not be surprising either that Negro children, growing a little older, will look back with cynicism and surely without forgiveness upon the white teachers who have denied them even this much self-knowledge and who have disseminated among them these crippling ideas and desiccating lies. . . .

Perhaps a reader would like to know what it is like to go into a new class-room in the same way that I did and to see before you suddenly, and in terms you cannot avoid recognizing, the dreadful consequences of a year's wastage of real lives. [Editor's note: Kozol is now describing a different school.]

You walk into a narrow and old wood-smelling classroom and you see before you thirty-five curious, cautious and untrusting children, aged eight to thirteen, of whom about two-thirds are Negro. Three of the children are designated to you as special students. Thirty per cent of the class is reading at the Second Grade level in a year and in a month in which they should be reading at the height of Fourth Grade performance or at the beginning of the Fifth. Seven children out of the class are up to par. Ten substitutes or teacher changes. Or twelve changes. Or eight. Or eleven. Nobody seems to know how many teachers they have had. Seven of their lifetime records are missing: symptomatic and emblematic at once of the chaos that has been with them all year long. Many more lives than just seven have already been wasted but the seven missing records become an embittering symbol of the lives behind them which, equally, have been lost or mislaid. (You have to spend the first three nights staying up until dawn trying to reconstruct these records out of notes and scraps.) On the first math test you give, the class average comes out to 36. The children tell you with embarrassment that it has been like that since fall.

You check around the classroom. Of forty desks, five have tops with no hinges. You lift a desk-top to fetch a paper and you find that the top has fallen off. There are three windows. One cannot be opened. A sign on it written in the messy scribble of a hurried teacher or some custodial person warns you: DO NOT UNLOCK THIS WINDOW IT IS BROKEN. The general look of the room is as of a bleak-light photograph of a mental hospital. Above the one poor blackboard, gray rather than really black, and hard to write on, hangs from one tack, lopsided, a motto attributed to Benjamin Franklin: "Well begun is half done." Everything, or almost everything like that, seems a mockery of itself.

Into this grim scenario, drawing on your own pleasures and memories, you do what you can to bring some kind of life. You bring in some cheerful and colorful paintings by Joan Miro and Paul Klee. While the paintings by Miro do not arouse much interest, the ones by Klee become an instantaneous success. One picture in particular, a watercolor titled "Bird Garden," catches the fascination of the entire class. You slip it out of the book and tack it up on the wall beside the doorway and it creates a traffic jam every time the children have to file in or file out. You discuss with your students some of the reasons why Klee may have painted the way he did and you talk about the things that can be accomplished in a painting which could not be accomplished in a photograph. None of this seems to be above the children's heads. Despite this, you are advised flatly by the Art Teacher that your naïveté has gotten the best of you and that the children cannot possibly appreciate this. Klee is too difficult. Children will not enjoy it. You are unable to escape the idea that the Art Teacher means herself instead.

For poetry, in place of the recommended memory gems, going back again into your own college days, you make up your mind to introduce a poem of William Butler Yeats. It is about a lake isle called Innisfree, about birds that have the funny name of "linnets" and about a "bee-loud glade." The children do not all go crazy about it but a number of them seem to like it as much as you do and you tell them how once, three years before, you were living in England and you helped a man in the country to make his home from wattles and clay. The children become intrigued. They pay good attention and many of them grow more curious about the poem than they appeared at first. Here again, however, you are advised by older teachers that you are making a mistake: Yeats is too difficult for children. They can't enjoy it, won't appreciate it, wouldn't like it. You are aiming way above their heads . . . Another idea comes to mind and you decide to try out an easy and rather well-known and not very complicated poem of Robert Frost. The poem is called "Stopping By Woods on a Snowy Evening." This time, your supervisor happens to drop in from the School Department. He looks over the mimeograph, agrees with you that it's a nice poem, then points out to you — tolerantly, but strictly — that you have made another mistake. "Stopping By Woods" is scheduled for Sixth Grade. It is not "a Fourth Grade poem," and it is not to be read or looked at during the Fourth Grade. Bewildered as you are by what appears to be a kind of idiocy, you still feel reproved and criticized and muted and set back and you feel that you have been caught in the commission of a serious mistake.

On a series of other occasions, the situation is repeated. The children are offered something new and something lively. They respond to it energetically and they are attentive and their attention does not waver. For the first time in a long while perhaps there is actually some real excitement and some growing and some thinking going on within that one small room. In each case, however, you are advised sooner or later that you are making a mistake. Your mistake, in fact, is to have impinged upon the standardized condescension on which the entire administration of the school is based. To hand Paul Klee's pictures to the children of this classroom, and particularly in a twenty-dollar volume, constitutes a threat to this school system. It is not different from sending a little girl from the Negro ghetto into an art class near Harvard Yard. Transcending the field of familiarity of the administration, you are endangering its authority and casting a blow at its self-confidence. The way the threat is handled is by a continual and standardized underrating of the children: They can't do it, couldn't do it, wouldn't like it, don't deserve it . . . In such a manner, many children are tragically and unjustifiably held back from a great many of the good things that they might come to like or admire and are pinned down instead to books the teacher knows and to easy tastes that she can handle. This includes, above all, of course, the kind of material that is contained in the Course of Study.

Try to imagine, for a child, how great the gap between the outside world and the world conveyed within this kind of school must seem: A little girl, maybe Negro, comes in from a street that is lined with car-carcasses. Old purple Hudsons and one-wheel-missing Cadillacs represent her horizon and mark the edges of her dreams. In the kitchen of her house roaches creep and large rats crawl. On the way to school a wino totters. Some teenage white boys slow down their car to insult her, and speed on. At school, she stands frozen for fifteen minutes in a yard of cracked cement that overlooks a hillside on which trash has been unloaded and at the bottom which the New York, New Haven and Hartford Railroad rumbles past. In the basement, she sits upon broken or splintery seats in filthy toilets and she is yelled at in the halls. Upstairs, when something has been stolen, she is told that she is the one who stole it and is called a liar and forced abjectly to apologize before a teacher who has not the slightest idea in the world of who the culprit truly was. The same teacher, behind the child's back, ponders audibly with imagined compassion: "What can you do with this kind of material? How can you begin to teach this kind of child?"

Gradually going crazy, the child is sent after two years of misery to a pupil adjustment counselor who arranges for her to have some tests and considers the entire situation and discusses it with the teacher and finally files a long report. She is, some months later, put onto a waiting-list some place for once-a-week therapy but another year passes before she has gotten anywhere near to the front of a long line. By now she is fourteen, has lost whatever innocence she still had in the back seat of the old Cadillac and, within two additional years, she will be ready and eager for dropping out of school.

Once at school, when she was eight or nine, she drew a picture of a rich-looking lady in an evening gown with a handsome man bowing before her but she was told by an insensate and wild-eyed teacher that what she had done was junk and garbage and the picture was torn up and thrown away before her eyes. The rock and roll music that she hears on the Negro station is considered "primitive" by her teachers but she prefers its insistent rhythms to the dreary monotony of school. Once, in Fourth Grade, she got excited at school about some writing she had never heard about before. A handsome green book, brand new, was held up before her and then put into her hands. Out of this book her teacher read a poem. The poem was about a Negro — a woman who was a maid in the house of a white person — and she liked it. It remained in her memory. Somehow without meaning to, she found that she had done the impossible for her: she had memorized that poem. Perhaps, horribly, in the heart of her already she was aware that it was telling about her future: fifty dollars a week to scrub floors and bathe little white babies in the suburbs after an hour's street-car ride. The poem made her want to cry. The white lady, the lady for whom the maid was working, told the maid she loved her. But the maid in the poem wasn't going to tell any lies in return. She knew she didn't feel any love for the white lady and she told the lady so. The poem was shocking to her, but it seemed bitter, strong and true. Another poem in the same green book was about a little boy on a merry-go-round. She laughed with the class at the question he asked about a Jim Crow section on a merry-go-round, but she also was old enough to know that it was not a funny poem really and it made her, valuably, sad. She wanted to know how she could get hold of that poem, and maybe that whole book. The poems were moving to her . . .

This was a child in my class. Details are changed somewhat but it is essentially one child. The girl was one of the three unplaced special students in that Fourth Grade room. She was not an easy girl to teach and it was hard even to keep her at her seat on many mornings, but I do not remember that there was any difficulty at all in gaining and holding onto her attention on the day that I brought in that green book of Langston Hughes.

Of all of the poems of Langston Hughes that I read to my Fourth Graders, the one that the children liked most was a poem that has the title "Ballad of the Landlord." The poem is printed along with some other material in the back part of this book. This poem may not satisfy the taste of every critic, and I am not making any claims to immortality for a poem just because I happen to like it a great deal. But the reason this poem did have so much value and meaning for me and, I believe, for many of my students, is that it not only seems moving in an obvious and immediate human way but that it *finds* its emotion in something ordinary. It is a poem which really does allow both heroism and pathos to poor people, sees strength in awkwardness and attributes to a poor person standing on the stoop of his slum house every bit as much significance as William Wordsworth saw in daffodils, waterfalls and clouds. At the request of the children later on I mimeographed that poem and, although nobody in the classroom was asked to do this, several of the children took it home and memorized it on their own. I did not assign it for memory, because I do not think that memorizing a poem has any special value. Some of the children just came in and asked if they could recite it. Before long, almost every child in the room had asked to have a turn.

All of the poems that you read to Negro children obviously are not going to be by or about Negro people. Nor would anyone expect that all poems which are read to a class of poor children ought to be grim or gloomy or heart-breaking or sad. But when, among the works of many different authors, you do have the will to read children a poem by a man so highly renowned as Langston Hughes, then I think it is important not to try to pick a poem that is innocuous, being like any other poet's kind of poem, but I think you ought to choose a poem that is genuinely representative and then try to make it real to the children in front of you in the way that I tried. I also think it ought to be taken seriously by a teacher when a group of young children come in to him one morning and announce that they have liked something so much that they have memorized it voluntarily. It surprised me and impressed me when that happened. It was all I needed to know to confirm for me the value of reading that poem and the value of reading many other poems to children which will build upon, and not attempt to break down, the most important observations and very deepest foundations of their lives. . . .

. . . I was standing in front of the class and they were listening to a record I had brought in. The record was a collection of French children's songs. We had been spending the month reading and talking about Paris and about France. As lunch-time drew near I decided to let the children listen to the music while they were having their meal. While the record was playing, a little signal on the wall began to buzz. I left the room and hurried to the Principal's office. A white man whom I had never seen before was sitting by the Principal's desk. This man, bristling and clearly hostile to me, as was the Principal, instantly attacked me for having read to my class and distributed at their wish the poem I have talked about that was entitled "Ballad of the Landlord." It turned out that he was the father of one of the white boys in the class. He was also a police officer. The mimeograph of the poem, in my handwriting, was waved before my eyes. The Principal demanded to know what right I had to allow such a poem — not in the official Course of Study — to be read and memorized by the children in my class. I said I had not asked anyone to memorize it but that I would defend the poem and its use against her or anyone on the basis that it was a good poem. The Principal became incensed with my answer and blurted out that she did not consider it a work of art. I remember that I knew right away I was not going to give in to her. I replied, in my own anger, that I had spent a good many years studying poetry and that I was not going to accept her judgment about a poem that meant that much to me and to my pupils. Although I did not say it in these words, it was really a way of telling her that I thought myself a better judge of poetry than she. I hope that I am.

The parent attacked me, as well, for having forced his son to read a book about the United Nations. I had brought a book to class, one out of sixty or more volumes, that told about the U.N. and its Human Rights Commission. The man, I believe, had mistaken "human rights" for "civil rights" and he was consequently in a patriotic rage. The Principal, in fairness, made the point that she did not think there was anything really wrong with the United Nations, although in the report that she later filed on the matter, she denied this for some reason and said, instead, "I then spoke and said that I felt there was no need for this material in the classroom." The Principal's report goes on to say that, after she dismissed me to my own room, she assured the parent that "there was not another teacher in the district who would have used this poem or any material like it. I assured him that his children would be very safe from such incidents."

As the Principal had instructed, I returned to my class, where the children had remained quiet and had not even opened up their lunch because I had not told them to and they were patiently waiting for me to come back. We had our lunch and listened to more music and did the rest of our lessons and at quarter to two, just before school ended, the Principal called me back again. She told me I was fired. This was about eight days before the end of school. I asked her whether this was due to the talk we had had earlier but she said it was not. I asked her if it was due to an evaluation, a written report, which I had sent in on the compensatory program about a week before. This was a report that I had written, as all teachers had, in answer to a request from the School Department and in which I had said that the program seemed to me to be very poor. I was told, at the time I passed it in, that the Principal had been quite angry. But again she said it was not that. I asked her finally if my dismissal was at her request and she said, No, it came from higher up and she didn't know anything about it except that I should close up my records and leave school and not come back. She said that I should not say good-bye to the children in my class. I asked her if she really meant this and she repeated it to me as an order.

I returned to my class, taught for ten more minutes, then gave assignments for the following morning as if I would be there and saw the children file off. After all but one were gone, that one, a little girl, helped me to pile up the books and posters and pictures with which I had tried to fill the room. It took an hour to get everything out and when it was all in my car it filled up the back seat and the space behind it and the floor, as well as the floor and half the seat in front. Outside my car, on the sidewalk, I said good-bye to this one child and told her that I would not be back again. I told her I had had a disagreement with the Principal and I asked her to say good-bye to the other children. I regretted very much now that I had not disobeyed the Principal's last order and I wished that I could have had one final chance to speak to all my pupils. The little girl, in any case, took what I had said with great solemnity and promised that she would relay my message to the other children. Then I left the school.

The next morning, an official who had charge of my case at the School Department contradicted the Principal by telling me that I was being fired at her wish. The woman to whom I spoke said the reason was the use of the poem by Langston Hughes, which was punishable because it was not in the Course of Study. She also said something to me at the time that had never been said to me before, and something that represented a much harder line on curriculum innovation than I had ever seen in print. No literature, she said, which is not in the Course of Study can *ever* be read by a Boston teacher without permission from someone higher up. When I asked her about this in more detail, she said further that no poem anyway by any Negro author can be considered permissible if it involves suffering. I thought this a very strong statement and I asked her several times again if that was really what she meant. She insisted that it was.

I asked if there would be many good poems left to read by such a standard. Wouldn't it rule out almost all great Negro literature? Her answer evaded the issue. No poetry that described suffering was felt to be suitable. The only Negro poetry that could be read in the Boston schools, she indicated, must fit a certain kind of standard or canon. The kind of poem she meant, she said by example, might be a poem that "accentuates the positive" or "describes nature" or "tells of something hopeful." Nothing was wanted of suffering, nothing that could be painful, nothing that might involve its reader in a moment of self-questioning or worry. If this is an extremely conservative or eccentric viewpoint, I think that it is nonetheless something which has to be taken seriously. For an opinion put forward in the privacy of her office by a School Department official who has the kind of authority that that woman had must be taken to represent a certain segment of educational opinion within the Boston school system and in some ways it seems more representative even than the carefully written and carefully prepared essays of such a lady as the Deputy Superintendent. For in those various writings Miss Sullivan unquestionably has had one ear tuned to the way they were going to come across in print and sound in public whereas, in the office of a central bureaucratic person such as the lady with whom I now was talking, you receive an absolutely innocent and unedited experience in what a school system really feels and believes.

The same official went on a few minutes later to tell me that, in addition to having made the mistake of reading the wrong poem, I also had made an error in bringing in books to school from the Cambridge Public Library. When I told her that there were no books for reading in our classroom, except for the sets of antiquated readers, and that the need of the children was for individual reading which they would be able to begin without delay, she told me that that was all very well but still this was the Boston school system and that meant that you must not use a book that the Cambridge Library supplied. She also advised me, in answer to my question, that any complaint from a parent means automatic dismissal of a teacher anyway and that this, in itself, was therefore sufficient grounds for my release. When I repeated this later to some Negro parents they were embittered and startled. For they told me of many instances in which they had complained that a teacher whipped their child black and blue or called him a nigger openly and yet the teacher had not been released. It seemed obvious to them, as it seems to me, and would to anyone, that a complaint from a white police officer carries more weight in the Boston school system than the complaint of the mother of a Negro child.

I asked this official finally whether I had been considered a good teacher and what rating I had been given. She answered that she was not allowed to tell me. An instant later, whimsically reversing herself, she opened her files and told me that my rating was good. The last thing she said was that deviation from a prescribed curriculum was a serious offense and that I would never be permitted to teach in Boston again. The words she used were these: "You're out. You cannot teach in the Boston schools again. If you want to teach why don't you try a private school someday?"

6

Our Children Are Dying

Nat Hentoff

Nat Hentoff is a provocative journalist; here he writes about the work of Principal Elliott Shapiro. Hentoff uses the techniques of his craft to develop an enthusiastic yet objective account of an attempt by an administrator in a Harlem school to serve children. Despite its title, Our Children Are Dying *is a fundamentally hopeful book.*

Hentoff is a prolific writer on a variety of subjects, including jazz, pacifism, and politics, and a frequent contributor to magazines. As the excerpt opens, Shapiro is talking to Hentoff.

We walked into the hall and a gaggle of children rushed by. "They look lively, don't they?" said Shapiro. "And they're very charming. But our children are dying. The way they look conceals the fact that they're dying. It's not like being killed by a car. There's no blood on them, and because there is no visible injury, nobody in the middle class is aghast at the sight. Nobody gets really involved. Let me give you an example of what I mean. Fourteen years ago, two years before I came here, of one hundred and twenty-two children in the sixth grade, only three were reading at grade level. That means one hundred and nineteen children had been separated very effectively from society. They're now twenty-five or twenty-six years old. What kinds of jobs do you think they have? I don't know for sure, but I can make an informed guess. That year one hundred and nineteen children died. And thousands and thousands of other children in this city have been dying because their brain cells have never been fully brought to life. But the white middle class doesn't *see* this. Living in a ghetto, the children are out of sight and out of conscience."

A twelve-year-old boy ambled along the corridor. "Hi," Shapiro waved. The boy smiled. Miss Carmen I. Jones, a Negro, an assistant principal in charge of the lower grades from pre-kindergarten through the second grade, joined us as we walked. "We did begin to do a little better," Shapiro went on, "but not nearly well enough. By 1961, of one hundred and sixty-seven children in the sixth grade, forty-five were reading at grade level or above. That doesn't mean the children fourteen years ago were inferior. It means that we were helping some of our children learn to read somewhat more effectively. But since, in this affluent economy, education is still financed out of a principle of scarcity, there was a precipitous drop in the achievement level of that 1961 sixth grade below the top forty-five. We were too badly outnumbered to give the rest of those sixth graders all they needed. And they died. One example of how outnumbered we were is that from 1955 to 1962 the first and second grades and part of the third grade were on double shifts. They'd come in from eight to twelve or from twelve to four. They didn't even get a full day of schooling. Now that's stopped, but we're still outnumbered.

"From 1961 on, in terms of sixth-grade reading levels, we've been going downhill. The reason is that, after the third grade, we send our best achievers away to Intellectually Gifted Children's classes. We encourage parents to use the free-choice transfer policy to send their children to schools with an I.G.C. Program in other areas, thereby also promoting integrated education. Sure, losing their very best achievers is discouraging for our teachers, but we owe it to the children to let them get into those I.G.C. classes. When we move into our new school, I'm going to try to develop our own I.G.C. Program and then encourage class leaders from other schools to come to us. Better yet, obviously, would be heterogeneous classes with children at varying achievement levels. But to make those work, you need much, much smaller ratios of adults to children."

I asked whether the I.G.C. classes weren't harmful in the sense that they might create a feeling among those selected of being part of an elite, and a feeling of inferiority among those left out.

"As long," said Miss Jones firmly, "as they have those programs in other neighborhoods and other schools, we have to follow the concept."

"Besides," Shapiro added, "it doesn't hurt for a Negro child to feel superior."

"But," Miss Jones countered sharply, "they feel superior to other Negro children."

"That's why," Shapiro said, "I try to have our bright achievers sent into other neighborhoods than predominantly Negro ones." . . .

. . . "When I first came, I began to relax the discipline in the school — in the narrow sense of that word — and there were parents who interpreted that action as indicating I was just another white man who didn't care about their children. If I cared, I'd discipline them more. I think we've proved we do care, but there are still parents who feel our discipline isn't strong enough. They go off to work and are worried about their children being alone. So the threat of severe corporal punishment if the child misbehaves is always in the air, almost like a wireless between the parent and the child. They want us to 'protect' the child in the same way they do. I keep telling them it would actually be easier for us to use strong discipline — in that narrow sense — but that our staff tries to develop the children's liveliness. Being 'good' in a rigid sense gets in the way of learning. The child begins to give the teacher only what the teacher wants and loses his appetite for learning, his curiosity, and part of his identity.

"We're trying to help them develop an *inner* discipline. A child must have enough energy left in him to remain courageous. By that I mean the ability to question rather than always saying, 'Yes, sir,' and 'No, sir.' I think it's good that many of our children are able to question the wisdom of the adults in this building. It's particularly important for Negro children. They've been taught it's safe to be respectful. We want them to understand that they're citizens and they *can* question. That is, they're citizens except for one right — the right not to go to school. It's a very important right, and since we've taken it away from them, it's our responsibility to make the school as interesting as possible. You know, at Junior High School 136, where many of our children go when they leave here, our kids are considered outstanding in behavior in that they're not hostile to the teachers. Being able to question them, they can respect and trust them.

"The children in Mr. Marcus's fifth-grade class, incidentally," Shapiro said with evident satisfaction, "have been doing some important questioning. They analyzed a sizable number of social studies textbooks and they found every one to be wanting. Then they wrote letters to the publishers and to some of the people in the school system pointing out that certain matters of opinion were being treated as facts. The statement in one book, for example, that on the whole, the slaves were happy on the plantations. The children got many replies, and not being satisfied with some of them, they wrote again."

I asked Shapiro what the reaction had been from on high in the school system.

He smiled. "There were inquiries. Nothing was said that was an outright condemnation, but implicit in the questions was: 'How could you let this happen?' Among the inquiries were: 'What kinds of lessons are being given in that social studies class? Was the teacher biased? Did you discuss this project with the children? Perhaps there were better textbooks in the catalogue that were not analyzed?' Those are the kinds of questions that keep teachers passive. My answer was that at this point there is no social studies textbook which treats the Negro fairly, and that the children's questions were a true culmination of their research and were an excellent learning experience.

"Another residue of criticism from the parents," Shapiro continued, "is that the children aren't achieving well enough. It's obvious to some parents of sixth-grade children, for instance, that their kids are not reading at sixth-grade level. Some say, 'Why don't you hold the child back?' We do hold some back, but we don't have the facilities to do much good if we were to keep a lot of them back. And we do have Reading Improvement Teachers who take small groups out of the classroom for remedial reading work and who also work with teachers inside the classroom by concentrating on a particular group and leaving the teacher free to focus on the rest of the class. We do more of that than most schools. But we don't have enough teachers and small enough classes to do all that has to be done. The parents have a very real grievance. Two-thirds of our children in the sixth grade are not reading at grade level. That's better than ninety-nine per cent when I came, but it's hardly a triumph. If every teacher in the school were superior, we'd be able to reduce that proportion to one-third — even with big classes. But the human race being what it is, it's impossible to get that many superior teachers, just as it's impossible to find that many superior doctors, psychiatrists, and engineers. Therefore, we have to make conditions for teaching so good that the average teacher can become effective. If the context for teaching is superior, the average teacher will do as well as a superior teacher would have done in a bad setting."

Miss Jones, the assistant principal in charge of the lower grades, came in. With her was a young second-grade teacher. "Exciting news!" said Miss Jones, pointing to the teacher. "Thirteen in her class have finished *Our New Friends*." The teacher beamed. "That's only a first-grade book, of course, but Gus is really reading. He's picked up lots of new words." The teacher left. "That's when we get the rewards." Miss Jones turned to me. "You feel you're up against a blank wall, and suddenly one day light dawns and the child unfolds. No wonder a teacher feels like shouting when that happens. And you have no idea of the months of energy and effort that went into getting Gus to read. They didn't nickname him 'Granite Gus' for nothing."

"That sort of thing gets through to the parents too," said Shapiro. "I mean the great emotional investment our teachers have in getting the children to learn. The depth of that kind of concern only becomes clear over a long period of time . . .

In addition to involving himself and his staff in neighborhood conditions, Shapiro has also — particularly within the past five years — been concerned with emphasizing American Negro and African history and culture in the curriculum. Three years ago, with Shapiro's encouragement, thirty-five of the staff, under the direction of Miss Beryle Banfield, now an assistant principal at P.S. 175 on 134th Street in Manhattan, prepared a manual for teachers on ways of introducing African material into elementary school classwork.

The seventy-five-page manual includes sections on African folklore, family life, games, music, dances, art, foods, and history along with a bibliography for teachers and another for children. In the preface, Shapiro wrote:

> The history of Africa's earlier civilizations has been virtually omitted from textbooks and curricula of schools of every level, from elementary to college, everywhere in the world.
>
> In a real sense, this hiatus, this long silence, has been a stilling of the voice of conscience. The fact that a strong and glorious voice was stilled is a measure of the avarice of those who profited from the canard that Africa has no history.
>
> Now, at last, this long silence is coming to an end. Let us hope that our newly found ability to hear the voice of early Africa indicates that we now possess the will to live in the universal brotherhood that is absolutely essential for our survival.
>
> The material presented in the following pages is a breaking of that silence. More and greater voices will be heard as early Africa receives its due, but it is to the everlasting credit of Miss Beryle Banfield and the committees of teachers who worked so devotedly with her that the first voice to be heard in any educational system anywhere was theirs.
>
> Truly, they have been the pioneers, for we have been in the wilderness.

Requests for the manual have come from public school systems, church groups, social agencies, colleges, and individuals throughout the country. In the summer of 1964, sixty copies were in use in Mississippi Freedom Schools. There was also a demand for the manuals from the neighborhood. "People would come in off the street," Shapiro recalls, "and ask, 'Where is our history?' "

The one place from which interest in wider distribution of the guide did not come was the Board of Education. Copies had been sent to each of its members and to supervisory personnel. For a long time there was no response at all. Finally, two polite notes — but no offers to make the manual available throughout the school system — came from a member of the Board and from an assistant superintendent in charge of integration. The cost of preparing the manual had been borne entirely by the staff of P.S. 119, and much of its distribution was financed through a church group to which Mrs. Arthur Lanckton, a volunteer teacher at P.S. 119, belongs.

On the cover of the guide is a quotation from Edmund Burke: "A people will never look forward to posterity who never look backward to their ancestors." Shapiro has continued to operate on that conviction. In addition to classroom work on the Negro past, there have been African days and nights at the school. In 1964, for instance, some sixty of the children were trained in African dance by a professional African dancer. They performed at P.S. 119 before an overflow audience that included guests from African missions to the United Nations. Later the P.S. 119 dancers brought African culture to City Hall. For the event at the school, P.S. 119 parents prepared African food. "Our guests from the U.N.," Shapiro notes with pride, "certified that they were indeed African dishes."

7

The Lives of Children

George Dennison

It is difficult to excerpt from The Lives of Children, *for many of George Dennison's best insights are contained in his detailed reporting of interrelationships among students and staff. But the account of José's problems reproduced here provides some insights into the way Dennison conceives of the curriculum and the learner. Denni-*

Excerpts from *The Lives of Children*, by George Dennison, pp. 3–10, 73–80. Copyright © 1969 by George Dennison. Reprinted by permission of Random House, Inc.

*son's book should be read as a whole, for the experiences and moods
of both teachers and learners at the First Street School changed
throughout the year as described in* The Lives of Children.

*Dennison has taught in preschool, primary, and preparatory
schools, and has worked with severely disturbed children. The First
Street School closed in part because of lack of funds.*

There is no need to add to the criticism of our public schools. The critique
is extensive and can hardly be improved on. The processes of learning and
teaching, too, have been exhaustively studied. One thinks of the books of
Paul Goodman, John Holt, Greene and Ryan, Nat Hentoff, James Herndon,
Jonathan Kozol, Herbert Kohl; and of such researches as those of Bruner
and Piaget; and of Joseph Featherstone's important *Report.* The question
now is what to do. In the pages that follow, I would like to describe one unfamiliar approach to the problems which by now have become familiar. And
since "the crisis of the schools" consists in reality of a great many crises in
the lives of children, I shall try to make the children of the First Street
School the real subject of this book. There were twenty-three black, white,
and Puerto Rican in almost equal proportions, all from low-income families
in New York's Lower East Side. About half were on welfare. About half,
too, had come to us from the public schools with severe learning and behavior
problems.

Four things about the First Street School were unusual: first, its small size
and low teacher/pupil ratio; second, the fact that this luxurious intimacy,
which is ordinarily very expensive, cost about the same per child as the $850
annual operating costs of the public schools; third, our reversal of conventional structure, for where the public school conceives of itself merely as a
place of instruction, and puts severe restraints on the relationships between
persons, we conceived of ourselves as an environment for growth, and accepted the relationships between the children and ourselves as being the very
heart of the school; and fourth, the kind of freedom experienced by teachers
and pupils alike.

Freedom is an abstract and terribly elusive word. I hope that a context of
examples will make its meaning clear. The question is not really one of
authority, though it is usually argued in that form. When adults give up
authority, the freedom of children is not necessarily increased. Freedom is
not motion in a vacuum, but motion in a continuum. If we want to know
what freedom is, we must discover what the continuum is. "The principle,"
Dewey remarks, "is not what justifies an activity, for the principle is but
another name for the continuity of the activity." We might say something
similar of freedom: it is another name for the fullness and final shape of activities. We experience the activities, not the freedom. The mother of a child
in a public school told me that he kept complaining, "They never let me
finish anything!" We might say of the child that he lacked important free-
doms, but his own expression is closer to the experience: activities important

to him remained unfulfilled. Our concern for freedom is our concern for fulfillment — of activities we deem important and of persons we know are unique. To give freedom means to stand out of the way of the formative powers possessed by others.

Before telling more of the school, I must say that I was a partisan of libertarian values even before working there. I had read of the schools of A. S. Neill and Leo Tolstoy. I had worked in the past with severely disturbed children, and had come to respect the integrity of the organic processes of growth, which given the proper environment are the one source of change in individual lives. And so I was biased from the start and cannot claim the indifference of a neutral observer. Events at school did, however, time and again, confirm the beliefs I already held — which, I suppose, leaves me still a partisan, though convinced twice over. Yet if I can prove nothing at all in a scientific sense, there is still a power of persuasion in the events themselves, and I can certainly hope that our experience will arouse an experimental interest in other parents and teachers.

But there is something else that I would like to convey, too, and this is simply a sense of the lives of those who were involved — the jumble of persons and real events which did in fact constitute our school. The closer one comes to the facts of life, the less exemplary they seem, but the more human and the richer. Something of our time in history and our place in the world belongs to Vicente screaming in the hallway, and José opening the blade of a ten-inch knife — even more than to Vicente's subsequent learning to co-operate and José to read. So, too, with other apparently small details: the fantasy life and savagery of the older boys, the serenity and rationality of the younger ones, teachers' moments of doubt and defeat. Learning, in its essentials, is not a distinct and separate process. It is a function of growth. We took it quite seriously in this light, and found ourselves getting more and more involved in individual lives. It seems likely to me that the actual features of this involvement may prove useful to other people. At the same time, I would like to try to account for the fact that almost all of our children improved markedly, and some few spectacularly. We were obviously doing something right, and I would like to hazard a few guesses at what it might have been. All instruction was individual, and that was obviously a factor. The improvement I am speaking of, however, was not simply a matter of learning, but of radical changes in character. Where Vicente had been withdrawn and destructive, he became an eager participant in group activities and ceased destroying everything he touched. Both Eléna and Maxine had been thieves and were incredibly rebellious. After several months they could be trusted and had become imaginative and responsible contributors at school meetings. Such changes as these are not accomplished by instruction. They proceed from broad environmental causes. Here again, details which may seem irrelevant to the business of a school will give the reader an idea of what these causes may have been. A better way of saying this is that the business of a school is not, or should not be, mere instruction, but the life of the child.

This is especially important under such conditions as we experience today.

Life in our country is chaotic and corrosive, and the time of childhood for many millions is difficult and harsh. It will not be an easy matter to bring our berserk technocracy under control, but we *can* control the environment of the schools. It is a relatively small environment and has always been structured by deliberation. If, as parents, we were to take as our concern not the instruction of our children, but the lives of our children, we would find that our schools could be used in a powerfully regenerative way. Against all that is shoddy and violent and treacherous and emotionally impoverished in American life, we might propose conventions which were rational and straightforward, rich both in feeling and thought, and which treated individuals with a respect we do little more at present than proclaim from our public rostrums. We might cease thinking of school as a place, and learn to believe that it is basically relationships: between children and adults, adults and adults, children and other children. The four walls and the principal's office would cease to loom so hugely as the essential ingredients.

It is worth mentioning here that, with two exceptions, the parents of the children at First Street were not libertarians. They thought that they believed in compulsion, and rewards and punishments, and formal discipline, and report cards, and homework, and elaborate school facilities. They looked rather askance at our noisy classrooms and informal relations. If they persisted in sending us their children, it was not because they agreed with our methods, but because they were desperate. As the months went by, however, and the children who had been truants now attended eagerly, and those who had been failing now began to learn, the parents drew their own conclusions. By the end of the first year there was a high morale among them, and great devotion to the school.

We had no administrators. We were small and didn't need them. The parents found that, after all, they approved of this. They themselves could judge the competence of the teachers, and so could their children — by the specific act of learning. The parents' past experience of administrators had been uniformly upsetting — and the proof, of course, was in the pudding: the children were happier and *were* learning. As for the children, they never missed them.

We did not give report cards. We knew each child, knew his capacities and his problems, and the vagaries of his growth. This knowledge could not be recorded on little cards. The parents found — again — that they approved of this. It diminished the blind anxieties of life, for grades had never meant much to them anyway except some dim sense of *problem*, or some dim reassurance that things were all right. When they wanted to know how their children were doing, they simply asked the teachers.

We didn't give tests, at least not of the competitive kind. It was important to be aware of what the children knew, but more important to be aware of *how* each child knew what he knew. We could learn nothing about Maxine by testing Eléna. And so there was no comparative testing at all. The children never missed those invidious comparisons, and the teachers were spared the absurdity of ranking dozens of personalities on one uniform scale.

Our housing was modest. The children came to school in play-torn clothes.

Their families were poor. A torn dress, torn pants, frequent cleanings — there were expenses they could not afford. Yet how can children play without getting dirty? Our uncleanliness standard was just right. It looked awful and suited everyone.

We treated the children with consideration and justice. I don't mean that we never got angry and never yelled at them (nor they at us). I mean that we took seriously the pride of life that belongs to the young — even to the very young. We did not coerce them in violation of their proper independence. Parents and children both found that they approved very much of this.

Now I would like to describe the school, or more correctly, the children and teachers. I shall try to bring out in detail three important things:

1) That the proper concern of a primary school is not education in a narrow sense, and still less preparation for later life, but the present lives of the children — a point made repeatedly by John Dewey, and very poorly understood by many of his followers.

2) That when the conventional routines of a school are abolished (the military discipline, the schedules, the punishments and rewards, the standardization), what arises is neither a vacuum nor chaos, but rather a new order, based first on relationships between adults and children, and children and their peers, but based ultimately on such truths of the human condition as these: that the mind does not function separately from the emotions, but thought partakes of feeling and feeling of thought; that there is no such thing as knowledge *per se*, knowledge in a vacuum, but rather all knowledge is possessed and must be expressed by individuals; that the human voices preserved in books belong to the real features of the world, and that children are so powerfully attracted to this world that the very motion of their curiosity comes through to us as a form of love; that an active moral life cannot be evolved except where people are free to express their feelings and act upon the insights of conscience.

3) That running a primary school — *provided it be small* — is an extremely simple thing. It goes without saying that the teachers must be competent (which does not necessarily mean passing courses in a teacher's college). Given this *sine qua non*, there is nothing mysterious. The present quagmire of public education is entirely the result of unworkable centralization and the lust for control that permeates every bureaucratic institution.

In saying this, I do not mean that the work in a free school is easy. On the contrary, teachers find it taxing. But they find it rewarding, too — quite unlike the endless round of frustrations experienced by those at work in the present system. . . .

Perhaps after these excerpts from the journal, something of our intimate, informal style may be apparent. What may not be so obvious is that there was any connection between this style and the advances in learning made by the children. And here we come to one of the really damaging myths of education, namely, that learning is the result of teaching; that the progress of the child bears a direct relation to methods of instruction and internal relationships of curriculum. Nothing could be farther from the truth. Naturally we want good teachers. Naturally we want a coherent curriculum (we need not impose it in standardized forms). But to cite these as the effective causes of learning is wrong. The causes are in the child. When we consider the powers of mind of a healthy eight-year-old — the avidity of the senses, the finesse and energy of observation, the effortless concentration, the vivacious memory — we realize immediately that these powers possess true magnitude in the general scale of things. Beside them, the subject matter of primary education can hardly be regarded as a difficult task. Yet the routine assumption of school professionals is that somehow or other learning is difficult.

Why is it, then, that so many children fail? Let me put it bluntly: it is because our system of public education is a horrendous, life-destroying mess. The destruction is primary. The faculties themselves, the powers of mind, are nipped in the bud, or are held inoperative, which eventually comes to the same thing.

There is no such thing as learning except (as Dewey tells us) in the continuum of experience. But this continuum cannot survive in the classroom unless there is reality of encounter between the adults and the children. The teachers must be themselves, and not play roles. They must teach the children, and not teach "subjects." The child, after all, is avid to acquire what he takes to be the necessities of life, and the teacher must not answer him with mere professionalism and gimmickry. The continuum of experience and reality of encounter are destroyed in the public schools (and most private ones) by the very methods which form the institution itself — the top-down organization, the regimentation, the faceless encounters, the empty professionalism, and so on.

Eléna and Maxine suddenly began assimilating schoolwork at a fantastic rate. Their lessons were brief and few, yet in a year and a half both girls covered more than three years' work. Maxine, who had been behind in everything, was reading three years beyond her age level. But the truth is that there was nothing unusual in this, though certainly it seems to be rare. I mean that the girls found it *easy*. José gradually reversed his long-standing habit of total failure. He began to learn. His progress was slow, but his experience was much like that of the girls. I mean that he discovered — just barely glimpsed — the easiness of learning. And invariably, when he glimpsed it, a very particular laughter bubbled out of him, expressing release.

The experience of learning is an experience of wholeness. The child feels the unity of his own powers and the continuum of persons. His parents, his friends, his teachers, and the vague human shapes of his future form one world for him, and he feels the adequacy and reality of his powers within this world. Anything short of this wholeness is not true learning. Children who store up facts and parrot the answers (as John Holt has described in *How Children Fail*) invariably suffer a great deal of anxiety. If they are joined to the continuum of persons, it is not by the exercise of their powers, but by the suppression of their needs. Rebellious children are more loyal to their instincts, but they suffer the insecurity of conflict with the persons who form the continuum of life.

The really crucial things at First Street were these: that we eliminated —
to the best of our ability — the obstacles which impede the natural growth of
mind; that we based everything on reality of encounter between teacher and
child; and that we did what we could (not enough, by far) to restore something of the continuum of experience within which every child must achieve
his growth. It is not remarkable that under these circumstances the children
came to life. They had been terribly bored, after all, by the experience of
failure. For books *are* interesting; numbers are, and painting, and facts about
the world.

Let me put this in more specific terms by saying a few words about José.
At the same time, I would like to show that what are widely regarded as
"learning problems" are very often simply problems of school administration.

José had failed in everything. After five years in the public schools, he
could not read, could not do sums, and had no knowledge even of the most
rudimentary history or geography. He was described to us as *having* "poor
motivation," *lacking* "reading skills," and (again) *having* "a reading problem."

Now what are these *entities* he possessed and lacked? Is there any such
thing as "a reading problem," or "motivation," or "reading skills"?

To say "reading problem" is to draw a little circle around José and specify
its contents: syllables, spelling, grammar, etc.

Since we are talking about a real boy, we are talking about real books, too,
and real teachers and real classrooms. And real boys, after all, do not read
syllables but words; and words, even printed words, have the property of
voice; and voices do not exist in a void, but in very clearly indicated social
classes.

By what process did José and his schoolbook come together? Is this process
part of his reading problem?

Who asks him to read the book? *Someone* asks him. In what sort of voice
and for what purpose, and with what concern or lack of concern for the outcome?

And who wrote the book? For whom did they write it? Was it written for
José? Can José actually partake of the life the book seems to offer?

And what of José's failure to read? We cannot stop at the fact that he
draws a blank. How does he do it? What does he do? It is impossible, after
all, for him to sit there *not listening*. He is sitting there doing something. Is
he daydreaming? If so, of what? Aren't these particular daydreams part of
José's reading problem? Did the teacher ask him what he was thinking of?
Is his failure to ask part of José's reading problem?

Printed words are an extension of speech. To read is to move outward
toward the world by means of speech. Reading is conversing. But what if
this larger world is frightening and insulting? Should we, or should we not,
include fear and insult in José's reading problem?

And is there a faculty in the mind devoted to the perception and recollec-
tion of *abc*? Or is there just one intelligence, modified by pleasure, pain, hope,
etc. Obviously José has little skill in reading, but as I have just indicated,
reading is no small matter of syllables and words. Then reading skills are no

small matter either. They, too, include his typical relations with adults, with other children, and with himself; for he is fiercely divided within himself, and this conflict lies at the very heart of his reading problem.

José's reading problem is José. Or to put it another way, there is no such thing as a reading problem. José hates books, schools, and teachers, and among a hundred other insufficiencies — *all of a piece* — he cannot read. Is this a reading problem?

A reading problem, in short, is not a fact of life, but a fact of school administration. It does not describe José, but describes the action performed by the school, i.e., the action of ignoring everything about José except his response to printed letters.

Let us do the obvious thing for a change, and take a look at José. This little glimpse of his behavior is what a visitor might have seen during José's early months at the First Street School.

He is standing in the hallway talking to Vicente and Julio. I am sitting alone in the classroom, in one of the student's chairs. There is a piece of paper in front of me, and on it a sentence of five words. The words appear again below the sentence in three columns so that each word is repeated a number of times. Now since José came to us with a reading problem, let us see what relation we can find between these one dozen syllables and the extraordinary behavior he exhibits.

He had been talking animatedly in the hall. Now as he comes to join me, his face contracts spasmodically and the large gestures of his arms are reduced to almost nothing. There is no one near him, and he is absolutely free to refuse the lesson, yet he begins to squirm from side to side as if someone were leading him by the arm. He hitches up his pants, thrusts out his lower lip, and fixes his eyes on the floor. His forehead is lumpy and wrinkled like that of a man suffering physical pain. His eyes have glazed over. Suddenly he shakes himself, lifts his head, and squares his shoulders. But his eyes are still glassy. He yawns abruptly and throws himself into the chair beside me, sprawling on the tip of his spine. But now he turns to me and smiles his typical smile, an outrageous bluff, yet brave and attractive. "Okay, man — let's go." I point to the sentence and he rattles it off, for his memory is not bad and he recalls it clearly from the day before. When I ask him to read the same words in the columns below, however, he repeats the sentence angrily and jabs at the columns with his finger, for he had not read the sentence at all but had simply remembered it. He guffaws and blushes. Now he sits up alertly and crouches over the paper, scanning it for clues: smudges, random pencil marks, his own doodles from the day before. He throws me sagacious glances, trying to interpret the various expressions on my face. He is trying to reconstruct in his mind *the entire sequence* of yesterday's lesson, so that the written words will serve as clues to the spoken ones, and by repeating the spoken ones he will be able to seem to read. The intellectual energy — and the acumen — he puts into this enterprise would more than suffice for learning to read. It is worth mentioning here that whenever he comes upon the written word "I," he is thrown into confusion, though in conversation he experiences no such difficulty.

Now what are José's problems? One of them, certainly, is the fact that he cannot read. But this problem is obviously caused by other, more fundamental problems; indeed, his failure to read should not be described as a problem at all, but a symptom. We need only look at José to see what his problems are: shame, fear, resentment, rejection of others and of himself, anxiety, self-contempt, loneliness. None of these were caused by the difficulty of reading printed words — a fact all the more evident if I mention here that José, when he came to this country at the age of seven, had been able to read Spanish and had regularly read to his mother (who cannot read) the post cards they received from the literate father who had remained in Puerto Rico. For five years he had sat in the classrooms of the public schools literally growing stupider by the year. He had failed at everything (not just reading) and had been promoted from one grade to another in order to make room for the children who were more or less doomed to follow in his footsteps.

Obviously not all of José's problems originated in school. But given the intimacy and freedom of the environment at First Street, his school-induced behavior was easy to observe. He could not believe, for instance, that anything contained in books, or mentioned in classrooms, belonged by rights to himself, or even belonged to the world at large, as trees and lampposts belong quite simply to the world we all live in. He believed, on the contrary, that things dealt with in school belonged somehow to school, or were administered by some far-reaching bureaucratic arm. There had been no indication that he could share in them, but rather that he would be measured against them and be found wanting. Nor did he believe that he was entitled to personal consideration, but felt rather that if he wanted to speak, either to a classmate or to a teacher, or wanted to stand up and move his arms and legs, or even wanted to urinate, he must do it more or less in defiance of authority. During his first weeks at our school he was belligerent about the most innocuous things. Outside of school he had learned many games, as all children do, unaware that they are engaged in "the process of learning." Inside the school this ability deserted him. Nor had it ever occurred to him that one might deliberately go about the business of learning something, for he had never witnessed the whole forms of learning. What he had seen was reciting, copying, answering questions, taking tests — and these, alas, do not add up to learning. Nor could he see any connection between school and his life at home and in the streets. If he had heard our liberal educators confessing manfully, "We are not getting through to them," he would have winced with shame and anger at that little dichotomy "we/them," for he had been exposed to it in a hundred different forms.

One would not say that he had been schooled at all, but rather that for five years he had been indoctrinated in the contempt of persons, for contempt of persons had been the supreme fact demonstrated in the classrooms, and referred alike to teachers, parents, and children. For all practical purposes, José's inability to learn consisted precisely of his school-induced behavior. . . .

8

Epilogue: The Key Word is Relevance

William Van Til

The editor's epilogue is a reminder that the quest for relevance leads through a curriculum based on learners, social realities, and human values. As the compassionate critics rightly insist, the curriculum must be related to the individual learner. A curriculum which ignores the learner's experience will have no meaning for him, and thus relevance will be unattainable.

Yet a child-centered curriculum alone is not enough, despite the eloquence of the compassionate critics. Unless the curriculum illuminates social realities and clarifies values for mankind, it is not sufficiently germane to contemporary society.

At least so the editor suggests, citing illustrations of irrelevance and suggesting both fundamental changes and adaptations in the contemporary curriculum.

Let us begin with an admission: Some of the content we teach in American schools is not as relevant as it might be to the lives of the young people we teach, to the society in which they are growing up, or to the clarification of democratic values.

Some illustrations are obvious. For instance, one of the many Puerto Rican schools I visited during a New York University survey of education in Puerto Rico was in a village high in the mountains of the interior. The villagers were very poor and afflicted with the problems that go with poverty — poor nutrition, inefficient agriculture, dilapidated housing, bad health, and the rest.

Only a handful of young people of the village and the surrounding countryside ever enrolled in any kind of educational institution beyond high school. Yet, what were the young people studying in the secondary school in this little mountain village? In a social studies class, they were memorizing lists of products of South American countries. Their mathematics work had no relationship to the problems they might encounter in the school shop or at home or elsewhere. In an English class, students were reading eighteenth and nineteenth century British novels: At the time of my visit one class was dissecting *Ivanhoe*. (This mountain school and community, I hasten to say, was not typical; many other Puerto Rican schools were more relevant to learners, society, and values, and many other communities had higher living standards.)

Recognizing the lack of relevance in education in an exotic, faraway setting is easy. Such was the case when I visited a home economics class in a town of mud hovels in Iran: The girls were making scrapbooks of pictures (clipped from very old magazines) that portrayed the clothes and foods of prosperous Americans and Europeans.

The closer to home we get, however, the harder it becomes for a teacher to recognize irrelevance. Take Doris Smith and Harry Jones, for instance. She teaches in the suburbs in the Midwestern United States; he, in the slums of a West Coast city. Both of them would quickly recognize the lack of meaning in the two faraway examples cited. Yet, both might have difficulty recognizing that they have their own problems in making the content of their classes meaningful to some students.

Doris Smith teaches social studies in an affluent suburb that is among the first places where new national projects and proposals are tried. A genuine innovator, she uses a variety of methods and materials with versatility. She uses simulation techniques, for example, and has just completed an academic game with her eleventh graders. The game deals with economics; the players adopt roles and the ones who make the most money are the winners.

Margaret, one of Miss Smith's better students, went through the motions of the game but was fundamentally uninvolved. Why? Because, like Benjamin in *The Graduate*, Margaret had painfully learned from the lives of her parents and their friends that affluence did not necessarily result in a good life. Why, wondered Margaret, were teachers blind to what was most relevant to young people? For instance, why didn't the teacher see that the most important thing about this game would be to examine the materialistic goals which were taken for granted as desirable?

During follow-up discussions, Miss Smith raised questions with the class about the strategy of moves made during the game. Margaret's responses were correct but unrelated to her concern for values.

Harry Jones teaches language arts in an intermediate school in a slum neighborhood. Though Mr. Jones is white and most of his students are black, racial differences have not been a barrier to mutual liking and respect. The class is now reading a selection in a new anthology which is quite appropriate to the level of the students' reading abilities. Mr. Jones notices that Jess isn't reading the assigned selection, but instead is simply leafing through the pages. It isn't as though I'd asked the class to read dull, difficult material simply because it's supposed to be an English classic, Harry thinks. I guess Jess just doesn't care.

Jess is thinking: I can't find black men in this book. Where's the brothers? This is Whitey's book. How can a good guy like Mr. Jones be so dumb? Not for me, baby.

"What are you doing, Jess?" asks Harry. "Just lookin'," says Jess.

Good teachers though they are, even Miss Smith and Mr. Jones sometimes attempt to teach content that is unrelated to the lives of learners. Some teachers have even greater difficulty in achieving relevance than do methodologically skilled Doris and well-liked Harry. Classes do exist in your community and mine in which an uninterrupted academic content bores young people. Classes do exist where subject matter is quite unrelated to the dilemmas and struggles and aspirations of many prospective learners.

The teacher who realizes that his content of instruction isn't meaningful has two viable alternatives. He can change his content from the irrelevant to the relevant. Or, if he cannot change the required content, he can teach it in such a way as to give it relevance.

Yes, a third possibility does exist. One can continue with the meaningless content, break his heart trying to teach, and achieve very little.

A teacher does not need extensive instruction in educational psychology to realize that his teaching must be connected with the student's background, drives, and life if any learning is to take place. Experience soon teaches a teacher this axiom.

The obvious and sensible thing to do is to replace the irrelevant with the relevant through changing the content. Remember, for instance, the poverty-stricken Puerto Rican mountain village in which the students were memorizing products, being taught mathematics without application, and reading *Ivanhoe*. Here was a setting characterized by a host of problems in the areas of health, sanitation, housing, nutrition, safety, use of resources, production, and consumption. Here were Puerto Rican youngsters who would face bewildering life problems including those presented by the continuing restless migration from the rural ways of the *barrio* to the urbanized ways of San Juan; from the hospitable island of their birth to the impersonal, tenement-lined canyons of New York City, with its strange folkways and less-than-warm welcome to those regarded as "foreigners."

Reality could be introduced into their education. In social studies, students might well learn of the real problems of the village, the island, the mainland. In mathematics, they might see a relationship between mathematics and the problems they encounter in school shop and in their homes. In English classes, students might well acquire the bilinguality they need by reading English-language newspapers and magazines, as well as books of fiction and nonfiction by Puerto Rican and mainland Americans, plus a sampling of British authors. Fortunately, the better Puerto Rican schools do introduce such realities into their programs.

In mainland America, too, the obvious and sensible approach is to change the content if it is not germane. Most educators will readily grant that a teacher must begin at the actual level of accomplishment of those who are to be educated — not to stay there but begin there. Most will grant that pitching the learning at an unreachable level is an exercise in futility. But additionally we must recognize the vital importance of selecting suitable content.

The curriculum should be made more relevant to the lives of the children and youth for whom the curriculum exists. Through their reading materials, for example, city children must often meet people like themselves, rather than always encounter the legendary Dick and Jane and Spot of suburban life. The world of the city must itself become part of the subject matter if young city dwellers are to improve human relations, develop citizenship, widen horizons, and meet the problems of urban living. In Harry Jones's class, and those of his colleagues, surely the contributions of Negro-Americans should be an integral part of the American literature curriculum for both Negroes and whites.

Nor are the suburbs exempt from the blight of irrelevance. Though some suburban young people have an economic head start in life, they, too, are sometimes cheated. When communities are bland and homogenized and indifferent to reality, the young are sometimes cheated of the opportunity to know people of varied races, religions, nationality backgrounds, and social classes.

When high school students are regarded as college fodder, they are sometimes cheated of sufficient experience in home economics, music, fine arts, and industrial arts. When the only god worshipped is academic success in formal learning, students are sometimes cheated of the opportunity to explore seriously their allegiances to values, their relationships to the adult world, their ways of finding satisfaction, and their participation in political action and social change.

"But," a teacher may say, "I cannot change the required content to make it relevant. I am not a board of regents or a local board of education or a curriculum bigwig attached to the central office staff." He may add, "I am just a humble teacher, a prisoner of the syllabus, the required textbook, and the system in which I am caught. Deviation is not permitted. THEY would not allow it."

Maybe so, but I doubt it. Before the teacher resigns himself to a prisoner's life, he might wish to reexamine his chains. Perhaps they are not as strong as he assumes.

In today's world, more and more educators and laymen are realizing that not all of the answers to the problem of curriculum are in. Since the early 1960's, increasing numbers of educators have attempted to develop curriculums that are more important to the culturally disadvantaged or, in a plainer phrase, the poor.

Now recognition is growing that we are far from having achieved the best of all possible worlds with respect to the education of the economically advantaged. In 1969, still more educators will be looking for curriculums appropriate for young people from affluent backgrounds. Paradoxically, today's disenchanted young people, including democratic activists and serious and sensitive students as well as hippies and nihilists and revolutionaries, stem mostly from the middle and upper classes.

Possibly the chains of established content are not as binding as assumed. Teacher power grows. In a time of teacher shortage, few need stay as teachers in repressive atmospheres, for some administrators are seeking change-minded teachers.

In those cases where, through a variety of circumstances, the chains do prove real and teachers simply must use some prescribed content which is not as relevant as they would wish it to be, how can they make their work more meaningful?

Rather than making fundamental changes in the content, some teachers use the second alternative mentioned and adapt the content to make it more relevant. Illustrations are legion: In literature, teaching *Julius Caesar* in relationship to contemporary dictatorships; in history, preparing and contrasting attitudes toward past American wars with present attitudes on war in Viet Nam; in biology, relating the study of human blood to false claims and misleading mythologies as to blood differences between races; in modern languages, teaching the culture as part of the culture's language; in language arts, stressing those readings in anthologies which have most meaning to the particular learners. Miss Smith, for instance, could have discussed with the class the value assumptions behind the economic game that was the required content.

Some readers may ask for the prescription good teachers use for adaptation of content. There isn't any. Sorry about that. If there were a single sovereign remedy, it would have been discovered long ago. The good teacher uses his intelligence in relating the required content to the world of the learner. Good teachers have been doing so for a long time; adaptation is no revolutionary doctrine.

In making content more relevant, there is no substitute for knowing the social realities which characterize the environment of the student. There is no substitute for knowing the learner as an individual. There is no substitute for having a philosophy which gives direction to the educational enterprise. So armed, one can relate much of the content to the learner, the class, the school, and the community.

9

Epilogue: Crisis in the Classroom

Charles E. Silberman

> *Charles E. Silberman is a distinguished journalist and a first-rate scholar. His first major book,* Crisis in Black and White, *predicted and brilliantly analyzed some of the trends in Negro–white relationships which were currently emerging in America. The Myths of*

Automation, *his next book, was rational and well-balanced; it refuted much of the common scare-talk about men and machines. His vigorous and controversial book,* Crisis in the Classroom, *published in late 1970 after a 3½-year study by the Carnegie Corporation, is a spectacularly ambitious attempt to deal with American education as a whole.*

Silberman is critical of some of the compassionate critics. Yet they would endorse the overwhelming majority of the elementary school practices, and many of the secondary school procedures, that Silberman approves. However, he is fearful that the child-centered compassionate critics may oversimplify basic educational issues. One such issue which he repeatedly calls to the attention of his readers, as the excerpt which follows indicates, is the need for centrality of purpose and philosophy in education. He argues that the failure of the recent curriculum reform movement, which focused on rebuilding the separate academic disciplines, related to the inability of scholars to recognize the central importance of the questions raised by the leaders of the progressive movement in education.

Silberman has been on leave from Fortune *magazine while he directed the Carnegie Study of the Education of Educators.*

It is one thing to say that education must be purposeful; it is another to say what those purposes should be. The fashion in contemporary American writing about education holds that talk about purpose is a frightful bore. Dr. James B. Conant, probably the most prestigious and influential contemporary student of education, has confessed that "a sense of distasteful weariness overtakes" him whenever he hears someone discussing educational goals or philosophy. "In such a mood," he writes, "I am ready to define education as what goes on in schools and colleges" — a definition that has prevented him from asking whether what now goes on should go on. Martin Mayer, an influential educational journalist, is equally disdainful of talk about goals. "It is well to rid oneself of this business of the 'aims of education,'" he states flatly in his book *The Schools*. "Discussions on this subject are among the dullest and most fruitless of human pursuits."

But philosophical questions neither disappear nor resolve themselves by being ignored. Indeed, the question of purpose kept intruding itself throughout the course of the research, and even more, through the course of the writing. Writing is always painful, for it is a continuous process of dialogue with oneself, of confrontation with one's thoughts, ideas, and feelings. "As is true of any writing that comes out of one's own existence," Lillian Smith has said — and no serious writing can entirely avoid that source — "the experiences themselves [are] transformed during the act of writing by awareness of new meanings which settled down on them . . . the writer transcends her material in the act of looking at it, and since part of that material is herself, a metamorphosis takes place: *something happens within:* a new chaos, and then slowly, a new being." [Emphasis hers]

It was not until I was well into the writing, therefore — not until I had, over a summer, completed and abandoned a first crude draft — that I began to realize what a metamorphosis had taken place in me and in my thinking about education. In struggling to find my theme, I discovered that my views had changed profoundly. I had not thought hard enough about educational purpose until the agony of writing forced me to; I thought I *knew* what the purpose of education should be: namely, intellectual development. "The United States today is moving away from progressivism," I had argued in 1961, and still believed when I started the study, "not because it is 'false' in some absolute sense, but because it badly serves the needs of our own time. The growing complexity of organization and the explosive pace of technological and social change are creating an enormous demand that is without historical precedent. Society has always needed a few men with highly developed and disciplined intellects; industrial society needed masses of literate but not necessarily intellectual men. Tomorrow requires something that the world has never seen — *masses of intellectuals.*" . . . [Emphasis in the original][1]

. . . I am indignant at the banality of the mass media: no one concerned with the quality of American life can avoid a sense of sickening disappointment over the Vast Wasteland that public as well as commercial television has turned out to be. Nor can much more satisfaction be derived from contemplating the rest of the mass media. I am indignant, too, at the narcissism of so many college professors and administrators who, at least until prodded by student rebels, refused to think about the nature and content of liberal education, particularly about the ways in which knowledge may have to be reordered to make it teachable to a new generation. And I am indignant at the smug disdain with which most academicians view the problems of the public schools.

Most of all, however, I am indignant at the failures of the public schools themselves. "The most deadly of all possible sins," Erik Erikson suggests, "is the mutilation of a child's spirit." It is not possible to spend any prolonged period visiting public school classrooms without being appalled by the mutilation visible everywhere — mutilation of spontaneity, of joy in learning, of pleasure in creating, of sense of self. The public schools — those "killers of the dream," to appropriate a phrase of Lillian Smith's — are the kind of institution one cannot really dislike until one gets to know them well. Because adults take the schools so much for granted, they fail to appreciate what grim, joyless places most American schools are, how oppressive and petty are the rules by which they are governed, how intellectually sterile and esthetically barren the atmosphere, what an appalling lack of civility obtains on the part of teachers and principals, what contempt they unconsciously display for children as children.

And it need not be! Public schools *can* be organized to facilitate joy in learning and esthetic expression and to develop character — in the rural and urban slums no less than in the prosperous suburbs. This is no utopian

---

[1] Charles E. Silberman, "The Remaking of American Education," *Fortune*, April 1961.

hope; as I shall argue and demonstrate in the chapters that follow, there are models now in existence that can be followed.

What makes change possible, moreover, is that what is mostly wrong with the public schools is due not to venality or indifference or stupidity, but to mindlessness. To be sure, teaching has its share of sadists and clods, of insecure and angry men and women who hate their students for their openness, their exuberance, their color or their affluence. But by and large, teachers, principals, and superintendents are decent, intelligent, and caring people who try to do their best by their lights. If they make a botch of it, and an uncomfortably large number do, it is because it simply never occurs to more than a handful to ask *why* they are doing what they are doing — to think seriously or deeply about the purposes or consequences of education. . . .

If mindlessness is the central problem, the solution must lie in infusing the various educating institutions with purpose, more important, with thought about purpose, and about the ways in which techniques, content, and organization fulfill or alter purpose. And given the tendency of institutions to confuse day-to-day routine with purpose, to transform the means into the end itself, the infusion cannot be a one-shot affair. The process of self-examination, of "self-renewal," to use John Gardner's useful term, must be continuous. We must find ways of stimulating educators — public school teachers, principals, and superintendents; college professors, deans, and presidents; radio, television, and film directors and producers; newspaper, magazine, and TV journalists and executives — to think about what they are doing, and why they are doing it. And we must persuade the general public to do the same. . . .

One need only sit in the classrooms, in fact, and examine the texts and reading lists to know that, with the possible exception of mathematics, the curriculum reform movement has made a pitifully small impact on classroom practice. The criteria for deciding what should be in the curriculum, Jerome Bruner of Harvard, one of the chief architects of curriculum reform, has suggested, should be to ask "whether, when fully developed, [the subject or material] is worth an adult's knowing, and whether having known it as a child makes a person a better adult. If the answer to both questions is negative or ambiguous, then the material is cluttering the curriculum."[2]

The answer is negative to both questions for an incredibly high proportion of the elementary and secondary school curriculum. There is a great deal of chatter, to be sure, about teaching students the structure of each discipline, about teaching them how to learn, about teaching basic concepts, about "postholing," i.e., teaching fewer things but in greater depth. But if one looks at what actually goes on in the classroom — the kinds of texts students read and the kind of homework they are assigned, as well as the nature of classroom discussion and the kinds of tests teachers give — he will discover that the great bulk of students' time is still devoted to detail, most

2 Jerome S. Bruner, *The Process of Education*, Cambridge: Harvard University Press, 1960. Bruner's book was perhaps the most important and influential to come out of the curriculum reform movement.

of it trivial, much of it factually incorrect, and almost all of it unrelated to any concept, structure, cognitive strategy, or indeed anything other than the lesson plan. It is rare to find anyone — teacher, principal, supervisor, or superintendent — who has asked why he is teaching what he is teaching. . . .

What happened? Why did a movement that aroused such great hopes, and that enlisted so many distinguished educators, exert so little impact on the schools?

A large part of the answer is that what was initially regarded as the curriculum reform movement's greatest strength — the fact that its prime movers were distinguished university scholars and teachers — has proven to be its greatest weakness. In part because the movement was based in the scholarly disciplines, in part because it grew out of the scholars' revulsion against the vulgarization of progressive education and against the anti-intellectualism that that vulgarization in turn had spawned, the reformers by and large ignored the experiences of the past, and particularly of the reform movement of the 1920s and '30s. They were, therefore, unaware of the fact that almost everything they said had been said before, by Dewey, Whitehead, Bode, Rugg, etc.; and they were unaware that almost everything they tried to do had been tried before, by educators like Frederick Burk, Carleton Washburne, and Helen Parkhurst, not to mention Abraham Flexner and Dewey himself.[3]

One result of this failure to study educational history, particularly the history of progressivism's successes and failures, was that the contemporary reformers repeated one of the fundamental errors of the progressive movement: they perpetuated the false dichotomy that the schools must be *either* child-centered *or* subject-centered. Ignoring the warnings of men like Dewey, Boyd Bode, Harold Rugg, and Carleton Washburne, the progressive reformers had opted for the former; their preoccupation with child-centeredness made them content, in Dewey's phrase, "with casual improvisation and living intellectually hand to mouth." It was this "absence of intellectual control through significant subject-matter," Dewey wrote, "which stimulates the deplorable egotism, cockiness, impertinence and disregard for the rights of others apparently considered by some persons to be the inevitable accompaniment, if not the essence, of freedom."[4]

The reformers of the 1950s and '60s made the same mistake, except that they opted for the other side of the dichotomy. They placed almost all their emphasis on subject matter, i.e., on creating "great compositions," and for the most part ignored the needs of individual children. As Dewey wrote

---

[3] Cf. Lawrence A. Cremin, *The Transformation of the School* and *The Genius of American Education*: John I. Goodlad, "Curriculum: A Janus Look," *Teachers College Record,* November 1968; J. Stuart Maclure, *Curriculum Innovation in Practice,* Third International Curriculum Conference, Oxford (Her Majesty's Stationery Office, 1968); Patricia A. Graham, *Progressive Education: From Arcady to Academe,* New York: Teachers College Press, 1967; Harold Rugg and Ann Shumaker, *The Child-Centered School: An Appraisal of the New Education,* New York: World Book Co., 1928.

[4] John Dewey, "How Much Freedom in New Schools?", *The New Republic,* July 9, 1930.

of the progressive educators whose one-sidedness he deplored, the new re-formers "conceive of no alternative to adult dictation save child dictation." Reacting against the banality that child-dictated education had become, they opted for adult dictation. They knew what they wanted children to learn; they did not think to ask what children wanted to learn. Some of the reformers, however, now realize their error. Thus it was Zacharias, at the 1965 White House Conference on Education, who made a passionate plea that educators think about children and their needs.

Because the reformers were university scholars with little contact with public schools or schools of education, moreover, and because they also neg-lected to study the earlier attempts at curriculum reform, they also tended to ignore the harsh realities of classroom and school organization. The courses they created were, and are, vastly superior to the tepid and banal fare most students now receive. But without changing the ways in which schools operate and teachers teach, changing the curriculum alone does not have much effect.[5]

To some degree, this error reflected the reformers' innocence and naïveté. Because they had so little firsthand experience with the elementary or sec-ondary school classroom (in contrast to most of the great figures of the progressive movement), they somehow assumed that students would learn what the teachers taught; that is, if teachers presented the material in the proper structure, students would learn it that way. Thus, they assumed im-plicitly that teaching and learning are merely opposite sides of the same coin. But they are not, as we have seen in Chapter 4.

The error reflected academic hubris as well: not content with ignoring the classroom teacher, the reformers, in effect, tried to bypass the teacher alto-gether. Their goal, sometimes stated, sometimes implicit, was to construct "teacher-proof" materials that would "work" whether teachers liked the materials or not or taught them well or badly. "With the kind of casual arrogance only professors can manage, when they conceived of lower schools," Dean Robert J. Schaefer writes, the curriculum reformers' goal was "to pro-duce materials which permit scholars to speak directly to the child." They viewed teachers, if they thought of them at all, as technicians, and they conceived of the schools, Schaefer suggests, as "educational dispensaries — apothecary shops charged with the distribution of information and skills deemed beneficial to the social, vocational, and intellectual health of the immature. The primary business of a dispensary," Schaefer continues, "is to dispense — not to raise questions or to inquire into issues as to how drugs might be more efficiently administered, and certainly not to assume any authority over what ingredients should be mixed."[6]

The effort was doomed to failure. For one thing, the classroom teacher

[5] Cf., for example, Blythe Clinchy, "School Arrangements," in Jerome Bruner, ed., *Learning About Learning: A Conference Report,* U.S. Office of Education, Cooperative Research Monograph No. 15. The Clinchy essay is one of thirty in this volume; it is the only one directly concerned with the ways in which schools and classrooms operate.

[6] Robert J. Schaefer, *The School as a Center of Inquiry,* New York: Harper & Row, 1967.

usually is in an almost perfect position to sabotage a curriculum he finds offensive — and teachers are not likely to have a high regard for courses designed to bypass them. For another, many of the "teacher-proof" curricula have turned out to be more difficult to teach than the courses they replaced; certainly the "discovery method" makes far more demands on the teacher than does rote drill or lecturing. But insofar as they thought about in-service education of teachers, the reformers tended to assume that the problem was to get teachers to know — to really know — the subject they were teaching. This was crucial, of course, but experience with National Defense Education Act Institutes and the like have made it painfully clear that mastering the subject matter does not begin to solve the problem of how to teach it.

The failure to involve ordinary classroom teachers in the creation and modification of the new curricula, moreover, tended to destroy, or at least inhibit, the very spirit of inquiry the new courses were designed to create. Curriculum designers are not likely to attract students to the life of the mind if they fail to entice the students' teachers as well. "How can youngsters be convinced of the vitality of inquiry and discovery," Dean Schaefer asks, "if the adults with whom they directly work are mere automatons who shuffle papers, workbooks, and filmstrips according to externally arranged schedules?" Since the spirit of inquiry "necessitates a live sense of shared purpose and commitment," the teachers *must* participate in the scholar's search if the effort is to succeed.

The most fatal error of all, however, was the failure to ask the questions that the giants of the progressive movement always kept at the center of their concern, however inadequate some of their answers may have been: What is education for? What kind of human beings and what kind of society do we want to produce? What methods of instruction and classroom organization, as well as what subject matter, do we need to produce these results? What knowledge is of most worth?[7]

---

[7] Cf. especially Lawrence A. Cremin, *The Genius of American Education*, and John I. Goodlad, "Curriculum: A Janus Look."

B. The Critics of Compulsory Education

10

Freedom and Learning: The Need for Choice

Paul Goodman

For several decades Paul Goodman has been a forthright and insistent critic of society and the schools. In the following article on an issue which has long concerned him, he argues that learners must be allowed to make their own choices rather than submit to coercion by the school machinery. Goodman calls for mini-schools (such as Dennison's First Street School) on the elementary school level, for small preparatory academies on the secondary level, and for a community of scholars on the university level. He suggests apprenticeship, travel, self-directed study, reconstruction projects, work camps and the like as better ways of learning than schools for some students. To Goodman, the community itself is the greatest potential educator.

Paul Goodman is the author of Growing Up Absurd, Compulsory Mis-Education, The Community of Scholars *and other books. He is a prolific writer of articles for magazines.*

The belief that a highly industrialized society requires twelve to twenty years of prior processing of the young is an illusion or a hoax. The evidence is strong that there is no correlation between school performance and life achievement in any of the professions, whether medicine, law, engineering, journalism, or business. Moreover, recent research shows that for more modest clerical, technological, or semiskilled factory jobs there is no advantage in years of schooling or the possession of diplomas. We were not exactly savages in 1900 when only 6 per cent of adolescents graduated from high school.

Whatever the deliberate intention, schooling today serves mainly for policing and for taking up the slack in youth unemployment. It is not surprising

Paul Goodman, "Freedom and Learning: The Need for Choice," *Saturday Review,* May 18, 1968, 73–75.

that the young are finally rebelling against it, especially since they cannot identify with the goals of so much social engineering — for instance, that 86 per cent of the federal budget for research and development is for military purposes.

We can, I believe, educate the young entirely in terms of their free choice, with no processing whatever. Nothing can be efficiently learned, or, indeed, learned at all — other than through parroting or brute training, when acquired knowledge is promptly forgotten after the examination — unless it meets need, desire, curiosity, or fantasy. Unless there is a reaching from within, the learning cannot become "second nature," as Aristotle called true learning. It seems stupid to decide a priori what the young ought to know and then to try to motivate them, instead of letting the initiative come from them and putting information and relevant equipment at their service. It is false to assert that this kind of freedom will not serve society's needs — at least those needs that should humanly be served; freedom is the only way toward authentic citizenship and real, rather than verbal, philosophy. Free choice is not random but responsive to real situations; both youth and adults live in a nature of things, a polity, an ongoing society, and it is these, in fact, that attract interest and channel need. If the young, as they mature, can follow their bent and choose their topics, times, and teachers, and if teachers teach what they themselves consider important — which is all they can skillfully teach anyway — the needs of society will be adequately met; there will be more lively, independent, and inventive people; and in the fairly short run there will be a more sensible and efficient society.

It is not necessary to argue for free choice as a metaphysical proposition; it is what is indicated by present conditions. Increasingly, the best young people resolutely resist authority, and we will let them have a say or lose them. And more important, since the conditions of modern social and technological organization are so pervasively and rigidly conforming, it is necessary, in order to maintain human initiative, to put our emphasis on protecting the young from top-down direction. The monkish and academic methods which were civilizing for wild shepherds create robots in a period of high technology. The public schools which did a good job of socializing immigrants in an open society now regiment individuals and rigidify class stratification.

Up to age twelve, there is no point to formal subjects or a prearranged curriculum. With guidance, whatever a child experiences is educational. Dewey's idea is a good one: It makes no difference *what* is learned at this age, so long as the child goes on wanting to learn something further. Teachers for this age are those who like children, pay attention to them, answer their questions, enjoy taking them around the city and helping them explore, imitate, try out, and who sing songs with them and teach them games. Any benevolent grownup — literate or illiterate — has plenty to teach an eight-year-old; the only profitable training for teachers is a group therapy and, perhaps, a course in child development.

We see that infants learn to speak in their own way in an environment where there is speaking and where they are addressed and take part. If we tried to teach children to speak according to our own theories and methods and schedules, as we try to teach reading, there would be as many stammerers as there are bad readers. Besides, it has been shown that whatever is useful in the present eight-year elementary curriculum can be learned in four months by a normal child of twelve. If let alone, in fact, he will have learned most of it by himself.

Since we have communities where people do not attend to the children as a matter of course, and since children must be rescued from their homes, for most of these children there should be some kind of school. In a proposal for mini-schools in New York City, I suggested an elementary group of twenty-eight children with four grownups: a licensed teacher, a housewife who can cook, a college senior, and a teen-age school dropout. Such a group can meet in any store front, church basement, settlement house, or housing project; more important, it can often go about the city, as is possible when the student-teacher ratio is 7 to 1. Experience at the First Street School in New York has shown that the cost for such a little school is less than for the public school with a student-teacher ratio of 30 to 1. (In the public system, most of the money goes for administration and for specialists to remedy the lack of contact in the classroom.) As A. S. Neill has shown, attendance need not be compulsory. The school should be located near home so the children can escape from it to home, and from home to it. The school should be supported by public money but administered entirely by its own children, teachers, and parents.

In the adolescent and college years, the present mania is to keep students at their lessons for another four to ten years as the only way of their growing up in the world. The correct policy would be to open as many diverse paths as possible, with plenty of opportunity to backtrack and change. It is said by James Conant that about 15 per cent learn well by books and study in an academic setting, and these can opt for high school. Most, including most of the bright students, do better either on their own or as apprentices in activities that are for keeps, rather than through lessons. If their previous eight years had been spent in exploring their own bents and interests, rather than being continually interrupted to do others' assignments on others' schedules, most adolescents would have a clearer notion of what they are after, and many would have found their vocations.

For the 15 per cent of adolescents who learn well in schools and are interested in subjects that are essentially academic, the present catch-all high schools are wasteful. We would do better to return to the small preparatory academy, with perhaps sixty students and three teachers — one in physical sciences, one in social sciences, one in humanities — to prepare for college board examinations. An academy could be located in, and administered by, a university and staffed by graduate students who like to teach and in this way might earn stipends while they write their theses. In such a setting, without dilution by nonacademic subjects and a mass of uninterested fellow students, an academic adolescent can, by spending three hours a day in the classroom, easily be prepared in three or four years for college.

Forcing the nonacademic to attend school breaks the spirit of most and foments alienation in the best. Kept in tutelage, young people, who are necessarily economically dependent, cannot pursue the sexual, adventurous, and political activities congenial to them. Since lively youngsters insist on these anyway, the effect of what we do is to create a gap between them and the oppressive adult world, with a youth subculture and an arrested development. .

School methods are simply not competent to teach all the arts, sciences, professions, and skills the school establishment pretends to teach. For some professions — e.g., social work, architecture, pedagogy — trying to earn academic credits is probably harmful because it is an irrelevant and discouraging obstacle course. Most technological know-how has to be learned in actual practice in offices and factories, and this often involves unlearning what has been laboriously crammed for exams. The technical competence required by skilled and semiskilled workmen and average technicians can be acquired in three weeks to a year on the job, with no previous schooling. The importance of even "functional literacy" is much exaggerated; it is the attitude, and not the reading ability, that counts. Those who are creative in the arts and sciences almost invariably go their own course and are usually hampered by schools. Modern languages are best learned by travel. It is pointless to teach social sciences, literary criticism, and philosophy to youngsters who have had no responsible experience in life and society.

Most of the money now spent for high schools and colleges should be devoted to the support of apprenticeships; travel; subsidized browsing in libraries and self-directed study and research; programs such as VISTA, the Peace Corps, Students for a Democratic Society, or the Student Nonviolent Coordinating Committee; rural reconstruction; and work camps for projects in conservation and urban renewal. It is a vast sum of money — but it costs almost $1,500 a year to keep a youth in a blackboard jungle in New York; the schools have become one of our major industries. Consider one kind of opportunity. Since it is important for the very existence of the republic to countervail the now overwhelming national corporate style of information, entertainment, and research, we need scores of thousands of small independent television stations, community radio stations, local newspapers that are more than gossip notes and ads, community theaters, high-brow or dissenting magazines, small design offices for neighborhood renewal that is not bureaucratized, small laboratories for science and invention that are not centrally directed. Such enterprises could present admirable opportunities for bright but unacademic young people to serve as apprentices.

Ideally, the polis itself is the educational environment; a good community consists of worthwhile, attractive, and fulfilling callings and things to do, to grow up into. The policy I am proposing tends in this direction rather than away from it. By multiplying options, it should be possible to find an interesting course for each individual youth, as we now do for only some of the emotionally disturbed and the troublemakers. Voluntary adolescent choices are often random and foolish and usually transitory; but they are the likeliest ways of growing up reasonably. What is most essential is for the youth to see that he is taken seriously as a person, rather than fitted into an institutional system. I don't know if this tailor-made approach would be harder or easier to administer than standardization that in fact fits nobody and results in an increasing number of recalcitrants. On the other hand, as the Civilian Conservation Corps showed in the Thirties, the products of willing youth labor can be valuable even economically, whereas accumulating Regents blue-books is worth nothing except to the school itself.

(By and large, it is not in the adolescent years but in later years that, in all walks of life, there is need for academic withdrawal, periods of study and reflection, synoptic review of the texts. The Greeks understood this and regarded most of our present college curricula as appropriate for only those over the age of thirty or thirty-five. To some extent, the churches used to provide a studious environment. We do these things miserably in hurried conferences.)

We have similar problems in the universities. We cram the young with what they do not want at the time and what most of them will never use; but by requiring graded diplomas we make it hard for older people to get what they want and can use. Now, paradoxically, when so many are going to school, the training of authentic learned professionals is proving to be a failure, with dire effects on our ecology, urbanism, polity, communications, and even the direction of science. Doing others' lessons under compulsion for twenty years does not tend to produce professionals who are autonomous, principled, and ethically responsible to client and community. Broken by processing, professionals degenerate to mere professional-personnel. Professional peer groups have become economic lobbies. The licensing and maintenance of standards have been increasingly relinquished to the state, which has no competence.

In licensing professionals, we have to look more realistically at functions, drop mandarin requirements of academic diplomas that are irrelevant, and rid ourselves of the ridiculous fad of awarding diplomas for every skill and trade whatever. In most professions and arts there are important abstract parts that can best be learned academically. The natural procedure is for those actually engaged in a professional activity to go to school to learn what they now know they need; re-entry into the academic track, therefore, should be made easy for those with a strong motive.

Universities are primarily schools of learned professions, and the faculty should be composed primarily not of academics but of working professionals who feel duty-bound and attracted to pass on their tradition to apprentices of a new generation. Being combined in a community of scholars, such professionals teach a noble apprenticeship, humane and with vision toward a more ideal future. It is humane because the disciplines communicate with one another; it is ideal because the young are free and questioning. A good professional school can be tiny. In *The Community of Scholars* I suggest that 150 students and ten professionals — the size of the usual medieval university — are enough. At current faculty salaries, the cost per student would be a fourth of that of our huge administrative machines. And, of course, on such a small scale contact between faculty and students is sought for and easy.

Today, because of the proved incompetence of our adult institutions and the hypocrisy of most professionals, university students have a right to a large say in what goes on. (But this, too, is medieval.) Professors will, of course, teach what they please. My advice to students is that given by Prince Kropotkin, in "A Letter to the Young": "Ask what kind of world do you want to live in? What are you good at and want to work at to build that world? What do you need to know? Demand that your teachers teach you that." Serious teachers would be delighted by this approach.

The idea of the liberal arts college is a beautiful one: to teach the common culture and refine character and citizenship. But it does not happen; the evidence is that the college curriculum has little effect on underlying attitudes, and most cultivated folk do not become so by this route. School friendships and the community of youth do have lasting effects, but these do not require ivied clubhouses. Young men learn more about the theory and practice of government by resisting the draft than they ever learned in Political Science 412.

Much of the present university expansion, needless to say, consists in federal- and corporation-contracted research and other research and has nothing to do with teaching. Surely such expansion can be better carried on in the Government's and corporations' own institutes, which would be unencumbered by the young, except those who are hired or attach themselves as apprentices.

Every part of education can be open to need, desire, choice, and trying out. Nothing needs to be compelled or extrinsically motivated by prizes and threats. I do not know if the procedure here outlined would cost more than our present system — though it is hard to conceive of a need for more money than the school establishment now spends. What would be saved is the pitiful waste of youthful years — caged, daydreaming, sabotaging, and cheating — and the degrading and insulting misuse of teachers.

It has been estimated by James Coleman that the average youth in high school is really "there" about ten minutes a day. Since the growing-up of the young into society to be useful to themselves and others, and to do God's work, is one of the three or four most important functions of any society, no doubt we ought to spend even more on the education of the young than we do; but I would not give a penny to the present administrators, and I would largely dismantle the present school machinery.

11

Educating *Contra Naturam*

Theodore Roszak

Theodore Roszak is a vital spokesman for today's counter-culture. He rejects the compulsory public school as a product of the rigid social orthodoxy of industrial society. As for students, he counsels, "Let them go. Help them to escape, those that need to escape." He suggests "talking up the natural rights of truancy and the educational possibilities of hooky."

Theodore Roszak is Professor of History at California State College at Hayward. He is the editor and a contributor to The Dissenting Academy *(New York: Pantheon Books, 1968) and the author of* The Making of a Counter-Culture *(Garden City, N.Y.: Doubleday Anchor Books, 1969).*

Suppose — instead of applauding, praising, but inwardly insisting that we know better — we heard and affirmed what the poet proclaims: that "heaven lies about us in our infancy", that the child comes to us shaped by nature's hand, a

> Mighty prophet! Seer blest!
> On Whom those truths do rest
> Which we are toiling all our lives to find. . . .

Well then . . . what would education be but the fine art of watching and waiting, and in good time, of summoning forth from the child all that abides within: kingdoms, powers, glories . . . ? So — the task of the teacher would be that of fire-minder: keeper and feeder of the indwelling flame.

Yet if — believing this — we look about us at the world of men which is the result of our labor, what can we do but echo Wordsworth's lament?

> Whither is fled the visionary gleam?
> Where is it now, the glory and the dream?

Our pedagogy deals poorly with these visionary gleams, does it not? How many of us would recognize them if we saw them? In truth, did we ever really believe they were there — within ourselves, as much as in the young?

There is a drawing by William Blake: Age applying the scissors to the wings of Youth. The image tells us what *our* education is all about, *must* be all about in schools financed by church or state and enforced upon the young by compulsion. Tolstoy put the point vividly more than a century ago when, throughout the West, compulsory public school systems were coming into fashion with the unqualified approval of all progressive opinion. He was among the few who saw through this pedagogical fad which was destined to become the iron social orthodoxy of every industrial and industrializing society.

> Education [Tolstoy said] is a compulsory forcible action of one person upon another for the purpose of forming a man such as will appear [to society] to be good. . . . Education is the tendency toward moral despotism raised to a principle. . . . I am convinced that the educator undertakes with such zeal the education of the child because at the base of this tendency lies his envy of the child's purity, and his desire to make him like himself, that is, to spoil him.[1]

A harsh judgment. I wince at it as much as you do. For it comes from one who was not only a supreme prophetic spirit, but a gifted teacher of children. And like you I ask, *must* it be so? Is there no other possibility?

Of course there is. There is the possibility Tolstoy himself explored at his own voluntary school for peasant youngsters, Yasnaya Polyana, where, as he put it, "the criterion of pedagogics is only liberty."

"The people," said Tolstoy, "love and seek education, as they love and seek the air for breathing. . . . Some want to teach and others want to learn. Let them teach as much as they can, and let them learn as much as they will."[2]

That is the other possibility: to teach in freedom, in complete freedom, in response to the native inclination of the student; to be a teacher only when and where and insofar as the student authorizes us to be.

But that libertarian possibility has nothing to do with our schools — our "free" public schools, where "free" refers, not to an existential relationship between teacher and student, but to a budgetary arrangement for the financing of a coercive institution.

"*Let* them learn," said Tolstoy. He did not say, "*Make* them learn," because he knew that true education satisfies a natural appetite. Why then resort to force-feeding?

And yet, how much of our educating proceeds from the assumption that the young must be *made* to learn? Made to learn . . . tricked into learning . . . charmed . . . inveigled . . . cajoled . . . bribed . . . as if in truth education were *contra naturam* and required clever strategies.

[1] Leo Tolstoy. *Tolstoy on Education.* Translated by Leo Wiener. Chicago: University of Chicago Press, 1967, pp. 110–11.
[2] *Ibid.*, p. 5.

If we do not work from that assumption, then why is education ever anywhere a "problem"? A "problem" requiring, mind you, professional, specialized, full-time, and Herculean attention . . . and prodigious amounts of money?

WHY THE COMPULSION?

If we do not work from that assumption, then why the compulsion? And I do not refer only to the legal compulsion of our lower grades, but to such forms of compulsion as military conscription, which has given us a male college population largely made up, not of young scholars, but of refugees seeking sanctuary in draft-deferrable occupations: the coercive process General Hershey once referred to as "choice under pressure." I speak too of the more subtle compulsions: the lure and the goad of jobs, status, licenses, and credentials.

Now it cannot be unknown to any informed person that in so-called primitive societies, as in many pre-modern civilizations, the whole of vast and profound cultures was easily and naturally transmitted from generation to generation without the intervention of an educational establishment. Rather, the burden of cultural continuity rested on what Paul Goodman has recently called "incidental education": learning in the home, on the job, especially at play, by way of observation and imitation, now and then, here and there, from whoever happens to know, as and when the spirit moves . . . above all, without fuss and bother. The pedagogical theory of all this has been neatly summarized by George Dennison in his book *The Lives of Children.*

> These two things taken together — the natural authority of adults and the needs of children — are the great reservoir of organic structuring that comes into being when arbitrary rules of order are dispensed with.
>
> The child is always finding himself, moving toward himself, as it were, in the near distance. The adult is his ally, his model — and his obstacle (for there are natural conflicts, too, and they must be given their due).[3]

"Incidental education" . . . how precarious this must sound to us. And yet each generation of Eskimos or Bushmen has stepped forth into life in full possession of the culture. This is not because the culture of primitives is "simpler" than our own: a preposterously ethnocentric assumption. What we mistake for the "complexity" of our culture (when we are not simply confessing to our own sad confusion) is really its technical and academic specialization — the correct measure of which is quantity, not complexity. Quantity is a blunt measure of disorganized amount; complexity measures the richness and integrity of the cultural whole within which all things known and valued should properly find coherence.

In this respect — with reference to coherent moral, religious, aesthetic,

[3] George Dennison. *The Lives of Children.* New York: Random House, Inc., 1969. p. 25.

mythological, and ritual content — primitive cultures are often far more complex than the down-at-the-heels, *Reader's Digest* and Sunday-supplement version of Western civilization most of our fellow citizens are carrying about haphazardly in their heads. There is even a vast store of purely technical know-how every Eskimo and Bushman must learn — a much greater store than most of us need learn who undo the technical snags in our lives by looking in the Yellow Pages and dialing seven numbers.

I grant you, there have been primitive groups in which harsh forms of indoctrination existed; but I call your attention to the others where little of this has been necessary because the culture, after its own fashion and style, gracefully gave expression to the many dimensions of human personality: the workaday practical, the metaphysical-speculative, the sexual, the communal, the creative, the visionary. Oddly enough, the single aspect of primitive culture many civilized people find least palatable is the often grueling rites of passage — especially those that transpire at puberty. But even these rituals have had at least a natural sanction: they have been the culture's way of dramatizing and illuminating an irrepressible constant in the nature of man — and so of integrating it into the personal and communal pattern of life.

How ironic and revealing it is that in our schools we permit children to be hurt, bullied, and browbeaten if they display too much healthy animal energy in the classroom, or if they fail to revere what the school authorities pose as the social orthodoxies. These conformist demands that arise outside the child's experience may be severely enforced. But as for the biological imperative of puberty which arises mightily within the child . . . of this hardly a candid word may be whispered in many schools. Either teachers play dumb, assuming a comic and unbecoming chastity; or the so-called "problem" is treated by way of the most fastidiously anti-erotic sex instruction.

Our schools would be chagrined to graduate a student who did not know the ritualistic pledge of allegiance to the flag; but they feel no shame whatever to graduate adolescents who would be (for all their schools had taught them) sexual ignoramuses. And is this not in itself heavy evidence of how pathetically little our own culture knows of the nature of man: that we take a superficial national emblem to be more worthy of ritual elaboration than the deep demands of erotic experience?

Thus, even where primitive cultures have tended to be far more physically brutal than you or I would approve, they have by and large been true to Tolstoy's dictum: "Every instruction ought to be only an answer to the question put by life."

Water finds its level, the swallows fly south in winter, children learn. It is just that simple. That is what Tolstoy knew; that is what the primitives knew. And so they could say, "Let them learn." Societies that trust their culture can let nature take its course, knowing that in their own good time — and usually very promptly — the children will come round and learn what it looks interesting and important to learn; that indeed, their young lives, unless stunted or sidetracked, are nothing but the inquisitive unfolding of potentialities.

But when a society begins to fear that its culture is not interesting or important to the young — that indeed its culture violates nature — then it concludes that education must be *made* to happen: must be organized strenuously into existence and enforced by professionals. And then we have much heavy talk about methods, discipline, techniques, discipline, incentives, discipline, inducements, discipline, the "crisis in our schools" . . . and discipline. We also have blue-ribbon committees, top-level conferences, exhaustive surveys, bold reforms, daring experiments, courageous innovations . . . and the educational establishment grows and grows and grows.

Let us postulate a law: the less secure the culture, the larger the educational establishment. All of us readily recognize that a society in need of heavy policing must be in serious trouble — for the laws have surely lost their power to command respect. Similarly: a society that professionalizes and anxiously aggrandizes its educational establishment — its cultural cops — is also in serious trouble — for the culture has surely lost its capacity to command interest and involvement. The now chronic top-to-bottom state of emergency in our schools does not exist because the educational establishment is not good enough and needs repair. The crisis is that the culture is not good enough. The educational establishment, with all its compulsions, its disciplinary hang-ups, and — yes — even with its constabulary forces patrolling the corridors — all this only exists in the first place because of the insecurity of the culture.

Once we realize this, we can perhaps see that the feverish efforts of even good-hearted educators to inspire and motivate their students are as pathetic as the belated efforts of our Special Forces in Vietnam to win the hearts and minds of the very people they have degraded and brutalized. Within the context of coercion all efforts to ingratiate are vitiated from scratch. As Tolstoy observed with respect to teachers who seek to achieve "greater freedom" in the schools,

> Those gentlemen . . . resemble a man who, having brought up some young nightingales and concluding that they need freedom, lets them out of the cage and gives them freedom at the end of cords attached to their feet, and then wonders why the nightingales are not doing any better on the cord, but only break their legs and die.[4]

Now if the law we have postulated is true, it leads us to an ironic conclusion about modern Western civilization. If there has ever been a civilization obsessed with what we call "free, public education," it is ours. We invented this quaint institution and we invest a special historical pride in it. We take it as an indisputable sign of social progress that we have built such colossal, affluent, and broadcast school systems. Until, at last, we begin to anticipate that education will soon become our largest "industry" — the major preoccupation of the society. Far from perceiving in this prospect the advanced cultural insecurity it betokens, we feel this is not only right, but ideal. How better to use our wealth, our leisure, and our know-how than to train more teachers, build more schools, process more students?

[4] Leo Tolstoy, *op. cit.*, p. 130.

AN ADJUNCT OF NATIONAL POWER

Why does industrial society do this? Tolstoy's contemporary, Bismarck, knew why. "The nation that has the schools," Bismarck observed, "has the future."

Education as an adjunct of national power: a shrewd insight . . . one worthy of such a grim broker in blood and iron. But one did not have to be a Prussian autocrat and militarist to accept the hard-bitten logic of Bismarck's argument. William E. Forster, who led the good fight for compulsory public education in Great Britain, was a solidly bourgeois Quaker: an industrialist and a self-denying public servant. And here, very revealingly, is how Forster sized things up in 1870 in presenting his successful elementary education bill to Parliament:

> Upon the speedy provision of elementary education depends our industrial prosperity. It is of no use trying to give technical teaching to our artizans without elementary education; uneducated labourers . . . are, for the most part, unskilled labourers, and if we leave our work-folk any longer unskilled, notwithstanding their strong sinews and determined energy, they will become over-matched in the competition of the world. . . . Civilized communities throughout the world are massing themselves together, each mass being measured by its force; and if we are to hold our position among men of our own race or among the nations of the world, we must make up the smallness of our numbers by increasing the intellectual force of the individual.[5]

Note the tell-tale imagery of the argument: energy . . . force . . . power . . . mass. Education as mental steam engine; the school as brain-production factory. No doubt today the metaphors would draw upon computer technics or information theory. But the argument would nonetheless be the same. "Knowledge is power" said Francis Bacon more than three centuries ago at the dawn of the scientific revolution. And from Bismarck to Project Apollo, that fateful dictum has been the ensign of public policy throughout the developed and developing countries.

Tolstoy, whose healthy anarchist instincts were quick to sense which way the power-political winds of our time were tending, gauged the situation shrewdly. This time he speaks of higher education, but the criticism strikes at the same authoritarian-utilitarian vice which was for Tolstoy the curse of all state-supported education:

> No one has ever thought of establishing universities on the needs of the people. . . . The universities were founded to answer certain needs, partly of the government and partly of higher society, and for the universities was established all that preparatory ladder of educational institutions which has nothing in common with the needs of the people. The government needed officials, doctors, jurists, teachers, and the universities were founded in order to train these. . . . It is generally said that the defects of the universities are due to the defects in the lower institutions. I affirm the opposite: the de-

[5] J. Stuart Maclure, editor. *Educational Documents: England and Wales, 1816–1967.* London: Chapman & Hall, Ltd., 1965. Pp. 104–105.

fects of the popular . . . schools are mainly due to the false exigencies of the universities.[6]

The words are as telling in the age of the multiversity as they were a century ago. Yet how easily we have come to accept the assumption — almost as if it were printed on every dollar our schools receive (for in effect it is) — that education exists, not to debate, but to serve the preordained national priorities. How nicely it simplifies everything to define the good student as he who gets the grades that get the job — a deferential simplification that, incidentally, takes on no greater ethical complexity even if the pigmentation of the students who are pressed into service becomes as various as the rainbow.

In the dim and dismal past, there was indeed a time when aristocratic and feudal elites jealously defended a deep vested interest in the plain brute ignorance of peasant masses. Those days are gone forever. Industrial society requires, not illiterate serfs and peons, but trained workmen and trained consumers, bound together in the tight coordination of urban life. As rural routines break down before the thrust of modernization, the well-adjusted citizen must be capable of rapidly assimilating new stores of data; he must respond snappily to the myriad signals, commands, instructions of a change-ful new world. The peasant guides his conduct by custom; the industrial worker by information. The peasant lives by tradition; the industrial worker by the news of the day. This is what accounts for industrial society's peculiar obsession with literacy: its facile and unexamined assumption that someone who cannot read is, of necessity, "backward," "underdeveloped."

THE "ROYAL ROAD TO PROPAGANDA"

In 1968, while I was in London, Granada Television produced a documentary film on the civil war that has been raging in Portuguese Guinea for the past several years: an embryonic African Vietnam being contested by Portugal (armed by the United States via NATO) and the Guinean National Liberation Front. The report was presented wholly from the NLF side and it captured much of the idealism of these youthful rebels who are out to free themselves from the dead hand of the imperialist past and to usher their society into the modern world.

At one point, we were shown an NLF jungle school where guerrilla teachers were drilling away at children from the bush — and at students considerably older too. One guerrilla, we were told, had only learned to read at the age of 30 — and this was now his proudest achievement. We saw the man poring laboriously over a sheet of paper, ponderously shaping out each word with his lips as his finger underlined it, and smiling broadly as each sentence of the text was conquered. It might have been an image out of our own American past: the familiar picture of the Polish or Italian immigrant learning his letters in night school, making the great leap forward into literacy and citizenship.

[6] Leo Tolstoy, *op. cit.*, pp. 30–31.

But what was it our night-school immigrants went on to read once the breakthrough had been made? Legend has it that they all went on to Shakespeare, Tocqueville, and John Stuart Mill. Surely some did. But mostly they went on to the local Hearst press . . . the *Police Gazette* . . . Horatio Alger . . . the Sears catalog. And what was the text our proud Guinean guerrilla was draining of all its insight? Of course: a party bulletin — especially prepared for the feebly literate. It was all his formal education allowed him to cope with. And it was, in any case, about all the party was prepared to give him . . . though perhaps he will eventually graduate to the *Thoughts of Chairman Mao.*

Thus, for the peasant revolutionary as for the vast majority of our own more affluent youngsters, literacy is the royal road to propaganda. Why does industrial — or would-be industrial — society crusade so fanatically against illiteracy? It is hardly because illiterate people are necessarily stupid. They *may* be. But not necessarily so. Recall that high civilizations have been reared on this earth without the aid of the written word. It is hardly because literate people are necessarily smart. They *may* be. But not necessarily so. And to judge by what most of our almost universally literate citizenry patronizes in the way of newspapers, magazines, political oratory, and television entertainment — to judge especially by its gullibility in the marketplace — literacy would seem to bear about as much relationship to intelligence in our society as a Presidential convention bears to a town meeting. It is little wonder then that as of the year 1970, our political leaders come to the convenient conclusion that, in the arena of social controversy, the voice of the universally literate people is . . . a "silent majority."

The simple truth is: industrial society has no use for unschooled people, because unschooled people are too difficult to organize. Lacking the sense of discipline and responsibility the schools provide, lacking the minimal literacy they purvey, people will not pay what they owe, buy what they ought, report for work on time, appear for induction when summoned, dial the right number, sign on the dotted line, fill out the form correctly. They will not know what the advertisement says, they will not know where to put their mark on the ballot, they will not know why the war is necessary, they will not know wherein lie the genius and honor of their leaders. Unless equipped with a good, practical education — "an education for life" — they may even revert to employing the sense they were born with, put two and two together, and *not* come up with a good solid official five.

Of course I know there are exceptions to the standard: exceptional teachers, exceptional students. But let us be honest about our history: the free public school system is a product of industrial necessity within the context of the nation-state. I am not unaware of the genuine idealism that has been and still is entrusted to this institution. Idealism is often planted in barren earth. Believe it or not, in the high days of the French Revolution, the conscripted citizen army — the *levée en masse* — was regarded as a shining expression of liberty, equality, fraternity. Ask our youth today what they think of this great democratic institution. Institutions have such a tragic way of devouring the ideals they exist to foster.

The function of the educational establishment in industrial society is to treat industrialism and all that it demands as "given": necessary, good, inexorably so . . . a veritable force of nature toward which one must be "practical," not "critical." The schools are built because they produce the skills that will turn the populace into interchangeable, socially serviceable units of a productive economy: at the least, reading, writing, ciphering — but also the sophisticated technical skills necessary for elaborating the industrial plant.

In addition, the schools enforce the virtues of what is called "citizenship": meaning eager acquiescence in the national mystique, patriotic resolution, docility before official superiors, well-developed resignation before externally enforced discipline. In collectivized economies, the schools inculcate a deep and automatic appreciation of ideological inanity; in privatized economies, a profound piety for the privileges of property.

In brief, the elites of all industrial societies take their strength from technicians so narrowly proficient that there is no room in their busy consciousness for a single moral scruple, and from masses so minimally literate that nothing intellectually larger than a commercial advertisement or an official political stereotype can wedge itself into so abbreviated an attention span.

What, then, is the measure of the success of the educational establishment? Let me suggest two examples that vividly represent the excellence the establishment was in reality created to achieve. I could have chosen other examples, but I choose these two because they strike me as having required a superhuman effort in dealing with recalcitrant human material and, obviously, because they give us much to ponder.

"THE BALANCE OF TERROR"

The first of these is the gargantuan Russo-American weapons system we call "the balance of terror." It is hardly a secret that, since the end of World War II, the building of this juggernaut has been public business number one for both the U.S. and the U.S.S.R. Nothing in either society — no matter of social justice or humanitarian need — has received more trained manpower or money than these weapons have. Yet these is no system of social ethics — excepting those of Tamerlane, Al Capone, and Joseph Paul Goebbels — which offers a breath of support to this major international enterprise.

Translated out of the official casuistry which covers their true character, these weapons represent an institutionalized commitment to the doing of genocide — perhaps on a global scale. They exist to kill children. Among others, to be sure. Yet I call attention to the children because we are teachers and perhaps this does the most to tear the heart. These weapons are aimed at children, not by accident or unavoidable necessity — but directly, specifically, intentionally, with painstaking malice aforethought, and without apology or guilt. That is what "terror" means. So they have been designed; and so they will be used — when the time comes. They are, as Thomas Merton has called them, "the original child bomb."

Now consider how efficient an educational establishment is required to produce the scientists and technicians who will sell their necessary talents to such a project. Consider how carefully a curriculum must be designed to bring these specialists through 16, 18, 20 years of education without ever once unsettling their conscience. Consider how delicately their acquaintance with the religious and ethical traditions of their culture must have been arranged in order not to preclude their serviceability. Consider with what ingenious cunning they must have been maneuvered through the study of what we call "the humanities." Consider how diligently every inborn trace of moral inquisitiveness had to be surgically removed from their nature, along with every remnant of a sense of humanitarian service, pity, fellowship, or sheer existential disgust — until at last we had specialists whose only remaining ethical reflex would be, "What they do to us, we do to them — worse!" And how many of these men, one wonders, have come from schools which have fiercely defended their right to have the words of Amos, Isaiah, and Jesus read in class?

The second example I offer is an event now much on the public mind. I refer to what happened in the Vietnamese village of Songmy on March 16, 1968. What has followed from that event has led to a great deal of controversy — though I learn from one public opinion poll, taken at Christmas-time 1969, that 51 percent of those questioned refuse — like the Saigon government — to believe that anything untoward ever occurred in Songmy. But let us assume that the U.S. Army and its Commander-in-Chief know better and can be believed when they tell us that an atrocity there took place. In what grotesque sense of the word can that savage act be called a "success" of our educational establishment?

Once again, consider what a labor it must have been to produce the young Americans capable of such a deed. Such ordinary, such stolidly ordinary young men . . . a few years before they turned their guns on these women and children and shot them, they were perhaps going out for the high school basketball team, planning heavy weekend dates, worrying about their grades in solid geometry. No moral degenerates, these: no more so than Adolph Eichmann was. But given the order to kill, they killed. Not because they were monsters, but because they were good soldiers, good Americans, doing as they had been taught to do. Given the order to kill, they killed — the obviously innocent, obviously defenseless, crying out to them for pity.

Later, one of the men is reported as saying that he has bad dreams about the deed. Did he ever learn in school that there are such dreams? Was he ever asked to decide for himself what his duty is to the state? to his own conscience? to his innocent fellow man? Did he ever hear of the Nuremberg trials? Did he ever have a class dealing with the subject "orders one must consider *never* obeying"? Would any board of education, any PTA now demand that such a class be offered? Would the U.S. Department of Health, Education, and Welfare encourage it? Would the U.S. Department of Defense suggest it? Would the local Chamber of Commerce and American Legion permit it?

Well then: what respect has our culture for the moral nature of our young? Again to quote Tolstoy, our school system "trains not such men as humanity needs, but such as corrupt society needs."

I have said that the great problem with education in our time is that the culture it exists to transmit — the culture of industrial society — is largely worthless and therefore without inherent interest to lively and unspoiled young minds. Worse still, much that industrial society requires degrades all natural humanity. It trespasses against reason, gentleness, and freedom with a force that is plainly homicidal in intensity. That is why the schools, in their eagerness to advance the regimenting orthodoxies of state and corporation — property, power, productivity — have had to distort education into indoctrination. That is why so much is incurably wrong with the schools — all the things keener critics than myself have raised to the level of common knowledge. I need not discuss here what writers like John Holt, Edgar Friedenberg, Jules Henry, Paul Goodman, Jonathan Kozol, and James Herndon have so well analyzed: the compulsion of the system, the tyranny of "right answers," the surrealistic charade of lesson plans, methods, and learning resources, the obsession with discipline, above all the mercenary manipulation of competitive favors — grades, gold stars, good opinions, awards, jobs, status, power.

END TO INDUSTRIALIZATION?

Nor do I have the time here to persuade those of you who do not already feel it in your bones like the plague, that the West's 150-year experiment in industrialization is approaching a disastrously bad end. Our collective nightmares are available for all to consider: the bleak landscapes of the Brave New World and of 1984, hallucinations of thermonuclear extinction or total environmental collapse. If the bomb does not finish us, then the blight of our habitat very likely will. If not the atom's fire, then the poisoned air, water, earth: the very elements pronounce their sentence of death upon industrial society. Surely they will serve even for the least religious among us as the voice of God.

Whatever health remains in a corrupted culture gathers in the gift of prophecy or also perishes. And woe to the people who fail to recognize their prophets because they come in unlikely forms . . . for prophets are in the habit of so doing. The best and brightest of our young go barefoot and grow shaggier by the day; they scrap the social graces; they take despairingly to the streets to revile and cry doom; they abscond to the hinterlands in search of purity and simple dignities; they thrust themselves upon us in our public parks and on the stages of our theaters stripped naked and imploring us to "let the sunshine in." We can hardly be so ignorant of our own tradition that we do not recognize — for all the frequent zaniness and gaucherie — the gesture, the presence, the accusatory word that is here reborn before us. The prophet Micah, wild-eyed and wailing in the streets of Jerusalem:

> Arise and go, for this is no place to rest;
> because of uncleanness that destroys
> with a grievous destruction . . .

Your rich men are full of violence;
  your inhabitants speak lies . . .
Their hands are upon what is evil
  to do it diligently;
the prince and the judge ask for a bribe,
and the great man utters the evil desire of his soul;
thus they weave it together. . . .
For this I will lament and wail;
  I will go stripped and naked;
I will make lamentation like the jackals,
  and mourning like the ostriches.[7]

In the finest moments of their outrage and anger, what the young are demanding is what every prophet has demanded of his people: that they too strip away the defiled garment of society, turn away and inward toward the first principles of the conduct of life. The great question is always the same. It was asked of King David, of Imperial Rome, and now of Imperial America, playing self-appointed policeman to the nations and conquering hero to the whole of nature. "What shall it profit a man if he gain the whole world and lose his soul?"

For those of us who teach, the return to first principles means a return to Tolstoy's critique of compulsory, public education: an honest admission that what our existing pedagogical machinery is programmed to produce is the man that industrial society in its benightedness thinks it needs; and what industrial society in its benightedness thinks it needs of us is but the shriveled portion of our full humanity — how small a portion one must almost weep to say.

But lest we despair, we must remember that for Tolstoy this bleak fact was only a minor blemish on the face of an abidingly beautiful truth; that the spontaneous splendors of the human personality return to us whole in every child and will struggle fiercely to be educated in accordance with their nature. Because he believed this, Tolstoy was prepared — indeed, compelled — to sweep away the state's claim to all educational authority, which could only be the authority to pollute the wellsprings of learning. There can be no more precise way to frame the matter than as he did in raising the question: *who has the right to educate?* His answer:

There are no rights of education. I do not acknowledge such, nor have they been acknowledged nor will they ever be by the young generation under education. . . . *The right to educate is not vested in anybody.*[8]

It was out of this clear perception that authentic education derives only from the need of the child, not from the right of the adult, that Tolstoy appealed for that which presently animates campus rebellion throughout the Western world — now in the colleges; but soon enough I suspect our high

---

[7] *The Holy Bible.* Revised Standard Version. New York: Thomas Nelson & Sons, 1952, pp. 723–24, 726–27.
[8] Leo Tolstoy, *op. cit.,* pp. 111, 114.

schools too will be ablaze (not only figuratively) with the demand: "freely formed institutions, having for their basis the freedom of the learning generation."

A steep demand. A demand that is bound to seem unthinkable to those who mistake a proper sense of adult responsibility for automatic submission unto the higher powers of the social order and to the bizarre necessities that come down to us from these obsessive profit- and power-mongers. Such resignation in the name of responsibility can only drive us to cling to the established way of things as if it were all the deck there is and everything beyond, the cruel, cold sea. Nothing to do then but clap the would-be mutineers in irons, rearrange the cargo, patch up the leaks, and continue the cruise to oblivion.

But the deck is afire, while the sea, if not benign, is yet filled with a multitude of inviting islands: the possibilities of culture on the far-side of industrial necessity and nationalistic idolatry. The possibilities are there, though I think the diminished consciousness to which we are — most of us — beholden will see them only as mirages or not at all. That is why the expertise and technician-intelligence to which we habitually turn for solutions — as if with the reflex of duty well-learned — are really no help to us: more statistics, more surveys, more professional shoptalk and hair of the dog. As if there could be no knowledge of man that did not wear the official uniform of research.

But the poet Shelley tells us there are and have always been "unacknowledged legislators of mankind" whose age-old gift it is to "bring light and fire from those eternal regions where the owl-winged faculty of calculation dare not ever soar." A word from them does more than all our science and its dismal train of imitators to reclaim the wasted dimensions of our identity: the buried erotic powers, the truths of the imagination that yield meaning to song, dance, or ritual gesture, but which common literacy will never touch but to kill. Astonishments of the spirit . . . gods of the heights and of the depths . . . thrones and dominions that only the lamp of prophecy reveals . . and all these inborn glories of our nature useless, useless for achieving what the nations would achieve. We deal here in vistas of experience in which the orthodox ambitions of our society shrivel to nonentity. Yet what else would we have the education of the young be but such an adventure in transcendence?

So the demand is for "freely formed institutions": education beneath the sway of the visionary gleam. From where we stand, a revolutionary demand. And I can hardly be sanguine that many of us here who belong to the establishment will prove to be effective revolutionaries.

Should I be asked, however, "what then are *we* to do?" perhaps, for those having ears to hear, I can offer one minimal suggestion (since the maximum one can do is obvious enough): not a program, not a policy, not a method, nothing to be worked up into a research project or the grist of the conference mill — but only a silent commitment to be pondered in the heart and practiced with unabashed guile when opportunity permits. And it is this: might we not at least let go of our pretensions . . . and then simply let go of the students?

Let them go. Help them to escape, those that need to escape. Find them cracks in the system's great walls and guide them through, cover their tracks, provide the alibis, mislead the posse . . . the anxious parents, the truant officers, the supervisors and superintendents and officious superegos of the social order.

At least between ourselves and the young, we might begin talking up the natural rights of truancy and the educative possibilities of hooky — which is after all only matriculating into the school without walls that the world itself has always normally been for the inquisitive young.

And who knows? Once we stop forcing *our* education on the children, perhaps they will invite a lucky few of us to participate in *theirs.*

C. Criticism by the High School Radicals

12

The High School Revolutionaries

Marc Libarle and Tom Seligson

The High School Revolutionaries, *the book from which the following excerpts are taken, is a manifestation of the student revolution which has spread from the college campuses to the high schools. Eighteen-year-old David Romano of suburban Westport, Connecticut, reports that, given an option to attend or stay away from an experimental English class, the students stayed away. Sixteen-year-old Michael Marqusee of suburban Scarsdale declares that school and community "process" rather than educate students. N. K. Jamal of the New York City Black High School Coalition reports that the slum environment of the students is not taken into account in black schools. Sixteen-year-old Susan Snow (a pseudonym) finds the curriculum of her Erie, Pennsylvania, school uninspiring and the school board uninterested.*

The young contributors express themselves passionately, forthrightly, and sometimes obscenely; there is no mistaking their hostility to both school and society and their rejection of the curriculum of their schools. The editors of The High School Revolutionaries, *Marc Libarle and Tom Seligson have taught in the New York City schools and gathered the reports in their book nationwide from writings and tape recordings.*

I SAW AMERICA IN THE STREETS
David Romano

No matter how good the teacher may be, no matter how many books he may have published (there are many accomplished teachers at Staples: teachers with Ph.D.'s, teachers who have published, teachers who attended Harvard and Columbia), he is not going to be able to teach anything if his students don't come to class. It's almost impossible to get the kids to come to class now, and once they're in class the situation is so bad that instead of learning anything or even being in a neutral situation they have an adverse reaction to anything that is being taught to them. This student boredom is reflected in the large numbers of Staples' students who cut school and classes regularly. (Out of a school of about nineteen hundred students, approximately three hundred skip the entire day, every day, and the number of students who cut individual classes often totals up to nine hundred, or half the school.) I think this shows that students are not just bored with individual classes, but with school generally. The only students who attend classes consistently are those who are intimidated by their teachers. Staples is probably no better or no worse than most schools in this country.

I think the educational system from top to bottom, from kindergarten to college, is in pretty bad shape. The experience of a Staples Experimental English class is indicative of this. The course, instituted this year and open only to Seniors, allowed the students the option to either come to class or stay away. In class they were allowed to study anything they wanted, anything that interested them. With this freedom, almost all the Senior students, instead of putting it to good use, decided to stay away. After eleven years of stifling classroom experience, these students were unable to take advantage of this freedom. They'd come to class, sign out, and then they'd leave. They'd go down to the school lounge, or they'd smoke cigarettes, or they'd just leave campus. While a few students did put this opportunity to good use, most of them were too brainwashed to do so.

TURN LEFT AT SCARSDALE
Michael Marqusee

I have lived in Scarsdale for most of my life, and I write from the viewpoint of the affluent student turned radical. This contradiction between my political thinking and economic and social background may seem strange, but it is one of which I am constantly aware; in fact, it is my upbringing in this culture which has directly influenced my radicalization and is in some ways the cause of it.

The Scarsdale community can be described as an upper middle-class community. With the average income over $25,000 and a virtually all-white population, Scarsdale is the ideally insulated town, excluding the poor and the black. It is a community of family units in which the father usually commutes to New York City while the mother stays home to tend the children who attend, for the most part, one of the highly-rated Scarsdale public schools. The jobs that the men in Scarsdale commute to are almost all either in one of the professions or in business. In this community, my friends and myself are all the children of desk-sitters. Our fathers work in a 9 to 5, tie-and-jacket world where the guiding principle is usually that of finding the easiest path to the most money.

Obviously, laborers of any kind and low-ranking desk-job holders find no place for themselves in Scarsdale. In fact, for most of us, the only working-class people we ever have contact with are the employees our parents hire to clean house, do the gardening, or repair the washing machines, heaters, cars, stoves, and swimming pools.

Scarsdale prides itself on its cultural and intellectual interests. There are many patrons of Lincoln Center, frequent theater-goers, and supposedly avid book-readers. Most of us live in large, one-family houses, among which there is little variety. The town has a calm, serene mood, with its quiet, uncrowded streets, and absence of night activity. There is a generally restrained and almost unfriendly attitude toward one's neighbors. The mothers of the town engage in various "wifely" activities: watching the kids, directing her staff, chatting on the phone, shopping, playing tennis, or maybe some occasional stuffing letters at a local political office.

Finally, in this catalogue of Scarsdale family elements, there are the children, and we are in many ways the center of family and community attention. Virtually all parents see their child's function within school as the attainment of high grades, or in other words, academic success and a better chance for admission to a highly-rated college. This is the goal and primary function of our high schools. . . .

I return to the subject of school because finally it is the center of all our activity and is the primary tool with which the young of Scarsdale are molded into finished products. The word "process" has repeatedly cropped up here because it is indicative of the nature of existence in my community. Thus, Scarsdale High seeks to produce college graduates who are in turn directed into a field within the professional or business community. This "process" is not so far removed from the pattern whereby black kids in a ghetto school are trained for "niggerly" jobs (or no jobs) or where working-class kids are sent to vocational schools. As has been said, the student is universally a nigger. We are subservient to all authority and our lives are controlled by that authority from the selection of our careers to the development of our values. This is a system which should be abhorrent to all who hold supposedly "human," "progressive" values, yet it is endorsed by almost all in the adult world, for they see it as a necessary preface to that wondrous goal — a career.

Choose anything you want but have a career — a definite, disciplined job or skill that involves a routine of work. In that routine is security, happiness, and normalcy. This is a standard defense of the school system. They preach that this process aids in our attainment of fulfillment. It gives us opportunities. Bullshit. This process, as I and my friends in affluent Scarsdale have discovered, is one of limitation and misdirection. Imagine spending your entire thinking life attending classes which have been planned by someone thirty years older than you who usually has little in common with you; having your daily schedule worked out by someone who probably has never seen you; sitting down in assigned desks at the signal of a bell and standing up again fifty minutes later at the same signal, only to move to another pre-planned class and follow the same routine, all day, every day, in pursuit of a goal someone else has set for you and which, whether you believe in it or not, seems to offer as little excitement as the dreary schedule you now go through. This is the high school student, and that existence is one directed toward limitation, demoralization, and I repeat, manipulation. One of the weapons which the school uses in directing our course is a steady, subtle humiliation which starts the moment we learn in kindergarten that we must raise our hand (an absurd ritual) in order to get permission to go to the bathroom. It is continued in the hundreds of orderly lines we all form to move around elementary school, the disgrace we suffer when we make a wrong answer to an easy question, and the paranoia and tension that accompany the distribution of grades on all levels of education.

For a student, grades can become an obsessive force in life. All our activities in school revolve around our grades. However, few students actually believe they are an accurate measure of someone's intelligence or capabilities. Teachers often say they indicate a student's "performance." They picked the right word. Attaining high grades in school is usually just a matter of performing or acting out the role of dutiful student with a straight face. Given a talent for bullshitting, anybody can pull an A. The difference between one grade or another, even if it's between a B+ and an A, can absorb some students to the point of neurosis. The parents are almost all excessively concerned with their child's grades, and some will punish or reward their kids according to their quarterly standing. All of them encourage and even push their kids into working for a higher grade whether that means learning anything or not. Often, we find ourselves orienting everything toward creating a good impression the last few weeks of each marking period and then dropping it at the beginning of a new one until report-card time comes around again. . . .

RIGHT ON
N. K. Jamal

. . . Most black slum children are facing hard life every day. They walk down hot smelly streets in the summer. They walk down cold, slushy, dirty, dangerous streets during winter. Any season the sidewalks are strewn with uncovered garbage cans, some lying horizontally on the ground, trash falling into the children's paths. They walk past tall, dingy tenements on the way to school. They look up at the little old women who stare at them from three stories up — little women who sit there at the rusty, maybe broken and crumbled window ledge, reminiscing.

Traffic on the corner frightens children as they go to school. They never grow accustomed to the death-dealing automobiles that virtually fly past them in hordes in the early morning. They cross the streets, wary of broken glass that could cut them, possibly causing permanent injury.

On the school block, pimps coax the little girls as they walk past. Prostitutes pucker their lips at the little boys, telling them to come and see them when they grow up. Dope addicts nod, not at the children, not at anyone in particular, just nodding, in their vertical sleeping positions. Dope pushers attempt to sell the children little pieces of candy that are not as innocent as they look.

Further up the block gangs of boys and girls are giving one boy the shakedown. Others are yelling and screaming in fright or glee as two boys fight.

Still others yelp as someone throws a bowl of hot, scalding water out of the third floor window of the adjoining tenement.

This is life as the average black student lives it — every day. This is the sharp, focused world of reality. The world of the slum child.

Yet, once the student enters the classroom, this world mysteriously changes. The harsh roughness of existence is erased. The everyday life of Harlem, Watts, Detroit, Newark, or Washington, D.C. fades into the past. Everything that should have been used to determine the nature and direction of the student's education is discarded.

As David himself said, his education and mine have indeed been subtle. Education was not about the subjects of English, Math, and History, which were "taught," but rather about the workings of the system. Hypocritical education under false pretenses. The education we all received was actually about the subtleness of the structure that was educating us, the why of this subtleness, and the useful purposes we might later serve to the system. This was our education. We were awakening. David was awakening. We began to see a set, noted formula. A *pattern*. Guidelines by which the system knew it could prepare the student for his predetermined place in society.

The method? Soothe the student. Pull the kid out of the hard-hitting realities of life and push him up the path that leads into the soothing world of Mother Goose.

Kill the pessimism of his real life with the optimism of Honest Abe, the self-educated farmboy grown President.

Don't let him become aware of his color. Make him see no color. Let Dick and Jane become his everyday, colorless friends. Avoid questions about why Dick and Jane don't have a darker friend on their whole block.

Talk to him about Spot, and ask him if he has a dog of his own (don't let him trap you with discussion about the stray, rabid dogs roaming ghetto streets).

This was the formula — and if followed correctly, it worked.

The formula was set by the general society. Public education is society's baby. It arises from the need for society to determine what the individual should do with his life, and how he will live it. It arises from society's need to be able to control the individual — he belongs here, and she belongs there. Therefore, educate him to become this, and her to become that.

The formula is still being instituted by the entire school system, with the individual teacher being the most immediate and vulnerable component, the administration, principals, district supervisors, and the Board of Education and its members being the extensions, and *total control* being in the hands of a select group.

The method of institution of the formula is up to the individual teacher. In a circle of thirty or so teachers, there can be thirty stories about how each teacher managed to pull her student from the facts of his existence, to the bourgeois world of *Our Friends and Neighbors* — from the rugged tenements of Harlem to the clean-swept, mowed-lawn atmosphere of suburbia in a matter of minutes.

Then she will discourse on the success she has had in this transformation with minimal balking from her students during or after the transition. In short, she is proud that she can hide the discrepancy between life and the classroom from the student.

An amazing feat in itself, this process brings to mind the sad realization that the entire education the student receives is merely an escapist barbiturate to soothe and hold the student until he is ready to take his acceptable, preset place in society.

The nature of the education of the student is an incredible story. It would appear from the outset that the student's education should be geared to his environment. But, as has already been pointed out several times in the foregoing pages, the education was only to prepare the child for his "slot" in life (as a data-processing card has its slot in the computer, so has the student his "slot" in society).

The student can be going to school in a Harlem area — in fact, in middle Harlem, on 114th Street, down the block from one of the busiest dope and prostitution traffic corners in the world, and up the street from one of the most crime-ridden apartment buildings in New York City — and yet once he crosses the threshold of his school building and enters the classroom, a fantastic psychedelic illusion of truth, warmth, and everlasting beauty (as interpreted by the system), looms before him, inviting him to come in and be "educated."

He sees young boys and girls moving around in an impossible world of dreams and middle-class aspirations. He watches them, as they float in white shirts and ties that they cannot afford, blue skirts and blouses, doldrum uniforms reflecting the gray attitudes of the school administration.

Their thoughts and dreams aspire beyond reality — they reach for the white middle-class star that shines high above them. They prepare to make the necessary change — to usurp their inherited blackness to become half-white members of the "Negro Middle Class."

This is not their fault. This is their teaching. It is a fact that society's recognized position for these students is in the Negro Middle Class, where they best serve society as prime examples of "those who made it." These are the students who would, in centuries past, have been recognized as the former slave who escaped, got rich, and then decided that he needed a few black slaves of his own, because if "Massa has it, why cain't I . . . ?"

Then there are the others. Our student watches a group of kids walk by who do not conform. They don't obey the rules. They don't wear ties. They don't care about society. They fight, they lie, they cheat, and they steal. These are the victims of society. These are the ones most affected by their environment, and yet these are the ones who receive the least benefit from the school system. It is said of these, "They are too hard-headed," "He is uneducable," "She will never learn," and "I tried, but he won't listen." These are the students who *must* resign themselves to Gym, Shop, and Hygiene classes as their education. These are the ones who have only society's worst to look forward to—jobs as unskilled laborers, welfare, and the Selective Service.

Denise W—— goes to a junior high school in Harlem. It is an all-girls' school. It's in one of the worst neighborhoods of New York. Outside — rape, murder, robbery, and undermining. Inside the school, much of the same . . . only this time done to girls by girls.

Denise lives in a bleak, dangerous, slum neighborhood, and yet her education is geared to the type of student that lives in white middle-class Scarsdale, N.Y., with its bourgeois ideals and settings. The fact that she lives in the worst, sub-standard conditions of housing, mental and physical health, and emotional stability, is not taken into account at all. She is taught by a formula, not by her capacity to relate to the things she is taught. It would be much easier for Denise to learn if her teacher did talk about the stray Spots in the streets, the problems that Denise is having at home, the attitudes of the girls in the school toward one another, and the situations that arise in the community; but it is easier for the teacher to just give the lesson as she is told. This way, she doesn't have to breach the socio-economic and racial gaps between her and Denise. . . .

MY TEACHER IS A RACIST
Susan Snow

The courses offered are the basic academic subjects: English, Math, Science, History, and a foreign language. I've already mentioned how uninspiring and elementary they are. Many of the kids at Academy don't go on to college, and there are very few courses that will be helpful to them. There are some vocational courses given, but in skills that were useful twenty or thirty years ago. They teach drafting and metal working — things that are no good in 1969. I hear that some schools offer courses in Computer Programming, in which there are many jobs today; but Academy has nothing like that. When about 70 percent of Academy's graduates go looking for jobs right away rather than going to college, this lack of preparation speaks poorly for the school. A lot of the boys go right into the army after graduation, and it is there rather than at Academy that they learn trades for later life.

The teachers always seem to skirt certain subjects. For example, I've never had a lesson on Vietnam. Anything I know about Vietnam is through my own outside reading. There may be an occasional remark like, "We're escalating again," but we've never actually discussed what the situation was like before we got in there, and what's happening there now. The boys in my class will soon be asked to go over there, they'll be asked to kill, and they'll be asked to die; we don't even know what it's about — we're not told. We are told that Russia is "bad," but we're never told how the Russian society is different from America. I've never been taught what the communist doctrine is, I've never been taught about socialism or Marxism. Anything like this we have to find out on our own. It's not part of the curriculum; it should be, because it's part of the world picture. Some of our national problems are touched on in a course called Problems of Democracy, but even then everything is much too theoretical. For example, when learning about town government we learned about the different bureaus and agencies that make it up — how many councilmen there are, how long the mayor's term is, what the aldermen do. We didn't talk about how Erie's Mayor Tulio is the head of a party machine that controls the policemen and the firemen in addition to the school board in town. An actual case like this that contradicts the textbook is never discussed; and a teacher would never talk about what can be done to solve such problems as the war and Tulio's control.

Students should have a voice in decision about curriculum. As of now, we are never listened to. Once, when it was requested by students that a course in psychology be introduced, the school board came back with: "There are not enough funds." They've done this every time students have asked for something, yet they seem to find funds very conveniently when they need them. Giving up on help from the teachers and the administration, a group of students took the initiative to get the materials needed for a certain subject. We wanted to learn about the history of certain minority groups so we went out and got eleven sets of magazines to be used in the History classes. The magazines were put out by a scholastic firm, so the teachers couldn't say that they were radical or anything. They were a condensed version of Negro History which the teachers could teach from, but they never used them. They said, "Oh great, we'll work these into our curriculum," but only one teacher out of eleven ever did. I think some of them didn't want to teach Negro History because they were prejudiced, and many of them are just too darn lazy to work it into the programs that they do have. Some of the teachers use the same study plan for five or six years running. I guess they think that the world never changes.

Within the History curriculum, there was no Black History course offered. A few of the black students got together and asked two teachers if they would start an after-school Minorities' History class. They suggested that once a week kids would come in for about an hour to study a topic which they considered important but which was not included in the regular program. The two teachers agreed, and they got clearance from the administration to have this after-school class, to be open to all students, black and white. There was a pretty big turnout for it the first few weeks, but gradually the teachers lost interest. Maybe they were too tired from their regular classes, but whatever the reason was, they stopped coming. The class was held Monday afternoons, and we began to hear almost regularly on the public address system the announcement that "Minorities' History will not be held today." The last few months of school we lost all confidence in them, and there were no classes held at all.

I think there definitely should be a course in Minorities' History introduced into the regular curriculum. But as it looks now there won't be such a course this coming school year. At the end of last year, I went to one of the teachers and asked whether we were going to have a Minorities' History class next year. He said that he didn't know, and I thought this was odd because he was the one in charge of it. I don't think it should take that long to organize a new course like this, but the school bureaucracy in Erie stifles any real changes in the schools. Any reform proposal must first go to the school administration. If the administration approves it, then it must be presented before a meeting of the school board. Board members have the final say in a matter like this, and they usually take their time considering things. If they want to spend six months discussing it, well then they'll spend six months discussing it; meanwhile, the course will not be taught in the high school. All of the members of the Erie School Board are white, and they have no interest whatsoever in any black issues or Black Studies program. Sometimes I don't think they have any interest at all in our education. . . .

13

Our Time Is Now

John Birmingham

The high school underground press is another source of information about the attitudes of some high school students toward school and society, although some readers will be turned off by the obvious bitterness and frequent vulgarity of the writers.

John Birmingham is well-equipped to edit this material, not only because he himself developed an underground newspaper but also because he is an intelligent and reasonable young crusader. Seventeen years old when he wrote Our Time Is Now *(New York: Praeger, 1970), Birmingham is now a student at New York University.*

A *generation gap.* The one you hear about most is the gap between the over-thirty and the under-thirty. I'm seventeen, so I am supposed to say that if you are over thirty you are against me, and if you are under thirty you are with me.

Besides calling it cliché, I could criticize anyone who uses the term "gap," because it means putting people into groups — boxes. But I won't. I know enough to see that you can't get by as a human without putting people into boxes. My real objection to the way people talk about the gap is that they have made only two age-group boxes — the over-thirty and the under-thirty. If you are going to put people into boxes, the least you can do is give them a wide variety of boxes to fit into.

From *Our Time Is Now*, ed. John Birmingham (New York: Frederick A. Praeger, Inc., 1970), pp. 3–6, 193–194, 204–208. Reprinted by permission of Frederick A. Praeger, Inc.

A generation gap is the result of what has happened during the twenty years that lie between two generations. During this time, the younger generation has been forming a new culture, new politics, and new means of communicating with each other. At the same time, the older generation has been holding onto the culture, politics, and media that were developed twenty years ago. The more that times have changed during these twenty years, the more difference has developed between the generations.

Today the younger generation is typified in the eyes of most adults by the college revolutionaries. What does the younger generation do? They take over college buildings. That is the stereotype you are supposed to fit. But another — different — revolutionary movement has begun to erupt in the high schools. Of course, this movement does not get as much coverage by the over-thirty media because it is presently on a smaller scale than the college-campus rebellions. And the people involved in media generally put the high school revolutionaries into the same box as the college revolutionaries. This stereotype has to be dealt with before we can discuss the high school underground fairly.

The easiest way is to create a couple of new age-group boxes and point out a gap that is virtually unheard of — the gap between high school and college students.

Times change so fast that three years now can form a gap that might be equal to a gap formed by twenty years in the last century. College students — mostly the Students for a Democratic Society (SDS) — don't fully understand why they were unable to organize the high schools. In a way, they were ignoring the gap. Often they like to think of themselves as fathers to the high school underground, but, in reality, college revolutionaries play only a small part in the evolution of the high school revolution. Yes, a lot of high school SDS groups have been formed, in California and Washington especially, but these groups usually act on their own, without college-student influence. And high school SDS's are not as common as totally independent high school underground movements.

Last summer, the SDS sent out a newsletter that was directed to high school revolutionaries, urging them to start underground papers. This might seem to indicate that the SDS was partially responsible for organizing the high school students. But the opposite is true. This newsletter was only repeating what high school students had already said many times. And it was urging high school students to do what they were already doing — completely on their own. In fact, many high school revolutionaries whom I have spoken to talk of SDSers as though they are "over the hill." These high school students (myself included) believe that their own movement is far more important than the college movement. They believe that it is more important because it includes all youth. High school is responsible at one time or another for the education of all young people in America.

At seventeen, I am younger than some people and older than others. Things change fast enough in our society so that seventeen is not like twenty-one, nor is it like fifteen. I may not have as much experience in organizing students for a political revolution as some SDSers have, but, by the same token, I have not made their mistakes — destructive mistakes, such as trying to cause change through violence and violation of other students' rights. At the same time, I should not be lumped together with students much younger than me. Just because we both put out underground papers in our schools, I don't think I should be put into the same box as Joshua Mamis, who helped to put out a junior high school underground paper at the age of twelve.

And now that I have graduated, I will be going to college. This won't mean that I will be changing from one movement to another. That isn't what it will mean for most high school revolutionaries who go to college. Instead of joining the college movement as it exists today, they will change it into a new movement that will begin tomorrow. Joshua Mamis and others like him will then be changing the high schools.

Today the high school revolutionaries are looking for *really* new ideas. They won't just settle for standard proposals that have been handed to them by the SDS or some radical adults. Norman Mailer discovered this when he went to a meeting of students in the high school underground in New York during his campaign for the Democratic mayoral nomination. A girl there told him that he sounded just like her parents.

Probably the best way of destroying the stereotype is to let the high school underground speak for itself in all its variety of voices. Maybe only 5 per cent of high school students are actively involved in the underground movement, but that 5 per cent is enough to lead, to cause some change in the high schools, and to cater to the needs of high school students in a way that teachers and administrators never could.

The revolution began for me personally in May, 1969 — in the form of a crudely printed underground magazine called *Smuff*. Inside were eleven pages on the war in Vietnam, student radicalism, draft-dodging, and Hackensack High School. I was the editor-in-chief out of *necessity*. And I soon discovered that what was happening in Hackensack was also happening all over the high school scene, south as well as north, west as well as east. Out of *necessity* — everywhere. . . .

A common criticism of student radicals, in general, is that they put down everything and then offer no alternative. To an extent, this is a valid criticism. It is a lot easier to be destructive than creative. And, like other human beings, students often take the easiest way out. But this criticism is not entirely valid. A lot of adults close their ears after hearing only half of the students' story. This is understandable. They, too, are taking an easy way out.

Students in the underground offer no alternative, sometimes because there is no alternative. At least, there's no alternative that sounds like an alternative. With many restrictions, dress codes, for instance, the only alternative that the students want is no more dress codes.

Other times, concrete alternatives are being offered but not being taken seriously enough by the administration. Some of the alternatives have already been discussed in earlier chapters of this book. Meaningful student councils, self-censored and uncensored student newspapers, black studies courses, student power in general, these are all alternatives.

In fact, the underground itself is an alternative, and about as concrete an alternative as you will find. The underground press and the student-power organizations offer alternatives to students who are disillusioned with the overground counterparts.

This year, at my school, *Smuff* is offering another alternative, an independent study course that is run entirely by students. Our school has made ventures into the field of independent study for advanced students, but the subject matter and the independence of the student are restricted. Students have asked for independent study. Last year, the *Voice* had two editorials submitted that asked for it, and one of them was printed. But progress has not been made. "It takes time" is the excuse of most administrators. And perhaps for them it does. So now, the students who are involved with *Smuff* are doing it quickly. . . .

Curriculum is an area where a lot of reform is called for by the underground. The main criticism is of irrelevant courses. Too many courses are tailored to deal with the world as it was ten years ago, and too many teachers refuse to relate the subject matter to today. A wide variety of courses is offered, but not the right ones. Courses in music appreciation are offered at most schools, but how many schools offer courses in rock music? The curriculum in high schools today has virtually ignored the culture of the students it is educating. Rock is having a tremendous effect on the life-styles of young people in the world today; it is communicating to them. Yet many teachers will insist that it is not a serious kind of music, not one to be studied.

Actually, I have not seen enough underground papers touch on this area of curriculum reform. While I am sure most students would agree with me that curriculum should be related more to the youth culture, the subject has been neglected except by implication.

What is touched upon more often is the obvious irrelevance of the curriculum to the black community. The banning of *Soul on Ice*, by Eldridge Cleaver, from San Francisco high schools is an explicit example.

Here are two articles that deal with curriculum:

ATTENTION ALL TEACHERS!

We recommend that all biology teachers read the last chapter in the BSCS biology text. It explains that in one year, you (the students) will have forgotten about 85 per cent of the facts you learned in biology and that the purpose of the course was not to have you memorize facts, but to put you in a frame of thinking, in this case scientific.

The authors assume that if you don't go into science, you won't have much use for all the details, but that becoming a person more aware of yourself and environment will make you more easily adaptable to and comfortable in your surroundings. We wish that the course was taught on this assumption, as we wish all required courses were.

[1] *Mine* No. 8. Tucson, Arizona.

It is evident that a forced feeding of facts leads only to the forgetting of them, not to the making of a better student, or a better community, or a better world. In this age of specialization, though electives should be taught for job training, with whatever means necessary, required courses, after providing the basics necessary to life, should be a broadening influence, allowing the student to develop his own patterns of thought. School therefore, should be a place where in addition to being trained for performing the techniques necessary for earning money, a student is allowed to become a better person in all facets of his future life. Making a living is not restricted to the accumulating of monetary wealth, but includes searching for and achieving wisdom — understanding self and environment, i.e., others — and happiness.

It is then necessary to condemn the school in which the student is removed from the accumulating of wisdom and is not allowed to discover how to achieve happiness. Such a school is only a temple to pre-twentieth century rigamarole.

J. S. Catalina

When the administration of a high school makes a reform, the underground will usually be the first to recognize their accomplishment. This is because the students in the underground are constantly looking for reform. And sometimes the underground can use these reforms as examples to prove a point they have been making for a long time.

Given A Chance[2]
Bob Klein

A course entitled English 8x9x is offered in our school for the first time this term. This course requires two periods a day, yields two major credits, and is satisfying a long felt want of many of John Bowne's seniors.

What makes this course so different is that with the extra time we can do not only the required curriculum, but also whatever voluntary and in depth work we wish to carry on in class. We can do additional work either as one class or in seminar groups of five to fifteen people. The work done in these seminars is chosen by the students with suggestions offered by the teachers as to what ends each group should try to attain in its subject of interest.

Students in our school have demanded for some time the right to choose their own curriculum. In this class we are finally able to do that. Groups have studied Kafka, Pinter, Malcolm X, Carrol, and others already, and will soon reorganize themselves to start on a new series of topics and authors.

Some people are critical of students on the basis that students want rights, but are unwilling to accept responsibilities. I believe that this course disproves the misconceptions. Students in the class have given their own money to purchase extra books, spent time (not required) out of school for group work and for extra research. The teachers needn't check our homework because they know it has been done and done with interest.

Interest is the crux of the matter. A student can sit in a class all term, hand in homework each day and walk away with a mark, but without in-

[2] *The Observed* Vol. I, No. 4. Flushing, New York.

terest, will learn nothing and retain even less. If, as in this class, he can study those things of interest to him personally, he will enjoy doing so.

Given a chance, given the materials, given the encouragement we need, courses like this can help us, as students, to learn and love it.

D. Advocates of Affective Education

14

The Invisible Curriculum

Hanne Lane Hicks

Occasionally a brief reminder is as telling as a long article. This is the case with Mr. Hicks' "The Invisible Curriculum." As Hicks says, it is not that the visible curriculum "is not valuable, but that too often it is value-less."

Hicks is the coordinator of secondary student teaching for Indiana University in the Fort Wayne area.

There the rusting hulks of steel sit on the sand — with jagged holes where Mars has poked his finger like a moody child jamming a stick into the earth. And Samson's weapon of bone is still at work, though in a different capacity, in the capitals of what has been called the "cradle of Western civilization."

In a newer, more brash, and far more prosperous land of the West, acts of omission over the years have led to violence, and examples of happiness and peace are infrequent. And the wise of the land feel wise no more. And the people are worried. And one sighs and wonders if people will ever learn.

At times, it seems not.

And yet, there have been teachers. Oh, so many famous names dot the pages of man's biography as a race: Socrates, Jesus, Aristotle, Gandhi, Dewey, Voltaire. Social historians have little trouble tracing the teachings. But what of the learning? Perhaps it is best that we attempt nothing more than surmise.

But the effort is still present. The children are exposed to flexible scheduling, programmed instruction, team teaching. They are socialized in kindergarten, institutionalized in grade school, and homogenized in high school. And they are graduated, too often, unchanged, untouched, and uncaring. It is not that the curriculum of our schools is not valuable, but that too often it is value-less.

For this is the visible curriculum. Dick and Jane visit the farm in third grade; in junior high school they are cast adrift in a unit called "Adventure": they still have their problems in high school — only now they are called Macbeth and Lady Macbeth. And while lovers scurry to view the moon on the eve of St. Agnes, John views the athletic field through the grimy window, wondering if the scouting reports of Cathedral High are accurate. Little Susan doesn't pay much attention to the agonies of Desdemona. Why should she? She was rejected by her boyfriend last night — she knows the part well. Tad has his own problems too. He can't concentrate on his teacher's lecture about *Lear* and Shakespeare's comment on the breakdown of the family. His parents' divorce is pending and next week he has to choose one with whom to live. Within one classroom we find a microcosm of the world's insecurity and fear.

Is Keats unimportant? Is Shakespeare without value? Of course not! But until these parts of the curriculum are merged with the invisible curriculum they will remain meaningless and dry to the majority of students. What is this missing, invisible curriculum? What is this mysterious intangible that makes current curriculum a catalyst instead of a catastrophe?

It is difficult to say. After all, it *is* invisible, seldom appearing in curriculum guides. But perhaps some elements of it can be described.

Perhaps the invisible curriculum is made up of concern. The teacher who is concerned enough to realize his potential effect — positive and negative — on children is displaying a knowledge of the invisible curriculum. Students perceive the teacher as powerful, financially secure, and intellectually free. Students must be convinced, somehow, that these are not the reasons for the teacher's being in the classroom. The student must be assured that he is the only reason that teachers exist. This concern of the instructor for his "children" must be made obvious — it can never be taken for granted that the students will understand that the teacher has it. They probably won't, without evidence.

Perhaps the invisible curriculum is made up primarily of respect. Do teachers really listen to what students say? If so, do they hear? Does the student who says "You can't make me study!" really mean "Please make me pass!"? Students may be nonworkers sometimes, but they are never nonthinkers. If we listen, hear, and understand what the student is saying, we may be closer to creating a meaningful curriculum. But we listen to someone only when respect is present.

Perhaps a large part of the invisible curriculum is enjoyment. The chuckle that must inevitably come when a child states that "Russian spies like to hide behind ironed curtains" is surely part of the invisible curriculum. Has drudgery and dryness ever stimulated the mind of a child — or of anyone else? In every class in which the invisible curriculum is present there is a bit of the feeling one gets when Edmund Gwenn takes little Natalie Wood on his knee in *Miracle on 34th Street* and explains, "There is a French nation. There is an English nation. But the most wonderful nation of them all is the Imagination." Learning is exciting, adventurous, and fun — when it is a product of the invisible curriculum.

Perhaps this nebulous curriculum is based on care. A teacher working with this curriculum must care enough to risk heartbreak when a child "fails." The teacher must care so deeply about his children, his job, his responsibility, that he can never become blasé or calloused concerning the desperate needs of children.

In the final analysis, the invisible curriculum is attitude — a positive attitude. Without this and the other components, no visible curriculum can affect the life of a child, let alone the history of the world.

And the world, with its defoliated jungles in Vietnam, its hunger-bloated bellies in Biafra, its gutted shops in Detroit and Newark, is as much a concern of the curriculum as reading, social studies, or arithmetic. Can education be responsible for rebuilding those shops and making war between men, if not impossible, at least highly improbable? If so, then the invisible curriculum will be invisible no more.

15

Teaching the Young to Love

Jack R. Frymier

Jack R. Frymier edits Theory Into Practice, *a journal sponsored by Ohio State University's School of Education which presents significant ideas on the curriculum. He recently devoted an issue to the affective dimension in education. Here he suggests that in a time of hate and violence, "the need to teach the young to love transcends everything else."*

Jack R. Frymier is Professor of Education at Ohio State University.

It is time that those who work in schools teach children something about love.

Despite protests to the contrary, most schools in the United States teach about hate. Look at the diagrams on a social studies classroom bulletin board. Study the charts and pictures hanging on the wall. They usually

From Jack R. Frymier, "Teaching the Young to Love," *Theory Into Practice*, VIII (April, 1969), 42–44. Reprinted by permission of Jack R. Frymier and the College of Education, The Ohio State University.

relate to war. Books on desks, maps on walls, and projects assigned to children all add up to the indefensible fact that schools are unwitting participants in teaching young people about the negative aspects of human existence — about how to hate and how to kill.

Educators talk about attitudes, feelings, and emotions and their role in teaching and learning, yet they do little about them in schools. The widespread violence in our society the last four or five years and the continuing involvement of our country in war are real, tangible evidence talk is not enough.

Not only must men find a way to learn to live together in peaceful, loving, accepting ways, this must be taught as a way of life. It literally is.

It shouldn't be necessary to argue, this point of view is so obvious. But, when it comes to organizing educational effort with the objective of helping young people develop positive feelings and positive behaviors toward others, educators do not act as if it is.

Instead, large sums of money and great amounts of energy are spent on substantive aspects. In the many national curriculum reform efforts, for example, the emphasis has been on improving the nature of subject matter by sequencing information differently, identifying the conceptual bases, and building upon the structure of the disciplines. The problem of such efforts, however, is that when schoolmen start with subject matter to build goals and objectives, as they have in these reform attempts, then subject matter is where they must ultimately end up.

Man is the end. Objectives and purposes must be stated in human terms. Not in substantive terms, not in social terms, but in individual, personal, human terms. The means to achieve this goes far beyond helping people learn to read and write and to add and subtract — far beyond most of the substantive aspects of schools today. The need to teach the young to love transcends everything else.

There was a time when there was no great urgency, when it did not make so much difference. That was a time, though, when only a few people would possibly be hurt or killed. That time is gone. We all know that. The young people of this world know that. They are the first generation to grow up within the pale of our awesome destructive power. Concerned and aroused, they are taking drastic measures. Their mood and their methods may be questionable, but their message is not. Their message is real — subject matter, disciplines, rationality is not enough.

It was intelligent and rational thought that the Germans used so methodically to destroy human life in World War II. Nazi Germany's extermination of the Jews was one of the most highly rational activities ever accomplished by man up to that point. The men who were in charge of killing the Jews in the extermination camps were so proficient that they were able to devise schemes to make the Jews literally run to their deaths. They made the Jews run because they had carefully studied the problem of extermination and had found that a winded Jew died faster.

At one death camp, Treblinka, the Germans were so efficient that it took no more than forty-five minutes from the time Jews arrived there by train until their dead bodies were being removed from the gas ovens. In just 6 hours and 15 minutes, Treblinka could process twelve trains of twenty cars each. 24,000 human beings.

That was 25 years ago. Today, rational efforts have brought men to a new pinnacle. The truth of this age is that we possess the power to destroy all life entirely. Plant and animal. This is an impossible reality to comprehend, let alone deal with. Yet, this reality must be faced and it must be faced in ways that will make a difference.

It dare not be assumed that if people know that they will, therefore, behave in kind and humane ways — that children will automatically learn to think and behave positively rather than negatively. They have to be taught.

There are no packaged programs, no teacher's manuals, and no texts on teaching love as a unit. We are our best resource. Each of us. It is by what we are, our attitudes and the behaviors that reflect them, that we teach about love. Or teach about hate.

Speaking out against other people or saying negative things about them is the mildest example of unloving behavior. Allport, in an exploration of human prejudice, identified this manifestation of hate as antilocution. It is the first of five steps that become successively more negative. Avoidance is the second level. It is staying away from other people, not having contact with or approaching them. The middle level is discrimination, subjecting another person to an unpleasant or undesirable experience you are unwilling to impose upon yourself. Striking out against another person or physical attack is the fourth level. Extermination, killing or destroying life, is the final, ultimate, and irreversible level.

These five levels of rejective behavior show how we relate in negative, unloving ways to other people. But they are only one half of human potential. The other half projects positive attitudes and loving behaviors.

Speaking out in favor of another person, saying good things about other people which cause them to be better, is the first level of accepting or loving behavior. The counterpart for avoidance is seeking out other people, deliberately approaching and moving toward other persons and interacting positively with them. The next level of loving behavior is altruism, the unselfish doing of good things, the giving of yourself. Physically touching, caressing, embracing or positive loving behavior is the fourth level; it is showing other people in physical ways that they are good and worthwhile. The fifth level of loving behavior would theoretically be the creation of life. Obviously, the sexual act is this. It is the ultimate intimate relationship between man and woman and, in its potential for the creation of life, it represents the epitome of loving behavior.

It is the positive side of this continuum of behaviors that can be emphasized in teaching. Some people, though, maintain that if feelings are to become personal, they have to be caught not taught. While there is some truth in this, learning cannot be left to chance. Schoolmen have to work at it. They need to arrange circumstances, provide information, and most of all, generate human relationships to make catching these understandings possible. The place to begin in schools is with teachers. For, whether a child becomes negative or positive will depend upon the development of his concept of himself and teachers play a powerful part in its formation.

A child is born with neither a negative concept of himself nor a positive concept. His view of himself is what he sees reflected in others' actions and reactions. Teachers provide this kind of feedback every day. Some of it in the form of such things as grade cards or student conferences is formal. Most, however, is informal — it is what teachers say and do.

Teachers react to children hundreds and hundreds of times during the course of a given day. Almost all of their reactions are immediate, spontaneous, and momentary. Most teachers don't plan it this way. Their intentions are usually the opposite. They mean to be deliberate, thoughtful, and purposeful. Some of the time they manage this — before school when they organize lessons and learning experiences for the day and after school when they mull over their own and the children's successes.

All day long in the classroom, though, teachers simply "bounce" off the children — "What do you want Johnny?" "Everybody open your books to page 73." "Billy be quiet." "John, Helen, and Mary go to the board and do problems twelve, thirteen, and fourteen." There isn't time to be deliberate, thoughtful, and purposeful under the pressures of the teaching situation. The kind of human being a teacher is is what counts.

Some teachers are generally positive. "Atta boy." "Good work." "Keep it up." They feed back data hundreds and hundreds of times a day that tell students they are worthwhile, they are good, they are important, and they count. Other teachers have a basic style of bouncing which is negative. They scowl, they frown, they are discouraging. These teachers feed data back hundreds of times a day, thousands of times a week, and millions and billions of times during the school year with negative results for children.

Teachers have many serious, unconscious biases at work. Teachers, for example, unconsciously favor students in their class according to sex. One study showed that boys attempted to participate in classroom discussions eight times more often than girls (held up their hands, volunteered), but teachers called on girls ten times more often. Teachers differentiate negatively in other ways, too. Studies clearly indicate that youngsters from lower class homes receive less physical attention and less eye to eye contact than children from middle to upper middle class income families.

An in-depth study of 3,000 teachers in a major urban school district contains some of the most alarming data of all. These teachers considered their children below average, their children's motivation below average, and their children's aspirations below average. The tragedy is that children would have little chance to be anything but below average in the classrooms of teachers with views like these.

People become what they perceive — what they experience and psychologically consume. Just as the food we eat and the air we breathe become a part of us physically, so do the sights we see and the sounds we hear, the things and people we experience become a part of us psychologically.

If we degrade another person, then a degraded person becomes the substance of our perceptions. We become what we perceive — we degrade ourselves. The person who destroys another person thus actually destroys himself. It's as if you were to take an apple, sprinkle poison on it, and then eat it.

But when a person behaves positively, when he does things which make other people feel good and worthwhile and important and valuable, he feeds psychologically on good perceptual stuff and also becomes better. This obviously is the golden rule, and the best empirical data that we have today says that it is right. Anthropology, sociology, and social psychology show us that what we do toward our fellow man is what we tend to become.

This applies the same to children. Children tend to become like the people they perceive, like the people they experience and psychologically consume — the people their teachers are. These teachers may be their parents, their friends, or their school teachers. If their various teachers behave in positive ways, they will grow to become positive people.

Schools obviously cannot control all that a child encounters, but one thing can be controlled. Whatever role we play, the one variable over which we can exert the greatest control is ourselves and our own behavior. We have to learn to use ourselves in positive, creative, responsible ways to provide the kind of feedback to help younger and older children become the positive, loving human beings they can become.

The thing that counts is us. Subject matter, organization, and evaluative techniques are all important, but the major perceptual stuff for a child is other people. In education, the other people are the adults who work in schools.

A child is not born loving or hateful. Love and hate are learned. We have to learn to use ourselves to teach young people to learn to love.

16

Reach, Touch, and Teach

Terry Borton

The Philadelphia Public Schools, as part of their program of innovation, have sponsored the Affective Education Research Project. Terry Borton, as co-director of the project, helped teachers to deal

Terry Borton, "Reach, Touch, and Teach," *Saturday Review*, January 18, 1969, 56–58, 69–70. Copyright 1969 Saturday Review, Inc. Reprinted by permission of the author and publisher.

with psychological as well as logical processes. In "Reach, Touch and Teach" he reports on classroom experiences and teacher training techniques and discusses the problems of acceptance which affective education will undoubtedly encounter.

Terry Borton is a research associate at the Harvard Graduate School of Education. The article reproduced here was adapted from his book, Reach, Touch and Teach: Student Concerns and Process Education *(New York: McGraw-Hill, 1970).*

There are two sections to almost every school's statement of educational objectives — one for real, and one for show. The first, the real one, talks about academic excellence, subject mastery, and getting into college or a job. The other discusses the human purpose of school — values, feelings, personal growth, the full and happy life. It is included because everyone knows that it is important, and that it ought to be central to the life of every school. But it is only for show. Everyone knows how little schools have done about it.

In spite of this, the human objectives describe the things all of us cite when we try to remember what "made a difference" in our school careers: the teacher who touched us as persons, or the one who ground out our lives to polish our intellects; the class that moved with the strength and grace of an Olympic team, or the dozens of lessons when each of us slogged separately toward the freedom of 3 o'clock. What we learned, and what we became, depended to a significant degree on how we felt about ourselves, our classmates, and our teachers. The schools were right — the human purposes *were* important. But with the exception of those teachers who were so rare we never forgot them, the schools did little to put their philosophy into practice.

Recently, however, a variety of programs have begun to build curricula and teaching methodology that speak directly to the human objectives. These programs, stemming both from within the schools and from various branches of psychology, point the way to a school practice which not only recognizes the power of feelings, but also combines academic training with an education directly aimed at the student's most important concerns. Schools may soon be explicitly teaching students such things as how to sort out and guide their own psychological growth, or increase their desire to achieve, or handle their aggressive instincts in nonviolent forms.

The new impetus has a variety of names: "psychological education," "affective," "humanistic," "personological," "eupsychian," "synoetic." Some of these names are a bit bizarre, and none has yet gained wide acceptance. But taken together their presence indicates a growing recognition that in the world's present state of social and moral turmoil, the schools' traditional second objective can no longer be for show. Riots, poverty, war, student rebellion, swollen mental hospitals, and soaring crime rates have involved an enormous number of people. They have generated a broadening conviction that society is as responsible for the psychological well-being of each of its members as is each individual. And that conviction has created a receptive audience for new kinds of educational critics.

The new critics do not simply attack the schools for their academic incompetence, as did the Rickovers of a decade ago. They are equally concerned with the schools' basic lack of understanding that students are human beings with feelings as well as intellects. Jonathan Kozol has given a gripping sense of the "destruction of the hearts and minds of Negro children" in his *Death at an Early Age*. In *How Children Fail* John Holt has shown that even in the best "progressive" schools, children live in constant fear which inhibits their learning, and Paul Goodman's *Compulsory Mis-Education* has made a powerful case for his contention that "the present school system is leading straight to 1984." The intuitive warnings of these "romantic critics" have been backed up by statistical evidence from the largest survey of education ever conducted, James Coleman's *Equality of Educational Opportunity*. This survey correlates academic achievement with attitudes such as a student's self concept, sense of control over his fate, and interest in school. The study concludes that these attitudes and feelings are more highly correlated with how well a student achieves academically than a combination of many of the factors which educators have usually thought were crucial, such as class size, salary of teachers, facilities, curriculum.

The pressure to deal more directly with student feelings (increasingly a pressure from students as well as critics) has given rise to dozens of different projects. None of the three examples which I will discuss here has yet reached the size or influence of the giant curriculum centers (such as the Educational Development Corporation) which grew up as a result of the post-Sputnik criticism. But in the long run they may be much more important. For the post-Sputnik curriculum reforms were essentially attempts to find better ways to teach the traditional disciplines of math, science, or social studies — often with the effect of moving the college curriculum into elementary and secondary schools. The programs I am describing not only operate with different techniques, but also begin to define and develop new curriculum subjects and a new school orientation toward practical and applied psychology. If expanded, they will make a profound change in American education — hopefully a change toward a more humane educational process, and a more human student.

The project which I co-directed with Norman Newberg, the Philadelphia School Board's specialist in "affective education," is an example of such a curriculum. It is being developed from within the schools — in this case by a group of urban teachers trying to find a philosophy and method which would work with the students they were asked to teach. The program is based on the assumption that every person handles massive amounts of information, and needs to be taught both logical and psychological processes for handling it. Two semester-long courses, one in communications, and one in urban affairs, isolate such processes as symbolization, simulation, dreaming, and de-escalating pressure, and teach them in an explicit fashion. At the same time the classes are designed to tie these processes to the amorphous undercurrent of student concerns for self-identity, power, and relationship.

I dropped into a high school communications class one hot day during last summer's field testing, when the teacher was working on "taxonomy of process," or a way of looking at what, why, and how behavior occurs and changes. The purpose of the class was to show the students a simple technique for analyzing their own habitual forms of processing the world around them, and then to show them how they could develop new responses if they wanted to. The class was working in groups of twos, filling in "What Wheels" for each other. One boy in the back was without a partner, so I joined him, and we agreed that I would make a What Wheel for him, and he would make one for me. I drew a circle, filled in the spokes, and wrote down my first impressions of him: "strong, quick, Afro, shy, bright."

The teacher asked us to read each other our What Wheels, select one adjective which interested us most, and ask our partner to draw a "Why Wheel" to explain *why* that adjective was meaningful to him.

Charlie read me his What Wheel — he was perceptive, as students usually are about teachers. Then I read him mine.

"Why'd you write 'shy'? I ain't shy."

"Well, I just met you, so I can't fill out a whole Why Wheel about it. But when I first sat there, I noticed you looked down at your desk instead of up at me. So I just guessed you were shy with strangers — maybe just with strange teachers."

Charlie took his What Wheel from me and looked at it. "You know, that's the truth. I thought nobody, except maybe my mother, knew that about me, but well, it's the truth anyhow."

The murmur of the class's conversation quieted while the teacher told us how to make up "How Wheels" with our partners. We were supposed to write down the range of actions which would either increase or decrease the trait we had been discussing.

"Aw, man, it would be easy to increase being shy," laughed Charlie. "I just wouldn't look at nobody."

"And decreasing it?"

"I'd look at you like I'm looking at you right now," he said, looking me straight in the eye. "And more than that, I'd look at you like that when you first came in here. Teacher, or white man, I wasn't afraid of you; no reason why I should act like I was."

We talked for a while — about my wheels, about the effectiveness of the what, why, how process questions for looking at behavior, and about school. When the bell rang, we shook hands. "See ya around," he said.

"See ya around," I said.

While many teachers have been experimenting with techniques similar to ours, research psychologists usually have been rather disdainful of the messy problems in the schools. Increasingly, however, psychologists such as David McClelland of Harvard are beginning to work on problems of motivation and attitude in schools. The progression of McClelland's study is a good example of how basic research may be applied to problems in education. McClelland began working on problems of measuring the motivation of rats deprived of food, performed a series of experiments to measure hunger motivation in humans, and then devised a system for measuring "achievement motivation" in men by counting the frequency of its appearance in fantasy images. He defined the need for achievement (n-Ach) as a pattern of thought and fantasy about doing things well, and discovered that those people who had such a pattern were characterized by a preference for moderate risk goals, a desire for immediate feedback on their performance, and a liking for personal responsibility. McClelland reasoned that if a society had a great number of such individuals, the society itself should show outstanding achievement. Twenty years were spent in a mammoth research effort to substantiate his claim that achievement research provided a "factual basis for evaluating theories that explain the rise and fall of civilizations." The next step was to devise educational methods for increasing the achievement motive in people who did not have much of it, and to test out these methods in this country and abroad.

Dr. Alfred Alschuler, director of the Harvard Achievement Motivation Development Project, which is one result of McClelland's research, is in charge of a federally funded five-year research project to assess what factors lead to effective achievement training. The project has devised many classroom techniques for increasing achievement motivation in students, most of them involving experiential learning that takes place in a game situation. I visited one training program for teachers in a nearby city, and sat in on a session that used a contest in making paper airplanes to demonstrate to the teachers how achievement motivation affects their students.

There was a lot of joking around the table, as everyone was a little nervous.

"Now they're going to use the old carrot on us," cracked a little physics teacher sitting on my right.

The head of the math department, an enormous man, smiled broadly, first at the physics teacher, and then at me. "Feeling cut-throat?" he asked.

I didn't say so, but I was, and he knew it. My "n-Ach" was way up. We eyed each other while we set our own quotas for the number of planes we would make.

Dr. Alschuler gave us the start sign. I was making planes feverishly; out of the corner of my eye, I could see the math department head moving more slowly, but doing a better job — the quality control check at the end of the game might go in his favor. The physics teacher was using mass production techniques, making one fold at a time.

At the end of five minutes the game was up, and we were all laughing at the tension it had produced. The physics teacher had more planes than any of us, but his mass production assembly had failed — all the planes were missing one wing. I had the second largest number of planes, but several had sloppy folds and were disqualified.

"Nuts to this," said the physics teacher. "I'm not going to get another heart attack over a bunch of paper airplanes. Next time I'm dropping my quota in half. I'm only going to make six."

I was swearing at myself — I should have been more careful. Next time through the game I would set a slightly lower quota and do a better job.

The math teacher was smiling broadly. He had won.

Later we all talked about our experience in the game and how our own behavior did or did not reflect the characteristics of a high achiever. Did we set moderate risk goals? Did we utilize information on our success or failure? Then we began to dig into the more fundamental value issues that were involved. Suppose that we could use games like the paper plane construction to teach students the characteristics of a high achiever, and through a variety of such exercises could actually train him to think and act as one. Was that a good thing? Did we want to subject our students to the pressure that we had felt? Could we decide that achievement training was good for some students who were not achieving up to our standards, and bad for those who were too competitive? On what basis?

Just as researchers are becoming involved in the practical questions of education, so clinical psychotherapy is getting up off its couch and finding ways to add its skill to solving school problems. Dr. Carl Rogers, founder of client-centered therapy, is presently working with Western Behavioral Sciences Institute and a group of Catholic schools to devise ways to use "sensitivity groups" in the schools. (A "sensitivity group" or "T-group" is composed of about a dozen people who meet for the purpose of giving feedback on how each person's behavior affects the other people in the group.) The National Training Laboratory, an associate of the National Education Association, is now running a year-round series of T-groups and related experiences for teachers and administrators. And in San Diego, child psychiatrist Dr. Harold Bissell and educator Dr. Uvalo Palomares have set up the Human Development Training Institute which has written a two-year sequence of lesson plans to improve a primary school child's self-confidence and awareness, and has trained 1,000 teachers to use it.

One of the most eclectic approaches in the clinical tradition is the project run by Dr. George Brown of the University of California at Santa Barbara. Brown's project, sponsored by the Ford Foundation through the ebullient Esalen Institute, utilizes many different approaches, but particularly the theories of Gestalt therapy which attempt to get youth in touch with how they are feeling in the "here and now." With such theoretical orientations in their background, the teachers in Brown's project are encouraged to devise their own techniques to integrate academic with affective or emotional learning in order to achieve a more "humanistic education."

I joined the teachers at one of the monthly meetings where they learn about new ideas, and share with each other the techniques they have developed. Gloria Siemons, a pretty first-grade teacher, was describing an exercise that she had first conducted with the entire class, and then used when one child became angry at another. She lined the class up in two rows on the playground, had them find a partner, put their hands up facing each other, and push.

Push they did, laughing all over the field, especially at their teacher, who was being pushed around in a circle by several of the bigger kids.

Later, when two kids got into an argument at recess, Mrs. Siemons simply asked them: "Are you angry now? Would you like to push?"

"Yes, I'm angry. I'm angry at him."

Both agreed to the contest, pushed for a minute as hard as they could, and then collapsed into each other's arms giggling. Their anger was worked out, but without hurting each other.

"What would happen," I asked Mrs. Siemons, "if one kid pushed another hard enough to hurt him?"

"We have a rule about that. 'It's OK to be angry with someone, and it's OK to push, but it's *not* OK to push him into the rosebush.'"

Good teachers, particularly good first-grade teachers such as Mrs. Siemons, have always responded to the emotional side of their students' lives, and it is precisely this intuitive gift which Dr. Brown is capitalizing on. By systematizing such techniques and relating them to a general theoretical framework, he and the teachers of his staff have begun to generate hundreds of ways to integrate the feelings of students with the regular curriculum taught from kindergarten to high school.

The techniques being developed, the dozens of programs, and the various theories differ in many respects, but they have several features in common. First, and most important, all of them deal in a very explicit and direct way with the student's feelings, interpersonal relations, or values. It is the fact that they are so explicit and direct which sets them apart from the vague protestations that schools have usually made about this area. While schools were concentrating on math, science, or English, they often ignored or actively suppressed feelings. The new programs make what was covert behavior the subject of overt discussion; they make the implicit explicit. They legitimize feelings, clarify them for the student, and suggest a variety of behaviors which he can use to express them. They do so on the assumption that these feelings exert a powerful effect on a student's behavior, both in the present and in the future. If schools want to influence behavior, then it makes sense to deal directly with its major sources, not just with the binomial theorem, the gerund, or the Seventeenth Amendment.

A factor in the new field which often causes misunderstanding is that most of the programs use non-verbal experiences, either through physical expression and involvement, or through art, sculpture, or music. For the most part, this involvement with the *non*-verbal is not *anti*-verbal or *anti*-intellectual. Non-verbal educational techniques are based on the obvious but little-utilized fact that a child learns most of his emotional response patterns at a very young age — before he can talk. His knowledge of love, rejection, anger, and need does not come through words, but through his physical senses — touch, a flushed face, a gnawing in his stomach. Even later, when he begins to talk, the words he learns are "Mama," "doggie," "see" — words for things and actions, not feelings. Indeed, many children seem entirely unable to give a name to their current feelings — they have been taught how to say "I am bad," but not "I feel bad." Education that deals with feelings is often facilitated by skipping over the verbal labels which have been learned relatively late in life, regaining the other senses, and then reintegrating them with verbal thought and new behaviors.

Another common technique which causes confusion is the reliance of many of the programs on games, dramatic improvisations, and role-playing. Again, though those utilizing the techniques believe in fun and use games, few of them are simply advocating "fun and games." Their interest stems from an insight into the learning process of small children. By playing games — house, fireman, office, war — little children learn what it will be like to be an adult, and begin to develop their own style in that role. But our culture provides few such opportunities for older children or adolescents, even though the society is changing so fast that many of the response patterns they learned as a three-year-old may be no longer relevant, or even dangerous. Games and improvisation allow a simulation of the self. While they are real and produce real emotions, their tightly defined limits provide a way to try out new behavior without taking the full consequences which might occur if the same action were performed in ordinary relationships.

There are answers for questions about non-verbal and gaming emphasis, but there are many other questions which the programs raise for which there are no answers. At best, solutions will come slowly, and that is bound to produce tremendous strain in a time when events wait for no one. Many of these problems are already developing. Though Dr. Alschuler at Harvard and Dr. Willis Harmon at the Stanford Research Institute are both engaged in large surveys to find out what techniques and philosophies are presently being employed in the field, there is still no common theoretical base for the programs, and very little research on their effectiveness. The Achievement Motivation Development Project has by far the most extensive research program, and Dr. Alschuler's experience with it has made him feel strongly about the need for additional evidence before program expansion:

> We have very little hard evidence that programs in this new field accomplish much more than natural maturation. We have claims, promises, and fascinating anecdotes. But we should not institute these programs without first using the most sophisticated research techniques we have to improve them and explore their consequences.

In addition to unanswered questions about effectiveness, there are practical limitations to all of the programs. Few have done an adequate job of integrating their material with the usual skills and knowledge that everyone recognizes the schools must continue to teach. No attempt has yet been made to work together with the free-flowing academic programs (such as the Leicestershire movement) which seem natural complements. Though all of the projects I have discussed here stress their responsiveness to student concerns, it is not yet clear how they can do that and yet not be heavily dependent on the skills and personalities of a few teachers like Mrs. Siemons who can both legitimize anger and make the rosebush out of bounds.

Politically, programs with both the potential and liabilities of these are obvious hot potatoes. It is unclear as yet how projects designed by psychologists will fit in with current efforts toward more community control and what seems to be the resulting concentration on "teaching the basics." Even a mode of politics that is in consonance with the ideals and methods of the new programs is unknown, for the vision they present is often as utopian as that in George Leonard's exciting new book, *Education and Ecstasy*. How to get from here to there without waiting until 2001 is a complex political problem. Suppose, for instance, that a school district decided to adopt an entirely new curriculum and school organization based on the concepts I have been discussing. Would the teachers be able to change? Great care would have to be taken with their feelings and concerns, for not only are they as human as the children, but — as recent events in New York have indicated — they will strike if they feel they are being treated unfairly.

The most fundamental problem, and the one which is likely to get people the most upset, is the ethical question caused by changing the expectations of what schools are for. At present, students go to school to "learn stuff," and though they may expect schools to provide information, they do not expect schools to change them in any fundamental way, or even to offer that opportunity. As long as schools continue to have relatively little explicitly acknowledged impact on the students' values, attitudes, and behaviors, no one is likely to worry much about ethical issues. If schools consciously begin to make important changes in students' lives, people will suddenly become very concerned about what is happening to immature minds that are forced to accept this kind of education for twelve years. They will begin to ask whether there should be compulsory education, or whether students should be free to accept or reject schooling. And they will begin to ask hard questions about what should be taught, and how it should be presented.

If, for instance, all children should be motivated, should they also be "achievement motivated"? At what age? Who decides? And who teaches? What is to stop teachers from working out of their own needs rather than for those of their pupils? Should teachers who share an important confidence have the same legal privilege which a lawyer or a minister has? How can parents and children be assured of the privacy which is their right?

The ethical problems are likely to be compounded by the reporting of the mass media. The new field is peculiarly open to parody ("HARVARD PROF TEACHES PAPER AIRPLANE CONSTRUCTION") and to easy association with the exotic and erotic. (*Life* recently stuck a single misleading paragraph on Brown's project into a long article on Esalen Institute. By far the most arresting thing in the article was a two-page picture spread on a nude sensitivity group that had nothing to do with either Brown's project or Esalen.) Sensational publicity is not what the new field needs. It does need the time, the careful research and planning, and the critical reporting which will allow it to grow or decline on its merits. The alternative is a series of fads, created by ignorance and publicity, and death — after a short and enthusiastic life — in disillusionment.

The new programs are too important to allow that to happen. They are delicate, and they are moving into an area which is fundamentally new, so they can be expected to suffer from the attention they attract, to make mistakes, and to run into blind alleys. If it takes the big curriculum development corporations a million dollars and three years to build a single course in science or social studies, it will be even more difficult to build a fully developed curriculum in a new field. But the effort should be encouraged. For while it may not be novel to assert that a man's feelings are a crucial determinant of his public behavior and private well-being, there is no question about the novelty and significance of school programs that explicitly educate both the feelings and the intellect. Such programs raise many of society's basic questions about purpose and meaning — tough questions which will not be easy to answer. But they also offer a possibility for building a saner world — a world where people are more open about their feelings, careful in their thinking, and responsible in their actions.

PART TWO

Curriculum for the 1970's

As the decade of the Seventies opens, the commentators chronicle the good things about our times. In the United States, hopeful developments include a still-rising standard of living, relatively low unemployment, negotiations to reduce bomb and missile threats, men on the moon, an explosion of scientific knowledge, conquest of diseases, and expansion of educational enrollments. You can add others.

Yet the chroniclers also report our urgent problems. The war in the Vietnamese quagmire drags on. Black rage is bitter. A segment of the young revolt or drop out. The "silent majority" hardens its attitude toward dissent. Crime increases; violence strikes; assassinations take place. Some people are still hungry in America. The slums of the inner cities rot away. Welfare rolls increase. Inflation exacts its toll. Inadequate job preparation for the young, frequently the black, persists. The quality of the environment deteriorates in the air, on the land, and in the waters. Confrontations violate the majority conception of the democratic process. American unity weakens further. There is a crisis of confidence in the American dream.

As the decade of the Seventies opens, American educators relate good things about education, too. Education grows bigger and is better supported, and often takes place in better buildings with better equipment. Aid for governmentally favored fields has enhanced the quality of instruction in some curricular areas. Disadvantaged people begin to participate in the process of curriculum change.

Yet American educators must also report on problems that beset education. General education is inadequate; when it exists, it often fails to illuminate social realities, meet individual needs, and develop humane values. Integration of knowledge through the curriculum is lacking. Compensatory education does not obtain hoped-for results. More money is still badly needed. Inadequate schools persist. Children of the blacks, the other minority groups, and the poor are especially short-changed. Even young people from privileged backgrounds protest unreality in the curriculum. The disciplines proposal crests and ebbs; no socially oriented proposal for humanized education gathers sufficient support to rival subject-by-subject reform. The struggle among forces in society for control of curriculum change grows sharper.

Admittedly, my summary of the times and of education as the Seventies open is blunt. Yet, though rendered in bold strokes, it describes the setting in which the authors of the following selections write. Essentially, this is the nature of the American scene in which the authors set forth their proposals for a better curriculum in a nation which is part of a wider world marked by related problems.

You will find that there is much in common among our authors. Notably, they write with a sense of urgency. They know that they live in a time of crisis. Each in his own way quests for genuinely relevant education. Each seeks a curriculum which makes sense for the 1970's. Yet, naturally, they often support different means for achieving their curricular ends.

My role as editor is to comment on some of their ideas and, in the process, share some of my own convictions on curriculum for the 1970's. If I were you, I would read the authors' articles before reading further in this editorial. Then, after your own exercise of free play of intelligence, turn back here for my reactions.

There is much reflective thought combined with good will in the viewpoints of our authors. There is good sense in each of their proposals. One wishes that he might call for implementation of each proposal and avoid making choices.

Take, for instance, the four encompassing recommendations for the entire curriculum which are grouped in the section, "An Approach to Curriculum." Take Theodore Brameld's advocacy that at least half of the curriculum be experienced outside the schoolroom through direct participation and travel. Versions such as Brameld's of the community school and the social travel proposals — seminal ideas suggested in earlier decades yet largely disregarded — are urgently needed in today's social setting, in which young people struggle to make a difference through participation and seek to build relationships through meeting other people in other places. Take Arthur W. Foshay's aspiration for a synthesis of what is real with what is conceptual, particularly in the neglected social studies and arts. As Foshay warns, we should not jettison coolness and logic and settle solely for heat and involvement.

Take R. Thomas Tanner's socially sensitive proposal for new science themes to carry on such unfinished business in an unfinished country as improvement of the quality of the environment through interdisciplinary work involving social studies and other educators. Tanner's view is a clear recognition of the folly of any discipline attempting to go it alone without multidisciplinary programs and relationships. Take Lawrence E. Metcalf and Maurice P. Hunt's call for youth to examine and appraise their rejection of the adult world in order to clarify their own values and make their own social policies better grounded and internally consistent. The proposal reflects the inescapable necessity of using intelligence in human affairs.

Such proposals cannot be fully carried through in a curriculum tidily and tightly separated into discrete subjects. Though supportive of the achievements and potential of "the disciplines proposal," Foshay recognizes and defines its limitations in the present crisis: begging the question of the integration of knowledge, not dealing directly with the relationship between education and life, failing to take into account the nature and need for teacher education, and being directed to the college-bound rather than all children and youth.

There are two forms of curricular organization which might encompass characteristics these authors desire in curriculum reform: Brameld's participation, Foshay's integration of knowledge and relevance of knowledge to the real world, Tanner's neglected environmental quality, and Metcalf and Hunt's clarification of values and social policies. One possibility is a substantial block of time for interdisciplinary study focused on the real and pressing dilemmas of human beings and supplemented by needed education for diversity in broad curricular fields. The other form of viable curriculum organization utilizes distinct, yet closely cooperating, subject fields in order to teach young people about agreed-upon, overarching themes and central concerns of human beings faced by social realities.

Yet the separationist and isolationist forces which prevailed in curriculum development during the Sixties will undoubtedly oppose the use of such forms of curricular organization in the Seventies. The case for the disciplines proposal, stressing reconstruction of separate subjects, has had an attentive hearing in the Sixties. In the Seventies, cannot the case also be heard for the integration of knowledge relevant to the real perplexities and dilemmas of human beings? Interrelatedness and wholeness in curriculum development have too long been neglected.

Special new problems have emerged for curriculum-makers of the Seventies. For instance, in higher education black studies is a reality, though some opponents reject the proposal in toto and some proponents hail it with no more than two cheers. But black studies programs exist, with potential for scholarship or propaganda, for pluralistic participation or separation, for self-identity or racism. Charles V. Hamilton has a sound point in urging universities to make black studies work rather than pass the buck to the students. As Stephen J. Wright sees it, the proper response of a university to black studies is to treat the field as it treats other disciplines, stressing scholarship and eschewing propaganda and imposition, "eliminating much of the non-sense that has been generated in connection with black studies programs: suggestions and demands that the programs be closed to whites, that they be graded on different standards, that they be taught by the uneducated, that they be autonomous, etc." Black studies programs of all varieties, including Wright's thoughtful proposal, must encounter the questions raised earlier in this editorial as to whether the goals of curricular programs which propose to face realities and achieve integration of knowledge are better realized through discrete subjects or through interdisciplinary cooperation.

Educators of the 1970's have inherited from the 1960's debates over the proper work of the schools, especially questions of the worth of structural innovations in curriculum and an appropriate curriculum for the disadvantaged. The customary debate over innovation focuses on whether or not team teaching, independent study, the nongraded school, et cetera, have made any real difference. But Fred T. Wilhelms, without quibbling, sensibly accepts innovations which contribute to personalization. He believes that priorities in change efforts must go to helping each young person in his personal becoming and to dealing with the social agenda of the present. One can do little more than add a fervent "amen" to Wilhelms' eloquent presentation of the genuine priorities as to innovations. It is worth noting that Wilhelms too is concerned about curriculum fragmentation; he calls for interdisciplinary curriculum-building in each of his three major "streams": science-math, the social studies, and the humanities.

Robert J. Havighurst sees the solution to the problem of disadvantaged young people lying largely in social developments during the 1970's which should reduce the need for special education for the culturally disadvantaged. Still needed, he concludes, will be pre-school programs, more effective rewards, orderly classroom regimes, and small adaptations to meet knowledge deficiencies and self-image needs. As Havighurst himself perceptively recognizes, the reader's acceptance of his suggestions depends in large part on whether the reader anticipates, with Havighurst, increased real income and income stability, higher educational level of parents, a widespread acceptance of pre-school education, better methods in the primary grades, slowly decreasing racial and economic segregation, and a gradually decreasing gap in life styles between middle-class and disadvantaged people. The editor joins Havighurst in his long-range expectations as applied to the last three decades of the twentieth century. But whether the developments will occur rapidly enough in the 1970's, given the current conservative climate in politics, the attitudes of the silent majority, and the budgetary limitations placed on education, is open to question.

Donald W. Robinson reports on schools yet too new to settle upon a single name — the variously titled "alternative schools," "free schools," "schools without walls," "new schools," etc. All agree on sharp dissatisfaction with the status quo in education. But, naturally, the proposed approaches are as varied as their sponsors' ideologies. As the new schools appear and disappear, some in all probability will break genuinely new ground and others will simply naively reproduce errors of past infantile leftist ventures. The better of the programs, such as Philadelphia's Parkway School approach, will probably be given a black eye by the worst, even as well-balanced programs of progressive education from the 1920's through the 1940's were given a black eye by sentimental and inadequate purportedly progressive programs. That the ferment represented by "alternative schools" will mark the decade of the Seventies is a safe prediction. As to the educational outcome, the gods give no guarantees, as philosopher Boyd H. Bode often said.

Versions of the schism between C. P. Snow's two worlds persist into the 1970's. To those who value the humanities, it is heartening to hear Joseph Wood Krutch speak up for philosophy and the humane arts in a science-worshiping and gadget-ridden age. He persuades us that no substitute has yet been found for the contribution of the humanities to the struggle to improve man's condition. Through skillful understatement, he reminds us of Holmes' dictum that philosophy tells us a little bit about things that are extremely important. Even though we may be dubious of some of his conclusions as to desirable educational programs, such as his warning against language arts or communications courses, his dedication to the printed page alone, and his sweeping rejection of "machines," Krutch serves an important function in stressing the central place of values in any worthwhile curriculum.

David Engler, accompanying Krutch in the discussion of humanism and instructional technology, refuses to rise to Krutch's anti-machine bait. To Engler, there is no real conflict between humanism and educational technology; instead, he believes technology can further humanize education. He makes a strong case in his well-argued article. Yet tantalizing questions persist as to instructional technology and the curriculum. Granted that the new instructional technology can individualize instruction — can it ever personalize (and thus humanize) instruction? Is the new technology actually "value-free" and "neutral"? A working paper on new instructional technology which I recently prepared for John Dewey Society members stirred lively discussion, much of it centered on the latter question. Many discussants saw the new technology not as "neutral" but as necessarily geared to a B. F. Skinner type of behavioristic psychology and loaded in favor of a curriculum stressing fact accumulation rather than intellectual speculation.

Complicating the lively controversies over content, organization, media, and methods of the curriculum for the 1970's are problems concerning curriculum change. The supposed "good old days" of leaving all the curriculum decisions to the educators are past, if they ever actually existed. Now, in the words of the immortal Jimmy Durante, everybody wants to get into the act. As Ronald C. Doll points out, some forces seek power, some control the spending of governmental and philanthropic dollars, some proffer knowledge accumulated by scholars, and some foster the needs and concerns of pupils, educators, parents, and community members. As Muriel Crosby indicates, agents of change assume varied guises; they include accrediting agencies, universities, industry, federal agencies, state legislatures, and a multiplicity of dissenters. Today, curriculum change is hydra-headed.

Forward-looking educators have long urged that everybody get into the act. After all, the public schools do belong to the people. Consequently, current misgivings by some educators concerning teacher, student, parent, and community demands for participation have a hollow sound. For better or worse, so-called "outside" forces are "in," as our authors point out. We cannot and we should not try to turn back the clock to an educators' monopoly in curriculum change. Yet neither should educators abdicate their roles as participants and as leaders.

The challenge of the 1970's in regard to curriculum change is to establish a process in which multiple forces will be taken into account, yet reasonable decisions as to curriculum will be made. We cannot afford a paralysis created by endless discussion. Nor can we allow confrontation to prevail as the accepted way of making curriculum change. Today in curriculum change we are close to an anarchic situation in which the forces and agents with the most power reign temporarily in an eternal "king of the hill" struggle. We have to develop new ground rules for a wider sharing in curriculum decision making which utilizes more effective democratic processes than have ever been devised.

Curriculum for the 1970's must be for everyone, including the young and the old, as Harold G. Shane points out in his advocacy of a curriculum continuum for education in the future. Let us hope that educators and citizens of the future recognize, with many of our authors, the central place that should be occupied by social realities, the needs of individuals, and humane values. If we base our educational programs on social realities, needs and values, and if we stress integration of knowledge, education in the Seventies may have a fighting chance to make a difference in the quality of the lives of the individuals who inhabit this nation.

A. An Approach to Curriculum

17

A Cross-Cutting Approach to the Curriculum: The Moving Wheel

Theodore Brameld

A teacher of philosophy of education and an advocate of social reconstruction, Theodore Brameld proposes a cross-cutting, integrative curriculum in which a minimum of one-half of the entire time devoted to the school curriculum is used outside classrooms. He symbolizes his proposal with a "moving wheel" whose rim represents mankind's predicaments and aspirations, whose hub represents a central question, and whose spokes represent supporting areas or courses.

Brameld is visiting professor of urban life at Springfield College in Massachusetts, and emeritus professor of educational philosophy at Boston University. Author of a dozen books and numerous articles, he is regarded as the leading proponent of the hopeful reconstructionist theory of education, which encourages the schools to take an activist position with respect to social and political ills.

A number of presuppositions must underlie a cross-cutting approach to the curriculum, some of which, I am sure, are shared by one or another of my associates in this KAPPAN. Let me merely sketch several of these presuppositions.

1. The prime responsibility of the curriculum on any level, but most focally on the lagging senior high school and undergraduate college levels, is the confrontation of young people with the array of severe, indeed ominous, disturbances that now beset the "naked ape" himself.

2. These disturbances are by no means of exclusive concern to the "social studies." Rather, they pervade every aspect of human life across the planet — whether we are thinking either of the political, economic, esthetic, moral, and religious, or of the so-called "objective" sciences and skills of, say, chemistry, botany, and mathematics. Nothing that

From *Phi Delta Kappan*, March, 1970, 346–348. Reprinted by permission.

man has begun to understand or to utilize can any longer be considered as separable from the crucial roles that he now plays, and the extraordinary obligations that these roles entail.

3. The interpenetrating, interfusing, and evolving character of nature, including human nature, compels us to recognize the universality of the critical period through which we are passing. And education, in turn, is compelled to create new models of the curriculum that express and dramatize this universality.

4. By the same token, the new curriculum models and applications of them in experimental practice repudiate and supersede the entire conventional structure of subjects and subdivisions of knowledge that, for much too long a time, have reflected a grossly outworn, atomistic model of both the universe and man.

5. The legitimate place that special subjects and skills occupy in transformed conceptions of the curriculum undergoes its own metamorphosis. The part no more remains merely a part than does the heart or the hand when it becomes dissevered from the total human body.

6. To follow the same metaphor another step, the human species requires abundant opportunity to reach inward, outward, and upward toward increasing fulfillment of its ever-developing powers both individually and cooperatively. To the degree that men are denied this opportunity, life becomes a failure for them. When education is not completely geared to this same purpose, it too becomes a failure.

7. The necessarily comprehensive presuppositions that we have made above apply, as norms, to any period of culture and history. But they apply with peculiar urgency to our own period. Fearful warnings, often heard, that the birth of the twenty-first century may never be attended by any historian, because no historian will have survived on our planet 30 years hence, are not warnings that any serious-minded citizen, much less any serious-minded educator, can conscientiously ignore. Unless, of course, he chooses to scoff at such an absurdity.

I am aware that each of these bald statements could be refined and supplemented almost endlessly. Nevertheless, for purposes of discussion, I intend to point directly toward one prospective design for a secondary school curriculum constructed upon the bases that they provide. This is not at all to claim that only one defensible curriculum is possible. It is to claim, however, that models at least comparable to this model should be pulled off the drawing boards and put to the test.

What are the interrelated problems and issues that illustrate the educational agenda inherent in our several presuppositions? I shall state them, again baldly, and without pretense of either order of priority or novelty. They do, however, serve as catalysts for the model to follow.

1. Can the ordinary human being conceivably hope to approach anywhere near optimal fulfillment of his own capacities in the face of accelerating technologized and depersonalized forces?

2. Can the ordinary human being develop a sense of inner personal tranquility and harmony amidst the alienating, divisive, disillusioning experiences by which he is constantly bombarded?

3 Does one (that is, you or I) hold substantial expectations of maintaining any deep sense of relationship with others (that is, with one's mate or family, with one's friends or associates) either amidst chronic instabilities or under the aegis of the folk belief of modern Western culture that self-interest (however "enlightened") still remains the only "realistic" justification for one's daily conduct?

4. Can neighborhoods and other relatively homogeneous communities learn to work together in attacking their own difficulties, in acting concertedly to remove them, and in achieving even a modicum of well-planned, cooperatively organized programs of constructive change?

5. Can racial, ethnic, and other disadvantaged minorities learn to act similarly both among themselves and with other groups of differing backgrounds?

6. Is it actually plausible to expect that human conflicts — for example between the sexes, the generations, and socio-economic classes — can be ameliorated by more humane, viable patterns of living and working?

7. Can religious institutions, with all their rigidities of custom and tradition, still find ways to emulate the same general processes suggested above?

8. Can we reasonably aspire to the expectation that nations will find powerful means to conquer and control the ever-advancing threat of human annihilation?

9. Can the fine arts become a vastly wider, richer experience of unique as well as communal creativity for people across the globe, to be shared freely and openly among diverse cultures?

10. Can communication, in every form (such as travel) and through every medium (such as television), occur without restriction or intimidation not only within but between nations?

11. Can the sciences become equally available to all men, devoted to their welfare and advancement (for example, through the sciences of human health or of the control and growth of natural riches), without depletion and decay?

12. Can economic and accompanying political establishments be rebuilt so that people in every part of the earth have access to and become the exclusive directors of (through their chosen representatives) physical and human resources?

13. Can a converging awareness and unity of mankind as one species — a species with unique, life-affirming, life-controlling powers — be achieved, and will this awareness and unity prove translatable into workable guidelines for political, scientific, esthetic, religious direction and renewal?

14. Can education, finally, direct its attention and energy not only toward the past or toward the present of man's experience, but even more persistently and painstakingly toward man's future as well?

That this agenda is far from all-inclusive is surely obvious. Each question could proliferate into dozens of others; indeed, students themselves, stimulated by mankind-oriented teachers, could and should raise innumerable others. All of these questions, moreover, invite explorations into learning not only by means of books and laboratories; above all, they invite firsthand involvement in the experiences of people in nearby or more distant communities who frequently share the same kinds of questions and seek the same kinds of answers.

To approach the problem somewhat more directly, what does all this mean for the organization and operation of the cross-cutting curriculum? It is possible again to summarize only a number of potentialities. According to this normative model:

1. A minimum of one-half of the entire time devoted to the curriculum is spent outside the classroom — in the laboratory of direct participation with people and institutions, and always with the close support of teacher-consultants equipped to deal with whatever situations or issues have been selected for analysis and prognosis.

2. The circumference of this kind of participation is as wide as the earth, extending all the way from the family and neighborhood outward to the region, nation, and eventually to distant nations. Learning therefore occurs *directly* through intra- and international travel (let us not be deluded by financial bugaboos; more than adequate funds are available if we insist upon them enough), and *vicariously* through films, the fine arts, and contact with experts such as anthropologists. There are countless other resources.

3. "Team teaching," so often applied adventitiously these days, is supplanted by flexible partnerships of interdisciplinary study, research, and field involvement.

4. The structure of the curriculum may be symbolized (I have developed this proposal at length elsewhere) in the form of a moving "wheel." The "rim" is the unifying theme of mankind — its predicaments and its aspirations. The "hub" is the central question of any given period of learning (perhaps extending over one week, perhaps a semester), while the "spokes" are the supporting areas of concentrated attention that bear most directly upon each respective question. The "spokes" may thus be termed "courses" in art, science, foreign language, or any other pertinent subject or skills. But these are not to be construed as *mere* courses. At all times they are as supportive of the "hub" as it is of them.

5. To the extent that a particular student discovers whatever special interests and talents he may possess, the individual is given every opportunity to develop fields of concentration in his own "spoke." Never is he encouraged to do so, however, for the sake of completing a "major," or passing "college entrance examinations," or other dubious appendages of conventional school systems. Jerome Bruner's truncated concept of structured learning is also of secondary value, for the legitimacy of

high-level "excellence" is respected only within the full pattern of the moving "wheel." So, too, Joseph Schwab's cross-cutting but still amorphous schemes for the curriculum are superseded by the theme of post-organic evolution — that is, human evolution — amidst our own age of cultural transformation.

The normative target of this theme is, I contend, far more "practicable" than are most of those advocated in the name of "practicality." This is so because a cross-cutting curriculum of the kind I urge meets the ever more insistent demands of young people for audacious, unconventional, but directly meaningful experiences in both learning and action.

If it is to succeed, students themselves should, of course, share throughout in the planning and implementation of each year's program. Jointly with their teachers, they should decide what issues are most significant to concentrate upon in a selected period. They should help to pre-plan each successive year. They should take heavy responsibilities for all field involvements both in arranging and in following them through. They should support the deviant student who may not always be interested in "problems" at all, but rather in his own "thing" (music, for example). They should engage in the dialogic process of learning that demonstrates (as Martin Buber has so brilliantly urged) how it is possible to face the profound dilemmas of human existence through the mutualities of shared emotion, reflection, and aggressive action.

I suggest, in short, that the time is long overdue when theories of the integrative curriculum should be revived and reconstructed. The trend among influential curriculum experts who have managed during the post-progressive-education period to reverse those theories should itself now be reversed.

In all fairness, nevertheless, let us not pretend that the sufficient cause of anti-integrational and pro-structural curriculum building can be attributed to any such experts in themselves. Rather it is attributable much more fundamentally to imperious demands of the burgeoning industrial-oligarchical order. But, similarly, the causes for curriculum renewal that are now fast emerging become, in one sense, precisely antithetical to this dominant one. More and more independent-minded and future-directed young citizens, not only of America but of other countries, are demanding a radicalization of secondary and higher education. They are doing so both because they are penetrating the facades of conventionality, timidity, and sterility, and because they increasingly want what they rightly deserve: a curriculum that expresses and serves their own time and their own concerns. I entirely agree with them.

18

How Fare the Disciplines?

Arthur W. Foshay

A *researcher and curriculum theorist, Arthur W. Foshay brought
the disciplines proposal for curriculum development before the
Association for Supervision and Curriculum Development in his
1961 presidential address, entitled "A Modest Proposal." Here he
reexamines the advantages and limitations of the disciplines idea in
light of experience with the reconstruction of some disciplines in
the 1960's and the pressing need for a new curriculum in the
1970's.*

*Foshay has been connected with Teachers College, Columbia, for
many years, beginning as assistant principal of the Horace Mann–
Lincoln School in 1946. After a five-year period as director of the
Bureau of Educational Research at Ohio State University, he returned to Teachers College as executive officer, then director, of the
Horace Mann–Lincoln Institute for School Experimentation. In
1961 he became director and in 1964 associate dean for research
and field services at Teachers College. At present he is professor of
education there. His writing includes the twice-revised* Education in
the Elementary School (*with H. L. Caswell*) *and his widely used*
Handbook of Education.

The idea that the structure, or logic, of each of the scholarly disciplines
offers a way of learning the discipline itself was "in the air" during the
latter part of the Fifties, and was stated vividly by Jerome Bruner in his
The Process of Education in 1960. Here, we will call this idea the "disciplines proposal." Bruner's book was surely the most influential bit of educational writing of its time. While the proposal is not very clearly explained
in the book, it communicated a fresh insight to a large number of people.

The war between the Progressives and the subject matter specialists had
been going on for more than two generations. Within the National Education Association, the departments in the various subject matter fields and
the departments dealing with the school as a whole (such as the Association for Supervision and Curriculum Development, the Department of Elementary School Principals and the National Association of Secondary School
Principals) had drifted out of contact with each other. Each group — the

From *Phi Delta Kappan*, March, 1970, 349–352. Reprinted by permission.

generalists and the specialists — patronized the other and indicted it on the one hand for being fuzzy and on the other for being too narrowly subject-centered. Bruner's proposal offered a welcome way out of the impasse that had developed. If we could take subject matter as something becoming, instead of as something given, a ground for negotiation would be immediately apparent.

In these pages, I want to discuss what has become of the disciplines proposal since its wide promulgation in 1960, to indicate some of its built-in limitations and possibilities, and to offer certain suggestions for its future.

If anyone had asked the Progressives how they thought subject matter should be learned, they would, as good Deweyites, have responded that all subject matter had to conform to the same general laws of reasoning, and that subject matter ought to be pursued in an active, not passive, way. Of course, the subject matter specialists had the same thing in mind. It is entirely possible that what confused the issue between the generalists and the specialists in the years between 1920 and 1955 was their interpretation of Dewey's notion of the complete act of thought. I myself was present at a highly dramatic faculty seminar at Ohio State in 1956 when a bacteriologist pointed out to one of our principal Deweyites that the complete act of thought did not describe the way he conducted inquiry in his own discipline — that, specifically, it failed to take into account the problem of unknown variables operating in his experiments, and that bacteriologists had long since incorporated a way of dealing with unknown variables into the basic logic of their inquiry.

This was a shocker. The discussion foundered on this rock because, in the last analysis, it called into question the whole core curriculum. The seminar took the position that the function of teaching any given subject matter was to help students to learn how the members of the discipline thought — how they conducted inquiry. Similar discussions must have been going on all around the country. It was because of an audience that had been created by these discussions that Bruner's pronouncement struck fire so quickly.

The idea that the function of instruction is to develop in the student's mind several modes of inquiry is one of the very rare new ideas to have taken root in instruction. The idea has no important background in the tradition of elementary and secondary school instruction. While it probably had occurred to many people at many times, to my knowledge no group had ever coalesced around it before 1960. In the degree that it had any currency, it was found in certain projects within subject matter fields. Harold Fawcett had approached it in the Thirties with a project on mathematics instruction for the Progressive Education Association. No doubt many science teachers had used the idea without naming it during the preceding decades. But the grand tradition of education is not in science and mathematics, both of which are comparatively modern subjects in the curriculum. The grand tradition is in literature, history, geography. The disciplines proposal never had any currency in these fields.

The innovations in instruction of the Progressive era were either technical (like the "unit of work") or policy-oriented (like the "life problems" of the core curriculum). The function of the social studies program during the Twenties, Thirties, and Forties was to teach children how to identify and solve problems, using Dewey's complete act of thought as the means. It was this thrust that separated the Progressives from the subject matter groups.

But if one could take a subject matter as a mode of inquiry, then many of the problems that separated the groups would disappear. One could have an active learner, for he would be actively inquiring. One could have an inquiry-centered strategy which was enough like the "problem-centered" strategy to be recognizable. More important, the approach through inquiry promised a student who would be equipped to persevere in the subject matter he was learning. The older approach to subject matter, whatever its virtues, did not take perseverance as one of its stated objectives. It was, basically, statically conceived. The idea was to make mastery palatable and "meaningful" — but the palatibility and meaningfulness were to be found through ingenious applications of subject matter to real external life, thus demonstrating its utility. They were not to be found by equipping a student so that he could carry on inquiry independently within the subject matter field. On the other hand, the core curriculum was intended precisely to make the student able to carry on independent inquiry concerning social problems.

The disciplines proposal had developed first in the physics project (PSSC) under Jerrold Zacharias. It was his group which, having found that updating the existing physics curriculum resulted in an impossible load of subject matter, cut through the problem with the notion that the function of instruction physics was not to teach subject matter directly, but to teach it indirectly. Indirect teaching refers to the teaching of styles and methods of thought, as against teaching the myriad of facts that such thought deals with. Not surprisingly, the idea spread rapidly through the several science curriculum projects supported by the National Science Foundation after 1955. This same basic idea also appeared in the new mathematics programs then under development. It appeared in chemistry and biology almost at once.

There has been a substantial evolution of the idea in mathematics and science from that day to this. The new mathematics is said to be in its third generation now. The PSSC program has been followed by Harvard Project Physics and others. There were at least two prominent chemistry programs, each somewhat differently conceived, and three notable versions of biology.

Interestingly enough, the idea has not fared nearly so well in curriculum projects in other fields, such as literature and history. A distinction perhaps has to be made between fields of knowledge in which inquiry is central and other fields in which something like interpretation is central. One can have disciplined interpretation as well as disciplined inquiry, of course. However, the tradition of disciplined inquiry in literature has had two distinct branches, the historical and the critical; and literary scholars have not traditionally been concerned with the question of the structure of their discipline. In the case of history, although historiography has existed for a long time, writing in the field of historiography has not been nearly so central to historians as has been the writing of history itself. Only recently has a series of books been published to deal with the nature of history as a field of speculation and thought. Perhaps this is why the curriculum projects of the early Sixties in these two fields have not been so concerned with their areas as modes of inquiry as have mathematics and science.

Instruction in foreign language has an independent history that goes back to World War II and the widespread acceptance of the methods of the Army Language Schools. More recently, under the influence of Noam Chomsky, some beginnings are being made to bring contemporary linguistic science to bear on the approach to instruction in this field. Unfortunately, only beginnings are showing; the field is one of the last to respond to this change in the curriculum climate.

The disciplines proposal has suffered the fate of many ideas in education. That is, it has been trivialized, attacked as nothing more than the old enemy, subject-centeredness; it has been misapplied, equated with its opposite (i.e., the complete act of thought), thrown into contrast with creativity (as if there were no such thing as creative inquiry), and so on. We shall not concern ourselves here with this aspect of what has become of the idea. All educational ideas have to survive such pathologies. Rather, let us consider what the built-in advantages and limitations of the idea have turned out to be.

Primary among the advantages of the disciplines proposal is the fact that students are offered subject matter as if it were reasonable. So much of what is offered in school is not reasonable — it is a set of arbitrary codes to be learned, or a set of arbitrary statements to be given back upon demand or recalled when needed — that it is a relief to have subject matter thought of by students as something they can derive out of their own logical processes.

Teachers have wanted students to "understand" subject matter for as long as there have been teachers. We have not had an adequate operational definition of "understanding." The disciplines proposal offers one such. To understand is to be able to give reasons. To inquire is to develop reasons that adequately explain phenomena. The two, understanding and inquiry, finally match each other. The promise of the disciplines proposal is the promise of understanding itself.

Moreover, if pursued in sufficient depth, the approach through the disciplines offers a fresh and enriched view of the nature of general education. At the bottom of every discipline we teach, one may say, is general education. At the bottom, that is, not at the top. A superficial acquaintance with science or mathematics consists only of knowledge of technique. The conceptual material is somewhat deeper. But at the conceptual level the vocabulary of the learned fields turns out to be the intellectual vocabulary of general education. The fundamental concepts of the fields we teach in the lower schools have very wide applicability. *Inverse ratio*, for example, taken from mathematics, can be applied to all sorts of non-mathematical phenomena. There is probably an inverse ratio between the degree of selectivity of the school system and the breadth of knowledge held by the general population in the country. The idea that the more of one thing one has, the less of another, can be learned (it probably is learned) in elementary mathematics. With only slight help, children can see its general value. The notions of *fact, legend,* and *myth,* all from the field of history, have the same general applicability. The notions of *relative motion, the properties of objects, interaction,* and *systems* all arise in one of the better new elementary science programs. I have seen children using this vocabulary in non-science applications, yet with great precision and insight.

The fact that general education has a vocabulary has not been widely recognized. Part of the promise of the disciplines proposal is that the minds of children can be furnished with such a vocabulary, and that the possibility of a real general education is thereby enhanced.

What are the limitations of the disciplines idea? Does it, indeed, have any limitations? There are those who would say that there are none. But there are some.

First, the disciplines proposal begs the question of the integration of knowledge. We must recognize that the integrity of the fields of inquiry — the disciplines — must be preserved if they are to be learned. But this immediately makes it impossible in theory to combine disciplines into multi-disciplines for instruction. The subjects have to be taught separately, each in its own way, according to its own logic. To do otherwise is to relapse back into Dewey's complete act of thought, and to resume the old confusions. But to teach subjects separately leaves the problem of integration of knowledge to the student himself to carry out, more or less unaided.

Second, the disciplines proposal does not deal directly with the relationship between education and life — what we call "relevance." One of the oldest questions in education is how education is to be related to real life. The disciplines proposal deals with this question only in terms of the applications of separate fields of knowledge. It does not deal, of itself, with the kinds of life problems the core curriculum used to be concerned with, problems which do not come packaged in disciplines. One could study physics thoroughly and gain very little insight into problems of racial injustice or crime. One could study history — yes, even history — and gain little knowledge of real importance about the problems of poverty in Appalachia, or the nature of the poverty syndrome in our big urban ghettos. To the degree that we allow the school curriculum to be dominated by the disciplines proposal, we fail to offer students the opportunity to become more than superficially acquainted with great public problems.

Third, the disciplines proposal failed to take into account the nature of and need for teacher education. While all of the early science and mathematics programs provided teacher training, the training was brief, suited primarily to those who already had some knowledge of the discipline itself, and not suitable for pre-service education. There was no solid, or even recognizable, conception of teacher education operating in those early projects.

Fourth, the projects as originally conceived did not seek to deal realistically with all the children in the schools. The projects were conceived as suitable primarily for the college-bound, and indeed were mainly intended to improve the education of the college-bound. The 60 percent or so of the population that has no intention of pursuing education beyond high school was simply not taken into account in the early disciplines projects.

Of more fundamental importance is the fact that the disciplines proposal itself is a strictly rational affair. It is naive to assume that all of the problems of the world can be solved by rational men being reasonable with one another. They simply are not. To portray the major fields of knowledge as if they were sufficient is to tell a big lie. The disciplines proposal can be accused of having accidentally committed this grievous error. Man is much more than rational.

The most popular of the criticisms of the disciplines proposal is the lack of relevance of the curricula as developed to anything but further work in the selected disciplines. The projects were too exclusively committed to perseveration as a goal. During the years ahead, it is likely that increasingly sophisticated attempts will be made to show how conceptual knowledge of the kind developed in the disciplines does indeed apply to real problems in the world.

The questions of the integration of knowledge and the relevance of knowledge to the real world will not be denied. They demand a response from the school curriculum, one way or another. If the discipline-oriented curricula cannot respond effectively to these questions, then other responses will be found. It is predictable that we will reinvent the core curriculum, perhaps with some modifications, that a substantial incursion into the regular school day will be made by what were formerly thought of as co-curricular activities, and that students will increasingly refuse to undertake the discipline-oriented subjects. This last has already happened in the case of the physics program, the enrollment having dropped 10 percent during the last 10 years.

We must recognize that the assumptions of values upon which the disciplines proposal is based have come under radical examination during the past few years. Some people reject out of hand the proposal that we improve the present work-oriented system. "If we are foolishly willing to agree that experts are those whose role is legitimized by the fact that the technocratic system needs them in order to avoid falling apart at the seams, then of course the technocratic status quo generates its own internal justification: the technocracy is legitimized because it enjoys the approval of experts; the experts are legitimized because there could be no technocracy without them. . . . Thus, if we probe the technocracy in search of the peculiar power it holds over us, we arrive at the myth of objective consciousness. There is but one way of gaining access to reality — so the myth holds — and this is to cultivate a state of consciousness cleansed of all subjective distortion, all personal involvement. What flows from this state of consciousness qualifies as knowledge, and nothing else does." The above is quoted from a disturbing book, *The Making of a Counter-Culture,* by Theodore Roszak (Garden City, N.Y.: Doubleday, Anchor Books, 1969, pp. 207–08). It is in the cool, objective, logic-oriented quality of the disciplines proposal that the sensitive and aware young radicals find their greatest challenge. They demand precisely that knowledge be hot, involved, and personal. They would believe the account of scientific inquiry contained in *The Double Helix* before they would believe the account contained in the technical reports on DNA. It is personal knowledge they want, not objective consciousness.

It seems unlikely, given these limitations, that the disciplines proposal of the early Sixties will survive intact into the Seventies. The science and mathematics programs that have emerged out of this period are without doubt more engaging than their predecessors, more respectful of the students' intellectual attainments, less arbitrary, and more sensible. They are also more intellectual in character than the programs that preceded them. It is the quality of this very intellectuality that probably will have to change during the next decade, if the programs are to survive.

I do not mean to propose here that if these challenges are not met, we will go back to what we were doing before. I doubt that we would want to. But we could easily enter into a chaotic period, during which the nature of knowledge would come under fundamental reexamination. What is called for is a change in the spirit of the discipline-oriented curricula and a development of new curricula in the social sciences and in the arts that have something like the power and reach of those in the sciences and mathematics. This latter change is not yet happening in anything like the necessary volume or with the necessary determination.

It is precisely in the social sciences and in the arts that it is easiest to see the connection between education and life. If schooling is to be required to respond to the demand that it be "relevant" — and it seems clear that it has to respond to just such a demand — then the social sciences and the arts would seem to be the curriculum areas in which our efforts should be concentrated in the short run.

Over the long run, it is quite possible that some new version of what a school is and ought to become will be developed. The task is mind-boggling. Without sacrificing the intellectual quality (but at the same time changing its spirit) of the best of the new curricula, we have to find ways of allowing the real problems of the external world to come under searching examination in school. Our secondary school students are rapidly, it appears to me, challenging the concept of adolescence itself. They want to see themselves as participants in the world they live in, not as apprentices for it. They want the world to be in the school and the school in the world.

We cannot meet that requirement satisfactorily by going back to the "problem-centered" curriculum of a generation ago. We have to develop some new synthesis of what is real in the world with what is conceptual, and, as teachers, make all of this suitable for young people who know neither the reality nor the conceptual frameworks.

How fare the disciplines? To me they seem to have become a prologue for a new kind of curriculum theory, a new kind of curriculum organization, a new kind of conception of the meaning of instruction that is likely to come to some sort of fruition during the decade ahead.

19

The Science Curriculum: Unfinished Business for an Unfinished Country

R. Thomas Tanner

R. Thomas Tanner wants to build on past developments in the science disciplines through the inclusion of socially relevant themes. A socially concerned science educator himself, he describes some urgently needed themes related to the quality of our deteriorating environment. These, he argues, are the unfinished business of science education.

Tanner believes a multidisciplinary team approach involving social studies teachers and other educators is essential; we cannot depend upon science teachers alone.

Tanner is an assistant professor in the Department of Science Education at Oregon State University.

Although the science curriculum has undergone a major overhaul in the past 13 years, portents of new and needed changes are already blowing in the wind. In this article, I shall 1) summarize the developments of the recent past, 2) suggest some work still left undone, and 3) propose ways in which educators from other curriculum areas may participate in effecting these changes.

In science education, a reform movement of considerable dimensions began in the mid-1950's and has achieved fruition in the form of the "alphabet soup" high school courses now familiar to most of us (by name at least): BSCS biology, PSSC physics, CHEMS and CBA chemistry, ESCP earth science, plus a host of elementary school projects. Whereas previous texts were written by individual science educators, the new curricular packages were developed by writing teams in which practicing scientists played a

From *Phi Delta Kappan*, March, 1970, 353–356. Reprinted by permission.

dominant role. The content was not just updated; more important, the curricula were organized around the basic concepts of inquiry and structure.

Inquiry is epistemological. Students were to engage in laboratory work which was genuinely investigative rather than verificational. They were to infer from their own data rather than memorize a rhetoric of conclusions. They were to study the reasoning of scientists in the evolution of scientific concepts rather than commit to memory the associated names and dates. The processes and not just the products of science were emphasized.

Structure is ontological. First, the science course was to represent genuine science and was not to be a catchall for units in alcohol, smoking, narcotics, and the like. Secondly, and more fundamentally, the science course was not to be a hodgepodge of discrete facts or a series of mini-courses in physiology, anatomy, genetics, light, or mechanics; rather, it was to be given unity by a few overarching themes. For instance, the Biological Sciences Curriculum Study claimed nine themes as having guided its work throughout the writing of several texts and supporting materials. These themes include evolution, genetic continuity, and complementarity of structure and function, among ohers. The Earth Science Curriculum Project chose 10 themes, including universality of change, conservation of mass and energy in the universe, and uniformity of process as the key to understanding the past. The National Science Teachers Association prepared a much-debated list of seven "conceptual schemes" meant to guide future curricular efforts. The schemes are extremely broad generalizations regarding matter and energy; an example is, "All matter is composed of units called fundamental particles; under certain conditions these particles can be transformed into energy and vice versa."

This article is not concerned with inquiry, nor does it question the structures (the themes) which have been developed in the several courses. Rather, I wish to suggest some additional themes. The subject matter developed during the past 13 years may very well constitute a much-improved curriculum in science per se, but it does not go very far beyond science concepts in exploring the societal implications of the scientific enterprise, the interactions of science with society, culture, and human values. Scientists and science educators are beginning to express grave concern over this deficiency in the new status quo of science education.[1,2,3] Having long been in complete concurrence with this view, I would like to describe three new themes, which are intended mainly to be suggestive and catalytic. Hopefully, a cross-disciplinary conference of scholars and educators may arrive at a more profound list in the near future.

These three themes all deal directly with technology and thus indirectly with basic sciences upon which technology is founded. (Science is the on-

---

[1] Fred W. Fox, "A Better Climate for Science." Eugene, Ore.: Oregon State University, 1968 (mimeographed).

[2] Fred W. Fox, "Forces Influencing Education: Present and Future," in David P. Butts (ed.). *Designs for Progress in Science Education.* Austin: Science Education Center, University of Texas (in preparation).

[3] Paul DeHart Hurd, "The Scientific Enterprise and the Educated Citizen: An Unfinished Task." Paper presented at the meeting of the Kansas City, Missouri, Science Teachers, November 17, 1967.

going pursuit of basic principles of nature; technology is the concurrent application of these principles in developing new products and techniques. The layman often uses the term *science* when in fact he is referring to technology.) The themes:

TECHNOLOGY AND MANKIND: A MASTER-SERVANT RELATIONSHIP

Shall the technological revolution be directed by man for the greatest common good, or shall it sweep us all along toward an unplanned and unthinkable brave new world? Will man utilize technological possibilities "just because they are there," or will he weigh their assets against the sociocultural upheaval they instigate? Shall technology be used to aid in uplifting the minds of men, or shall mindless men be used to consume the surplus products of technology? These are the kinds of pressing questions which our students should explore.

The chasm between Snow's two cultures widens; our folkways, laws, institutions, and traditional modes of thought fall further behind our technological advances and their use by industry; social discontinuities proliferate. Automation threatens employability, self-respect, and pride of craftsmanship, while organized labor can respond with little more than featherbedding and hereditary privilege of union membership. Computers serve the interests of giant corporations while plaguing the individual with incorrect invoices, errorful records, and unresponsiveness to protest. The institutionalized uses of technology have created a populace with wealth, mobility, and free time, but the people are as yet uneducated for use of these benefits. Spaceships and peasants coexist paradoxically within a single nation. Medical technology controls death but laws still do not control birth. The weapons of complete and instant extinction are stockpiled as if they were only spears, rifles, or cannon.

It would appear that if ever we needed a utopia, we need it now. To this end, it is somewhat encouraging to note the birth of futuristics, the study of the future. The Commission on the Year 2000, the World Future Society, and similar organizations are beginning to chart desirable and feasible futures, as answers to the darker dystopias of Orwell and Huxley. Despite the skepticism traditionally accorded utopian thinkers, we must surely place increasing but humanitarian control over the future, if we are to be assured of having one. To continue the practice of brinksmanship in these times is to invite either a bang or a whimper.

TOMORROW'S TECHNOLOGY AND TODAY'S LICENSE

A common excuse for the exercise of greed, irresponsibility, and shortsightedness is that tomorrow's technology can clean up the resultant mess. Once it was easy to turn our backs on the fallacy and go West, leaving the scarred land behind, but now the frontier is gone (although the process is being repeated in "developing" nations). Nevertheless we continue to act as if the frontier were still there. Business equates growth with progress, and the depletion of natural resources is euphemistically referred to as development of natural resources. Population growth causes or intensifies many dilemmas of the day: pollution in all its insidious forms, depletion of natural resources, famine, loss of identity and individual freedom, degradation of the environment, extinction of species, and even war and racism.

Yet technology is optimistically applied to these problems while population growth and economic irresponsibility are accepted or even lauded. Smog devices, desalination plants, floating cities, and high-yield food production methods lull the public into a blind faith in technology, but these are only temporary, stop-gap measures — they are Band-aids applied to a cancer. Similarly, there is a tendency to ascribe to the process of research powers far beyond its capacities. For instance, alarm at the impending extinction of the great whales is assuaged by the assurance that research is being applied to the problem, when it should be obvious that no amount of research will save anything in the absence of strictly enforced international whaling laws.

Implicit in all this is a charge for the educator: A society which has replaced an unquestioning faith in God with a hind-sighted faith in science and technology has not made a very significant intellectual advance. Over-faith should be accorded the same derision as overkill.[4]

Man in Nature, Man over Nature

American man has traditionally considered nature to be opposed to his progress, and he has endeavored to conquer the natural world and its laws. This attitude, which we have inherited, has deep roots. From Europe's late Renaissance and Age of Reason, Western man brought to these shores the concept of progress through empiricism, in contrast with a former slavish acceptance of the fates. He said, "God helps those who help themselves." Here he found a wilderness which reinforced the attitude by yielding, albeit stubbornly, to his axe, rifle, and plow. At about the time that the frontier was disappearing, along with its opportunities for the common man, social Darwinism became the rationalization for industrial barons who conducted a highly successful "struggle for existence" against nature and against their fellow man. In this century, unionism has spread the wealth to many, and so the many have been cajoled into accepting the industrial revolution's continued battle against the natural world. Now, the technological revolution is succeeding the industrial revolution; it has already contributed to increasing the wealth a hundredfold and decreasing human physical effort by a similar order of magnitude.

This entire period, from Enlightenment to technological revolution, has

---

[4] A documented enumeration of our vast ecological problems is not within the scope of this article. These have been detailed at length in the popular press and in technical journals. The reader is referred to such periodicals as *BioScience*, *Natural History*, *Audubon*, and *The Living Wilderness*, and to the *Conservation Yearbooks* of the Department of the Interior. Stewart Udall's *The Quiet Crisis* (New York: Holt, Rinehart and Winston, 1963) and Paul Ehrlich's *The Population Bomb* (New York: Ballantine, 1968) are also recommended.

been marked by a new faith in science as the means of comprehending and thus controlling the environment.

Equilibrium theories such as Festinger's cognitive dissonance give educators a reasonable explanation of attitudes through this historical progression. The frontiersman wrested his homestead from a resisting wilderness, the captain of industry fought "fang and claw" to the top, and this century's laborers endured wars and depression to claim their share of the bounty. As Festinger might note, they all placed high value on the fruits of their labors because of the effort expended and hardships suffered to obtain those fruits. Thus the concept of a struggle with nature was easily rationalized by all. By the same token, today's restless youth (as epitomized by *The Graduate*) who question the value of great material wealth may be doing so, in part, simply because they themselves did not have to strive for its acquisition. One of our jobs as educators is to bring them to question not just the love of material wealth but also the dangerous concomitant concept of man over nature.

What are the character and the danger of this attitude? Its character is obvious when man boasts of "conquering disease" (but conquers not his procreative urge), when his mineral resources are "ingeniously wrested from a reluctant earth," when he poses proudly with boot and rifle-butt planted atop the carcass of a "savage killer" (unresponsive to the plight of the "killer's" dwindling numbers and insensitive to the ironic self-condemnation of the expression). The attitude is sired by egocentrism and spawned of ignorance. Its danger has already been alluded to under Theme II, above; in brief, an infinitely expanding population can seek infinite material wealth for only a finite period of time, since it exists in a closed system: a planet with finite resources of space and material. Mother Earth is where it is (what's left of it). Those who assume that some day we will find our iron on Jupiter, our water on Mars, or our tranquility in a distant solar system may be asking their posterity to pay the piper an impossible fee. Like it or not, we are *in* nature and it would behoove us to act that way; we can never be *over* nature. We must understand, even more profoundly than did Bacon, that "nature is only to be commanded by obeying her." If we insist upon making a fight of it, we must expect to lose.

A PROPOSAL

As bleak a picture as these themes present, they should not be interpreted as despairing; rather, they represent that enlightened brand of pessimism which anticipates the worst and plans against it, knowing that the only surprises available to the optimist are unpleasant ones, happy surprises being the exclusive delight of the positive pessimist. Furthermore, there is some assurance to be gained when one notes the responsiveness of politicians to the growing grassroots sentiment for conservation issues, and the widespread dismay over the papal position on birth control. Finally, the themes set forth here certainly do not constitute the full range of societal understandings which citizens might appropriately possess; they are only some of the possible candidates for inclusion in the curriculum.

The science teacher is unlikely to possess all of the competencies necessary to deal adequately with these themes or with others dealing with the interplay of science, technology, and mankind. Furthermore, he may require the moral support of others in his school as he deals with possibly controversial issues. This suggests a unified high school course with a multidisciplinary team approach (and that is why this article is being directed to educators other than those in science).

Examples of some possible units and materials are in order. History and science teachers could examine the audacious new way in which man began to view his world during the late Renaissance and the Age of Reason, and the contributions of Copernicus, Galileo, and Bacon to the crossing of the Great Divide. The history teacher might deal with revolutions, the degree to which they are directed by men or, conversely, sweep men along in their course. Sociocultural revolutions such as the pastoral, agricultural, industrial, and technological could be compared and contrasted with political revolutions. The science and social science teacher could contribute to discussion of the technological revolution and its societal concomitants. Teachers of social science, history, and perhaps geography could develop the various concepts of man's place in nature which are held by us and by other peoples, including some of the Indian tribes which preceded us as the human stewards of the continent's resources. Examination of current legislation and government policies would constitute no small part of the curriculum. Political cartoons, such as the conservation gibes of Ding Darling and R. Cobb, would constitute an interesting source of material and a lively vehicle for discussion.

The English teacher could guide the study of contemporary utopian and dystopian novels such as *Lord of the Flies, Walden Two, Fahrenheit 451,* or *Anthem,* as well as brief consideration of earlier utopias such as those of Bacon or More. The University of Southern California film *THX 1138,* by George Lucas, provides a kind of cinematic little *Brave New World* in the light-show, McLuhanish, *cinema verité* form which seems to communicate to many of today's young people. (Incidentally, it was obviously no series of random events which saw these bleak societies conceived of in a century of science rather than in a previous era.) Fletcher Knebel's suspenseful novel, *Vanished,* illustrates the social concern of the scientific community today. Species threatened by the advance of man are considered touchingly in Bodsworth's *Last of the Curlews* and profoundly in Gary's *The Roots of Heaven.* The poetry of Jeffers and the philosophy of de Chardin suggest themselves, among a plethora of possibilities. Even some of the day's popular songs are appropriate.

The construction of such a new curriculum might best be accomplished by the team writing approach used in creating the new science courses. Subject-matter scholars, professional educators, psychologists, school administrators, and classroom teachers would meet together to identify the students they are trying to reach, to state conceptual themes and subsumed objectives, to determine practicable schedules of teacher load and course organization, to effect pre- and in-service teacher training, and to direct the preparation of whatever materials are deemed appropriate — texts, films, exams, etc. The plan not only requires the two cultures to sit at table together, but to be joined there by newcomers from the space, oceanographic, environmental, information systems, and futuristic sciences.

Contemporary educators have often tended to embrace means that were either devoid of ends or connected by illogic to only the fuzziest of ends. The writing group would be charged with keeping sight of ends, both immediate and long-range. Some immediate goals must be the preparation of a curriculum which is resistant to degeneration into dogma, and which will not quickly be made obsolete by the very rapidity of change with which it will be concerned. Consideration of the former goal will necessarily include scrutiny of student evaluation, since objective testing for discrete and trivial facts is temptingly easy and therefore has always been highly contributory to the degeneration process.

A long-range goal is suggested by Max Lerner in an essay written a few years ago: Youth need be instilled with an élan, a "feeling of commitment and of being on fire, a sense of mission . . . of our country still being unfinished, a sense of the authentic revolutionary tradition which is in our history."[5] The youthful unrest which has subsequently become so evident surely constitutes, in part at least, an expression of or search for élan. As a necessary direction for the release of its energies, I submit for consideration the following national purpose: *America should take the lead in establishing and maintaining a varied environment which offers maximum freedom of choice to mankind and to its individual members, everywhere and in perpetuity.* This goal has been discussed elsewhere, along with its implications for our current concepts of economic growth and progress.[6]

This goal should be made explicit for the students in this curriculum. It should be capable of stimulating and directing their élan for some time to come: We are still very far from its achievement.

[5] Max Lerner, "Humanist Goals," in Paul R. Hanna (ed.), *Education: An Instrument of National Goals.* New York: McGraw-Hill, 1962, pp. 105, 116.
[6] R. Thomas Tanner, "Freedom and a Varied Environment," *The Science Teacher,* April, 1969, pp. 32–34.

20

Relevance and the Curriculum

Lawrence E. Metcalf and Maurice P. Hunt

Metcalf and Hunt have contributed a perceptive book on teaching the social studies through emphasis upon "the closed areas." Some of its major themes are sharply delineated here.

The authors propose that a curriculum, if it is to be relevant today, must assist young people in an examination of their own basic assumptions about society and its improvement. They call for study by young people of youth's rejection of adult culture, and they advocate the development by young people of relevant utopias and preferred worlds.

Maurice P. Hunt is professor of educational foundations at Fresno State College in California. Lawrence E. Metcalf is professor of secondary education and social studies at the University of Illinois, Urbana. Together, Hunt and Metcalf wrote Teaching High School Social Studies *(Harper and Row, 1968).*

Our assignment in this article is to indicate what we mean by a relevant curriculum. We shall define curriculum not as "all the experiences a child or youth has in school" but more traditionally as "the formal course-work taken by students." We believe that formal coursework acquires relevance whenever it impinges upon what students believe, and whenever it has the effect of producing a pattern of belief that is well-grounded and internally consistent.

Ours is a period of history in which youth on a mass and international scale reject the culture of the old. This rejection is not universal to all youth; some are more actively opposed to established traditions; many are in tacit support of changes initiated by the bolder and more aggressive young. To a large extent the rebellion of the young began with college students, has now been adopted by large numbers of high school students, and is beginning to filter down into junior high school. Young people are beginning to develop their own culture, and appear at times to learn more from one another than from teachers or parents. Some adults feel so turned off and rejected that they doubt that they can ever say anything that youth would accept as relevant.

From *Phi Delta Kappan*, March, 1970, 358–361. Reprinted by permission.

Youth's rejection of adult culture — "the whole, rotten, stinking mess of it" — has become a significant social movement. This movement has assumed international proportions — practically every modern, industrialized nation has felt its impact. Any school that has not made this social movement a subject of serious study on the part of its youthful clientele is about as irrelevant as it can get.

Rejection of adult culture is proclaimed overtly, not merely by verbal attack, but also by deliberate adoption of grooming habits or display of those artifacts which have been established or promoted as symbols of sophisticated rebellion. New hair styles, manners of dress, a new language (which relies heavily on traditional Anglo-Saxon monosyllables), a new music, an open sexual promiscuity, and the use of drugs or pot — all reflect a wholesale rejection of tradition and orthodoxy.

Many of the new values and customs are carefully chosen as goads to older persons. "What would my parents or grandparents least like to have me think and see me do?" When this question has been answered, often only after some tests of adult reaction, the young then adopt whatever they think will best demonstrate that they are *not* part of the main culture stream of earlier generations. In the case of males, it may require only long hair and a string of beads to make the point. For females, attendance at a love-in or rock festival attired in a mini-miniskirt may suffice. The movement has its uniforms, rituals, and badges of membership. Older people sometimes put on the uniform in order to demonstrate that they are not entirely out of sympathy with the ideas and ideals of youth. Others, who are not without sympathy, refuse the beard and beads simply because they detest all uniforms, whether worn by pigs, fascists, or revolutionaries.

But the rebelliousness of youth does not confine itself to the symbolisms of dress, language, and coiffure. Rejection of religion as traditionally practiced has become commonplace. New faiths are emergent, as among the hippies, and have more in common with Zen than anything orthodox to Christianity. Paul Goodman sees the young as primarily religious. If so, theirs is the kind of faith that mirrors John Dewey's distinction between religion and the religious.[1]

Equally significant is the anti-war and pro-love stance of our young rebels. When generalized to embrace a way of life, it runs contrary to most American traditions. We now see mass protests on a grand scale. Riots, marches, sit-ins, love-ins, and mass assemblies surpass anything in our history. When a war moratorium brings hundreds of thousands of persons into public arenas, it can truly be called a "happening." Adults are puzzled by it all, and somewhat frightened.

A CONCEPT OF RELEVANT CURRICULUM

Young people are particularly critical of established educational practice. A common charge is that education lacks relevance. Often this criticism harks back to some of the traditions of old progressives in education. Sometimes,

[1] See John Dewey, *A Common Faith* (New Haven: Yale University Press, 1934).

the charge means that education has not allied itself with the goals of revo-lutionaries, or that it has allied itself with business, labor, and the military.

What can education do these days that would be relevant? *We suggest that the schools incorporate in their curriculum a study of an important social movement, rejection by youth, and that this study emphasize examining, test-ing, and appraising the major beliefs caught up in this movement.* To pander to the instincts or impulses of rebellion would have little or no educational effect. The over-30 adult who simply "eggs on" his activist students does his clientele no service. A black studies program that fosters black nationalism or separatism would be equally obnoxious. If this is what youths mean by relevance, their wishes can not be served.

Students find it all too easy to spot contradictions in the beliefs of their elders, and to explain all such discrepancies as instances of hypocrisy. They are a good deal less proficient in spotting their own inconsistencies, and they are quite convinced of their own sincerity. We need the kind of educational relevance that would help and require young people to examine their most basic assumptions about the kind of world that exists, and how they propose to change the world from what it is into something preferable. Students who rebel not only against the establishment but also against logical analysis may not at first perceive the relevance of this kind of education.

In order to achieve this kind of relevance, teachers will have to familiarize themselves with the thought patterns of students — their attitudes, values, beliefs, and interests. This can be done. It helps just to listen carefully to what young people are saying. Sometimes teachers who listen do not bore deeply enough into the meaning of what has been heard. They learn much about the surface thought of students but little, if anything, about what students "really think."

If we look closely at what students today believe, four issues or propositions in social analysis and processes of social change seem to prevail within the movement. Taken together, these four issues suggest a rejection of the liberal-reformist tradition. Liberalism is anathema to our youthful rebels. Liberalism is a failure, they say. Liberals talk much and do little. Many of the young leaders resemble the romantics who supported totalitarian move-ments in pre-war Germany and Italy. A seldom observed and reported fact is that the candidacy of George Wallace in 1968 received more support from people under than over 30 years of age. A realignment in American politics that would place radicals and conservatives in alliance against liberalism is not without prospect.

A major issue that divides radicals from liberals is to be found in attitudes toward The System. Liberals tend to assume that the system can best be changed and improved by working within it. They may agree with radicals that much in the system requires fundamental and sweeping change, but they also believe that the system is basically sound in that it permits and values change when rationally determined and implemented. In contrast, the radical would work against the system from the outside. He wants no part of the system, which he views as rotten throughout.

Liberals who suggest that schools assist students to examine the system in order to determine whether it is as rotten as some claim it to be are regarded as advocates of a delaying action. Radicals tend to view analysis of this kind as a form of social paralysis. It is not clearly established how many of today's young can properly be classified as radicals. An increasing number do believe that social change must begin with a total rejection of the existing system. Drastic change is preferred to any attempt to patch the existing system.

A second assumption that divides young people from the mainstream of American liberalism is over the relationship of means to ends. Liberals tend toward the assumption that the achievement of democratic ends requires the use of democratic means. Every means is an end, and every end a means to some further end. The quality of any end we achieve cannot be separated from the quality of the means used to achieve it. In contrast, many of the young assume that our kind of society can be transformed into a more democratic system only as people dare to employ undemocratic methods. They see no inconsistency in advocacy of free speech and denial of such freedom to their opposition. Some liberals agree with radicals on the need for drastic changes in the system, but they are unwilling to achieve such change except through processes of reason and persuasion.

A third assumption expresses on the part of the young a preference for intuitive and involved thinking as opposed to rational and detached thought. Many of the hippies, for example, have voiced a distaste for the logic and rationality of middle-class Americans. In contrast, liberals have criticized middle-class Americans for not being rational enough.

A part of the issue here is over the nature of rationality. Liberals do not agree that rational thought is necessarily detached or without involvement. Thought springs from the ground of social perplexity and concern. Objectivity is not the same as neutrality. Objectivity is a means by which to express concern and achieve conclusions. It is not to be used as a method by which to avoid conclusions or commitments. In the hands of some liberals, however, it has appeared to be a method by which to avoid rather than make value judgments. When they perceive objectivity as avoidance, concerned youth will look elsewhere for their philosophy. An intuition or existential leap may be their solution to any confusion that inhabits their minds. The popularity of the drug experience as a source of awareness and insight is consistent with this preference for intuitive methods of problem solving. The growing interest in parapsychology, extrasensory perception, spiritualism, and various versions of the occult manifests the same tendency to retreat from the use of reason in the study of social affairs.

A fourth assumption, issue, or proposition is over the nature, worth, and necessity of violence. The liberal eschews violence except when an organized minority thwarts the will of the majority, if that will seems to be the outcome of free discussion and reflective study of alternatives. The young, on the other hand, often regard reason and discussion as forms of compromise. It is quite defensible to take the law into one's hands if the law is unjust. One does not obey an unjust law until one is able to persuade others of its injustice and thus get it changed. Evasion of the law or open refusal to obey the law is an acceptable form of social protest, if personal conscience so dictates.

Basic to this issue is the question of whether or not drastic system change can be achieved without use of violence. Advocates of violence have not always distinguished between impressionistic and instrumental violence.[2] Impressionistic violence is the kind of hot response that results from deep-seated frustration over existing social conditions. Instrumental violence is more disciplined in nature, and is followed deliberately and coolly as a method of social protest with social change as its objective.

The above four assumptions are basic in varying degree to the life outlook of young people who are in rebellion against established traditions. None of them is entirely new. Each has been tried and tested in a variety of social circumstances. Relevant history would reveal where such assumptions lead when acted upon under certain conditions. Yet none of these assumptions is today subjected to open, careful, and fair appraisal by a majority of schools or teachers. A relevant curriculum would take these assumptions seriously enough to make their study a major purpose of general education. Such study would help young people to understand their important personal problems but would also open up for serious study the large social problems of our time.

UTOPIAS, RELEVANT AND IRRELEVANT[3]

A curriculum that would assist young people in an examination of their basic assumptions about society and its improvement must deal with values and social policies. Yet attention to values and social policies is now almost totally foreign to public schools.

Young people today will be in the prime of life by the year 2000. They can begin to think now about what they want as a society by that time. Four questions are basic to a curriculum that would start now to build toward future-planning: 1) What kind of society now exists, and what are the dominant trends within it? 2) What kind of society is likely to emerge in the near future, let us say by the year 2000, if present trends continue? 3) What kind of society is preferable, given one's values? 4) If the likely and prognosticated society is different from the society that one prefers, what can the individual, alone or as a member of groups, do toward eliminating the discrepancy between prognostication and preference, between expectation and desire?

These questions are relevant to anyone, but they are particularly relevant to those young people who think in utopias and who agree with Buckminster Fuller that we now have to choose between utopia and oblivion.

We define utopia as any description of a society radically different from the existing one. Some utopias, as described, are relevant. Others are irrelevant. A relevant utopia is a model of a reformed world which not only spells out in specific and precise behavioral detail the contents of that new world but, in addition, provides a behavioral description of the transition to be made from the present system to the utopian one. Irrelevant utopias omit

---

[2] Charles Hamilton is to be credited with this distinction, as developed in a speech at Wingspread in 1968.

[3] We are indebted to Saul Mendlovitz of the World Law Fund, who is also professor of international law, Rutgers University, for development of the concept of relevant utopias.

all solutions to the problem of transition. They may be precisely defined in behavioral terms, as in Butler's Erewhon, but provide no suggestions as to how one gets from where he is to where he wants to be.

Most utopias stated or implied by today's youth are irrelevant. Youth are fairly clear as to what they oppose. They desire a drastically different kind of social system, but they are not clear in any detailed sense as to what they desire as a system, or how that undefined system might be brought into being. To be relevant, youth with encouragement from the schools will have to engage in the kind of hard thinking that results in construction of social models. Hard thinking and model building are not always prized by youth who rely upon intuition and hunches for solutions to problems. Intuition is good enough for stating irrelevant utopias. It will not work, however, for those who value precisely stated concepts and tested solutions to the problem of social transition.

The search for relevant utopias should have great appeal to those youth who feel or believe that a drastic change in the social system is required for solution of today's problems. Its appeal lies in the fact that the search for relevance requires one to take seriously, and not merely romantically, the problem of how best to achieve drastic system change. Since drastic system change has occurred in the past, some study of a certain kind of history — not the kind usually taught in the schools — should be relevant to this search.

RELEVANT UTOPIAS, PREFERRED WORLDS

We have defined as a relevant utopia any social vision or dream that has been expressed as a social model with due regard for problems of precise definition and successful transition. From studies of existing society numerous relevant utopias have been stated. In the area of international systems alone no less than nine models have been identified by Falk and Mendlovitz.[4] Each model may be used descriptively, predictively, and prescriptively. That is, each may be seen as a report of what already exists, as a prediction of what will soon exist, or as a prescription of what ought to exist in the near future. (Obviously, a model used only for descriptive purposes does not function as any kind of utopia, relevant or irrelevant. A person who sees the present international system in certain terms can encounter in another person a different description. Both persons may agree or disagree as to what they conceive utopia to be.) Much of the literature fails to make a clear distinction between descriptive and other uses of a model. The methodology of relevant utopias requires that such distinctions be consciously made. This methodology also requires us to take seriously any utopia that qualifies as relevant. But to take it seriously does not force us to prefer it.

One chooses his preferred world from the set of relevant utopias available to him. It is in the region of preferred worlds that individuality as prized by young radicals has a chance to express itself. A person who chooses his preferred world from a set of available relevant utopias must decide what

---

[4] Richard Falk and Saul Mendlovitz (eds.), A *Strategy of World Order*. New York: World Law Fund, 1966.

risks he is prepared to take; and obviously, persons differ greatly as to what risks they perceive and what risks they are willing to take.

An illustration from international relations and systems may serve to clarify this point. Grenville Clark and Louis Sohn have developed a relevant utopia that takes the form of limited world government. Their model consists of detailed amendments to the UN Charter which would give to the United Nations sufficient authority to prevent war, but without authority to intervene in the domestic affairs of nation states. Another model, developed by Robert Hutchins and his colleagues at the University of Chicago, envisages a much more sweeping kind of world authority. The relationship within their model between the world authority and the nation states resembles that which holds within the American federal system between the national government and the several states.

If one's choice is limited to these two models, which one should become one's preferred world? One can imagine a person who would say to himself: "The federal model is superior to the modified UN model for purposes of war prevention because it can get at the causes of war by intervening in the domestic affairs of nation states. But the likelihood that any such world authority will come into being by the year 2000 is very dim. Yet some kind of world government is necessary if we are to have any chance of avoiding large-scale nuclear war. Therefore, I choose Clark-Sohn as my preferred world." Someone else might argue as follows: "Without an effective world government, nuclear disaster is bound to occur. Clark-Sohn, although feasible by the year 2000, could not possibly work. Hutchins, though very difficult to achieve, is my preferred world. To work for anything less would be a waste of time. I'll risk everything on reaching for the impossible. Perhaps, my preference can even have some influence on the possibilities in the case."

Students have every right to differ with one another and with their teachers in their preferred worlds. They may also disagree as to whether a given utopia has been stated relevantly, as we have defined relevance. They may even disagree as to whether a particular utopia would be either effective, if adopted, or achievable if pursued with zeal and rationality. They may also disagree as to whether utopian solutions are as necessary as some social critics claim. But these various differences are not always qualitatively the same. Whether a given model would work, or whether a given model is achievable in the near future, are factual questions; such questions can be answered only by ascertaining as rationally as possible what the probable facts are. But a difference in opinion over preferred worlds is not always a factual difference. It may be a difference involving values, preferred risks, life styles, and even personal temperament. One may use logic and evidence in choosing his preferred world, but logical men in possession of all the facts may not always agree on the world they prefer.

PERSONAL DILEMMAS, SOCIAL CONCERNS

A relevant curriculum is sometimes defined as one addressed to the personal problems of youth. This is not good enough. *It is more relevant to engage young people in a study of the problems of the larger culture in which many of their personal problems have their origin. The culture of most significance to the young consists of those aspects that are problematic — that is, the large conflicts and confusions which translate into the conflicts and confusions of individuals.*

To take one example, young people who are opposed to the war in Vietnam are reluctant to take a position against all war because the larger culture from which most of their learning continues to come expresses the same reluctance. In fact, many of the young insist upon the right to be conscientiously opposed to the war in Vietnam without a requirement that out of conscience they oppose all war. When asked the four questions basic to the methodology of relevant utopias as applied to the Vietnamese (what is Vietnam like today, what will it be like in the near future if present trends are extrapolated, what would you like it to be, and what can you do about any discrepancy between extrapolation and values?), they are prone to reply that the fate of the Vietnamese is of no concern to them and that America should mind its own business. Their vaunted idealism is thus victimized by the widespread cultural preference for some form of isolationism. Although they don't like Nixon, they find it difficult to oppose his attempts to turn over the war to the Vietnamese. The methodology of relevant utopias would ask them to consider carefully whether or not Nixon's policies and their own view of those policies are at all adequate as steps transitional to a drastic change in the existing system of international relations. Unless they make an assessment of this kind, their opinions on a number of related personal and social matters are bound to reflect a great deal of confusion. They could end up as confused as the parents and grandparents whose views they reject.

Finally, what has been said about the use of relevant utopias in social analysis and prescription also applies to personal development and self-analysis. The significant questions are: What kind of person am I now? What will I become if present habits and trends persist? What kind of person would I like to become? What can be done now about tendencies and preferences that conflict? This approach to the problem of identity is more promising than some of the programs offered these days in the name of black studies, black history, and black pride. Historical and cultural studies have maximal relevance when they help us to predict the future or to make transition.

B. Black Studies

21

The Question of Black Studies

Charles V. Hamilton

A *scholar in political science, Charles* V. *Hamilton collaborated with Stokely Carmichael on* Black Power: The Politics of Liberation in America (1967). *He sees black studies as a political demand for academic innovation and urges higher education to deliver the empirical goods. The establishment response to date, he feels, is to kill the movement with nit-picking criticism.*

Hamilton *is professor of political science and urban studies at Columbia University. Author of several articles on race and education, he is currently completing a book,* They Demand Relevance: Black Students Protest (*Random House*).

Several years from now, when historians studying race and politics in the United States look back on the 1960's, they will see a decade of innumerable phrases and labels. They will see such terms as *integration, busing, nonviolence, violence, freedom now, law and order, black power, community control, white racism, institutional racism, separatism, black nationalism, revolution, black studies.* Hopefully, those historians will realize the intense political environment out of which these terms came. These terms were abbreviated ways — and therefore dangerous because of the great possibility of oversimplification — of explaining or projecting complicated phenomena. Arising out of an emotional, intense political struggle, these terms became less the subject for penetrating, in-depth analyses and more the basis on which a polemical, momentarily dramatic debate was engaged.

The black studies issue is one example of this sort of treatment. The term rose out of the protest demands of black students on college campuses in the late 1960's. The demands generally were summed up in another phrase: "a relevant education." The black students wanted their exposure to higher education to be "relevant" to them as black people. They were dissatisfied with the nature of the college curriculum as it existed in most places around the country — and they were specific in their criticisms, with particular em-

From *Phi Delta Kappan*, March, 1970, 362–364. Reprinted by permission.

phasis on the humanities, history, and the social sciences. They pointed out major substantive gaps in American academia, and many of them concluded that these gaps were as much a function of a value system that deliberately chose the kinds of subjects to include in the curriculum as they were simply the result of scholarship yet to be done. In other words, the failure to depict the true role of black people in American history, or the exclusion of black writers from the reading lists of courses in American literature, for example, was a clear reflection of the values of American academia. Law schools and other professional schools were vehemently criticized for offering a course of study which did not "relate" to the developmental needs of a depressed black community.[1]

Thus the students began to demand black studies as an academic mechanism to overcome these normative and substantive problems. One has to understand that these demands were *political* precisely because they reflected — explicitly and implicitly — a feeling among the students that the colleges and universities were not "legitimate." That is, the students were demanding that the institutions change in many ways: in how they recruited black students, in what they did with the black students once they were on campus, in how the schools related to black communities, in the recruitment of black professors, in the kinds of courses offered. Therefore, as *political* demands for *academic* innovation, the demands were subject to negotiation and compromise. At all times, the demands were focal points of a political struggle. The struggle was political in the sense that the right of the college and university to rule unchallenged in the traditional ways was being questioned. *This was the central question: the question of legitimacy.*

Most schools readily admitted that changes (in curriculum, recruitment, community relations) had to be made. But then ensued an unfortunate period when many of the specific alternatives — which had to be understood as products of a political struggle — were taken as absolute academic ends. And before there was time to examine perceptively the kinds of *academic* changes that could be made, many people began to join the polemical debate. Black studies were called "soul courses"; they were seen as places where a cadre of revolutionaries would be trained; respected scholars admonished that black students needed "higher education" in order to compete, not something called black studies.

If one examined closely some of the black studies proposals, there is no question that he would find many of them being concerned with issues of ideology and what might be called subjective matters. This is so precisely because the proposals were trying to — and in many instances did — articulate a new system of legitimacy. The proposals were rejecting, for example, traditional and widely accepted political science literature that argued in favor of the virtual inviolability of a two-party system. The proposals in that field called for courses that attempted to explore new ways to approach sociopolitical change in modern America — at least from the vantage point of black Americans. Perhaps those courses were aimed at "getting ourselves together"

---

[1] See mimeographed newsletter issued by Harvard Black Law Students Association, Spring, 1968.

and at developing political power among black people. Why are these "soul courses" — in the catharsis-serving and demeaning sense of that phrase? Have not some political science courses traditionally been dealing with how groups operated "effectively" in the society? Have not many of the economics courses not only dealt with mere descriptions of the existing economic order but also with ways to strengthen and make that order more viable? Are we unaware of the mass of research carried on on the college campuses by scholars under contract with the government in the natural, physical, and policy sciences? Indeed, virtually all of American education (and surely this would apply to any educational system) has served as a socializing process.

The black students — perceiving blatant weaknesses in that process vis-à-vis their own lives and experiences — were calling for a substantive alternative. They no longer believed in the myth that higher education was value-free, objective, above the social turmoil. Traditional American scholarship has been geared to maintenance of the status quo. The black studies proposals were out to alter that orientation. Professors Seymour Martin Lipset and Philip G. Altbach — who cannot be accused of being generally and un-equivocally sympathetic to the black student demands — made an interesting observation on the nature of the university:

> In the developing countries, there is an intrinsic conflict between the university and the society, thereby creating a fertile ground for student political awareness and participation. The university, as one of the primary modernizing elements in largely traditional societies, necessarily finds itself opposed to other elements in its society, and must often fight to protect its values and orientation. Students are often involved in these conflicts and are key protectors of the modern orientation of the university. . . . In the developed nations, on the other hand, no such conflict exists. The university is a carrier of the traditions of the society, as well as a training agency for necessary technical skills. It is a participant in a continuing modernizing development, rather than in the vanguard of such development. University students are not called upon to protect the values of their institutions against societal encroachments. In most cases, they are merely asked to gain the qualifications necessary for a useful role in a technological society.[2]

This is an interesting observation because the black students *are* asking their universities to be in the vanguard of development.

The black students and the black studies demands have a valid *political* point. If this is generally accepted, as very many thoughtful people have conceded, it would appear that the next step would be to begin to work out the kinds of *academic* changes those demands call for. Clearly, the students who have served as the catalyst for this should not be expected to come up with the final answers. Those people who style themselves scholars have the burden of proceeding to try to develop new knowledge consistent with a new orientation.

[2] Seymour Martin Lipset and Philip G. Altbach, "Student Politics and Higher Education in the United States," in *Student Politics*, Seymour Martin Lipset (ed.). New York: Basic Books, Inc., 1967, p. 242.

Much of the empirical work has yet to be done, because the questions have never been asked. What is the feasibility of massive economic cooperative ventures in rural and urban black communities? What is the nature of and significance of the black culture vis-à-vis new forms and styles of political action in the black community? Is it possible to talk about a peculiar "black experience" that has relevance to the way black Americans organize themselves and conduct their lives? What is the impact of the oral tradition on social, economic, and political phenomena? Black Americans have a heritage, a black experience of abrupt cultural transformation to traumatized conditions of slavery in a distant, alien land with a different language and different life styles; to legal freedom from legal slavery in the same place and economic position; to an urban, atomized, technological environment from a rural, intimate, agrarian environment. What is the meaning of this heritage and experience in terms of new adaptive cultural characteristics, characteristics that can sustain black Americans as a viable people? What are the implications of all this for enlightened public policy? What does it mean for the kinds of effort made to bridge tradition and modernity in the black community? What is meant by the "crisis-oriented" nature of the black political experience? What is meant by "political traumatization" (as opposed to "political apathy") that makes this distinction relevant to one trying to understand and deal with the problems of black community development?

These are some of the kinds of questions that their proponents want black studies to deal with. Are these "soul courses"? Are they "separatist," "violent advocacy of revolution," "catharsis-serving" courses? Do they take one *out* of "higher education"?

I believe that, *if these courses are carefully thought out, they will be the epitome of higher education.* They will prepare the student to engage the total society, not to withdraw from it. One is not going to know much about how to proceed with black economic development or with black educational development or with black political development without knowing a great deal about the total economic, educational, and political systems. And if one listens carefully to the major thrust of the student arguments — rather than focusing on particular polemical sentences here and there — this point will come through clearly.

One must understand that the demands made in a particular environment — political, suspicious, hostile — have many functions: They serve to wrench an entrenched, closed system into a new awareness; they serve to state specifically a rejection of old values and to state generally a framework for new values. The new directions *cannot* be very specific; they are new programs for experimental times. All answers are not known. There is a tendency on the part of some people to require certainty of results and consequences before they are willing to innovate. In social dynamics, this is hardly reasonable. Of course, there is the possibility of unanticipated consequences. But if those who led the fight in the American colonies to break with England in the 1770's had waited until they knew the precise consequences, they probably would not have moved. Or, to take a less "ruptured" case, those who began to implement New Deal measures in the crises of the 1930's could not wait until they had definitive answers about results. They were faced with crises, and, hopefully bringing the best judgment to bear, they had to act.

American higher education faces a serious series of crises. The demands for black studies simply point up one area of intense concern. It is unfortunate, but understandable (if one agrees with Lipset and Altbach) that some so-called culturally disadvantaged black students had to take the lead in pointing out serious educational weaknesses. And precisely because they had to assume the role of innovator in an area traditionally felt to be in the province of "experts," it is quite possible that many people in power positions have forfeited their claim to authenticity. Many of them have been lax and unimaginative and listless for so long that many black students now view them as anachronisms.

If all the colleges and universities now rushing to set up some sort of black studies department are sincere in agreeing to the validity of their moves, then why — the black students ask — did they not recognize the need before now? Why did they have to be prodded and poked and seized? (If they are acting now simply to avoid another sit-in or disruption, then they should be exposed as spineless hypocrites!) The point is that the credibility of many of the schools in the eyes of many black students is so low — the students, indeed, in some instances, question their integrity — that the students do not trust the traditional administrators and faculty to set up and implement a viable program. And this is the crux of the control problem. *The students do not want control because they want to insure easy grades, but because they want to insure a quality program.* They ask: How can the people who have been so negligent and value-oriented in harmful ways now be *trusted* to administer this exciting, vibrant new educational innovation? These are important questions.

In a sense, it is the *pride* of established academia that is hurt. And frequently their vanity requires its representatives to call for assurances that "high standards" be maintained — in evaluation of class work, recruitment of professors, etc. It is rather strange to hear such calls issue from a group that has admitted its own failure and ineptness. How could a scholar in American intellectual history, for example, not recognize the genius of W. E. B. DuBois? What sort of standards must have prevailed that permitted such a scholar to assume a position of authority?

Let us consider proposals for black studies submitted by black students. Do the black students have the answers? Obviously not; they are still in the early stages of their formal education. But they have enough insights gleaned from their black experience (a term which some people have come to see as delightfully mystic or just quaint) to know that much of what has been taught is inconsistent with — indeed, irrelevant to — the lives they lead as black Americans. *And it is this recognition that accounts for a great part of the thrust for black studies.* Many of the proposals may sound, and in fact are, extreme and farcical. But one should not be too quick to dismiss the entire "movement."[3]

[3] One writer made the following observation: "To recruit thousands of young blacks into hitherto restricted American universities and to fill their heads full of something called

A Harvard University faculty committee on African and Afro-American studies made the following statement:

> We are dealing with 25 million of our own people with a special history, culture, and range of problems. It can hardly be doubted that the study of black men in America is a legitimate and urgent academic endeavor.[4]

Is American academia seriously prepared to embark on such an important intellectual pursuit? Or will there continue to be nit-picking and polemics and energy-wasting efforts over momentarily glamorous and dramatic issues (kicking white students out of black studies classes, separatism, etc.)? The black students have performed an invaluable educational service by raising in a political context the hard academic questions — a political context, incidentally, which many students perceived to be absolutely necessary, given the arrogance, smugness, and entrenched nature of many sources of power. The question now becomes whether higher education can be perceptive and intelligent enough to deliver the empirical goods.

American professors and deans are not unfamiliar with political struggles on their campuses. Campus politics has a long history in this country: interdepartmental rivalries; personality clashes; competition for promotion and tenure; faculty-wife gossip and clashes; at times, in some places, vindictive vetoing of each others' Ph.D. candidates; bitter maneuvering for fewer and smaller classes (and larger office space) at choice (i.e., not 8 A.M.) hours of the day and week.

But the demands and the criticisms leveled by many black students today will make those perennial squabbles seem like tea parties — or perhaps one should say panty raids. The demands of the black students are not nearly so frivolous. The black students are raising serious politico-academic questions that cut to the core, to the very nature of the university and college systems. The black students are political modernizers vis-à-vis higher education in a way never before experienced on American campuses. And traditional American academia may well flunk the test (a metaphor not entirely unintended) if it does not do its homework (hard, empirical, relevant research and teaching).

black studies is to prepare them for nothing." Arnold Beichman, "As the Campus Civil War Goes On, Will Teacher Be the New Dropout?" *The New York Times Magazine,* December 7, 1969, p. 48.

[4] Report of the Faculty Committee on African and Afro-American Studies, Harvard University, January 20, 1969, p. 14.

22

Black Studies and Sound Scholarship

Stephen J. Wright

*A professor and administrator, Stephen J. Wright is an estab-
lished leader of the moderate Negro community. He rejects a doctrinaire, propagandistic approach to black studies, supporting a
program in which the basic subjects are disciplines built on sound
scholarship. He believes in a black studies program in which students apply their knowledge to benefit man and in which they
think for themselves "without the inhibiting influences of any imposed position."*

*Wright has been a professor, an administrator, and an organiza-
tion executive. Formerly president of Fisk University in Nashville,
Tennessee, and president of the United Negro College Fund, he is
now consultant to the president of the College Entrance Examination Board.*

Very few, if any, developments in all of education are as freighted with
confusion, controversy, emotion, and pressure for haste as black studies. Yet
institutions of higher learning are being called upon to make long-term commitments to faculty recruited for the emerging programs of black studies, to
make heavy investments in the books and periodicals needed to support
them, and to institute radical new policies incident to their administration
and operation, some of which would not be considered seriously for any other
department or division — the demand for departmental "autonomy" being an
example. The consequences of this situation could, during the coming
decade, be an educational disaster. It is imperative, therefore, that the situation be critically, dispassionately, and reflectively examined.

ISSUES AND PROBLEMS

The really fundamental issues — as distinguished from the problems of implementation such as recruiting staff, developing the specific types of courses,
procuring the necessary library holdings, etc. — are those of definition, objectives, rationale, and the general nature and character of the program. The
central question is whether the program as a whole (or its component parts),
is to be treated as a discipline or as a constellation of disciplines.

From *Phi Delta Kappan*, March, 1970, 365–368. Reprinted by permission.

The purpose of this article is to examine these issues and a few of the important problems and to suggest some approaches that may, hopefully, contribute to a more orderly and a more viable development of this very significant and urgently needed field. This examination is based on the following fundamental assumptions:

1. That the basic subjects that constitute the program of black studies are disciplines, or parts of disciplines in the usual academic meaning of the term; that they involve no mystique and can, therefore, be taught and "learned" by those *academically* competent to do so. (This assumption in no sense excludes appropriate and relevant field experiences.)
2. That competence to teach and learn in the area of black studies is not a function of race, creed, or color.
3. That there are sufficient materials and problems to justify minors, majors, and graduate study, but that they need to be arranged in a scholarly manner and taught in an effective way.
4. That programs of black studies can be organized and developed in both predominantly black *and* predominantly white institutions of higher learning.
5. That black studies should not be substituted, in any total sense, for the education necessary to understand and function effectively in the larger American society.
6. That individuals pursuing, or individuals who have pursued, a sound program of black studies are capable of making their own judgments and applications with respect to the knowledge and appreciations they gain.
7. That the black people of the nation will not become a "fifty-first state," living separately as a "nation" within a nation, but that they will, increasingly, become involved in all aspects of the economic, political, educational, and cultural life of the nation, while maintaining their cultural identity as do several other minorities — Jews, for example.

Such a set of assumptions will doubtless offend those black Americans who desire a more doctrinaire or propagandistic approach. Those espousing such an approach are deeply concerned, of course, with the commitment of black students to the problems of the masses of black people. While I am equally concerned with the commitment of black students to the problems of the masses of black people, it is my position that there can be no program of substance or of lasting value that is not built firmly on the tenets of sound scholarship. If a black studies program built on sound scholarship is taught by those who bring dedication, competence, and enthusiasm to it, then those who experience it as students are very likely to be infected by that enthusiasm and will, on their own, develop the commitment to apply appropriate aspects of their knowledge and appreciation both to themselves and to the masses of the black people. But of equal importance is the fact that such students will be able to think for themselves and continue their own education in the field without the inhibiting influence of any imposed position.

TOWARD A DEFINITION

Unfortunately, there is no definition of black studies on which the majority of those in the various contending groups — black students, white students, black educators, and white educators — agree. It should also be borne in mind that the differences *within* these groups may be greater than those *between* and among them. Accordingly, definitions may vary from one that conceives of black studies as a small collection of minor courses whose content could easily be factored into existing courses to definitions which are substantially synonymous with the notion of a black university — whose definition also varies greatly. However, the definition of a black university included in the demands presented to the president of Fisk University in December, 1969, by those student leaders who occupied the main classroom building is representative of recent definitions by some black students:

> Our objective is to make Fisk a black university. The Fisk University education should be geared to preparing its students for participation in the black community. It should not only provide us with skills, but black consciousness which would bring about the commitment of Fisk students to work with and for black people.
> Through this process, we will "develop the power to move ahead and to add our potential to other power producing levers for the further enrichment of the life of the nation as a whole."
> With this in mind, we hereby state the basic concepts of the black university:
> 1. As an institution structured, controlled, and administered by black people, devoting itself to the cultural needs of the black community.
> 2. As an institution set up to deal with the skills necessary for the black existence.
> 3. As an institution that addresses itself completely, identifying all black people as Africans under the ideological concepts of Pan-Africanism.
> 4. As an institutional structure that addresses itself completely to BLACK LIBERATION.

The key phrases in the foregoing statement are: "preparing its students for participation in the black community," "black consciousness," "commitment . . . to work for and with black people," "the skills necessary for the black existence," "identifying all black people as Africans under the ideological concepts of Pan-Africanism." While there is no specific allusion to black studies, per se, the implication is crystal clear.

Obviously, such an approach would be impossible in a predominantly white institution, for such an institution is not "structured, controlled, and administered by black people." It is also obvious that such a black university, or a program with similar purposes, would be heavily propagandistic in its conception and its approach.

I conceive of black studies as involving that body of knowledge that records and describes the past of the black man in Africa and the other sections of the world in which he is concentrated, with very special reference to the United States; that records, defines, and delineates his contemporary social, political, economic, educational, and cultural status and problems. As is characteristic of other disciplines, black studies should advance referenced knowledge through continuing research. Moreover, it is assumed, of course, that black studies will be pursued "in a context that is relevant to the contemporary life styles of the American black and to the learning and leadership of the American black community."[1]

For a program based on such definition there is, to be sure, an abundance of relevant material — literally thousands of books, monographs, articles, and pamphlets by and/or about black people, not to mention the art, the music, the oral history of the civil rights revolution now in the process of being recorded.[2] These works do indeed include the black man's past in both Africa and the New World. They also record, define, and delineate his contemporary situation. But there is an urgent need to relate the appropriate parts of this material to current problems. This is the task for the scholars and the graduate students.

RATIONALE

While a number of programs of black studies have been established solely as a response to insistent student demands, there is a sound rationale for their establishment:

1. The black experience, in any fair and substantial sense, has simply been omitted from the curriculum of higher education in America and, without it, neither black students nor white students are educated for the hard realities of their times. In fact, the same rationale used to introduce non-Western studies into the curriculum is applicable to black studies.

   Until quite lately higher education in the United States of America has been almost completely under the sway of an illusion shared by nearly everybody of European descent since the Middle Ages — the illusion that the history of the world is the history of Europe and its cultural offshoots; that Western experience is the sum total of human experience; that Western interpretations of that experience are sufficient, if not exhaustive; and that the resulting value systems embrace everything that matters.
   . . . This illusion has been shattered by confrontation with a world of new and renascent nations striving to satisfy the submerged needs of their awakening peoples and to secure a place of dignity and respect in the international community. The need to do what we can, if only for the sake of self-preservation, to steer this restless world into paths of peaceful and orderly development, has forced the American people to look outward. And, looking outward, we have begun to see ourselves more clearly and to recognize our

---

[1] Donald B. Easum, "The Call for Black Studies," *Africa Report*, May–June, 1969, p. 17.

[2] I have recently appraised, for a university, a private collection of some 7,000 titles which, among other things, included more than 2,000 books about Africa and Africans, all of the books written by the major black American writers, and more than 1,000 books written about black Americans.

illusion as the product of ignorance, which breeds racial snobbery and intellectual parochialism.[3]

2. The black student has a very special need for a sound program of black studies, for it serves at least two essential purposes: a) It helps him, perhaps more than anything else, to answer his persistent questions concerning his identity. "A man must come to see himself in relation to his total environment in space and time, and so to locate himself on the map of human experience."[4] b) It provides him with the information and the appreciation he needs, almost desperately, to perform his leadership responsibilities. For any effective leadership, especially of a minority people, must be based upon a knowledge of their past and a comprehensive knowledge of their present condition, out of which a sense of their aspirations and destiny grows.

3. The white student also has an urgent need for systematic exposure to at least the fundamental aspects of a black studies program. At the present time, every ninth person in the United States is black, and the burden of the information and experience of the typical white student lead him, fallaciously, to the position of being either anti-black, indifferent, or patronizing. The position results inevitably from biased or inadequate information. Such positions, during the decades immediately ahead, can lead only to disaster.

The report of the Harvard University faculty committee on African and Afro-American studies summarizes the rationale aptly when it states:

> Quite a number of courses recognize the existence of black men in the development of America; quite a bit of expertise is already available. However, merely recognizing black men as integral segments of certain overall social processes is not good enough. We are dealing with 25 million of our own people with a special history, culture, and range of problems. It can hardly be doubted that the study of black men in America is a legitimate and urgent academic endeavor. If this be so and if we are determined to launch this field of study successfully, far-sighted goals and programs are required. These goals and programs should maintain and even raise academic standards; should avoid experience isolation; and finally, should have meaning for all serious students — black and white.[5]

Stated another way, whatever deeply concerns man and promises significantly to benefit man is an appropriate matter for systematic study. Moreover, if this criterion were rigidly applied to many of the courses now included in the curriculum of higher education in America, those that would be eliminated would leave more than enough room for black studies.

---

[3] *Non-Western Studies in the Liberal Arts Colleges,* A Report of the Commission on International Understanding. Washington, D.C.: Association of American Colleges, 1964, p. 11.

[4] *Ibid.,* p. 12.

[5] Faculty of Arts and Sciences, Harvard University, "Report of the Faculty Committee on African and Afro-American Studies," January 20, 1969, pp. 14–15.

OBJECTIVES

The basic objectives of programs of black studies are inherent in the rationale for their establishment. These objectives should, nevertheless, be clearly stated, for they serve as guides for the selection of courses, experiences, and materials. In addition, they provide the basis for evaluating the programs.

The specific objectives for programs of black studies should include:

1. Acquainting the students with the history, literature, art, and music of black men — African and American.
2. Providing young black Americans with valid and reliable information concerning the social, economic, educational, and political problems confronting black people in the United States as a basis for their leadership responsibilities in and for the black community.
3. Providing young white Americans with essentially the same type of information indicated in No. 2 above as a de-mythologizing experience and as a basis for the understandings they will need to live responsibly in a multiracial society.
4. Examining the extent, causes, nature of, and possible remedies for racism in America.
5. Developing teachers and scholars in the field of black studies.
6. Stimulating research in the field of black studies.

PROBLEMS

The establishment of programs of black studies on what has amounted to a crash basis has generated, understandably, a plethora of problems — not the least of which is the presence of too many nonexperts in the development process. Undoubtedly, the most critical and urgent problem is the paucity of qualified teachers. And the only way to relieve this situation is to train teachers on a crash basis. The National Endowment for the Humanities has helped significantly with its institutes, but such institutes need to be conducted for longer periods and a significant number of adequately financed fellowships need to be established. A related and essential need is for the development of a few centers with the resources to train the teachers. Obviously, the quickest way to get highly qualified teachers is to limit the fellowships initially to post-doctoral study. Atlanta University has already announced what appears to be a promising program at the master's level, with a doctoral program offered in cooperation with Emory University.

The problem of providing the necessary library materials will offer some difficulty for a few years. Fortunately, however, several companies have begun to reprint a number of the out-of-print volumes. The Kraus Reprint Company has undertaken a major program in this area. The Arno Press has also begun a promising program. Also, films of the Schomburg Collection in New York are available.

There is, in the judgment of this writer, a need for a three-part program:

1. One of limited offerings which could become a part of the general education of interested students.
2. One for those who wish to major or minor at the undergraduate level.
3. One for those who wish to pursue study at the graduate level.

Since the field is relatively new, there is a need to develop more "standard" courses and curricula. One approach might be the creation of a task force composed of outstanding scholars who would take a year or perhaps more to develop some model courses and curricula, with recommended supporting materials. Such models could serve as guides — not blueprints — for interested institutions. Such a project would be excellent for an interested and concerned foundation.

Finally, there is the problem of eliminating much of the nonsense that has been generated in connection with black studies programs: suggestions and demands that the programs be closed to whites, that they be graded on different standards, that they be taught by the uneducated, that they be autonomous, etc. It is my position and conviction that the viability of programs of black studies will be contingent upon the extent to which they are handled as other disciplines. Otherwise, they are unlikely in the long run to receive the sustained financial support that is necessary to attract outstanding scholars who are absolutely essential to their development, or to attract, on a continuing basis, the able young men and women without whom there will be no programs.

C. The Work of the Schools

23

Priorities in Change Efforts

Fred T. Wilhelms

Fred T. Wilhelms, a versatile educator, issues a clear call for pro-
grams which go directly to the human person and to the great social
agenda of today. In his words, "It may seem odd to advocate an
'innovation' which consists simply of deciding on purposes first and
then finding subject matter and experiences to achieve these pur-
poses. But an 'innovation' it would be — the most important inno-
vation that I can think of."

Wilhelms has been a professor, a school administrator, and direc-
tor of organizations dealing with problem areas in education. He is
now executive secretary of the Association for Supervision and Cur-
riculum Development in Washington, D.C. It is the largest and
most influential such group in America.

I believe that there are two needs so pressing that they place absolutely
overriding demands on us to produce curriculum that does what it is meant
to do. One is for programs deliberately designed to offer maximum effective
help to each young person in his personal becoming. The other is for programs designed to go straight to the great social agenda of the here and
now.

Around these two peaks lie wide ranges of other important needs. We
must produce real mastery of knowledge and skills in a great diversity of
areas: in reading, for instance, in mathematics, and in all that complex
that makes up our scientific technology and the vocational life of people
in it. These needs are real and basic and important. We dare not ignore
them or slight them because the competencies they represent are vital both
to the persons in our society and to the society itself.

Yet I believe the two overriding demands I have named tower above all
the others, simply because they go directly to what is crucial to life in our
culture — and the survival of the culture itself.

I know of no objective way to declare one or the other of these two the

From *Phi Delta Kappan*, March, 1970, 368–371. Reprinted by permission.

more important, both being essential. Certainly our society is in a state of emergency. Along with its wonderful productivity, our technology has generated side effects that suddenly converge upon us with bewildering speed: pollution, contamination of the earth and sea and air, urban rot, the depletion of key resources, and simultaneously the prospect of annihilation and of more people than the world can hold — to mention but a few. Alongside these, perhaps out of different parentage, rushes the blessed but troublous urgency for social justice and equity, with all its hostilities of race and class.

Every one of these problems is massive. Every one of them demands resolution in an incredibly short time — or else. Even if they could be taken one at a time, no one of them would yield a quick, simple solution. Taken together — as they must be taken — they constitute the most formidable agenda ever to face any society. Obviously they demand a nation of aggressive, effective, and dedicated problem-solvers. Obviously our schools are not producing enough of them. Our social studies drone on. Our so-called civic education is mostly a sterile analysis of structure, almost without effect. The whole thing is out of touch with reality. Until painfully recently, even the attempts at improvement were dominated by goals of mere academic virtuosity. That is changing now; but the inertia of the system is awesome. Only a massive effort, bringing to bear resources of mind-stretching diversity, has any chance of generating programs that can bring each youth face-to-face with his realities and teach him to help. We cannot depend forever on the political socialization of the street corner.

Yet, subjectively, I believe there is a still higher order of need in our culture. The salient problems of our day lie *within the individual person — within us.* Historians will see it more clearly one day; it is hard to see clearly while we stand inside the whirlwind. [Old religions, old systems of values and morals and mores are crumbling. Life changes at a fantastic pace, and the old stabilizers are weakening. Very probably we stand at one of the great swing-points in human history. And no matter how courageously or even buoyantly we hold to the faith that what will emerge will be better, the present is a time of trouble.]

Future shock Elements

Our youth are especially (only especially, not exclusively) hard hit. One cannot lump them all together. They react in many different ways, make their search in many different corners. Some reject virtually the whole tradition — perhaps in sullen withdrawal, perhaps angrily or even violently. Some have a sweetness about them that has rarely been equalled. Many stay within the system and throw themselves into great idealistic ventures, putting into action the finest of the old tradition and maybe something more. And the great "silent majority"? What mature adult really believes that even they are the same as he was at their age?

[Underneath all the turbulence, surfacing often in forms that may seem bizarre to us, and sometimes in forms that may genuinely be subversive, destructive, and dangerous — beneath all this, it seems to me, lies a bedrock quest for "something better," for a higher social ethic, and a finer relation of man to man.] The vision is inchoate; the goals are seen dimly, if at all. The search for "leads" goes everywhere — into old, quietist oriental religions, into existentialist philosophies, into human-relations experimentation, and even into consciousness-expanding drugs. The search is daring and courageous, but it is also, to be blunt about it, inept, sensation-ridden, and fumbling.

And how much have we done to help, we gray-heads in whom so much wisdom resides? How much chance have we provided a learner in our school to dig down into the immanent questions of values, of the significance of life, of the possibilities inherent in his humanity? How much help do we ever offer him to see the great options he has as to how to spend himself? What is there in our program that helps him to hammer out his own personal set of values, make his own commitments, and decide what to *be*?

I believe our next great task is to work out programs that will *go directly to the human person* — disregarding subject-matter rubrics at first, searching for subject matter and experience, from whatever source, that will help the person realize himself — starting bare-handed with nothing but the determination to help human becoming to its ultimate.

That will be the toughest, most sophisticated job ever undertaken by our profession. But we know enough now about human potential and its actualization to make the try. Anyway, as the kids say, "that's where it's at." The job of a school is to assault the deepest problems of its time. And I believe I have named them.

All this may be an unconscionably long prelude to an article that is supposed to be about innovation. But it is not a put-down of those brisk new developments one thinks of first when the word "innovation" is used. We shall need them — and more — if we are to master the challenges sketched above.

Obviously, if we are to have programs that "go directly to the human person," we have got to develop something beyond individualization — *personalization* — and yet keep it in a milieu of intimate human contact. Team teaching will be near-essential. Flexible scheduling that leaves much of each student's time free (and, hopefully, unpoliced) will help greatly. Assuming a considerable dependence on literature, art, and music, we shall need a wide array of materials that facilitate use by individuals or by two or three at a time — including books, but also including stereo record players with headphones, desk-size projection outfits, and so on, to the more complex devices. We need to be able to use motion pictures for even one student at a time. And we need individualized space for *doing* activities. The shapes of buildings and rooms will change radically, and all the new media for message-transmittal will be in great demand.

Yet it will be taking nothing from great adaptations such as these — which are commonly read as synonymous with "innovation" — to say that there must be other innovations of a far higher order. In teaching, for example. Consider for a moment the innovations in teaching that will be essential if we are to use literature optimally as an aid to human becoming.

The standard didactic mode upon which we chiefly rely in "teaching literature" is sufficient to do just what that phrase implies: to help students "know" a certain number of classics, to master lists of authors and their works, to survey literary movements, etc. But all this — important as it may be in an academic way — has very little to do with a young person's *use* of a poem or a novel as something to form himself upon. In all truth the standard didactic treatment gets in the way of such truly intrinsic learning.

It is hard even to visualize, let alone to practice, the sort of teaching that will let a youngster soak in literature that has direct meaning for him. I can scarcely imagine the tranquility, the warm, supportive environment, the uncrowded leisureliness it will take if individuals or small groups are to be free simply to look at themselves with clear eyes, talk through their deepest concerns, and forge out values to which they can commit themselves. I suspect that the highest forms of teaching will look to the unsophisticated observer like non-teaching. The sensitivity of feedback interpretation and progressive guidance will make the crude assign-quiz-test routine we now call teaching look as ridiculous as it is.

Probably the change in teaching need not be as radical in all areas as it must be in the deeply personal humanistic fields, but the change throughout must likely be in the same direction. What this will demand of preservice and in-service teacher learning staggers the imagination. In 10 years we have not been able to generate even the relatively simple teaching changes envisioned by the pioneers in science and mathematics. By and large, the visionary new ventures have suffered a massive regression to the mean as most teachers have translated the dreams of discovery learning into the comfortable routines of good old "standard didactics."

One hesitates to call a spade a spade in discussing the practice of teaching, because we have a fellow feeling for teachers, and we secretly know that they are not all that much to blame, being caught in a tradition and a system they didn't invent. But the cold truth is that, by any system of scoring with even the slightest element of the visionary in it, the typical teacher, if he were a golfer, would rarely break a hundred. The result is a dreary wasteland of mediocrity. And it is worse than that: From the viewpoint of the learner it is repression and all too often sheer oppression. There is really little use doing much of anything else in education unless we devise a system of education for teachers that sets them on a different track and then — more fundamentally important — help teachers toward a *way of life* consonant with what they are expected to deliver.

We are just "playing house" as long as we expect a high school teacher, for example, to think and feel deeply about individual learners, to innovate fundamentally in his use of subject matter — to reach for the stars — as long as he has to teach five classes a day, meeting a new group every hour on the hour, with maybe 15 or 20 minutes to prepare each lesson. He is ground down by the system; he goes home bone-tired — all the wearier because he knows in his heart that much of his work has been futile.

There has been a great deal of talk and some action — valuable enough in its way — about relieving teachers of clerical, milk-money duties. It is time we got up the nerve to talk about the sheer, massive volume of teaching-at-classes. Try saying sometime to an educational audience that teachers have to be able to live in the life-style of an intellectual, even of a scholar — and watch the blank looks. It is, to say it softly, not a part of our dream. How many educational leaders even believe that every secondary teacher needs a private office, with the appurtenances of systematic pursuit of study, and with room to confer privately with one or a few students? It is, to me, literally shocking, what we reveal we think about teachers. Maybe the most profitable innovation of them all would be to get serious about the total way of life that superior teaching has to be based on.

Just how to get at the necessary changes remains mostly to be worked out. But let us, at the least, face up to a grim truth: Unless somehow we provide teachers a breakaway from the stultifying school life we now force upon them, most of them will remain virtually inaccessible to new ideas and new insights. The savants in the schools of education may go on elaborating their intricate "scenarios" for educational revolution; the scholars in the background may penetrate deeper and deeper into the mysteries of human potential and the ways of learners; but the typical teacher will go on, practically untouched by it all, placidly administering the old routines of standard didactic method.

It is a tempting target for contempt. Teachers ought to be "professional," we tell ourselves; they ought to be alert to new knowledge, new insights, new content, and new materials. But who among us could or would do all that if we carried the load they carry and lived in the environment that people like us have made for them? If we want anything significant in further improvements in our schools — anything more fundamental than the sharpening of existing competencies — we had better make ourselves "tribunes for the teachers" and fight for a way of life that will free them for a quest a lot of them want to make.

And then there is the curriculum. Obviously it is too chopped up. John Donne might almost have had it in mind when he moaned,

> 'Tis all in peeces, all cohaerence gone;
> All just supply, and all relation.

In the past decade we have had splendid developmental work on many of the "peeces." The next great innovative surge had better be toward unification.

My own perception is that to begin by trying to balance and integrate the whole curriculum at one time is to court defeat; the job is just too big. On the other hand, confining ourselves to the individual course only accentuates fragmentation. I propose that we start serious work with each of what I see as the three great streams in the common curriculum:

> Science-Math
> The Social Studies
> The Humanities

I suggest that in each of these broad areas we ("we" meaning variously a single school, a school system, a state, a professional association, etc.) form a comprehensive "area committee."

In terms of personnel, such an area committee should include broad representation of parents, the public at large, and students as well as professionals of all appropriate types. About half of the professionals should deliberately be drawn from *outside* the disciplines directly affected; e.g., the humanities area committee should include science persons, physical educators, vocational education staff members, etc.

In terms of purpose, each area committee should be charged primarily to inquire into the *kind of program* needed; e.g., what should an entire social studies program be designed to *do?* Only very slowly should such a committee move into specific organizational plans and content areas. It should never dictate details of particular courses — that is a job for specialists.

Such a committee, because of its heavy loading of nonspecialists, can work wonders to move the emphasis in curriculum-forming back to where it belongs — to the *purposes to be achieved*, with subject matter selection in an ancillary role. The fundamental mistake we make over and over is to start with subject matter.

In fact, the fundamental mistake lies even deeper. To put it in terms of systems analysis, *we have confused input with output.* So we keep acting as if "putting across" informational content (input) is our job, and as if the students' knowing it is the output. Most of the time nothing could be further from the truth. For example, a history teacher may labor mightily to put across chronological details of presidential administrations (input); if she is honest she knows that nearly all of those details will quickly be forgotten. If, then, there is no other output than the students' knowing those details, there is nothing left — and the teacher is essentially goal-less in her teaching.

That confusion of output with input — and that consequent goal-lessness — are extremely deepseated in American education. It may seem odd to advocate an "innovation" which consists simply of deciding on purposes first and then finding subject matter and experiences to achieve those purposes. But an "innovation it would be — the most important innovation I can think of.

And if we go at it that way we shall reap one other benefit. To unify curriculum across wide areas is very difficult if we start with subject matter, for the disciplines are discordant among themselves. To integrate around fundamental purposes is relatively easy. If we go to the fundamentals, organization will fall into place rather naturally.

24

Curriculum for the Disadvantaged

Robert J. Havighurst

An experienced student of human development, Robert J. Havig-hurst is an active participant in controversies concerning the work of the schools in relation to disadvantaged people. He predicts changes in the social setting of the Seventies which could eliminate need for a special curriculum for the disadvantaged child (except for a pre-school system), reorientation of teachers to rewards and an orderly classroom regime, and relatively small adaptations to fit specific knowledge deficiencies and self-image needs.

Havighurst has been a member of the University of Chicago education staff since 1941. His many books and articles include Education in Metropolitan Areas, 1966, *and* The Public Schools of Chicago, 1964.

In writing usefully about school programs which will be valid for the coming decade in the education of the economically disadvantaged, it is important to look ahead at the shape of things to come, and to avoid being turned to stone by the backward look at the ways of the past.

What is the probable social setting in the 1970's for children of the poorest 20 percent of the American population? With considerable assurance we can predict the following:

1. Increased real income and greater stability of that income. Some reform of the welfare system is sure to come very soon to provide a basic family allowance for every poor family. It will operate to keep fathers and mothers together with their children.

2. Higher educational level of low-income parents. The increase in grade-level attainment since the war is reflected in the young adults whose children are now beginning to enter school. Lower-income parents will be better able to appreciate the school experience of their children, to read to them, etc.

3. Pre-school education for at least one year before the age of five. An improved and amplified Head Start program is now ready for widespread use, and teachers trained in one of several programs proven successful will be available in increasing numbers. These successful programs are raising the I.Q. level of disadvantaged children by an average of 10 to 15 points

From *Phi Delta Kappan*, March, 1970, 371–373. Reprinted by permission.

and keeping this gain for three years, at least. In another year or two, we will know whether these children retain their improved learning ability up to the third- or fourth-grade level. If they do, we will be able to employ a curriculum for the intermediate grades which is based on the assumption of very little reading retardation of children in inner-city schools.

4. Improved methods of working in primary grades with disadvantaged children. This is part of the situation we have just described. Once a child from a disadvantaged family has been aided substantially by a pre-school program, he will continue to be aided by primary school teaching that gears in with his Head Start experience.

5. Slowly decreasing racial and economic segregation in the schools. The pattern of residential segregation by race and income which was set in the 1950's and supported by public housing practices will only slowly be overcome by the forces now at work to produce integration in the central city and the suburbs. While we may expect substantial change in the direction of integration, it will not affect large proportions of disadvantaged children during the decade immediately ahead.

6. A gradually decreasing gap in material style of life and in social attitudes and values between the middle class and the disadvantaged lower-class group. Though the gap will continue throughout the decade, it will become less noticeable. The "subculture of poverty" which dominates the life style of many poor families today will lose much of its grasp.

To some readers this may appear to be an overoptimistic view of the immediate future, but it seems essentially realistic to me. It is far better for the schools to "tune up" to the future than to prepare for a disappearing past.

The goal of education for all children, rich or poor, from literate or illiterate families, is the same if it is expressed in general terms. This is to help the child become a competent and happy person, now and in the future, in a democratic, productive, and increasingly urban society. There is no distinction here between social classes. It does not make sense in this society to talk about "turning a lower-class child into a middle-class child" as though this were a good or a bad thing to do. There are common goals of competence and happiness in a productive and socially integrated society. Children will differ individually, because of social group differences, in their progress toward these goals. The school's mission is to help all children move toward these common goals.

There are two important questions to be answered with respect to the curriculum for economically disadvantaged children. One has to do with *methods* of teaching, the other with *content* of the curriculum.

METHODS FOR THE DISADVANTAGED

There is a growing body of data on the relation of reward to learning among children which supports the following propositions.[1]

---

[1] These propositions are developed more fully in my article on "Minority Subcultures and the Law of Effect," *American Psychologist*, 25 (April, 1970), 313–322.

1. There are differences among socioeconomic groups and ethnic subcultures in the reward systems they teach and use with their children. External rewards (material, or intangible — such as praise) and punishments are to be contrasted with internal (superego and ego) rewards and punishments.

2. In general, external rewards (material or intangible) have greater positive value for disadvantaged or failing children.

3. Appropriate teaching methods can help a child evolve from the external to the internal reward system.

Thus a system of deliberate external rewards (material things like toys, gold stars, edibles) and praise should be employed with disadvantaged pupils.

A CHILD-ORIGINATED CURRICULUM?

When children do not learn well in school, we naturally ask ourselves whether there is something wrong with the curriculum or the way it is presented to the pupil. There are two contrasting answers to this question. One is that we adults are imposing a limited, rigid curriculum on children and putting their minds in a strait-jacket. The other is that we do not present the curriculum in such a way that the child can understand what he is doing and where he is going.

The first view has had considerable play during the last few years, in a revival of the child-centered curriculum movement which was popular in the 1920's and 1930's. Among its persuasive presenters are John Holt and George Dennison, authors of books recently published. Holt, in his book, *How Children Learn*,[2] says, "Only a few children in school ever become good at learning in the way we try to make them learn. Most of them get humiliated, frightened, and discouraged. They use their minds, not to learn, but to get out of doing the things we tell them to do — to make them learn. In the short run, these strategies seem to work. They make it possible for many children to get through their schooling even though they learn very little. But in the long run these strategies are self-limiting and self-defeating, and destroy both character and intelligence. The children who use such strategies are prevented by them from growing into more than limited versions of the human beings they might have become. This is the real failure that takes place in school; hardly any children escape. . . . What is essential is to realize that children learn independently, not in bunches; that they learn out of interest and curiosity, not to please or appease the adults in power; and that they ought to be in control of their own learning, deciding for themselves what they want to learn and how they want to learn it."

As expounded by Holt, this proposition seems to apply more to middle-class children than to the economically disadvantaged group. However, Herbert Kohl's *36 Children*[3] appears to present much the same kind of case, based on experience in a Harlem ghetto school.

[2] John Holt, *How Children Learn*. New York: Pitman Publishing Company, 1967.
[3] Herbert Kohl, *36 Children*. New York: New American Library, 1967.

Kohl describes how he worked for a year with a class of 36 Negro slum children who were below average in academic skills. He did get results. There is no reason to doubt this. His method of encouraging them to write about their fears, their hates, and their likes, about the bad and good things they experienced in their homes and streets, loosened their pens and their tongues, added to their vocabulary, and got them interested in school.

What Kohl appears to have done was to attach school learning to the impulses of the children. By helping them to talk and write about the things that were most impelling in their daily lives, he made school relevant to them. To put this into psychodynamic terms, Kohl was marshaling the forces of the id on behalf of learning, just as Holt proposes to do. But Holt talks in "safe" middle-class terms about children's curiosity and interests, while Kohl faces the slum realities of children's fears and hates.

But how far can a system based on children's felt needs go? How far can a slum child (or a middle-class child) go toward mastery of arithmetic, of English sentence style, of knowledge of science and history, if he is motivated only by his drive to express his feelings or to satisfy his curiosity, or possibly also by his desire to please his friendly and permissive teacher?

We do not know how far this kind of reward will carry a child's learning. We might guess that it would carry children up to about the seventh-grade level. Therefore, we should ask Kohl and others of this school of thought to prove that their methods will carry children to the eighth-grade level. No such claims appear to have been substantiated, except in the case of socially advantaged children, such as those attending A. S. Neill's school at Summerhill, England. And some observers of this school argue that it can only work with children who have a strong British middle-class superego, and can profit from teaming their somewhat starved id with the superego in the pursuit of learning.

The contrasting view of curriculum calls for more rather than less adult-created structure than the pupil generally gets today, but a structure which is carefully fitted to the student's present knowledge and to his motives. It aims to achieve "a real dialectic of authority and empathy in the classroom," which Donald Barr, headmaster of the Dalton School, called for in his criticism of Holt's position.[4]

The essential element is the pupil's perception of the connection between what he does in the classroom or in his school work and a result which he wants. When this condition is met, the pupil's ego can come into action to guide his effort and reward his success.

Programmed learning is an example, where it is used skillfully. The pupil accepts an assignment to learn a particular lesson or set of facts, and he is informed immediately of every successful step he takes toward this goal.

According to this view, the pupil must accept the notion that he has hard work to do which will require effort on his part in order to achieve the goal that he sees clearly.

[4] Donald Barr, "The Works of John Holt," *The New York Times Book Review, Special Education Book Supplement*, September 14, 1969.

Another example is the Mastery Program which Benjamin Bloom has helped to work out in schools in Puerto Rico, a program now ready for general use. The work assignments are divided into relatively small units with frequent tests for mastery. The pupil works for the mastery of his assignment and keeps on working until he has demonstrated mastery. No matter how slow he is, compared with the rest of his class, he achieves mastery before going on to the next assignment. Bloom has found that the slow pupils move along much more rapidly than he had expected. Not only do pupils learn more effectively, they also come to enjoy learning. Bloom says,[5] "The clearest evidence of affective outcomes is the reported interest the student develops for the subject he has mastered. He begins to 'like' the subject and to desire more of it. To do well in a subject opens up further avenues for exploration of the subject. Conversely, to do poorly in a subject closes an area for further study. The student desires some control over his environment, and mastery of a subject gives him some feeling of control over a part of his environment. Interest in a subject is both a result of mastery of the subject [and] a cause of mastery."

The successful innovative programs for high-school-age students also contain this element of motivation toward a clearly understood goal. For example, the storefront academies that give high school dropouts a chance to prepare for the G.E.D. test and high school diploma equivalency probably are successful because they work with young people who have become convinced that they need more education; they see clearly the connection between their study in the storefront academy and the achievement of this goal.

The Upward Bound and High Potential programs for disadvantaged high school and college youth, where they are successful, seem to combine the element of motivation to succeed with a clearly outlined program of study for a summer or a semester. Such programs can be seen as a long step forward by the student.

EMPHASES FOR THE DISADVANTAGED

The argument to this point has been as follows: Economically disadvantaged children have difficulty in the school system for two reasons:

1. Their family environment limits their perceptual, conceptual, and linguistic experience in their early years, thus preparing them poorly for school. But this family factor is improving, due to the reduction of poverty and the increasing level of education among low-income parents.
2. Teaching methods in the schools have not been well-adapted to the learning styles of economically disadvantaged children. But recent research has shown the way to improved methods of teaching these children.

[5] Benjamin S. Bloom, "Learning for Mastery," *Administrator's Notebook*, April, 1968 (Midwest Administration Center, University of Chicago). See also B. S. Bloom, J. T. Hastings, and G. Madaus, *Formative and Summative Evaluation of Student Learning.* New York: McGraw-Hill, 1970.

This line of reasoning suggests that there is no special need for a special curriculum for the disadvantaged child.

Still, there are certain topics and subject areas that might well be given special stress in a school that serves disadvantaged children and youth. These have one or the other of two kinds of value:

1. *To meet specific deficiencies in the life of the child.* — For example, it is well established that the diet of children in poor families is very likely to be inadequate, partly because the family lacks money to pay for essential foods and partly because the child and his family lack knowledge about nutrition. Therefore it would seem wise to put special emphasis on the study of nutrition at two levels of the school — the third- or fourth-grade level, with simple and clear rules about diet, and the ninth- or tenth-grade level, with science-based information about nutrition.

2. *To meet self-image needs in the child and adolescent.* — Several disadvantaged minority groups have been given shabby treatment in American history and literature, which gets into the school curriculum and tends to undermine the self-esteem of children of these groups when they meet this material in front of their classmates. Three groups have suffered the most from this kind of experience — Negroes, American Indians, and Mexican-Americans.

For the sake of all American youth, the study of these minority groups should be more accurate, truth-based, and positive.

For the sake of minority group members whose forefathers are presented as inferior, cruel, savage, or servile, and who are themselves subject to discrimination in contemporary society, there may be some value in special readings and projects which give them a more positive picture of the past and present status of their own ethnic group.

CONCLUSION

Thus my conclusions concerning the education of the economically disadvantaged are:

1. We need a pre-school program of at least one year's duration aimed at improving the cognitive and language development of disadvantaged children.
2. Elementary school teachers need to learn more effective methods of rewarding disadvantaged children for effort and achievement in school.
3. Elementary school teachers need to create and maintain an orderly classroom regime in which pupils are convinced that they will be rewarded in the future for consistent effort today.
4. A relatively small adaptation of the ordinary school curriculum should be made to fit specific knowledge deficiencies and self-image needs of disadvantaged children and youth.

25

"Alternative Schools": Challenge to Traditional Education?

Donald W. Robinson

A part of the educational unrest of our time, "alternative schools" apply variant viewpoints on curriculum and methodology to the education of children. The growing movement, heavily sprinkled with "super-Summerhills," is reported by Donald W. Robinson, associate professor of secondary education at Indiana University

Over 700 independent schools have been founded during the past three years, as teachers, parents, and students seek alternatives to the stultifying climate of so many public schools. Two or three new "alternative" schools are born every day, and every day one dies or gives up its freedom, claims Harvey Haber, founder of the New Schools Exchange.

In existence less than a year, the New School Exchange (2840 Hidden Valley Lane, Santa Barbara, Calif. 93103) describes itself as the only central resource and clearinghouse for all people involved in "alternatives in education." The exchange publishes a directory of experimental schools, acts as a placement bureau for teachers, and publishes a newsletter (29 issues to date, 2,000 subscribers, $10 per year).

The exchange provides a sense of community among radical educators. As one visitor recently expressed it, "The information that is moving through things like the *New Schools Exchange Newsletter* is primarily a feeling, and only incidentally a body of data. It's that Woodstock complex, a ritual magic to ward off the stunning desolation that sweeps across the land sometimes like a cold wind. But then feelings are very powerful. They can swell and topple empires."

These feelings constitute the fuel that is firing the revolution that manifests itself alone in the New Schools movement, but equally in the student revolts and in the writings of such authors as Leonard, Kohl, Kozol, Holt, Herndon, and Glasser.

The feelings are of frustration and resentment because schools are so

From *Phi Delta Kappan*, March, 1970, 374–375. Reprinted by permission.

regimented, administration so unsympathetic, teachers so hamstrung, and learning climate so sterile.

The directory issued by the New Schools Exchange lists several hundred innovative schools and educational reform groups in 28 states, the District of Columbia, and Canada. The largest number, over 100, are in California. There is also a considerable concentration in New England. (The private schools springing up in the South are not experimental in the same sense!)

A similar directory is available (for $10) from the Teacher Drop-Out Center (University of Massachusetts, Amherst, Mass. 01002). This center is operated by two graduate students, Leonard Solo and Stan Barondes, who queried 400 reputedly innovative schools and published statements from 60 replies.

These replies reflect the spirit of the schools:

"We believe in the right of every individual to be free to experience the world around him in his own way."

"We encourage kids to live their own lives. Classes are not compulsory; self-government runs the school."

"We believe that in a loving, accepting environment in which emotional needs are met, children will feel free to grow; and that feeling free, they *will* grow, *will* follow their natural curiosity, *will* do whatever they find necessary to meet their needs."

More extreme is this statement from an Oregon school:

"Philosophy: A cross of Skinner and Neill and Leary and IWW. The school is an integral part of a farm commune research organization crazy house. Prospectus and appropriate political material available."

Of course not all of the reform movement lies outside of the public schools, and several city systems are listed in the Drop-Out Center's directory of innovative situations. The statement submitted by John Bremer, director of Philadelphia's much-publicized Parkway Program ("School Without Walls"), includes this unconventional bit:

"It is true that we teach some unconventional subjects, but the study groups are mostly small, under 10 students, and the old ways of classroom teaching just do not make any sense. So students and faculty are redefining what we mean by teaching and learning. Our faculty members teach, but when they do, it is not in a classroom; it is in the city, in an office building, in City Hall, in the street, depending on what they are teaching."

Such statements exemplify the sentiments of Solo and Barondes, whose goal is "to identify the schools — elementary and secondary, public and private — that want the unusual teacher, the teacher who believes in letting students grow into individual, alive, and aware humans, the teacher who breathes controversy and innovation." Their second goal is to locate these unusual teachers and to serve (without charge) as a clearinghouse to bring innovative teachers and free schools together. They find that the number of eager teacher applicants far exceeds the school openings. The center receives eight to 10 letters a day from teachers wanting to move to a freer school.

Still another manifestation of the freedom movement is *The Teacher*

Paper, a quarterly publication produced by high school English teacher Fred Staab, assisted by his wife and a volunteer staff. *The Teacher Paper* (280 North Pacific Ave., Monmouth, Ore. 97361, $2 per year) exudes a tone of congeniality with the spirit of the new schools, though its constituency is essentially the corps of teachers who have elected to reform the public schools rather than desert them. Staab started his paper last year to provide a forum for teacher expression and to improve communication between teachers and the public. He feels that too much of the local communication about education is filtered through the administration and that even in national education journals the teacher's voice is much too muted. He claims his publication is neither anti-administration nor anti-establishment, only pro-teacher and pro-student. And indeed both the feature article in the December, 1969, issue titled "Bulletin Boards as a Guerilla[1] Tactic" and a foldout "Guerilla Manual" listing 162 disruptive tactics should provide a modern superintendent with more chuckles than scowls. Militant rhetoric has become part of the scene.

Staab predicts that the rapid growth of *The Teacher Paper* will continue and is seeking a part-time job so he can devote more time to making it grow. His present 1,200 subscribers in 30 states include roughly 900 teachers and 300 parents, two-thirds of them Oregonians. He is confident that circulation will expand because other journals lack style, seriousness, and bite and do not reflect teacher views.

These three voices of dissent, the New Schools Exchange, the Teacher Drop-Out Center, and *The Teacher Paper*, are heralds of a protest movement that is gaining steam in its crusade to humanize education. (The founders and managers of all three are over 30.) While some educators are dedicated to extending the applications of computer assisted instruction and systems analysis, these teachers and parents are more concerned with humaneness, sensitivity, and freedom of the student to be a free, inquiring person, with human help from teachers.

The New Schools Exchange is beginning to attract attention. It has been visited by writers, foundation representatives, and government consultants, and dares to hope it may receive some grant money, while admitting that without additional support it cannot survive many more months.

Most representatives of recognized establishment groups admit that they know too little about the new schools to hazard an opinion. However, Cary Potter, director of the National Association of Independent Schools, recognizes them as one segment of the current wave of frustration with traditional education. "They represent a mixed bag," he says, "a terrific spectrum, out of which may come some useful ideas. Some of the black schools especially show something about independence which is good." . . .

Many of the conspicuous demands of the new school movement are being pushed in public schools also, but too slowly, too uncertainly, to satisfy the mood of "action now." Some public schools are becoming ungraded, introducing sensitivity training, calling on parents and other adults to contribute

---

[1] Webster spells it "guerrilla," but "free school" people tend to apply the same standard to spelling that they apply to conduct: Do your own thing.

their expertise as resource people, and even taking school completely out of the school building, as in the Philadelphia Parkway School already referred to.

One advocate of experimental schools has prepared a list of ways these "alternative schools" can relate to the public schools. The suggestions include: providing community resource specialists to supplement public school activity; giving creative parties for students from public schools; supporting radical students and teachers, if for no other reason than to let them know they are not alone, odd, insane, or whatever else the "system" might be trying to make them believe of themselves; organizing joint experimental school and public school student projects; offering student teachers practice teaching opportunities in experimental schools; and exchanging services of experimental school and public school teachers in after-hours activities.

The names of the new schools reflect the tone of the movement: Student Development Center, All Together New Free School, Alternative Foundation, School for Human Resources, Community Workshop School, Halcyon School, Involvement Education.

They represent a fairly wide spectrum of educational thought, with a heavy sprinkling of super-Summerhills. About half of them are inner-city schools. Haber estimates that approximately 80 percent are designed to accommodate students from pre-school through high school. Organization, curriculum, and financing vary widely. Some operate entirely on tuition, some rely wholly on other sources, and many combine the two.

Many of these new schools are not carefully planned; many do not survive. Haber estimates the average length of life of a new school at 18 months, after which it may die completely, merge with another school, or alter its course so severely as to cease to be a radically innovative institution.

The entire movement may prove ephemeral. But even if few alternative schools survive, the movement will have made its contribution to reform, much as third parties in our political history have forced the established parties to adopt social reforms.

D. Humanism and Instructional Technology

26

A Humanist's Approach

Joseph Wood Krutch

Joseph Wood Krutch was a literary figure whose interests ranged from drama criticism to nature commentary. He was a frequent spokesman for the humanities; here Krutch defends the claims of philosophy and the humane arts against such pretenders as science and machine teaching.

Krutch was one of America's most prominent authors, editors, and critics. Representative of his many works are Human Nature and the Human Condition, *1959, and* The Measure of Man, *1954 (recipient of the National Book Award). He wrote a number of articles criticizing education from the humanist's viewpoint. He died in 1970, shortly after this, perhaps his last article, first appeared.*

Within a very short time there has been a drastic change in the attitude of the intellectual community toward what are called (somewhat vaguely) "the humanities." As recently as 1953 I was, I think, entirely justified in describing the situation as it then existed in these words:

> In his sentimental moments even the tycoon sometimes puts in a word for the good old days and he may, like Henry Ford, support a museum to preserve their relics. In somewhat similar fashion nearly everybody professes to regret "the neglect of the humanities." Any discussion of education or contemporary civilization is likely to include a formal bow in the direction of "culture," much like the equally formal bow in the general direction of religion. "O yes, I almost forgot. There is also God and humanities—very important things, of course, though I haven't time to discuss them now."

> Compare the contents of any class magazine with that of a corresponding publication in the nineteenth century. Compare, for example, the modern *Harper's* or *Atlantic* with the same magazine two generations ago. Politics, sociology, and — to a lesser extent — science have now almost a monopoly. Any sort of writing whose appeal is primarily to what is still sometimes somewhat vaguely called "cultural interests" is almost nonexistent. Yet it

From *Phi Delta Kappan*, March, 1970, 376–378. Reprinted by permission.

was the staple of these same magazines not so very long ago. About such things their public has obviously ceased to care very much.

Today those who represent science, technology, and industry itself are no longer so sure as they once were that their aims and methods are the only ones necessary for the creation of a good life for mankind. It is, for example, no longer a cause for surprise that *Bell Magazine*, the house organ of the American Telephone and Telegraph Company, was glad to publish an article in which I elaborated upon the statement made by Herman Kahn (formerly of the Rand Corporation) and Anthony Wiener (formerly of the Massachusetts Institute of Technology) in their recent study called *The Year Two-Thousand*: "Practically all the major technological changes since the beginning of industrialization have resulted in unforeseen consequences. . . . Our very power over nature threatens to become itself a source of power that is out of control. . . . Choices are proposed that are too large, too complex, too important and comprehensive to be safely left to fallible human beings."

Two other scientists, speaking of the fact that biochemistry has almost in its grasp the power to control men's minds and to determine what the characters of future generations shall be, have remarked that such powers also are too great to be left to undirected applications. And since "fallible human beings" are the only kind likely to be available, the most pessimistic conclusion — namely, that we are in actual fact headed for self-destruction — seems possible at this very moment when our power is greater than any previous age would have dreamed possible. In a somewhat less hopeless mood René Dubos, the distinguished biochemist of the Rockefeller University, wrote an article for the *Saturday Review* of which the thesis is simply that science alone cannot be trusted to determine the future of man and of his civilization.

Readily deductible from the opinions expressed by the authors of *The Year Two-Thousand*, and explicitly expressed by Professor Dubos, is something which the humanist has always maintained; namely, that science cannot make value judgments and therefore can tell us only what can be done, never what we ought to do. The decision concerning what ought to be done or, if you prefer, what it would be wise to do, can be made only by taking into consideration the nature of the human being, his wants and his needs, instead of merely what science can find out and what technology can accomplish. We cannot cease to be fallible human beings but we can become truly *human* beings, not monsters of objectivity concerned only with wealth, power, and determinable facts rather than with the good life for such creatures as we feel ourselves to be.

What all this comes down to can be simply stated: Those of us who call ourselves humanists are no longer reluctantly tolerated but are appealed to and challenged. Often implicitly and sometimes explicitly, we are being asked, "What aid can you give us?"

Perhaps some of us would rather retire to the obscure corner we have occupied for so long than face the challenge. You must, so our one-time enemies demand, tell us (if you can) what truth you profess to know that our science has not been able to reveal and just how you establish the values which should guide us in deciding, not merely what we can do, but what we ought to do. Science has, at least, they go on, made enormous progress in solving the kind of problems it has set itself to solve, but have 2,500 years of philosophy and the arts made any progress at all? Are there any ethical truths or is there any hierarchy of what you call human values more clearly established or more generally accepted than it was in Plato's time? If your answer is, in some sense at least, a simple "no," then what kind of hope can you hold out to us?

Before we can give any sort of answer to that embarrassing question, we must ask ourselves seriously just what we mean by "the humanities" or "the humane studies," for we cannot afford to rest content with those vaguely assumed answers which sometimes reduce the humanities to a collection of merely pleasant fantasies into which we can escape from the realities science has demonstrated. "Do not all charms fly at the touch of cold philosophy?" is a very weak reply, either to those who want our help or those who continue to dismiss us as irrelevant.

We all know what the word "humanist" meant originally: a learned man concerned with worldly rather than with divine things, or more narrowly still, with the literature of Greece and Rome which, not being Christian, was naturally irrelevant to religion. That definition will hardly do, but we might begin by saying that if to the Renaissance the humanities were whatever was not relevant to theology, so to us they are everything which is not and cannot be brought within the purview of science.

Having said that, we may then go on to say what things we do regard as within the purview of science and what remains outside of it, being very careful, as it seems to me we should be, not to represent the humanities by such semi-sciences as sociology and experimental or statistical psychology, both of which make not very satisfactory attempts to answer humanistic questions by the methods of science.

Science, we should be ready to admit, is the only acceptable method of dealing with those things which can be investigated experimentally, and, especially, with those which can be measured. The humanities, on the other hand, include every sort of consideration of those human concerns which cannot be treated experimentally and usually cannot be measured — such as right and wrong, the ugly and the beautiful, the nature of happiness, the characteristics of the good life, and so forth — all of which, as soon as they are enumerated, are seen to be the things with which most men are more immediately concerned than with the facts established by science.

Judge Oliver Wendell Holmes once said that science tells us a great deal about things that are not very important; philosophy a little bit about things which are extremely important. And that statement (or at least the second half of it) should be the motto of the humanist. He must be prepared to admit that as long as he remains within the realm of the humanities and keeps away from the semi-sciences he cannot prove anything, although, as the scientists quoted at the beginning of this discussion are beginning to be willing to admit, the things which cannot be proved, cannot be established scientifically, will in the end determine whether what science has taught us how to do will be in the end a blessing or a curse.

The unregenerate positivist will, of course, reply by declaring that what cannot be proved cannot be useful or more than that sort of pseudo knowledge which has too long plagued mankind with fanciful religions and queer notions concerning the proper conduct of our individual lives and the structure of society. In rebuttal, the humanist should point out that nothing has, fortunately or unfortunately, so greatly affected mankind as those things which the positivist dismisses cavalierly and the absence of which is responsible for precisely the threat which such biologists as Professor Dubos and such students of the future as Messrs. Kahn and Wiener have pointed out. The indisputable fact is simply that though nonscientific thought has never proved the validity of any philosophical system or any hierarchy of values, it has always been responsible for those which have been accepted.

The positivist's ideal, a life where conduct is never influenced by anything except verifiable facts, is simply unrealizable. Everyone will, consciously or not, make many decisions based upon both ethical value judgments and upon preferences which lie without the realm of the scientifically demonstrable. To take an extreme example, there is the case of the Nazis' mass experiments upon Jewish prisoners. There is nothing in the science of medicine which can decide whether or not their actions were legitimate. The difference of opinion between them and most of their American colleagues is simply a difference between the humanities (or anti-humanities) to which they had been exposed. As William James once said, we may philosophize well or ill but philosophize we must. Those who recognize the influence of humane learning upon their nonscientific convictions have examined their convictions. Those who refuse to recognize it simply do not know where they came from or why they hold them.

The humanities prove nothing because the things with which they are primarily concerned are not susceptible to scientific proof. But the humanities can and do *carry convictions*, and they are able to do so because they describe human life in terms which we recognize as true to our own inner experience. Science cannot prove that compassion is better than cruelty. But anyone who has responded to a familiarity with the humanistic tradition knows that for him it is better, however impossible it may be for science to demonstrate the fact.

Such are in very brief and incomplete form some of the reasons why the humanities are important, and especially so in a world which has tended to reject them until, at the present moment, it is beginning to realize that the science and technology to which it has devoted itself seem less and less likely to solve the problems of a deteriorating human condition. It will make a great difference indeed whether it is violent and sadistic movies or great music and literature which convince contemporary man that their implications are true by the light of his experience.

What, then, are some of the conclusions which the humanist may draw concerning his approach to his newly urgent responsibilities? I suggest the following:

1. His emphasis should be on the fact that the humane arts are not primarily ornaments but things essential to any good life, since it is only in the light of the convictions which the humanities have carried that it is possible to make consciously the value judgments we are bound to make for good reasons or for none at all.

2. His emphases should be upon those pure arts which do not pretend to prove anything but rely chiefly upon their ability to carry conviction, rather than upon the quasi-sciences which pretend to demonstrate what cannot be demonstrated.

3. Since all the humanistic arts embody responses to human experiences involving value judgments and the assumption that human life has meaning, he should let them speak for themselves and concentrate upon an examination of the convictions which they imply, rather than upon arguments like those which have been set forth in this article. If art carries conviction, argument or preaching very often inspires resistance instead.

4. In choosing works to be studied, preference should be given to those which conspicuously imply the value judgments which science cannot confirm but which the reader or the observer is most likely either to accept or reject simply because he does or does not recognize in them something corresponding to his own experience. This does not necessarily mean a major stress upon either the classics or the contemporary, but it should recognize the fact that to choose always what the student regards as "relevant" is often to neglect what, in the long run, he might most profit by. One of the aims of education should be to reveal what actually is, though it may not at first seem to be, "relevant."

5. Beware of substituting courses in "communication" or "language arts" for those called literature, philosophy, art, etc. What is most lacking today is not better means of communication but a sounder concept of what is worth communicating. The printed page is the most important means of communication ever invented and any student who does not learn how to take full advantage of it has failed to learn the most important thing schooling can teach. Teaching machines and "audio-visual aids" have their place, but they are impediments to continuing education if they diminish the student's ability to give proper attention to the printed word. Unless he has "learned to read" in the fullest sense of the phrase he will never be more than half educated.

The most complicated computer is very simple by comparison with the human brain, and its responses to questions or its evaluation of answers is bound to be unimaginative almost to the point of imbecility. Can you imagine one asking an intelligent question or appreciating a subtle answer? The more mechanical devices are depended upon, the more they make education a matter of cut and dried facts and "correct" answers, where none such exist in the largest areas of human intelligence and wisdom. In an overpopulated and overcrowded educational system it may be necessary to fall back upon them, but they are a poor substitute for contact with a mind rather than a mind with a machine. We have already gone rather too far in that direction with the multiple-choice examination. Let's not go any further.

27

Instructional Technology and the Curriculum

David Engler

David Engler is concerned with the adaptation of newer media of communication to education. He sees the supposed conflict between humanism and technology as a red herring. He calls for getting on with the use of technology to further humanize education and to achieve the goals of supporters of the humanities. Engler is a vice president for industrial technology in a major publishing firm, McGraw-Hill.

There is a widespread and unfortunate tendency in education these days to regard instructional technology as being synonymous with such things as computers, teaching machines, and audio-visual devices of all sorts, and to express concern about the possibility that the advent of such machines will mechanize and therefore dehumanize education. The image of the machine, cold and impersonal, manipulating our children as it manipulates rats and pigeons in the laboratory, is a haunting reminder of Huxley, Orwell, and others who have painted for us the frightening picture of the demise of humanism.

This is an unfortunate tendency, because in focusing on the machine as a threat to humanistic education, it is pursuing the scent of the red herring and ignoring the real problems of technology, humanism, and their relationship to each other.

Our thesis here is that the conflict between a humanist curriculum and instructional technology is more apparent than real; that it is, in fact, the product of semantic confusion and fuzzy definitions; that it is based on the assumption that we now have a humanistic curriculum but do not utilize instructional technology, an assumption which on both counts is at best debatable and at worst fundamentally erroneous; that, in fact, we must deal with a problem that is not technological but rather is ecological.

Let's consider first our definitions.

Instructional technology is defined in two rather different ways. First, and most commonly, it is defined as hardware — television, motion pictures, audio-tapes and discs, textbooks, blackboards, and so on; essentially, these are

From *Phi Delta Kappan*, March, 1970, 379–381. Reprinted by permission.

implements and media of communication. Second, and more significantly, it is defined as a process by means of which we apply the research findings of the behavioral sciences to the problems of instruction.

Defined either way, instructional technology is value-free. Gutenberg technology, which is widely used but not often recognized as a technology in schools, can produce the Bible, *Mein Kampf*, and *Portnoy's Complaint* with equal indifference. Television can present brilliant insight into the human condition as well as mindless and brutalizing violence with equal clarity. Technology as hardware is neutral. Notwithstanding Marshall McLuhan's preachments to the contrary, the message is the message.

The process of instructional technology is similarly value-free. It can be used to achieve good objectives or bad objectives; it can help to better define objectives and to better measure the achievement of those objectives, but it will work equally well for almost any objective. It is a tool, and like all tools, it is morally and philosophically neutral.

Historically, curriculum, by which we mean the sum total of the content of education, has been largely unaffected by any changes in technology. Motion pictures, radio, phonographs, television, and other widely used hardware have had no significant effect on the curriculum. Where they have been used, it has been to deliver the existing curriculum.

On the other hand, changes in curriculum have rarely required any changes in instructional technology. The vast curriculum reform movement of the past decade led to substantial changes in the goals and the content of many subject matter areas, but virtually all of these reforms relied on the traditional technology. Modern mathematics was taught through the same technology with which traditional mathematics had been taught.

In retrospect, one would be hard put to cite an example of significant curriculum change that was the result of any new technology. This is because decisions about curriculum are largely value judgments, and technology, being value-free, is simply not very meaningful in making such value judgments.

Thus, to raise questions about the conflict between humanism and technology is to tilt at windmills. There can be no curriculum, humanist or otherwise, without some means of delivering instruction to the learner and some strategy that will facilitate learning on his part. There can be no curriculum without an instructional technology. The real question is: Can we devise an instructional technology that will further humanize our curriculum?

To answer this question we must first consider the extent to which our curriculum is now humanistic, as well as the extent to which our prevailing instructional technology facilitates the transmission of that humanistic curriculum from school and society to each individual.

In fact, our society, our times, offer abundant symptoms of a widespread failure of humanism in our educational system. Song My may turn out to be one of the most shattering of these symptoms, but others abound in the crime, racism, alienation, and other sociopathic behavior produced by individuals who are the products of our educational system. If humanism is a significant aspect of our curriculum today, it is not succeeding in humanizing massive numbers of our citizens.

Beyond these social manifestations of the failure of our schools to humanize a significant segment of our population, there is the question of whether or not this failure is the result of an inadequate emphasis on humanism in our curriculum, or an inadequate method of transmitting that humanism to all of our population, or both.

However, to answer the question of whether or not our curriculum is humanistic enough requires one to make value judgments about ideas on which there are many philosophical and ethical differences of opinion among people. That task we shall leave to each individual reader.

The students who picket their university with signs saying, "Do not fold, spindle, or mutilate" bear witness not to the cold impersonality of computers but to the dehumanization that characterizes an educational system which does not value their human individuality. The ghetto dropout bears witness to the same problem. So, in fact, does virtually every youngster who experiences failure in school. Thus, to attempt to transmit a humanistic curriculum by means of a technology that fails to accommodate human individuality is to negate the essence of humanism.

The assumption that our traditional methods of instruction do not constitute a technology seems utterly indefensible. This is so whether one defines technology as a process or as hardware. The most accurate statement one can make about our present methods is that they are an old technology. The basic media of instruction, such as textbooks, chalkboards, and teachers, have been used for many years. Today, teachers are better prepared, textbooks are better written and better designed, and chalkboards have changed color, but their functions and their relationships to learners have not changed essentially in over a hundred years. Moreover, the process by means of which instruction is carried on has not changed in any fundamental respect during this period. It remains teacher-centered, group-oriented, and textbook-based.

It is a technology derived from the impact of an industrial society on the role and methods of education. In its time, it was a technology that contributed enormously to humanizing education by making education accessible to vast numbers of children who had never before had such opportunities. It was a technology designed to implement a curriculum which had as two of its major objectives to raise the level of literacy and to prepare youngsters to function in society as workers and citizens. Its prototype was the Lancasterian model of large-group instruction which developed and spread in Britain and the United States early in the nineteenth century; and while this model has undergone many modifications over the past century and a half, the general configuration of mass-production education remains fundamental to this technology.

The industrial revolution ended in our society many years ago, however, and we are becoming increasingly aware of the fact that we live in a post-industrial society. Our curriculum is changing and will continue to change as our awareness of this reality increases.

What are the factors that lead people to question our present curriculum and its related technology? They include the dwindling social demand for semiliterate and functionally illiterate workers; the concomitant increase in the need for citizens who can cope with the accelerated rate of change that characterizes modern technological society; the emerging realization that there no longer exists a finite body of knowledge constituting at any level what an "educated" individual should know, but that, on the contrary, the so-called knowledge explosion has rendered such a view completely obsolete; the growing recognition that for all citizens education is the *sine qua non* of economic and social adjustment, to say nothing of success; the need for citizens who are capable of bringing critical analysis to bear upon the information aimed at them by government and industry through the powerful and pervasive mass media of communications.

The new curriculum as it develops today and in the years ahead will have to reckon with these factors. It will have to assume responsibility for the successful achievement of its objectives by *every* individual in school. It will have to concentrate on developing the ability to learn instead of imparting a fixed schedule of knowledge. It will have to nurture an independence of mind and related skills of analysis that are all too often missing in the products of our present curriculum.

All of this brings us, at last, to the question of ecology. If we view the ecology of education as the web of relationships between and among learners, teachers, and the environment in which they operate, then it becomes apparent that these relationships are largely defined by the prevailing technology of instruction. Certainly these relationships are not inherent in the individuals or things that are the component parts of education; rather, they are conventions that attach to the traditional goals of education and the methods that are associated with the achievement of those goals.

In the past, many attempts to change education, particularly those attempts to individualize instruction and to develop skills of independent inquiry, have failed because they did not include any mechanism for changing the ecological balance between teachers and learners. Usually, these changes were imposed on the existing ecology in which the teacher leads a group-based lock-step progression through the course of study. This ecology is inevitably characterized by a high degree of active involvement on the part of the teacher and a comparably high degree of passive involvement on the part of the learner. It accepts as normal a distribution of success and failure that can be described by a bell-shaped curve; in fact, results which do not produce a bell-shaped curve often lead teachers to wonder whether or not their objectives and/or tests are too easy or too difficult.

This ecology more often than not results in a fair amount of boredom in students because it often attempts to teach them things they already know; it results in a high degree of frustration in students because it often attempts to teach them things they are not prepared to learn; finally, it tends to produce among the students with whom it is successful the habit of conformity, since that is what produces the highest payoff in grades.

To change the ecology so that each individual can receive the attention and instruction that he needs is obviously no small task. For the institution of the school and for the teacher in particular to assume responsibility for the success of each and every child is to go beyond the scope of the resources presently allocated to education. To transform millions of students who have been well-trained to pass their tests, get their grades, and move on to the next subject into millions of independent learners whose most important rewards come from the pleasures of learning is an undertaking of staggering dimensions. It should be clear to us by now that our present strategies and instruments of instruction, the prevailing instructional technology, cannot provide us with the means for effecting these changes.

Only a new instructional technology can change the existing ecological balance in education. The state of the art in instructional technology is such today that many of the tools and techniques needed to effect such change are available and feasible. We can, for example, by individual, specific diagnosis and instruction eliminate the practice of teaching youngsters what they already know or of teaching them what they are not prepared to learn. We can devise the means and organize the instructional environment to permit individuals to master the basic skills and acquire the basic information that are necessary ingredients of analytical or problem-solving work in most subjects. We can leave to the teacher the functions of diagnosis, evaluation, decision making, and direct, individual interaction with the learner on the level of the higher order intellectual, esthetic, and ethical objectives that are the essential ingredients of a humanistic curriculum.

This technology will require significant changes in how space is utilized in schools, in how time is allotted for each individual, in how progress and achievement are measured, in how materials of instruction are designed and used, in how teachers and learners relate to each other, and, above all, in how learners relate to the process of learning. Instructional technology in the form of hardware will obviously be an ingredient of this ecology, just as it is today; but only instructional technology as process will have the power to alter the ecology of education so that it is more responsive to individual human differences.

The problem is to get off the pursuit of the red herring of conflict between humanism and technology and get on to the task — huge and long-term though it be — of using technology to further humanize education.

E. Changing the Curriculum

28

The Multiple Forces Affecting Curriculum Change

Ronald C. Doll

*A curriculum worker, professor, and administrator who special-
izes in the process of curriculum change, Ronald C. Doll writes
about and participates in curriculum development. Here he examines the current roles of four forces: power, the dollar, growth
and knowledge, and human needs and concerns.*

*Doll is professor of education at Richmond College of the City
University of New York. He is author of* Curriculum Improvement: Decision-Making and Process, *and other works.*

William Van Til, in his foreword to the 1953 yearbook of the Association
for Supervision and Curriculum Development, told of William H. Burton's
attempts during the Forties "to rouse the concern of the educational profession over new developments in forces affecting education."[1] During the
subsequent decade, educators were jarred from their lethargy when practices
in elementary and secondary education were virulently attacked or urgently
criticized. Educator concern about "outside" forces reached a peak after
October, 1957, when the Soviet Union launched its first Sputnik. Within the
decade of the Sixties, both beneficent and hostile influences have continued
to play upon American school systems.

Groups and individuals of varied rheums and viewpoints have, then, for
generations affected American schools. Today those of us in curriculum work
recognize that some agents of forces, and thus some forces themselves, affect
the curriculum intimately and consistently. These special and permanent
forces, with their temporary agents, tend to cause curriculum change, though

From *Phi Delta Kappan*, March, 1970, 382–384. Reprinted by permission.

[1] William Van Til (ed.), *Forces Affecting American Education*, 1953 Yearbook, Association for Supervision and Curriculum Development. Washington, D.C.: The Association,
1953, p. ix.

sometimes they hold it back. Because the curriculum is where people are, the special, permanent forces bringing about and otherwise affecting curriculum change are clearly human. Each force, in its quality of humanness, holds potential for good and potential for evil. Each lies deep in human motivation.

Four forces affecting curriculum change have become especially prominent: 1) the drive for power; 2) the appeal of the dollar; 3) growth in knowledge, with corresponding efforts at evaluating acquisition of knowledge; and 4) the needs and concerns of people in schools, within surrounding social and cultural milieux.[2]

THE DRIVE FOR POWER

Consider people's drive for power over the curriculum. During the Forties, for instance, this drive revealed itself in the urge of a man or a group to speak loudly, to alert other citizens to an alleged danger, to become nationally prominent, or, as we say today, "to shake up the troops." Sometimes the drive had a helpful end; often it seemed only a quest for power for power's sake. During eras of attack on the curriculum, school people tend to think of man's natural drive for power as being malicious and threatening. During quieter, saner moments, they think of the drive for power as a force which could possibly result in improvement.

Within recent years we have seen several major attempts at shifting loci of power over the curriculum. Among them are the following:

1. A push by scholars in the subject fields, often at the expense of professional educators and especially curriculum leaders, to give elementary and secondary school pupils choice content from their fields and, whether incidentally or not, to enhance their own status as curriculum workers.

2. Prods from the far left to promote particular brands of political education, with countering prods from the far right against alleged dangers like sex education and sensitivity training.

3. Militancy by teachers' organizations, which have learned that when one begins to talk about teacher welfare, he must soon discuss organization of schools and children's curricula, both of which matters have previously been in the preserve of boards of education and their administrative staffs.

4. The increasing strength of highly localized community groups, especially in the big cities, at the expense of centralized control of schools.

5. The militant behavior of youth, beginning in the colleges and moving to the secondary schools.

6. The new thrust of quasi-governmental regional or national agencies, like the Education Commission of the States, which have developed prestige and sometimes real power.

7. Forays toward control of the curriculum by the United States Office of

---

[2] Students in the course 76.701, Supervision and the Improvement of Instruction, winter semester, 1969–1970, at Richmond College have helped in defining these forces.

Education and other federal agencies, at the expense of state departments of education and local school districts.

8. Campaigns for a black curriculum and, to a minor degree, a red curriculum, a Puerto Rican curriculum, a Mexican-American curriculum, and so on.

While systems and formal arrangements for decision making about the curriculum have not materially changed during the 1960's, the persons who have initiated and sanctioned curriculum ideas have often come from groups other than teachers, administrators, and school board members. Power has shifted, in part, to scholars in the subject fields, conductors of summer in-service institutes, people who complain most loudly, those who have special programs to promote, the inner councils of teachers' unions and associations, self-appointed community leaders, paraprofessionals and other climbers on career ladders, designers and reviewers of project proposals, bureaucrats at state and federal levels of government, and specialists at sitting-in, impeding, and taking over meetings for decision making. These individuals and groups have sought power in obvious, open ways. Other quieter participants in a new drive for power, like owners of wealth and persons high in the power structures of communities, have also been at work.

Inasmuch as every action is likely to trigger a corresponding reaction, vocal demands for power have made current wielders of power "run scared." After making some initial resistance, the currently powerful have often said in effect, "Oh, all right, let *them* try to improve things. They'll soon find out how complex the whole problem is!" A consequence of this viewpoint has been a bending of the decision-making system so that decisions which are less-than-legal and sometimes — though not always — poorer than before have eventuated. In exercising their new-found power to make curriculum decisions, inexperienced participants have inevitably gained a certain amount of valuable experience.

The Appeal of the Dollar

A second fundamental force which has affected curriculum change in the United States is the strong appeal which money has for curriculum makers in a materialistic society. Always in need of funds to do what they have wanted to do for children, curriculum personnel have found a bonanza in grants-in-aid, which have frequently proved to be mixed blessings. Whereas under a time-honored arrangement school boards and administrators waited for all their funds to be sent them by tax collectors, state finance officers, and (sometimes) federal agencies, school officials have become seekers of special grants to augment school district income.

State governments, along with accrediting agencies, still have something to say about ways in which funds are to be used for supporting and expanding the curriculum. But state regulations concerning the curriculum have always been fewer than classroom teachers or laymen have realized. For example, the states have often limited subject requirements in elementary schools to reading, writing, arithmetic, and health, while subject requirements in secondary schools may consist only of English, American history, and health. In the language of school administrators, state aid has been almost exclusively "general" and therefore usable largely at the discretion of personnel in local districts.

On the other hand, financial aid supplied during recent years by the federal government has frequently been earmarked, designated, or "categorical." Both acts of the Congress concerning education and guidelines prepared by private foundations have so predetermined the scope, direction, and precise nature of curriculum reform supported by the federal government and independent grantors that these agencies have been said by some school officials to stifle creativeness and skill development among local planners, as well as to cause excessive dependence on persons who are geographically remote and have little understanding of pupil needs in local districts.[3]

While grants have emphasized, for example, particularized cognitive development and special attention to poverty areas, producers of educational materials have sought financial profit through new educational ideas and the increase in child population. The appeal of the dollar for these producers has brought a flood of instructional materials which are conditioning, increasingly, what children learn. Thus one may say that both the curriculum hobbies of grantors and the sales promotion schemes of businessmen are now having unprecedented impact on curriculum decision making. Priorities in the curriculum have been realigned as control has continued to follow the dollar.

GROWTH IN KNOWLEDGE

A third force persistently affecting curriculum change is growth in knowledge, which formerly occurred slowly and quite steadily but now shows marked, erratic bursts of speed. The teacher is no longer able to "cover the book." Instead, many books now cover the teacher. The eight-to-12-year doubling of knowledge in the natural sciences which Robert Oppenheimer noted has not been duplicated in other subject fields. Nevertheless, knowledge abounds embarrassingly in all fields, so that Herbert Spencer's question, "What knowledge is of most worth?" becomes more and more pertinent. Against a backdrop of educational objectives, curriculum planners are forced to seek new answers to Spencer's question.

Apparently the well-advertised reforms in subject matter content, sponsored by national curriculum projects, have not affected the achievement of pupils in American schools as much as sponsors had hoped they would. But the public seems to be convinced that after "softness" in the schools had been revealed during the Fifties, a subsequent period of "hardness" brought reassuring improvement in the curriculum. Interestingly, though the schools were blamed in 1957 for our failure to keep up with the Russians' space program, few persons have seriously credited teachers with helping to put men on the moon.

---

[3] See, for instance, Galen Saylor, "The Federal Colossus in Education — Threat or Promise?" *Educational Leadership*, October, 1965, pp. 7–14.

Though the scholars in subject fields have failed to affect the curriculum as thoroughly as they have wished, in part because they have not faced the hard, human problems in curriculum change, they have shown new interest in ideas which have been talked about for a long time: experimentation, discovery, acquisition of meaning, inquiry, development of major concepts, and intellectual excitement. Our experience with organizing human knowledge for teaching now suggests the need to team academic scholars with curriculum specialists, behavioral scientists, and specialists in research and evaluation.

With increased growth of knowledge have come definite attitudes toward the effects of its growth. While one of these attitudes has been concern with how to sort out elements of knowledge and place them within the curriculum, another attitude has been fear that even the former elements are not being learned. Hence a flurry of effort at evaluation and assessment. Enter, for instance, national assessment, research and development centers, and new contracts for firms which develop and sell tests.

Proponents of national assessment have declared its purpose to be evaluation of educational performance as a means of gauging strengths and weaknesses in schooling and of assisting research. It could, under the wrong conditions, become a direct determiner of the curriculum in the same way that Regents Examinations have been one of the determiners of the high school curriculum in New York State. Dangers in the current anxiety about evaluation may well include confusion of means and ends in the curriculum, pressures which pupils and teachers feel in preparing for major examinations, and a tendency to sacrifice all-round development of children to a new set of remote goals. Though the elementary and secondary schools obviously did not cause the current burgeoning of knowledge, they are seriously caught up in its effects.

THE NEEDS OF PEOPLE IN SCHOOL

A fourth major force affecting curriculum change is the needs and concerns of pupils, teachers, administrators, parents, and other persons who work together to provide the best education for children. To dedicated educators, this is the most satisfying, meaningful force with which they deal. Always the real needs and concerns of people have part of their foundation in societal, subcultural, and community milieux. Therefore, parents and other community members should be expected to contribute to in-school education and to education beyond the confines of the school. The experiences children have in schools must be related increasingly to the life space of youngsters throughout the day.

Findings in human development and learning and in the impact of social and cultural influences on learners have been accumulating throughout the twentieth century. Very recently, we have come to realize more poignantly what various forms of disadvantage do to children. An economic order assisted by a new technology requires that pupils be introduced to new sets of skills. Experiments in urban education call for us to face live social problems. Furthermore, the current crisis in values makes us seek better ways of educating in the affective domain. Attempts at shaping human behavior through reinforcement are being made by one school of psychologists, though these attempts are being opposed by other psychologists and educators. More encouraging views of human potential are being expressed; clearer understandings of cognitive development are seen as having important applications in curriculum making. Curriculum workers are striving to develop pupil experiences which use children's learning styles, stimulate learners intellectually, offer them new opportunities for success, encourage their reasoning and critical thinking, help them understand other persons, help them clarify their values, and increase their ability to cope with their world in other ways. All in all, we live in an exciting era for attending to the needs and concerns of people in schools, within changing social and cultural contexts.

A major concern of teachers and administrators is for pre-service and in-service development of teaching skills which will help teachers do their best in classrooms. Studies of the teaching act which have resulted in more than two dozen ways of analyzing teaching give promise of indicating new emphases in teacher education and educational supervision.

THE INTERRELATIONSHIP OF FORCES

Curriculum leaders find that the four prominent forces which have been discussed above sometimes become merged and blurred because human motivation is almost never single or pure. Actions which are taken by professionally minded teachers for the good of children may be aided, for instance, by teaching devices manufactured by profit seekers and by ideas developed by power-hungry community groups. Is it possible that when a society begins to age and to become more complex, the impact of single forces on the curriculum of its schools become less clear-cut and distinctive by combining at times into a major, fused force? If so, discussions of "outside forces" versus "inside" or institutional ones become unreal, and efforts to identify separate forces according to any criteria become more difficult.

29

Who Changes the Curriculum and How?

Muriel Crosby

Muriel Crosby has been a forthright and courageous practitioner of human relations education in the inner cities. Here she appraises curriculum changes and failures to change, examines the present active change agents, and calls for professional educators to exert leadership, especially in identifying the roles and functions of agents and forces now pressing for curriculum changes.

Miss Crosby is one of America's most active and devoted women educators. She served as president of the National Council of Teachers of English in 1966 and two years later was president of the Association for Supervision and Curriculum Development. In 1965 she received the Brotherhood Award from the National Conference of Christians and Jews. From 1951 to 1967 Miss Crosby was an assistant and associate superintendent of the Wilmington, Del., public schools. She retired from administration in 1968 after serving one year as acting superintendent, and is now a consultant in urban education.

The title, "Who Changes the Curriculum and How?" implicitly recognizes, first, that the curriculum *does* change, and second, that there is some doubt about where the responsibility lies and with whom. I propose to explore here the status of change and, more important, to discover the forces — whether issues, institutions, or people — which impinge upon the curriculum as change agents.

THE STATUS OF CHANGE

In the not too distant past, the professional educator looked upon the curriculum as *his* business. As a matter of fact, this claim is still prevalent among many educators today. Even in the past, the educator often claimed exclusive credit for bringing about changes which were largely the result of various other forces.

Until mid-twentieth century, the gap between effective education and the

From *Phi Delta Kappan*, March, 1970, 385–389. Reprinted by permission.

life needs of the American people was not great. Social change was slow; old value systems of a class and caste society prevailed; and while new value systems were emerging, the rate of change was moderate and not always consciously discernible.

The speedup of social change has become the eye of the hurricane. Following the Supreme Court decision on the desegregation of public schools, a series of events has focused the attention of the nation upon its greatest social revolution. Paralleling this social movement in the late 1950's were the attainments in atomic and space sciences by a competitive foreign power which brought recognition of threat to national survival.

The immediate reaction was a national look at the public schools — and they were found wanting. This judgment of the schools was in part realistic and in part the guilty conscience of a nation in search of a scapegoat.

That education then and throughout the 1960's has not been as effective as needed is supported by recognition of the condition of millions of poverty-bound citizens lacking the means of earning a living, by the prevalence of prejudice which has reduced millions of citizens to human degradation, and by the permeation of political institutions by corruption. While public education has not been totally responsible for these conditions, it must carry a share of the blame.

On the other hand, some of the measures of the effectiveness of education, and a refutation of blanket indictment of the public schools, can be found in the intellectual accomplishments of a people whose technology and space science conquests stagger the imagination, and whose economic standard of living exceeds that of any nation in the world. Certainly it would be hard to deny that education has had something to do with these achievements.

Where do the schools stand, then, in terms of a realistic perspective of their capacity for change? What must be the nature of change? And who is responsible for creating curriculum change which will enable the schools to fulfill their role as change agent in the life of the nation?

THE CHARGE OF FAILURE

Those who look upon the schools and find them wanting often make their judgments in the context of personal experience, opinion, or belief.

Billy has trouble learning to read and his parents generalize, "The schools don't know how to teach reading. When we went to school, *we* learned. These newfangled methods aren't any good."

Pastor Smith is indignant at the thought of sex education as a part of the school curriculum. "Sex education is ruining the morals of our children. We should remove our children from the public schools."

Some adolescents, severely retarded educationally, most of them almost totally deficient in command of their native standard English, boycott their school because Swahili is not included in the curriculum.

A twelve-year-old girl, nursing her five-month-old infant, deeply involved in a black power group which is spearheading a movement for racially segregated schools, claims that their racially integrated school is not "relevant."

A group of parents, dismayed at the racially changing enrollment of their neighborhood school, transfer their children to a private school, explaining that the public school has "watered down the curriculum and lowered its standards."

These examples of criticism of the effectiveness of public education are a sampling of endless similar occurrences reflecting a need for a realistic analysis of the multiple motivations behind them, in which the schools are often made the scapegoat of society and the recipient of hostility toward conditions not always controlled by the schools.

But the evidence of failure is frequently more pertinent, more realistic. That the pace and quality of change in curriculum leaves something to be desired is a fact supported by objective evidence.

In a study conducted by the Educational Testing Service of Princeton, New Jersey, covering 38,000 students from more than 7,500 academic high schools who took the College Entrance Examination Board achievement tests during 1965–66, it was found that more important changes had occurred in secondary school curriculum and teaching methods during the previous 10 years than in any earlier decade studied. Innovations having substantial effect were found in the teaching of mathematics and science. However, it was found that the teaching of history and social sciences had remained substantially the same in the last 10 years. Changes in English curriculum were reported as only moderate, with most English teachers still including the traditional authors such as Dickens, Twain, and Chaucer, and traditional anthologies, while few included contemporary authors found popular among the students, such as Golding, Tennessee Williams, Harper Lee, and Salinger.

The National Council of Teachers of English, in its studies of change in English curriculum and teaching methods in American high schools, found significant change in relatively few schools. Its study of the effectiveness of programs for the disadvantaged on all educational levels produced evidence of little change. The results of such programs can only be described as depressing.

Where quality curriculum change has occurred, it can be found chiefly in the major fields commanding national interest and financial support, those of mathematics and science. It is a sad commentary on the value systems of government and private foundations that no major thrust for human development, in which the social sciences and the English language could be most influential, has yet developed. While millions of dollars have gone into compensatory programs for the poverty-bound, failure to focus on language development as a major means of achieving personal development and economic self-sufficiency is probably the chief weakness of these programs and underlies, in my judgment, the failure of compensatory programs, admitted by the National Advisory Council on Education of Disadvantaged Children in January, 1969. Of some 1,000 programs studied, only 20 had produced a significant measure of academic achievement.

In summary, as we assess the charges of failure in curriculum change, it is realistic to conclude that the gap between social change and educational change has widened; that significant change is a characteristic of relatively few schools; that education for the 1970's must become a stimulant to and a means of achieving desirable social change, instead of dragging its feet behind forced change; and that those most vocal in their criticism are often motivated by factors which may restrict rather than release the potential capacity for schools to effect change in curricula.

CHANGE AGENTS

The present status of the curriculum, its weaknesses and its strengths, may be comprehended in some measure by examining current change agents at work.

Accrediting Agencies. An evaluation committee from a regional accrediting agency met with the staff of the science department in a large urban high school. It had previously visited classes and talked with teachers and youngsters. The committee expressed its concern over the modifications made by the teachers who were using materials from a science program, nationally famous, which had been developed by an organization of science scholars. The teachers explained that the ability level characteristic of the student body had changed during the last few years. The school had formerly sent 90 percent of its students on to college; now only 30 percent could be expected to gain admission. A large number of the students were severely handicapped, educationally and economically. The adaptations in the science program were necessary, the science teachers felt, in terms of the abilities and needs of the students presently enrolled. When the evaluation report was made by the accrediting agency, the high school's science department received a very low rating, with the explanation that modifications of the science program were unjustified.

While accrediting agencies have served a useful purpose in stimulating the upgrading of secondary education for many years, those schools which have participated have recognized that the basic premise upon which they are evaluated (that is, an assessment of the school in terms of *its* stated philosophy) is a fiction. Most evaluation committees have their own very definite convictions and biases which are reflected in the ultimate evaluation of a school. The pressure for accreditation, in a very real sense, frequently makes schools accommodate to the judgments of the accrediting agency. It can be claimed with reasonable validity that accrediting agencies are change agents, for few modern secondary schools can afford to risk their accreditation.

Universities. A group of social scientists and elementary teacher advisers spend a summer on campus, planning a new curriculum in economics education. In meeting with a consultant, they define concepts, select informational material, and identify activities for children which should lead to the development of the concepts identified. But the biggest problem, the group explains, and one for which a consultant's help is solicited, is how to "sell" it to the teachers in surrounding school districts. The project is financed through funds from the federal government and a private foundation interested in economics education and the perpetuation of the private enterprise system.

Universities harbor a vast number of staff members committed to the implementation of a range of theories in the spectrum of disciplines or subjects they teach. With the emphasis placed upon research as a mark of the modern university, it is natural, then, for these researchers to seek a proving ground, and the proving ground is usually one or more neighboring public school districts. Participation by schools often serves as a stimulus to desirable change. The fly in the ointment, however, is the fallacious concept held by many university staffs that schools can be more effective by adopting a "university-built curriculum." There is little doubt that universities look upon themselves as change agents whose effectiveness is facilitated or blocked by the degree of "cooperation" obtained from the public schools. For many schools, the neighboring university acts as change agent.

The Franchise Industry. *The National Observer*, in its February 26, 1969, issue, reported on plans by the franchise industry to turn its sights on nursery schools, specifically on the plan of Performance Systems, Inc., formerly Minnie Pearl's Chicken System, Inc., to open pre-school educational centers, beginning with its first center in Nashville, Tennessee, in the fall of 1969, and expanding to 1,000 in a nationwide operation within three years. The backers of the plan believe that the care and teaching of three- to six-year-old children can be organized and sold with the same techniques so successfully used to sell fried chicken.

The incompatibility of quality education and financial profit leaves little doubt that the curriculum of franchised nursery schools will be seriously affected; moreover, the "armchair educator" concept is raised to its zenith and those who become Chicken Little will know for a certainty that "the sky is falling." The free enterprise system has injected itself into the role of change agent for early childhood education and the results can only be awaited with trepidation.

Big Brother. On August 1, 1969, *Education U.S.A.*, in its *Washington Monitor*, quoted a major policy decision by U.S. Commissioner of Education James E. Allen: "Strong advocacy for relevance and change will become a central thrust of federal efforts in education."

Lest the unwary be overly optimistic, it is important to examine the federal government's traditional interpretation of the term "relevance." As one example among many, we might consider vocational education.

In the late nineteenth century, the government decided that vocational education was "relevant" and instituted its now historic financial support in the context of controls to assure effective preparation of the "workingman."

Justly or unjustly, supporters of vocational education are claimed to constitute the most powerful of the educational lobbyists in Washington, and there is little doubt that the funds appropriated for training in occupations, trades, and related jobs greatly exceed those for any other single type of specialized education.

It is reasonable to ask: "How effective is vocational education today under the aegis of a Big Brother who cares?" The first annual report of the newly created National Advisory Council on Vocational Education is a blistering attack on the vocational education programs of the nation's schools. Claiming that 25 percent of the youth who turn 18 each year are not educated to a level of adequate employability, the council report closes with this appeal: "We believe the reform American schools so desperately need will not come about if the federal government continues to invest nearly $4 in remedial manpower programs for every $1 it invests in preventive programs." And, of course, this "appeal" is reinforced by a request for even greater expenditures by the federal government for effective change.

I suggest that "buying more of the same thing that hasn't worked to begin with," a common approach in the funding of federally supported educational programs and projects, is not the answer to the millions of potential workers from America's minorities, but rather that the solution to this problem may be found by the simple strategy of delegating to local communities the right to determine what is relevant education for the people who live there.

In another educational arena we find the federal government rightly aware of its responsibility to make an accounting to taxpayers on its investments in education. Into every project proposal for funds submitted by schools and universities, great emphasis on "objective" evaluation must be injected. As an originator of many proposals for one school system, as a consultant for hundreds of school systems engaged in federally funded projects, and as a past evaluator for the U.S. Office of Education in advising the allocation of funds for projects submitted under the Civil Rights Act and NDEA, I have yet to see one project approved that did not require "statistical" evaluation. Subjective evidence is discouraged or infrequently allowed as a bit of frosting on the cake.

This failure to recognize subjective evidence and to develop strategies to make it respectable is perhaps the greatest weakness found in the testing instruments developed to date for the National Assessment of Education Program, now under way. The now famous battle against national assessment, aimed at the secrecy with which it was conceived and initiated, was equally a protest against the exclusively statistical approach to evaluating the quality of education and the very real threat of eventual curriculum conformity on a national basis.

That evaluative processes and instruments may be a potent block to innovation in education is supported by the recent report of the National Advisory Council on Education Professions Development. It charges that "meaningless evaluation is ruining the cutting edge of educational innovation," that "truly significant improvements in education come from attacking educational problems in new ways with imagination and daring," and that "there is an almost total preoccupation with so-called 'hard data' developed by the mass use of standardized tests." It further points out "the folly of requiring all projects to conduct full-scale evaluations, even when funds are scarce."

That curriculum workers are in a bind created by a number of forces at work, including the federal government, is the major focus of the January 1969 issue of *Educational Leadership* (journal of the Association for Supervision and Curriculum Development). Writing on the subject, "Captive to Funded Projects" (federal), Galen Saylor pungently points up the problems created by federal funding of projects all of which have direct or indirect influence on the nature and quality of curriculum change:

1. Extreme bias in determining the projects to be funded.
2. Uncertainty of continuity in project development and completion.
3. Unwarranted requirements in preparing applications for funds, with specific reference to procedures and evaluation.
4. Improper emphasis on certain aspects of the educational program which affect balance in the curriculum.
5. Multiplicity of funding agencies within the government and the ineptness of many local community agencies which control funds and how they will be used.

State Legislatures. State legislative bodies have always had an indirect influence on the quality of education through school budget legislation for the education of children and youth. This is a legitimate function of state legislatures. In recent years, however, there have been increasing instances of the attempt of lawmakers to administer the schools and determine the curriculum. Neither of these functions is legitimate. They have been achieved by elimination of specific educational staff positions and by withholding funds for specific programs. "Driver education" has been particularly an "on again, off again" program in many secondary schools, and the current drive of right-wing extremists to prohibit sex education in the curriculum poses a dangerous threat to those communities concerned with genuine relevance in education. One example of many suffices: *The Washington Star*, August 20, 1969, described current efforts to eliminate sex education in the Maryland schools and reported an announcement by a state senator of his plans to introduce a bill during the next Maryland General Assembly session to place a three-year moratorium on sex education courses in Maryland schools.

It can be rightfully claimed that state legislatures have wrongfully assumed the responsibility for many restrictive measures which have blocked effective curriculum change in the schools of the nation. One such measure which created an educational furor, both in and out of California, was the requirement that every child in the state's public elementary schools study a foreign language. That qualified teachers were not available and that many children were unable to participate in such a program were not considered by the legislators. California is not alone in its restrictive curriculum legislation.

Dissenters. All facets of American life have felt the force of dissension. The variety of dissenters proliferates at an amazing speed, and the schools have been caught in the middle between right- and left-wingers whose goals are completely opposite.

From college campus through junior high school, students are forcing an awareness upon educators that they must be recognized in all aspects of education decision making. While much of the focus of student demands is centered on the student's out-of-class activities, his right to control his time, behavior, and activities, while most of the protest is against administration and its policy-making function, many of the demands are curriculum-centered, focusing on curriculum content, the right to choose courses and teachers, and the right to waive admission requirements. To date, schools and colleges have largely met these demands by either complete capitulation or punitive measures. The result has been chaos.

Teachers are emerging as a significant factor in dissension. While pursuing their right to negotiate for better salaries and improvement in conditions for teaching such as class size, student load, and adequate materials of instruction, they frequently make curriculum demands which could lead to a de-professionalization of teaching. One recent contract gives the teacher the right to eliminate planning; another limits conferences and educational meetings to one per month of an hour's duration. One of the emerging controversies which faces the schools is the possible confrontation between students and staff when the right of the students to determine what shall be taught and how it shall be taught runs head-on into the academic freedom of teachers. A polarization of rights is in the offing.

A recent Gallup survey (February, 1969) revealed that the public "was so uninformed about educational innovation and so lacking in objective ways of judging school achievement that little, if any, pressure is exerted by them to make improvements or is likely to be exerted until they are more knowledgeable in this area."

This finding may well be true in certain types of communities which have not felt the pressures of demands by minority groups. In highly urbanized areas where minority groups are concentrated, the reverse is true. The major cities of the country offer numerous examples of action by minority group parents to shape the educational program, to determine curriculum, to hire and fire teachers and principals, and to administer the schools. Sometimes the action is of a retaliatory nature against "the establishment." Often, it represents real parental concern and disenchantment with the quality of education their children are receiving. In either case, the methods used to resolve the problem often result in school and community disorganization.

These illustrations of change agents having power to affect curriculum and the quality of education serve to highlight the critical nature of the basic issue: "Who *should* change the curriculum and how?" This is the real problem facing the school of the Seventies.

RESPONSIBILITY FOR CURRICULUM CHANGE

The public schools of the nation have been characterized as a barometer of public concern with the social issues of the time. Never has this characterization been more true than since the Supreme Court decision of 1954 on the desegregation of public schools. Those of us who have been on the front line of this greatest of social revolutions know that the expectations held for the public schools have been traumatic in their effect upon school staffs.

It is true, too, that great social issues become the matrix in which political forces function. To some of us, the schools seem to be the pawn in a political chess game. If this is so, those of us who call ourselves professional educators are largely responsible. In the long struggle to professionalize teaching we have neglected the teacher, practicing a paternalism which has led to the current teacher revolution. Yet the teacher working with youngsters is the real determinant of curriculum change.

In trying to create a profession, we have largely ignored the fundamental prerequisite for needed curriculum change by avoiding curriculum research and its findings, upon which theories to guide and steer change must be based. Without a sound base for change, we blow with the wind, lacking educational purpose and direction.

Our insecurity has held us behind the walls of the school and we have kept parents and community at arm's length. Yet parents have a rightful role in the education of their children.

If education is to become what it must, the prime instrument for social change, if it is to meet its responsibility for enabling the American people to achieve their political dream of social, economic, and human equality, the professional educator must give direction to an identification of roles and functions properly associated with parents, students, community agencies and groups, government, and the professional staff.

The true professional does not "resign" from his profession to become nursemaid to a machine. The true professional knows how to involve the many groups who must have a voice in education, but he remains in control of curriculum change. The true professional recognizes the danger of mistaking innovative proposals for change. He knows that proposed innovation is just an initiation of possible change and does not result in change until it reaches the supportive level of teachers in the classroom. The true professional knows that the education of human beings is much more than "reaching grade level" in reading. Curriculum change is "people change."

The educated man is one whose behavior is guided by self-insight and a value system he can live with. The educated man is able to put his knowledge, skills, sensitivities, and imagination to work on the solution of human problems. To develop the educated man is the task of the school of the Seventies.

Many people, institutions, organizations, and issues will contribute to the curriculum change demanded by a new world. Only the teacher can effect this change. Whatever the nature of political power and its impact on educational direction, there is a "constant" in the scene: the role of the teacher in bringing about curriculum change.

Nations, like men, are seeking an identity, a character, shaped by the great moments of their past. They are today creating a past for generations, who will look backward in their search for directions for their future. Carlos Romulo has said that "We must look to teachers — the teachers in every land — to provide educational leadership for a free world. We must look to the teachers to show young people that the goal of men must not be war — but peace — that the purpose of men is not hatred but friendship, and the happiness of nations lies not in dominance, but in harmony. We look to the teachers to give us knowledge without which mere technical information can be dangerous."

F. Looking to the Future

30

A Curriculum Continuum: Possible Trends in the 70's

Harold G. Shane

Harold G. Shane is a specialist in elementary education and a versatile writer on a variety of educational issues. Increasingly, he has been dedicating his energy to analysis of alternative futures for American society and American education. He calls for a curriculum continuum, "an unbroken flow of experiences planned with and for the individual learner throughout his contacts with the school."

Shane is university professor of education at Indiana University, where he was formerly dean of the School of Education. Author of dozens of books and articles, his recent major works include publications on improving language arts instruction and linguistics for the classroom teacher.

For generations most education in the U.S. has been divided into arbitrary segments. It also has been given labels such as "the elementary school" and "the secondary school." A century or more ago, in view of what was then known about teaching and learning, and when the school population was expanding rapidly in urban centers, such grade-level divisions instituted for administrative purposes made a great deal of sense. However, education now has reached a level of sophistication at which serious thought can and should be given to the development of a carefully reasoned and well-designed continuum of experience for the learner, one which can replace the disjointed divisions of the past and present.

Such a curriculum continuum presumably would provide an unbroken chain of ventures and adventures in meaningful learning, beginning with early childhood education. It would extend through post-secondary education and on into later-life education.

Urgent priority should be given to studying and experimenting with the development of genuine continuity in education for several reasons. First,

From *Phi Delta Kappan*, March, 1970, 389–392. Reprinted by permission.

learning itself is a continuous process. It begins no later than at birth and extends through time until one ultimately learns the meaning of death. Since the input of experience is continuous, there is no reason for sectioning the curriculum into four- or six-year time blocks and for "keeping school" on the basis of a nine- or 10-month academic year.

Second, we have been wasting our time. Despite decades of talk about "articulating" the units of public education, this objective has never been achieved because it *cannot* be achieved. We have simply squandered our time and energy on refining the errors inherent in the graded school when we should have thrown away the "graded" and "segmented" concepts years ago.

Third, if we intend seriously to improve the psychology of teaching and learning (a task which is difficult enough in itself), we need to remove the uncoordinated divisions which presently serve as barriers or hurdles to the educational progress of children and youth.

A fourth reason for giving priority to the task of bringing continuity to education is perhaps more subtle than the first three. The challenge of building a sound, well-conceived curriculum continuum is one *which can help educators to find themselves* in a confused and confusing culture. Today most educators over 30 years old are pioneers in a new, unfamiliar pedagogical world. Whether we be elementary teachers or college deans, all of us have three educational deficiencies carried over from the pre-1940 period to overcome: 1) an experientially limited, hence inaccurate, concept of the past, 2) a perception of the present diminished by our incomplete auditory and visual input related to education during the last three decades, and 3) a concept of possible educational futures which is defective because it is based on faulty, linear projections of the past into tomorrow.[1]

As we move toward better continuity, the implications for changes in contemporary, arbitrary segments of education (such as the secondary school) become tremendous. Indeed, as the curriculum continuum becomes a reality, such divisions as the elementary school and the secondary school will literally cease to exist as academic or administrative units. Since this may strike some persons in elementary and secondary education alike as a draconian type of educational reform, careful heed must be given to an explanation of the nature of the curriculum continuum concept, its psychological value, and the desirable changes toward which increased continuity can carry educational practice.

WHAT IS A CURRICULUM CONTINUUM?

As indicated above, an educational or curriculum continuum may be described as an unbroken flow of experiences planned with and for the individual learner throughout his contacts with the school. Much current thought and research suggests that the program should begin no later than in early childhood and should continue to provide educational opportunities as long as the school has anything to offer the learner. In other words, persons in

[1] For example, the "over-thirties" in education are likely to think of the computer as an addition to our stockpile of resources in the education warehouse rather than as the foundation for an entirely new warehouse.

their sixties or even older would be served methodically when the continuum concept is eventually extended to its upper ranges.

Continuity in learning implies that schooling shall extend throughout the year. Furthermore, it may begin officially at any time during the year that a child is deemed mature enough to be present (e.g., at age three), not at a legislated date such as "by the year in which he becomes six years of age on or before midnight on the 30th of November." Vacation periods would be scheduled at any time during the calendar year and for any length of time upon which agreement was reached. This would constitute no problem when the young learner is assigned to a team of teachers rather than to grade level or to a class. Teachers likewise could be off-duty during any interval for study, travel, rest, and so on. Deliberate "overstaffing," i.e., five teachers attached to a basic four-teacher unit or team, would permit one to engage in non-teaching activities in February just as readily as in July.

In a curriculum continuum, educational experiences also are personalized. The *personalized* curriculum differs from *individualized* instruction in at least one major respect. Individualized instruction, which has been attempted for many years, was intended to help a child meet group norms or standards, but at his own rate of progress.[2] The personalized curriculum continuum serves as a means of making the school's total resources available to a child so that his teachers can figuratively help him to "create himself" without reference to what his "average" chronological age-mates may be accomplishing.

The meaning of a personalized continuum type of curriculum can be clarified further by means of literary allusion. The curriculum of the 1930-vintage graded school was one in which the child was forced to fit the program. That is, it was analogous to the mythological bed of Procrustes. This was an iron bedstead on which the ancient, unfriendly Greek giant bound the unwary traveler, then cut off his victim's legs, or stretched them to fit.

The individualized, and sometimes nongraded, approach to instruction was a distinct improvement, since it endeavored to shorten or lengthen the Procrustean bed to fit the child. The personalized curriculum continuum, on the other hand, is one in which the child, with teacher guidance, is encouraged — indeed expected — *to build his own bed.*

Some Psychological Values of the Continuum Concept

"Continuity" in education is not merely a mechanical or organizational plan for locking together or more closely articulating the present arbitrary units of education which precede and follow the secondary school years. Rather, in many ways, it is psychological concept, a way of conceiving the learner's ongoing experiences as a smoothly flowing stream with an "educational current" that is properly paced to match the skill and speed with which he can ride its eddies and rapids.

[2] In the "Winnetka Plan" as begun by Carleton W. Washburne, for instance, the curriculum was basically the same for all children in a given grade, but the *rate* of progress varied. The rapid learner was kept from moving beyond the company of his age-mates by providing him with enrichment activities and similar paracurricular experiences.

In a school characterized by the psychologically supportive qualities of the continuum, the learner begins to find answers to three questions which during the past decade have begun to be recognized as queries of basic importance:

1. "Who am I?" (self-identity)
2. "What am I doing?" (self-orientation)
3. "Where am I going? (self-direction)

Self-awareness and, hopefully, a wholesome self-concept are developed as answers are found to question one. Through seeking and gradually acquiring an answer to point two, the learner progressively "finds himself" in the process of searching for inner integrity. He likewise develops the skills of social interaction and the coping behaviors in which self-confidence resides. Finally, in discovering answers to question three the learner establishes a personal compass course or sets in motion an inner gyroscope which, if all goes well, leads to desirable personal-social contributions, to acceptance by others, and to consequent personal happiness.

It may be conjectured that only through a personalized curriculum continuum can we construct a humane educational milieu or matrix in which the learner can safely, and with a sense of security, *discover* the world and *create* himself. We do not know enough, we cannot clearly predict enough, of the twenty-first century world (in which the infant, child, or adolescent of the 1970's will spend the larger portion of his lifetime) to gamble on a less flexible concept of the curriculum than the one proposed here. We must eschew in the realm of content the impossible dream of *what* explicit fundamentals children and youth shall learn; we must espouse the more tangible goal of teaching them *how* to learn.

And we ourselves need to unlearn the unexamined educational *beliefs* that often guide our conduct, while striving to learn the value that resides in *believing* in what education can accomplish.

NEW DIRECTIONS TOWARD WHICH CONTINUITY IN EDUCATION CAN LEAD

In the years immediately ahead, the educational world seems likely to continue to be invigorated by continued change. Probable future developments which research and trend-projection suggest include substantial increases in whatever it is that I.Q. tests measure, in the continued spread of man's 13 major languages (especially English, Spanish, Mandarin, and Russian), and the development of a phonetic English alphabet with approximately 30 consonants and 15 vowels. The schools also seem likely to be influenced by major improvements in the status of women, by legislation requiring compulsory psychiatry, by a five- or six-hour day and an eight-month working year, and by the growing need to cope with problems stemming from overbreeding, pollution, accumulating garbage and diminishing resources, and man's ancient propensity for attempting to settle his disputes through warfare.

To the exciting and sometimes unnerving educational mix of the future, bona fide continuity in the curriculum *is* likely to bring further vitality. To illustrate, in schools with a curriculum continuum:

There would be no failure or "double promotion." One learner would merely live differently, and at a different rate, from others.

"Special education" and "remedial work" would cease to exist. All education of all learners would be "special," regardless of whether they were handicapped, gifted, or in the wide "normal" range between.

Annual promotion would become a thing of the past. What we now speak of as promotion would become a *direction* rather than a yearly hurdle.

There would be no dropouts. At present we have created a needless dropout problem. In a personalized program, with suitable guidance resources available, the secondary school student would not drop out to accept a position. Instead, the school, employer, student, and (when possible) his family would reach a consensus that it was desirable for him to extend the flow of his curriculum continuum outside the school to include the world of work. Weeks or months later he could, if he chose, pick up the thread of his in-school experiences. The absence of grades, formal class assignment, and so on, would encourage his return with no stigma attached.

Compensatory education would terminate. There would be no need for compensating, since education in a continuum is designed to maximize talents, minimize environmental inequities, and be inherently "supportive" in the sense that it builds on and sustains the unique assets which each learner acquires because of his membership in any given U.S. subculture.

Report cards and marks would vanish. In a continuum, reporting becomes a "spot check" on where the learner appears to be rather than an invidious semestral agony foisted on individuals clumped together for purposes of comparison.

And so on. . . .

CHANGES THE CONTINUUM CONCEPT CAN BRING TO EDUCATION IN THE FUTURE

What are some of the changes that are likely to occur in today's high school as the fact of continuity in learning and in education is more widely acknowledged and as teachers and administrators frankly face the opportunities — and problems — of a transition to an uninterrupted and personalized sequence of learning for children and youth?

Organizational changes. For one thing, as noted earlier, a discrete secondary school program would cease to exist. But so would the elementary school on one hand and college on the other. Graduation exercises would become obsolete, since one cannot graduate from a continuum.

Almost inevitably, there would be a significant downward extension of education. Ideally, the school would establish its first contacts with the child no later than at age two during a "non-school pre-school" interval.

Here children would be examined for psycho-physical or environmental impediments to learning prior to beginning direct school contacts in the "mini-school," at age three, for their first methodically planned sensory input.

Patently, when schooling begins for children three to four years sooner than is now generally the rule, the structures we now call elementary and secondary schools will be dealing with a psychologically different type of client with a distinctly different background. He would not have been enrolled in kindergarten, for instance. Instead, he would have spent an indeterminate "make-ready" period in a pre-primary continuum and entered the primary years anywhere between, say, five and seven or even eight years of age. By the end of the middle school era (i.e., at the close of what is now grade eight), he may have spent anywhere from seven to 12 years in elementary education following a seamless personalized program. He has worked under teacher-team guidance, and, quite conceivably, is the beneficiary of technological developments which have helped to widen and deepen his background.

The organization of the secondary school and the nature of its curriculum, as they exist in 1970, seemingly will need to go through a complete mutation as a continuum approach spreads upward. It is not too soon to begin speculating as to how the coming splice between elementary and secondary education can be made both smoothly and so as to serve the potential new product as he moves from early to later adolescence.[3]

Almost certainly, there will be major changes in the traditional high school-college relationship, too. At present, the college often expects U.S. secondary schools to provide a subject-content background so that the adolescent can achieve his "real education" during his university years, i.e., examine, expand, and apply the "beginnings of knowledge" presumably supplied by the time a diploma is conferred. As early childhood education becomes commonplace, as the personalized continuum becomes established, it may not be illogical to expect that, in effect, the secondary level of the 1980's will, with a more sophisticated clientele, be reorganized to replace the college years of today so that the "college-bound" secondary student of a decade hence can immediately enter upon a program at the university which is of graduate school caliber.

Changing policies and practices. Imbedded in the concept of continuity are various changes in policy. Typical of these is a decrease in age homogeneity among children working together. In the absence of rigid allocations of subject matter (e.g., studying the Middle Ages in grade six, biology in grade 10) the continuum may well draw together in year-long or in short-lived special purpose groupings children and youth who differ in age by as much as four or even six years.

Pupil interchange from school to school, district to district, and even country to country also becomes feasible if not essential when a personalized

---

[3] One is led to the tentative conclusion that, as education attains the continuity it has lacked, the portion of education now thought of as "secondary" will become at least as flexible as the "elementary" portion. Thus it would be of indeterminate length, without a graded structure — in short, a part of the stream of personalized, seamless education that would lead us into post-secondary programs of many kinds.

educational continuum replaces graded and nongraded schools. Teacher exchanges at an unprecedented level are a concomitant. By the 1980's it may be little more than routine to find a mature student (who today would be in high school) doing a year's work in Scotland or Ecuador. Perhaps his textual material would be transmitted from his home campus in facsimile form at appropriate intervals.

Undoubtedly, education will draw upon various instructional systems centers associated with the schools as supportive agencies for a continuum. Perhaps by the Eighties some forms of computerized instruction and information retrieval will be in general use.

The practice of making adult education an integral part of what is now secondary and collegiate education comes to mind when one extends a lifelong educational experience-chain to the middle years (40 to 70) and to early old age (70 years plus). With increases in leisure time, with rapid change making some skills and knowledge obsolete in a few years, and with the active life-spans of many people due to extend into the 90's within a decade or two, it seems reasonable that some people may profitably enroll in a secondary school interval appropriate to their personalized curriculum. Such re-enrollments, for as long as a year or two, might occur in the forties for the person seeking new vocational avenues and in the sixties or seventies as partial retirement draws near and new interests and hobbies are in need of cultivation. Who knows? We may have *old* married housing projects opening on the 1988 campus!

New deployment of faculty members. There will probably be much more vertical deployment of teachers in the continuum school as it becomes evident that learners need access to a greater variety of stimulating faculty minds. Today's second-grade teacher may find herself on a team working with a mixed cluster of 12- to 18-year-olds twice weekly in a human development-sex education project, working with senior citizens on several afternoons, and helping to supervise paraprofessionals working with three-year-olds in a minischool complex during the remainder of the week.

The effective use of paraprofessionals seems certain to be an important challenge to the school which uses differentiated staffs to achieve personalized instruction.

Perhaps the most demanding task, and certainly one of the most important as the seamless curriculum materializes, is that of redirecting teacher education — including inservice re-education. Particularly, some secondary teachers and many college teachers who have been predominantly subject-oriented may find it difficult to become skilled in the flexible, creative use of educational resources in identifying with interdisciplinary teams, and in working with groups of students in situations in which new criteria for group membership and for assessing success are taking form.

Selecting content for a curriculum continuum. For decades, research studies have suggested that, except for central tendencies created by widely used textbooks, the U.S. curriculum has been a Joseph's coat sewn of many pieces. Even now there is little agreement as to what should be taught and when. As a result, it is unlikely that conceptualizing the curriculum as a continuum can increase the general disarray. In fact, it is likely that a continuum will bring a measure of order.

One reason that much disagreement has marked curriculum development is that schools generally have grouped children chronologically, then failed to find any way of coping with problems of instruction brought about by the inevitable range in ability that ensued. The personalized curriculum reduces this problem to a minimum, since it rejects, as an undesirable goal, any idea of increasing the correlation between chronological age and uniform achievement norms.

As continuity is brought to education, the scope and sequence of the child's inner curriculum, i.e., the sum of what he has internalized from his school-sponsored experience, becomes uniquely personal. In the secondary continuum school, the individual adolescent would be guided in the wise exploitation of the school's total resources. His program would be *derived* from his status and needs, not predetermined by impersonal requirements.

BETTER TOMORROWS THROUGH GREATER CONTINUITY

In a recent book, Peter F. Drucker referred to the present as an age of discontinuity. His purpose in writing was to ask *not* "What will tomorrow look like?" but "What do we have to tackle *today* to make tomorrow better?"

Likewise, in education we should not speculate about tomorrow until our speculations become an opiate that keeps us from improving the schools as they exist today. At the same time, decisions made today shape the future. Since this is so, it seems prudent for educators at all levels, including secondary education, to give consideration to the idea of an uninterrupted, personalized flow of educational experiences, a seamless curriculum. Decisions that create greater continuity are likely to lead to the distinctly better education that the U.S. has always relied on the schools to produce.

PART THREE

Curriculum for the Future

A new development has emerged in contemporary curriculum-making. Professional educators, including curriculum workers, are joining scholars in other disciplines in speculating on the alternative futures which lie ahead for Americans.

Today's futurists often encounter skepticism among colleagues who remind them of the failures of previous efforts by intellectuals to predict the future. The skeptics point to the long history of utopian thought, from Plato to the optimistic nineteenth-century writer Edward Bellamy, and to the new phenomenon of negative antiutopian prophecies characteristic of the twentieth century, such as the fantasies of H. G. Wells and the despairing visions of George Orwell and Aldous Huxley. (The latter forecasts are more accurately described as Infernos than as Utopias.)

The editor has observed elsewhere that the 1970's, best described by borrowing Dickens' phrase "the best of times and the worst of times," have seen the arrival of neither Utopia nor Inferno. Instead, the residents of the United States experience a peculiar blend of both realms. Since neither the Utopian dream nor the Infernal nightmare has yet materialized, some skeptics maintain that speculation on the future is akin to astrology and that the work of scholars who deal with futurism is about as reliable as farmers' almanacs.

Yet speculating on the future is different from prophesying Utopia or Inferno. For one thing, today's futurists have better tools with which to shape their speculations than their predecessors had. More important, the most perceptive of today's futurists speculate on alternative futures rather than setting forth a single static prediction. Contemporary futurism recognizes the existence of "system breaks," which is Kenneth E. Boulding's perceptive phrase for the discontinuities, turning points, and surprises which occur in modern society. Consequently, today's futurism is much more than extrapolation from current trends or the whimsical projection of some tendency which has impressed a particular writer.

A frequent criticism of futurism is that it is escapist. Futurists are charged with dodging present problems by keeping their heads in the clouds of the future. Actually, the opposite is true. Studying alternative futures is a way of clarifying the alternative courses and possible value options available in the present. In other words, the study of alternative futures is a highly effective method of forcing human beings to confront their present problems and to consider the results of their present choices.

Futurism has a long history in Europe. More recently it has been taken up by American intellectuals. One of the best recent explorations of alternative futures was conducted by the American Academy of Arts and Sciences for the Summer 1967 issue of Daedalus. The issue was devoted to a report by the Academy's Commission on the Year 2000, which offered outstanding scholars the opportunity to present papers on various aspects of the future and to interact with each other on ideas concerning the future. The issue was then published in book form. The prestige of the American Academy of Arts and Sciences gave the futurist movement substantial momentum. The Year Two-Thousand, by Herman Kahn and Anthony J. Wiener (New York: Macmillan, 1967), provided futurists an extremely helpful factual basis for speculation concerning the future. Unfortunately, these publications give practically no attention to education and, consequently, implications were not drawn for the curriculum.

This defect was soon remedied by educators themselves. In the late 1960s, a project titled Designing Education for the Future and sponsored by eight Western states (Arizona, Colorado, Idaho, Montana, Nevada, New Mexico, Utah, Wyoming) cooperatively published a series of books. Scholars and educators in a variety of disciplines and specializations collaborated on books about education and the future. Among the better volumes are those on prospective changes in society, the educational implications of such changes, and on teacher education to meet emerging needs. Prospective Changes in Society by 1980 is composed largely of articles by scientists and humanists dealing with their own fields of specialization. Implications for Education of Prospective Changes in Society consists of speculation by educators on possible educational directions; it is a lively and provocative volume which takes into account the extrapolated trends and system breaks described in the earlier volume. Only rarely does a contributor interpret his role as a futurist to be that of supplying support for an educational innovation with which he is already associated. Preparing Educators to Meet Emerging Needs deals forthrightly with teacher education for the future.

Meanwhile, nineteen contributors were at work on their reactions to a chapter in Kimball Wiles' The Changing Curriculum of the American High School (Englewood Cliffs, N.J.: Prentice-Hall, 1963) in which Wiles had speculated on the curriculum of 1985. The 1970 symposium, a memorial volume for Wiles, is titled The High School of the Future and deals perceptively with possible futures for American secondary education. Another useful book is The Unprepared Society: Planning for a Precarious Future by Donald N. Michael (New York: Basic Books, 1968), an expansion of a John Dewey Society lecture. Michael clearly believes that difficulties are in store for the "unprepared society," unwilling to plan ahead.

Many excellent speculations on alternative futures have appeared in article or pamphlet form, and are thus less readily available to curriculum specialists than the books cited above. Consequently, the third and final part of this anthology offers to the reader selected articles and pamphlets by educators commenting on possible futures. The rest of this introduction will comment on interrelationships among the ideas they espouse.

A prologue by the editor deals with possible futures for very young children, while his epilogue discusses alternative futures for mature learners engaged in teacher education in the year 2000. Between prologue and epilogue is a series of articles dealing largely with elementary and secondary education.

"The Temper of the Times," written by the editor for the readers of Childhood Education, reports today's mood of violence, anger, and frustration, and urges a recognition that the lives of children in the year 2000 will be heavily influenced by how the reader lives today.

John I. Goodlad is also concerned about action now for a better tomorrow. He reminds us that while we are necessarily moving from human-based instruction to man–machine interaction, the goal must remain humanization. According to Goodlad, the question we must keep in mind as we move into the future is, "What kinds of human beings do we wish to produce?" Thus, Goodlad plays a role in speculation on the future similar to that he played in the 1960s by reminding scholars and philanthropic foundations that a balanced curriculum was necessary and that the whole child should be the essential concern of educators.

In "Youth Revolt: The Future is Now," Margaret Mead suggests that it is later than we think and that the future is actually upon us. In synthesizing ideas from her book, Culture and Commitment (New York: Doubleday & Co., 1970), she urges that we must relocate the future in the present as elders work with the young on the questions which only the young can think to ask. Since Mead regards the future as unknown and unknowable, she would probably regard with skepticism both Van Til's suggestion that the temper of the times in 2000 will partially depend upon action by today's adults and Goodlad's implication that today's educators can influence the kinds of human beings we wish to produce. We are, both young and old, strangers in an unknown land, says Mead, and we can only attempt to insure communication between elders and children and seek answers to children's questions.

Carl R. Rogers, in his speculation on alternative routes we may take in interpersonal relationships as we move toward the year 2000, interrelates two forces: the ability of democratic societies to deal with human survival problems, and the spread of such intensive group experiences as sensitivity training, encounter groups, and T-groups. Rogers, a proponent of such experiences, sees great promise for society and education if the trend toward openness, love, and reality in relationships prevails. Not only will the schools be environments for learning, but industry will also be increasingly humanized and religion will be related to a sense of true community.

Harold G. Shane, who frequently collaborates in writing about the future with June Grant Shane, is one of the most knowledgeable and widely-read educators studying the future and the curriculum. In the Kappan articles included in this anthology, Shane supplies an excellent background for readers interested in the development of futurism and most particularly in coping with future shock and using future-planning to influence the lives of human beings. In the first of his articles reproduced here, Shane deals with future shock, a term coined by Alvin Toffler in a 1965 article and popularized in Toffler's significant 1970 book, Future Shock. Shane considers the disorientation brought about by the premature arrival of the future and, in particular, its present and anticipated influence on the curriculum. He suggests some ways of coping with future shock through better programs of instruction. In his second article, Shane and his wife present a brief and useful history of futurism and stress that future-planning (the emphasis is theirs) involves "systematic conjecture based on analysis and projection of data." Consequently Shane is now engaged in a research study on "the status of current attitudes and opinions toward the future of education in the United States" for publication in the early 1970s.

Those who speculate upon the future must come to grips with the role of technology. The place of machines, especially the computer, is particularly important in any consideration of future curriculums.

Patrick Suppes, who is known for his pioneering in computer-assisted instruction, describes individualized instruction as presently and prospectively practiced. He examines and refutes criticisms of the use of computers, while admitting the potential that exists for abuse of the new technology. Suppes tells us that computer-assisted instruction has tremendous implications for the future of education if we are wise enough to use our modern instruments well.

Harold E. Mitzel supplies a helpful overview of the development of technology in his "The Impending Instruction Revolution." He examines the development of individualized instruction, including five concepts of individualization which have emerged. He predicts that adaptive education, involving the tailoring of subject-matter presentations to fit each learner, will be a next step. Such adaptive programs should be accompanied by teaching for student mastery. With the revolution growing out of computer-assisted instruction should come new concepts in student appraisal and adaptation to the increasing heterogeneity among students. Mitzel looks forward with confidence to his version of a genuine instructional revolution.

But a curriculum worker in the Montgomery County (Maryland) Public Schools, Elizabeth C. Wilson, is less sanguine, for she recognizes that "conventional wisdom regarding the task of the school dies hard" and that conservatism persists regarding electronic media. She calls for policy planning in a time when the electronic revolution is hard upon us. She points out the necessity for stressing areas such as the arts which do not lend themselves readily to technological devices, and emphasizes that lasting personal contacts must not be overlooked. In other words, she considers the development of a good curriculum foremost, and regards the matter of whether or not it can be computerized a second order of priority.

The editor's viewpoint on the coming technological revolution is set forth in a working paper distributed to members of the John Dewey Society for the Study of Education and Culture through a Commission on Educational Technology and Professional Practice which he chaired. He believes that educational technology is here to stay and that it carries both promise and dangers. He calls for educators to interact with the emerging technological complex and to participate in thinking through the relationship of educational technology to practice.

Broad speculation on the curriculum of the future, as a means of fostering intelligent decision-making on the alternatives and directions before us today, is essential. Statesmanlike reflection on goals and reminders of the central place of individuals in any consideration of the future are necessary, as the contributions of the above authors testify. But, in addition, discussion of alternative futures, to be maximally helpful, must also deal with specific areas of the curriculum. Consequently, the remainder of the selections in this part deal with such specifics.

Leonard E. Klopfer in "Science Education in 1991" deals with varying patterns of science education for prospective scientists and for nonscientists who require scientific literacy as part of their education. He visualizes the two streams of scientific education and dramatizes them by descriptions of possible school programs for the last decade of the twentieth century. His vision of the future should be of interest not only to science teachers but to that larger group of nonscientists whom Klopfer hopes will be educated for scientific literacy in the years ahead.

Max S. Bell in "Teaching and Learning Mathematics: 1991" is impressed by both positive and negative aspects of the present situation in mathematics. Unlike Klopfer, he presents both an optimistic vision of 1991 and a less hopeful vision extrapolated from negative aspects. He believes that the latter vision is more likely to be realized, and calls for "repentance" by educators to avoid his less desirable future alternative. Klopfer illustrates the uses of futurism in forcing people to re-examine their options.

In "Teaching of Social Sciences, 1991," Mark M. Krug puts major stress on the teaching of history, and we are excerpting from his long article only his comments on that particular field. Krug sees history as both art and science, and as essentially a more humanistic than scientific study. He disagrees with the "structuralists." He does not envision particular classroom settings as do Klopfer and Bell, but he does discuss the potential conflict on the teaching of history which may take shape in the decades ahead. There may be still more contenders in the field, including those who regard history as a tool to be used in dealing with social problems.

Howard Lee Nostrand chooses a shorter time span for his look into the future than the authors who precede him in this anthology. He modestly confines himself to the next few years in "Foreign Language Teaching in 1975." Though Nostrand recognizes the importance of the technological revolution to the teaching of foreign languages, he sees as even more crucial questions about the use of foreign languages in the lives of students and consideration of the most relevant content for study. Nostrand looks at foreign language teaching from a social point of view rather than limiting himself, as do some of his colleagues, to concern for the technological processes of communication.

We turn again to the Shanes for a discussion of social changes likely to occur in the near future and the implications of such developments for the curriculum of American schools. In this article, the Shanes, though aware that the future must be understood in terms of alternatives, forecast the developments considered most likely by scholars in the various disciplines. They assume that such "system breaks" as modification of personality by drugs and scientific modification of hereditary factors are even more than possibilities but are among tomorrow's likelihoods.

As an epilogue, the editor contributes a pamphlet he has written on teacher education and the year 2000. Because consideration of the future of teacher education necessarily involves attention to broader matters, the last selection includes comments on speculating on the future, a description of alternative futures before American society, a discussion of the consequent alternatives available to American education as a whole and culminates in speculation on possible directions for teacher education in the year 2000. The editor foresees conflict between technologists, who may be charged with stressing things and ignoring people, and the social emphasizers, who may be charged with stressing people and ignoring things.

A. Alternative Futures

31

Prologue: The Temper of the Times

William Van Til

"The Temper of the Times" opened an issue of Childhood
Education *devoted to social problems. The editor chose to use
futurism as a way of reminding readers that their present action or
inaction on social issues could make a difference in the year 2000
in the lives of the present two- to twelve-year-olds who are the concern of this magazine and its readers.*

*The younger one's students, the more crucial is the need for con-
sideration of the alternative futures in which they might live. The
youngest children now alive in the United States will live most of
their years in the twenty-first century.*

What is the temper of the times? Presumably, the times as experienced
by the reader. And, presumably, the times as experienced by the children on
whose behalf this journal is published.

Let us look first at the times as experienced by the reader. More likely
than not, the reader is a woman who is concerned with childhood education.
She is probably a student or a teacher or a community worker or a mother
or some combination of these. She could be of any age; for our purposes in
relating her to the times and in making a comparison, we will call her
thirty-eight years old in January 1969.

The times that our selected reader has experienced include the past. She
was born during the Great Depression. During her entire childhood the
President of her country was Franklin Delano Roosevelt. While she was still
a child, emphasis shifted from the New Deal to the war against fascism in
Europe. By the time the United States dropped the atomic bomb on
Hiroshima, she was a young adolescent. (She was out of college and well
into advanced studies before man launched into space.)

The temper of her times during her childhood? Grim but exciting. Tough

William Van Til, "The Temper of the Times," *Childhood Education*, January,
1969, 243–246. Reprinted by permission of the author and publisher.

but determined. Threatened by authoritarianism but marked by belief that somehow democracy would pull through.

TODAY'S MOOD INESCAPABLE

Now she lives in the present. . . . It is a time when her oldest son, now approaching the age of military service, is thinking about his relationship to the draft. It is a time when more than half of the world goes to bed hungry. It is a time when many American people still live in poverty. Yet, as a whole, hers is an affluent society in which the employment rate is high, the Gross National Product is climbing, and ingenious uses of leisure are increasing.

The temper of the times in which she lives today has turned violent, angry, frustrated. Not that she cannot escape it through varied sanctuaries and privatisms whether at home or through cultural resources or through entertainment. She can and often does. But the underlying ugly mood of her times is inescapable.

There is a climate of frustration in these times marked by the war in Vietnam, by the bitterness in mean city streets, by the assassination of our leaders, and by feelings of political impotence.

Anger is in the air on the part of aroused blacks and backlashing whites; on the part of alienated young people who protest against the industrial-military complex and against universities where nobody knows their names; on the part of poor people who want their share now; on the part of screaming, chanting hecklers who shout down candidates and diminish the democratic discourse; on the part of militant peace demonstrators and of repressive overreacting police forces under boss rule.

Our reader finds herself living in a world where, for the first time in history, people living in the country feel more safe from violence than people living in the large cities. This was not true in Greece or Rome or the Europe of the Middle Ages; nor was it true in eighteenth- and nineteenth-century America, or even in the America in which she was a child. Yet this is the way it is today; Americans feel unsafe in cities haunted by nuclear devastations, by unregistered weapons, by poverty, by organized crime, and by disorganized rioting.

For our selected reader, the rest of the twentieth century represents about all of her future that is left. When the year 2000 rolls around, she will have retired. Essentially she will then be a spectator, an onlooker.

THE CHILD OF TODAY

How about the times of the children on whose behalf CHILDHOOD EDUCA-TION is published as a "magazine for those concerned with children two to twelve"? To choose a child in order to compare him with our selected reader, let's break in half the ten-year CHILDHOOD EDUCATION span from two to twelve. We will choose a boy seven years old in January 1969.

The past of our seven-year-old, born in 1962, is briefer than that of our reader. But it already includes the most unpopular war in American history, the murder of a President and a Presidential candidate, the launching of a struggle against poverty, the increasing momentum of the Negro Revolution, the student revolt against the university establishment.

As to his life today, he too has his sanctuaries and his privatisms. For him, they are usually found in home and in family, in school and in play. Yet the temper of the times sometimes spills over into his world, since violence and anger and frustration are no respecters of childhood.

Some children are more protected from the temper of the times, whatever it might be; others are more vulnerable. Our chosen child learns early that he is Negro or white and that whichever he is makes a difference. He learns early what it is like to be poor or middling or affluent. He may go to the best of schools or the worst of schools or a school somewhere in between. At his school he may find adults waging wars, which are only partially comprehensible to him, over where he goes to school or who controls his education. Sometimes a relative of his, close or distant, disappears into the maw of the armed forces and, occasionally, never comes back. He learns early about streets that, for a child, are much more than thoroughfares to be traveled. Sometimes his streets are tree-lined and pleasant; sometimes they are rank with winos, junkies, and queers.

The Future World of the Child

As to the times he will experience, our chosen child differs from our selected reader in one irrevocable way — there is more of the future ahead of him. For instance, in the month that opens the year 2000, he will be thirty-eight years old, the age our selected reader is right now. He may retire somewhere in the 2030's, the exact date dependent somewhat on what the biological revolution contributes to longevity through transplants and other body bolsterings. The world of space will be a taken-for-granted part of his environment. It is quite possible that he will live several years beyond the mid-point of the twenty-first century.

During His Productive Years

What will his world be like when he is near his productive peak in 2000 and when our selected reader has retired? Those who speculate on alternative futures before us tell us. . . . He may be living in a megalopolis, a sprawling metropolitan complex. Perhaps his megalopolis will be Boswash (the Boston to Washington complex), with about one-fourth of the population; perhaps Chipitts (the Chicago to Pittsburgh complex), with one-eighth of the population; perhaps Sansan (the Santa Barbara to San Diego complex), with one-sixteenth of us, as suggested by Kahn and Wiener in *The Year Two-Thousand*. There is a substantial possibility that he will be living in a United States where the Gross National Product per capita has at least doubled and may have gone to about three and one-half times the current GNP per capita. The prophets foresee that he will be living in a time of continuing knowledge explosion, of extensive use of computers, of space conquest and of high emphasis upon the importance of education.

Of course, all bets as to his future are off if marked discontinuities, termed "system breaks" by some analysts of futures, do develop. For instance, in the case of worldwide nuclear war, our selected child might be among the millions dead. In the case of world famine, it is unlikely that the United States and other developed nations could or would remain islands of high living standards. In case violence grew to catastrophic proportions and overwhelmed our social institutions, then anarchy might prevail as the dominant characteristic of the times of our child. On the other hand, in the case of biological revolution, there might be a different population than expected, with a higher potential for achievement. In the case of a more advanced degree of technological growth than is now foreseeable, there might be abundance to share with the entire world.

PLAYING IT NEUTRAL OR WRONG

What will be the temper of the times of our child in 2000 when he has reached the age of our 1969 reader today? It depends. On what? It depends, in part, on what our reader does in the meantime. It also depends on what our child, growing up and grown up, does in the meantime.

One possibility is that our child and our reader (multiplied by millions of us) do nothing. Perhaps our child and our reader will play it neutral and settle for privatism. C. P. Snow said in his lecture in Fulton, Missouri, "We draw . . . the curtains, and we try to make an enclave of our own." Edmund Burke analyzed this alternative well: "All that is necessary for the forces of evil to win in the world is for enough good men to do nothing."

Another possibility is that our child and our reader (multiplied by millions) do the wrong things. Then our child and, for a while, our reader may be living in an American apartheid, two separate racial societies in the United States created by white segregationists and black separatists. They may even live in the time of the Stupid War between white race and black race in a world that ignorantly denies the existence of only one race, the human race.

Or child and reader may be struggling to exist in the unlivable city characterized by water and air pollution, organized crime, anarchic violence, festering poverty, slum housing, clogged streets, and too many people.

Or our child and reader may be living in a world of recurrent small wars, supported and stoked by the large powers, in a weapons culture of accelerated and expensive defenses and offenses fostered by the military-industrial alliance, in a time of a grim balance of terror as Big Brother watches from outer space for hostile moves. Or, indeed, our child and our reader may be engulfed in the holocaust of war.

IT ALL DEPENDS . . .

But there are other possibilities too. Our child and our reader (multiplied by millions) may be living in a nation and a world that has overcome the barriers of race. Our reader and our child may have rebuilt the old cities, developed new ones fit for civil habitation, and reached a stage of "no more people than the earth can take." They may have created workable controls over hate and suspicion and achieved a world society where the technological equivalent of beating swords into plowshares has been accomplished for mankind.

What the temper of the times will be like in 2000, when our chosen child is the age of our selected reader, is not written in the stars. It all depends. It depends on whom? In part, on you. After all, you do have *some* time left, and some of you have considerably more than others. Largely, the temper of the times in 2000 depends on him, our child, growing and grown. Essentially, the world of 2000 will be his world in which to live well or poorly.

32

Learning and Teaching
in the Future

John I. Goodlad

John I. Goodlad, one of America's best known curriculum leaders, speculates in this article on education in the future. Always humanistically oriented, he reminds us of the need for dialogue on the kinds of human beings we wish to produce.

Goodlad is dean of the Graduate School of Education at the University of California in Los Angeles and director of the Research Program at the Institute for Development of Educational Activities. Despite these administrative responsibilities, he is a prolific writer on curriculum.

As a member of the teaching profession, each of us is convinced that education is a powerful force for the improvement of man and mankind. But to assume that the school, as it now exists, carries the central thrust in changing human behavior is to be misled.

First, what the school does in educating the young appears to be less or, at best, no more effective than other factors in determining what the child learns and becomes.

John I. Goodlad, "Learning and Teaching in the Future," *Today's Education: NEA Journal*, February, 1968, 49–51. Reprinted by permission of the author and publisher.

Second, the incidence of nonpromotion, dropouts, alienation, and minimal learning in school suggests that today's schools are obsolescent. They were designed for a different culture, a different conception of learners and learning, and a different clientele.

Third, success in school, as measured by grades, appears to bear little relationship to good citizenship, good work habits, compassion, happiness, or other significant human values which our civilization prizes.

Fourth, a relatively new medium, television, has entered into the business of transmitting to children a large segment of our culture. If the years before a child begins school are taken into account, television occupies more of his hours than schooling from his birth to the time he graduates from high school.

Our immediate goal as educators should be to increase the intensity of the school so that it can again play a major role in educating the young. We must look to the possibilities of the future in order to provide responsible leadership in planning the kind of education that is to come.

We live in a time when one era of instruction is in full bloom, another is well begun, and a third is embryonic. Let us take a look at all three.

The era that is in full bloom and is about to fade is human-to-human instruction. The prime exhibit of this era is the human-based school — a school almost without machines. Here, we like to believe, children and youth are inducted into the culture, their individual potentialities are discovered and developed, they take on a sense of identity and ultimately transcend themselves, and they are inculcated in those values that make for the ideal adult. Increasingly, however, we have become aware that school is not accomplishing these things with a large segment of our population. Indeed, present-day education appears to increase the gap between the haves and the have-nots.

Nonetheless, we are in an inventive period, and old ways of doing things are tumbling before our drive to increase the effectiveness of the school. We have not yet eliminated track systems, with their self-fulfilling prophecies, nor have we broken down the grade barriers, with their nefarious adjustment mechanism of nonpromotion, nor have we learned to teach inductively, with the child learning for himself the skill of inquiry. But we have caught the spirit of these things.

The challenge now is much less one of inventing than of implementing the several powerful and viable innovations that have appeared during recent years. Human-based instruction in the schools will undergo no revolution during the next 15 years, nor has it undergone one during the past 15. It *will* see an accelerating evolution in curriculum, school organization, and instructional practices, while nonhuman-based instruction will loom ever larger on the horizon.

The era of instruction that will supersede the era of human-based instruction is to be one of man-machine interaction — and the machine is the computer. Although we have lived in the shadow of the computer for a long while, we have used it so little in teaching that we may be inclined to believe its future and our own to be things apart. Nothing could be further from the truth. Computers are already demonstrating their usefulness in teaching spelling, mathematics, reading, and a host of other cognitive skills. Tapes, screens, records, and other audiovisual devices, coupled with the computer, make possible a unique instructional system of sight, sound, and touch.

The computer will continue to march relentlessly into our instructional lives, and there is no reason to believe that it will not come right into the school building. To put a computer terminal into every elementary school classroom in the United States would cost, at current prices, about $1 billion; however, if we were to decide to do such a thing, competition within the industry would undoubtedly cut this figure in half. There are problems involved, especially in hooking up terminals to the computer-instructional system at some remote point, but this can be solved by improving communications connections or by having small computers closer to the schools they serve.

Providing programed sequences by way of computers offers us an efficient means of communicating educational lore. What the teaching profession must do is to *legitimatize* the computer as instructor in those basic areas that can be carefully programed. Then we must explore the question of how computers and people are to live together productively in education.

An important goal for the teaching profession now is to humanize the means of instruction. By this I mean emphasing our very best human values in the substance of the curriculum, and showing concern for both the individual and mankind in the teaching-learning environment. I believe these tasks to be at once so formidable and so important that I welcome the computer and charge it with teaching some of those basic skills and concepts that are only the beginning of educating the compassionate, rational man.

I do not see the computer as the teacher's competitor. Not at all! I see it rather as replacing the teacher for certain instructional tasks that I believe it can and will do better than any human teacher can perform them.

The research challenge is to catalogue those aspects of instruction that are most appropriate for the machine and for the teacher. We must *not* make the teacher a supervisor or coordinator of the computer, or he will become its servant. The teacher may very well contribute to programing, but the interaction should be between student and machine.

For us to take our traditional conservative position with respect to this electronic teacher is to delay progress in education and in the long run to endanger the highly relevant role of the human teacher. The significant task for educators, one that may very well be accomplished better if we turn over some of the other tasks to the untiring machine, is to discover how human beings and machines are to live together productively in tomorrow's learning-teaching environment.

A third era, only dimly visible at this point, is much more hazy in its outlines, and we can only speculate on its characteristics, assets, and liabilities.

When we try to envision the school of tomorrow, we must not be limited by our concept of the school of today. Education is not a static process, and the school of today cannot be considered a sacred or unchangeable institution. After all, every decision governing schools was at one time or another made by man. At the time the decisions governing today's schools were made, fewer data were available.

The men who made those decisions were no brighter than schoolmen today, and they were less well-educated. Therefore, it behooves us to re-examine every decision about schooling: size of building and whether we want one at all, numbers of teachers and whether we need a fully certificated teacher for every 28.5 children, whether the library is to be one that houses real books or computerized microfiche. (A fully automated library with no books but only microfiche is now out of the realm of science fiction into the actuality of college and university planning in the United States.)

We must not continue to assume that tomorrow's school will have X number of qualified teachers for Y number of children or that we will construct a school building large enough for all of the children to be housed. There is no reason at all why we could not employ half the usual quota of fully qualified teachers, using the balance of our money for part-time specialists and a host of instructional aids. And there is no reason at all why we could not plan an educational program that requires a school building only half the usual size, with the balance of the money going for trips, special projects, and individualized activities supervised by the staff or even programed by a computer.

A school is not necessary to teaching and learning. We do not need a school to guide children and youth in grasping their culture. And, certainly, we do not need a school to teach the fundamentals of reading, writing, and arithmetic. But we do need a formal process of instruction with the most able members of our society giving their time to it in planning and programing instructional materials, in computerizing varied programs for learning, and in interacting with other humans in the delightful business of learning from one another.

The computer, which we must legitimatize for learning and teaching in an imminent era, probably will contribute significantly in a still later era to the demise of what we now call school. We shall regard this as undesirable only if we lack faith in the ability of man to fashion a better world.

In viewing learning and teaching for the year 2000 and beyond, it is easier to predict what will *not* be than what will be. A prescribed age for starting school will be meaningless. The computer console with an array of devices for stimuli and feedback will be as natural for the child of the twenty-first century as television is for today's two-year-old. Teaching and learning will not be marked by a standard 9 to 3 day, or a standard September to June year, or a year for a grade of carefully packaged material. The child's age will not be a criterion for determining what he is to learn.

Will learning be any less because there will be no periods, no Carnegie units, no bells, no jostling of pupils from class to class? I think not. The student will be free to concentrate exclusively on a given field for weeks or months or to divide his time among several fields. The variability and comprehensiveness of programed learning sequences will be such that the student, unaided by human teachers, will control a significant portion of his curriculum.

Clearly, the role of teachers will change markedly. Hundreds of hours of their time will go into what will occupy each student for an hour or two. But because thousands or even millions of students might eventually select this hour, the teachers' preparation time will be well spent. And the quality of education will be vastly improved.

School as we now know it—whether egg crate or flexible space—will have been replaced by a diversified learning environment including homes, parks, public buildings, museums, and guidance centers. It is quite conceivable that each community will have a learning center and that homes will contain electronic consoles connected to it. This learning center will provide not only a computer-controlled videotape, microfiche, and record library, but also access to state and national educational television networks. It is even possible that advanced technology will return the family to center stage as the basic learning unit.

The most controversial issues of the twenty-first century will pertain to the ends and means of modifying human behavior and who shall determine them. The first educational question will not be "What knowledge is of most worth?" but "What kinds of human beings do we wish to produce?" The possibilities defy our imagination.

The nerve cells of the brain, far more than muscles or any other organs, are highly sensitive to small electric currents, to a variety of chemicals, and to changes in blood supply. Sedatives, barbiturates, tranquilizers, and various psychedelics provide powerful ways of controlling behavior by direct action on the brain. Similarly, we can manipulate behavior by applying electric currents to regions of the brain. Experiments are now under way with drugs and brain extracts designed to enhance learning or memory.

Aldous Huxley long ago introduced us to the possibilities of genetic selectivity through the availability of sperm and ovum banks. The means of drastically altering the course of human development through artificial insemination, chemical treatment, and electric manipulation are with us. We are already tampering with human evolution. The possibilities for further doing so will be enormously enhanced and refined as we move into the twenty-first century.

We of the teaching profession have tended to get bogged down in the narrow details of our calling, in details pertaining primarily to means: buildings, classrooms, textbooks, and so on. We have seldom gone beyond these trivialities to recognition of the fact that education and teaching are much bigger than schools. Schools are only a convenient means to more important ends, means that may no longer be relevant several decades from now.

As individual leaders, we must assert by our very competence that we know how to manage the means. Our constituencies lose faith in our competence when we hesitate, falter, and in desperation turn to the community for guidance in technique. But the charge to the organized profession is a much larger one. We must raise the level of the dialogue to the truly significant questions of educational ends, and we must be as diligent as our lay citizens in laying bare instructional deficiencies in the pursuit of these ends.

As to ends, let me put them as questions to ask about the educational enterprise:

1. To what extent are our young people coming into possession of their culture?
2. To what extent is each child being provided with unique opportunities to develop his potentialities to the maximum?
3. To what extent is each child developing a deep sense of personal worth, the sense of selfhood that is a prerequisite for self-transcendence?
4. To what extent are our people developing universal values, values that transcend all men in all times and in all places?

A fifth question is the most important, challenging, and frightening of all, now that men possess such manipulative powers: *What kinds of human beings do we wish to produce?* As a citizen and an educator, I cherish the right to participate in the dialogue about it.

33

Youth Revolt:
The Future is Now

Margaret Mead

The indefatigable Margaret Mead is a distinguished anthropologist and an effective mediator between young and old. This selection is an overview of her recent book, Culture and Commitment: A Study of the Generation Gap *(New York: Doubleday, 1970). Unlike the futurists, Mead believes that the emerging prefigurative future is unknown and unknowable, and thus stresses questing for answers to questions only the young can raise in a future which is already upon us. In Mead's view, there are no guides for the new immigrants in time.*

Margaret Mead is the author of many books in anthropology. She has served as curator of ethnology for the American Museum of Natural History and since 1968 has been chairman of the social sciences division of Fordham University, where she is also a professor of anthropology.

Our present crisis has been variously attributed to the overwhelming rapidity of change, the collapse of the family, the decay of capitalism, the triumph of a soulless technology, and, in wholesale repudiation, to the final breakdown of the Establishment. Behind these attributions there is a more basic conflict between those for whom the present represents no more than an intensification of our existing cofigurative culture, in which peers are more than ever replacing parents as the significant models of behavior, and those who contend that we are in fact entertaining a totally new phase of cultural evolution.

Most commentators, in spite of their differences in viewpoint, still see the future essentially as an extension of the past. Edward Teller can still speak of the outcome of a nuclear war as a state of destruction relatively no more drastic than the ravages wrought by Genghis Khan, and historians can point out that time and again civilization has survived the crumbling of empires. Similarly, many authorities treat as no more than an extreme form of adolescent rebellion the repudiation of present and past by the dissident youth of every persuasion in every kind of society in the world.

Theorists who emphasize the parallels between past and present in their interpretations of the generation gap ignore the irreversibility of the changes that have taken place since the beginning of the Industrial Revolution. This is especially striking in their handling of modern technological development, which they treat as comparable in its effects to the changes that occurred as one civilization in the past took over from another such techniques as agriculture, script, navigation, or the organization of labor and law.

One urgent priority, I believe, is to examine the nature of change in the modern world, including its speed and dimensions, so that we can better understand the distinctions that must be made between change in the past and that which is now ongoing. To do so, I make distinctions among three different kinds of culture: *post-figurative*, in which children learn primarily from their forebears; *cofigurative*, in which both children and adults learn from their peers; and *prefigurative*, in which adults learn also from their children.

Although it is possible to discuss both post-figurative and cofigurative cultures in terms of slow or rapid change without specifying the nature of the process and to compare past and present situations when the focus is kept on generation relationships and on the type of modeling through which a culture is transmitted, it is only when one specifies the nature of the process that the contrast between past and present change becomes clear.

The primary evidence that our present situation is unique, without any parallel in the past, is that the generation gap is world-wide. The particular events taking place in England, Pakistan, the United States, New Guinea, or elsewhere are not enough to explain the unrest that is stirring modern youth everywhere. Recent technological change or the handicaps imposed by its absence, revolution or the suppression of revolutionary activities, the crumbling of faith in ancient creeds or the attraction of new creeds — all these serve only as partial explanations of the particular forms taken by youth revolt in different countries.

Concentration on particularities can only hinder the search for an explanatory principle. Instead, it is necessary to strip the occurrences in each country of their superficial, national, and immediately temporal aspects. The desire for a liberated form of communism in Czechoslovakia, the search for "racial" equality in the United States, the desire to liberate Japan from American military influence — these are particularistic forms. Youthful activism is common to them all. The key question is this: What are the new conditions that have brought about the revolt of youth around the world?

The first of these is the emergence of a world community. For the first time human beings throughout the world, in their information about and responses to one another, have become a community that is united by shared knowledge and danger. As far as we know, no such single, interacting community has existed within archaeological time. The largest clusters of interacting human groups have always been fragments of a still larger unknown whole, and the idea that all men are, in the same sense, human beings always has been either unreal or a mystical belief.

The events of the past twenty-five years changed this drastically. Exploration has been complete enough to convince us that there are no humanoid types on the planet except our own species. World-wide air travel and globe-encircling TV satellites have turned us into one community, in which events taking place on one side of the earth become immediately and simultaneously available to peoples everywhere else. No artist or political censor has time to intervene and edit as a leader is shot or a flag is planted on the moon. The world is a community, though it still lacks the forms of organization and the sanctions by which a political community can be governed.

Men who are the carriers of vastly different cultural traditions are entering the present at the same point in time. It is as if, all around the world, men were converging on identical immigration posts, each with its identifying sign: YOU ARE NOW ABOUT TO ENTER THE POST-WORLD-WAR-II WORLD AT GATE 1 (GATE 23, etc.). Whoever they are and wherever their particular points of entry may be, all men are equally immigrants into the new era. They are like the immigrants who came as pioneers to a new land, lacking all knowledge of what demands new conditions of life would make upon them. Those who came later could take their peer groups as models. But among the first comers, the young adults had as models only their own tentative adaptations and innovations.

Today, everyone born and bred before World War II is such an immigrant in time as his forebears were in space — a pioneer struggling to grapple with the unfamiliar conditions of life in a new era. Like all immigrants and pioneers, these immigrants in time are the bearers of older cultures, but today they represent all the cultures of the world. And all of them, whether they are sophisticated French intellectuals or members of a remote New Guinea tribe, land-bound peasants in Haiti or nuclear physicists, have certain characteristics in common.

Whoever they are, these immigrants grew up under skies across which no satellite had ever flashed. Their perception of the past was an edited version of what had happened. Their perception of the immediate present was limited to what they could take in through their own eyes and ears and to the edited versions of other men's sensory experience and memories. Their conception of the future was essentially one in which change was incorporated into a deeper changelessness. The industrialist or military planner, envisaging what a computer, not yet constructed, might make possible, treated it as another addition to the repertoire of inventions that have enhanced man's skills. It expanded what men could do, but did not change the future.

When the first atom bomb was exploded at the end of World War II, only a few individuals realized that all humanity was entering a new age. And to this day the majority of those over twenty-five have failed to grasp emotionally, however well they may grasp intellectually, the difference between any war in which, no matter how terrible the casualties, mankind will survive, and one in which there will be no survivors. They continue to think that a war, fought with more lethal weapons, would just be a worse war. Our thinking still binds us to the past — to the world as it existed in our childhood and youth.

We still hold the seats of power and command the resources and the skills necessary to keep order and organize the kinds of societies we know about. We control the educational systems, the apprenticeship systems, the career ladders up which the young must climb. Nevertheless, we have passed the point of no return. We are committed to life in an unfamiliar setting; we are making do with what we know.

The young generation, however — the articulate young rebels all around the world who are lashing out against the controls to which they are subjected — are like the first generation born into a new country. They are at home in this time. Satellites are familiar in their skies. They have never known a time when war did not threaten annihilation. When they are given the facts, they can understand immediately that continued pollution of the air and water and soil will soon make the planet uninhabitable and that it will be impossible to feed an indefinitely expanding world population. As members of one species in an underdeveloped world community they recognize that invidious distinctions based on race and caste are anachronisms. They insist on the vital necessity of some form of world order.

No longer bound by the simplified linear sequences dictated by the printed word, they live in a world in which events are presented to them in all their complex immediacy. In their eyes the killing of an enemy is not qualitatively different from the murder of a neighbor. They cannot reconcile our efforts to save our own children by every known means with our readiness to destroy the children of others with napalm. They know that the people of one nation alone cannot save their own children; each holds the responsibility for all others' children.

Although I have said they *know* these things, perhaps I should say that this is how they *feel*. Like the first generation born in a new country, they listen only half-comprehendingly to their parents' talk about the past. For as the children of pioneers had no access to the landscapes whose memories could still move their parents to tears, the young today cannot share their parents' responses to events that deeply moved them in the past. But this is not all that separates the young from their elders. Watching, they can see that their elders are groping, that they are managing clumsily and often unsuccessfully the tasks imposed on them by the new conditions. The young do not know what must be done, but they feel that there must be a better way and that they must find it.

Today, nowhere in the world are there elders who know what the children know, no matter how remote and simple the societies are in which the children live. In the past there were always some elders who knew more than any children in terms of their experience of having grown up within a cultural system. Today there are none. It is not only that parents are no longer guides, but that there are no guides, whether one seeks them in one's own country or abroad. There are no elders who know what those who have been reared within the last twenty years know about the world into which they were born.

True, in many parts of the world the parental generation still lives by a post-figurative set of values. From parents in such cultures children may learn that there have been unquestioned absolutes, and this learning may carry over into later experience as an expectation that absolute values can and should be re-established.

There are still parents who answer such child's questions as why he must go to bed, or eat his vegetables, or learn to read with simple assertions: Because it is *right* to do so, because *God* says so, or because *I* say so. These parents are preparing the way for the re-establishment of post-figurative elements in the culture. But these elements will be far more rigid and intractable than in the past because they must be defended in a world in which conflicting points of view, rather than orthodoxies, are prevalent.

Most parents, however, are too uncertain to assert old dogmatisms. They do not know how to teach these children who are so different from what they themselves once were, and most children are unable to learn from parents and elders they will never resemble. In the past, in the United States, children of immigrant parents pleaded with them not to speak their foreign language in public and not to wear their outlandish foreign clothes. They knew the burning shame of being, at the same time, unable to repudiate their parents and unable to accept simply and naturally their way of speaking and doing things. But in time they learned to find new teachers as guides, to model their behavior on that of more adapted age mates, and to slip in, unnoticed, among a group whose parents were more bearable.

Today, the dissident young discover very rapidly that this solution is no longer possible. The breach between themselves and their parents also exists between their friends and their friends' parents and between their friends and their teachers.

These young dissidents realize the critical need for immediate world action on problems that affect the whole world. What they want is, in some way, to begin all over again. They are ready to make way for something new by a kind of social bulldozing — like the bulldozing in which every tree and feature of the landscape is destroyed to make way for a new community. Awareness of the reality of the crisis (which is, in fact, perceived most accurately not by the young, but by their discerning and prophetic elders) and the sense the young have that their elders do not understand the modern world, because they do not understand their children, has produced a kind of rebellion in which planned reformation of the present system is almost inconceivable.

Nevertheless, those who have no power also have no routes to power except through those against whom they are rebelling. In the end, it was men who gave the vote to women; and it will be the House of Lords that votes to abolish the House of Lords — as also, in the final analysis, nations will act to limit national sovereignty. Effective, rapid evolutionary change, in which no one is guillotined or forced into exile, depends on the co-operation of a large number of those in power with the dispossessed who are seeking power.

These, in brief, are the conditions of our time. These are the two generations — pioneers in a new era and their children — who have as yet to find a way of communicating about the world in which both live, though their perceptions of it are so different. No one knows what the next steps should be. Recognizing that this is so is, I submit, the beginning of an answer.

I believe we are on the verge of developing a new kind of culture, one that is as much a departure in style from cofigurative cultures as the institutionalization of cofiguration in orderly — and disorderly — change was a departure from the post-figurative style. I call this new style "prefigurative," because in this new culture it will be the unborn child, already conceived but still in the womb — not the parent and grandparent — that represents what is to come. This is a child whose sex and appearance and capabilities are unknown, but who will need imaginative, innovative, and dedicated adult care far beyond any we give today.

No one can know in advance what the child will become — how swift his limbs will be, what will delight his eye, whether his tempo will be fast or slow. No one can know how his mind will work — whether he will learn best from sight or sound or touch or movement. But knowing what we do not know and cannot predict, we can construct an environment in which a child, still unknown, can be safe and can grow and discover himself and the world.

Love and trust, based on dependency and answering care, made it possible for the individual who had been reared in one culture to move into another, transforming, without destroying, his earlier learning. It is seldom the first generation of voluntary immigrants and pioneers who cannot meet the demands of a new environment. Their previous learning carries them through. But unless they embody what is new post-figuratively, they cannot pass on to their children what they had acquired through their own early training — the ability to learn from others the things their parents could not teach them.

Parents, in a world where there are no more knowledgeable others to whom they can commit the children they themselves cannot teach, feel uncertain and helpless. Still believing that there should be answers, parents ask how they can tell their children what is right. So some try to solve the problem by advising their children, very vaguely, that they will have to figure it out for themselves. And some parents ask what the others are doing. But this resource of a cofigurative culture is becoming meaningless to parents who feel that the "others" — their children's age mates — are moving in ways that are unsafe for their own children to emulate, and who find that they do not understand what their children figure out for themselves.

It is the adults who still believe that there is a safe and socially approved road to a kind of life they have not experienced who react with the greatest anger and bitterness to the discovery that what they had hoped for no longer exists for their children. These are the parents, the trustees, the legislators, the columnists and commentators who denounce most vocally what is happening in schools and colleges and universities in which they had placed their hopes for their children.

Today, as we gain a better understanding of the circular processes through which culture is developed and transmitted, we recognize that man's most human characteristic is not his ability to learn, which he shares with many other species, but his ability to teach and store what others have developed and taught him. In the past men relied on the least elaborate part of the circular system — the dependent learning by children — for continuity of transmission and for the embodiment of the new. Now, with our greater understanding of the process, we must cultivate the most flexible and complex part of the system: the behavior of adults. We must, in fact, teach ourselves how to alter adult behavior; we must create new models for adults who can teach their children not what to learn, but how to learn, and not what they should be committed to, but the value of commitment.

In doing this we must recognize explicitly that the paths by which we came into the present can never be traversed again. The past is the road by which we have arrived where we are. Older forms of culture have provided us with the knowledge, techniques, and tools necessary for our contemporary civilization.

The freeing of men's imagination from the past depends on the development of a new kind of communication with those who are most deeply involved with the future — the young who were born in the new world. In the past, in cofigurational cultures, the elders were gradually cut off from limiting the future of their children. Now the development of prefigurational cultures will depend on the existence of a continuing dialogue in which the young, free to act on their own initiative, can lead their elders in the direction of the unknown. Then the older generation will have access to the new experiential knowledge, without which no meaningful plans can be made. It is only with the direct participation of the young, who have that knowledge, that we can build a viable future.

Instead of directing their rebellion toward the retrieval of a grandparental utopian dream, as the Maoists seem to be doing with the young activists in China, we must learn together with the young how to take the next steps. Out of their new knowledge — new to the world and new to us — must come the questions to those who are already equipped by education and experience to search for answers. The children, the young, must ask these questions that we would never think to ask, but enough trust must be re-established so that the elders will be permitted to work with them on the answers.

I feel that we can change into a prefigurative culture, consciously, delightedly, and industriously, rearing unknown children for an unknown world. But to do it we must relocate the future.

Here we can take a cue from the young who seem to want instant utopias. They say the future is now. This seems unreasonable and impetuous, and in some of the demands they make it is unrealizable in concrete detail; but here again, I think, they give us the way to reshape our thinking. We must place the future, like the unborn child in the womb of a woman, within a community of men, women, and children, among us, already here, already to be nourished and succored and protected, already in need of things for which, if they are not prepared before it is born, it will be too late. So, as the young say, the future is now.

34

Interpersonal Relationships:
U.S.A. 2000

Carl R. Rogers

Carl R. Rogers is a distinguished psychologist and a pioneer in the development of open interpersonal relationships. In this article, based on his contribution to a symposium entitled "USA 2000," sponsored by the Esalen Institute, Rogers hopefully stresses the promise inherent in intensive group experiences for the realization of future interpersonal relationships. He presents a "new picture of man — this flowing, open, expressive, creative person."

Rogers, a former president of the American Psychological Association and a guiding force in client-centered therapy, psychotherapy, and study of personality, is now a member of the Center for Studies of the Person in La Jolla, California.

I want to make it very clear at the outset that I am not making predictions about the year 2000. I am going to sketch possibilities, alternative routes which we may travel.

One important reason for refusing to make predictions is that for the first time in history man is not only taking his future seriously, but he also has adequate technology and power to shape and form that culture. He is endeavoring to *choose* his future rather than simply living out some inevitable trend. And we do not know what he will choose. So we do not know what man's relation to man will be in this country thirty-two years from now. But we can see certain possibilities.

MAN'S GREATEST PROBLEM

Before I try to sketch some of those possibilities, I should like to point to the greatest problem which man faces in the years to come. It is not the hydrogen bomb, fearful as that may be. It is not the population explosion,

Carl R. Rogers, "Interpersonal Relationships: U.S.A. 2000," *Convergence*, II, 3 (1969), 40–46. Reprinted by permission. Abstracted from an article published in *The Journal of Applied Behavioral Science*, IV (1968), 265–80. This article was part of a symposium entitled "U.S.A. 2000," sponsored by the Esalen Institute and held in San Francisco, Calif., January 10, 1968.

though the consequences of that are awful to contemplate. It is instead a problem which is rarely mentioned or discussed. It is the question of how much change the human being can accept, absorb, and assimilate, and the rate at which he can take it. Can he keep up with the ever increasing rate of technological change, or is there some point at which the human organism goes to pieces? Can he leave the static ways and static guidelines which have dominated all of his history and adopt the process ways, the continual changingness which must be his if he is to survive?

There is much to make us pessimistic about this. If we consider the incredible difficulties in bringing about change in our great bureaucracies of government, education, and religion, we become hopeless. When we see how frequently the people take action which is clearly against their long-range welfare — such as the resolute refusal to face up to the problem of the urban ghettos — we become discouraged.

But I see two elements on the other side of the balance. The first is the ability of the Western democratic cultures to respond appropriately — at the very last cliff-hanging moment — to those trends which challenge their survival.

The second element I have observed in individuals in therapy, in intensive encounter groups, and in organizations. It is the magnetic attraction of the experience of change, growth, fulfillment. Even though growth may involve intense pain and suffering, once the individual or group has tasted the excitement of this changingness, persons are drawn to it as to a magnet. Once a degree of actualization has been savored, the individual or the group is willing to take the frightening risk of launching out into a world of process, with few fixed landmarks, where the direction is guided from within. So, in this field of interpersonal relations, though there is much reason for despair, I believe that if our citizens experience something of the pain and risk of a growth toward personal enrichment they will grasp for more.

With this context of uncertainty about our ability or willingness to assimilate change, let us look at some specific areas of interpersonal relationships.

Urban Crowding and its Possible Effects

The world population will more than double in the next thirty-two years, a ghastly trend which will affect us in unknown ways. The population of the United States, which was comfortably remembered in my grammar school days in 1915 as 100 million, fifty-two years later reached 200 million, twenty-two years from now is predicted to reach 300 million, and in the year 2000 will be between 320 and 340 million, though hopefully it will be starting to stabilize itself at about that time. The great bulk of these millions will reside in a great megalopolis, of which there will probably be three. One trend which we may follow is to crowd more and more closely together, as we are now crowded in our ghettos. I understand that Philip Hauser, the noted demographer, has stated that if all of us were crowded together as closely as the residents of Harlem, all of the people in the entire United States could be contained in the five boroughs of New York City. The future may resemble this, if we choose to push in more and more closely together.

Such crowding has consequences. Even in rats, as Calhoun[1] has so vividly shown, overcrowding results in poor mothering, poor nest building, bizarre sexual behavior, cannibalism, and complete alienation, with some rats behaving like zombies, paying no attention to others, coming out of their solitary burrows only for food. The resemblance to human behavior in crowded rooming house areas, the complete lack of involvement which permits people to watch a long-drawn-out murder without so much as calling the police, the poor family relationships — this could be a trend which will be carried even further by the year 2000.

On the other hand, we could learn to decentralize our great urban areas, to make them manageable, to provide not only for more efficiency but for warmer and more human interpersonal relationships. We could use more space, build smaller cities with great park and garden areas, devise plans for neighborhood building which would promote humanization, not dehumanization. What will the choice be?

CLOSENESS AND INTIMACY IN THE YEAR 2000

In my estimation, one of the most rapidly growing social phenomena in the United States is the spread of the intensive group experience — sensitivity training, basic encounter groups, T groups (the labels are unimportant). The growth of this phenomenon is rendered more striking when one realizes that it is a "grass roots" movement. There is not a university nor a foundation nor a government agency which has given it any significant approval or support until the last five or six years. Yet it has permeated industry, is coming into education, and is reaching families, professionals in the helping fields, and many other individuals. Why? I believe it is because people — ordinary people — have discovered that it alleviates their loneliness and permits them to grow, to risk, to change. It brings persons into real relationships with persons.

In our affluent society the individual's survival needs are satisfied. For the first time, he is freed to become aware of his isolation, aware of his alienation, aware of the fact that he is, during most of his life, a role interacting with other roles, a mask meeting other masks. And for the first time he is aware that this is not a *necessary* tragedy of life, that he does not have to live out his days in this fashion. So he is seeking, with great determination and inventiveness, ways of modifying this existential loneliness. The intensive group experience, perhaps the most significant social invention of this century, is an important one of these ways.

What will grow out of the current use of basic encounter groups, marathons, "labs," and the like? I have no idea what *forms* will proliferate out of these roots during the coming decades, but I believe men will discover

[1] J. B. Calhoun, "Population density and social pathology," *Scientific American,* 206, 2 (1962), 139–50.

new bases of intimacy that will be highly fulfilling. I believe there will be possibilities for the *rapid* development of closeness between and among persons, a closeness which is not artificial, but is real and deep, and which will be well suited to our increasing mobility of living. Temporary relationships will be able to achieve the richness and meaning which heretofore have been associated only with lifelong attachments.

There will be more awareness of what is going on within the person, an openness to all of one's experience — the sensory input of sound and taste and hearing and sight and smell, the richness of kaleidoscopically changing ideas and concepts, the wealth of feelings — positive, negative, and ambivalent, intense and moderate — toward oneself and toward others.

There will be the development of a whole new style of communication in which the person can, in effect, say, "I'm telling you the way it *is*, in me — my ideas, my desires, my feelings, my hopes, my angers, my fears, my despairs," and where the response will be equally open. We shall be experimenting with ways in which a whole person can communicate himself to another whole person. We shall discover that security resides not in hiding oneself but in being more fully known, and consequently in coming to know the other more fully. Aloneness will be something one chooses out of a desire for privacy, not an isolation into which one is forced.

In all of this I believe we shall be experimenting with a new ideal of what man may become, a model very *sharply* different from the historical view of man as a creature playing various appropriate roles. We seem to be aiming for a new *reality* in relationships, a new openness in communication, a love for one another which grows not out of a romantic blindness but out of the profound respect which is nearly always engendered by reality in relationships.

I recognize that many individuals in our culture are frightened in the depths of their being by this new picture of man — this flowing, changing, open, expressive, creative person. They may be able to stop the trend or even to reverse it. It is conceivable that we shall go in for the manufactured "image," as on television, or may insist more strongly than ever that teachers are *teachers*, parents are *parents*, bosses are *manipulators* — that we may rigidify every role and stereotype in new and more armorplated ways. We may insist with new force that the only significant aspect of man is his rational and intellectual being and that nothing else matters. We may assert that he is a machine and no more. Yet I do not believe this will happen. The magnetism of the new man, toward which we are groping, is too great. Much of what I say in the remainder of this paper is based on the conviction that we are, for better or for worse, in labor pains and growth pains, turning toward this new view of man as becoming and being — a continuing, growing *process*. . . .

LEARNING IN INTERPERSONAL RELATIONSHIPS

What of education in the year 2000, especially as it involves interpersonal relationships? It is possible that education will continue much as it is — concerned only with words, symbols, rational concepts based on the authoritative role of the teacher, further dehumanized by teaching machines, computerized knowledge, and increased use of tests and examinations. This is possible, because educators are showing greater resistance to change than any other institutional group. Yet I regard it as unlikely, because a revolution in education is long overdue, and the unrest of students is only one sign of this. So I am going to speculate on some of the other possibilities.

It seems likely that schools will be greatly deemphasized in favor of a much broader, thoughtfully devised *environment for learning*, where the experiences of the student will be challenging, rewarding, affirmative, and pleasurable.

The teacher or professor will have largely disappeared. His place will be taken by a facilitator of learning, chosen for his facilitative attitudes as much as for his knowledge. He will be skilled in stimulating individual and group initiative in learning, skilled in facilitating discussions-in-depth of the *meaning* to the student of what is being learned, skilled in fostering creativity, skilled in providing the resources for learning. Among these resources will be much in the way of programmed learning, to be used as the student finds these learnings appropriate; much in the way of audiovisual aids such as filmed lectures and demonstrations by experts in each field; much in the way of computerized knowledge on which the student can draw. But these "hardware" possibilities are not my main concern.

We shall, I believe, see the facilitator focusing his major attention on the prime period for learning — from infancy to age six or eight. Among the most important learnings will be the personal and interpersonal. Every child will develop confidence in his own ability to learn, since he will be rewarded for learning at his own pace. Each child will learn that he is a person of worth, because he has unique and worthwhile capacities. He will learn how to be himself in a group — to listen, but also to speak, to learn about himself, but also to confront and give feedback to others. He will learn to be an individual, not a faceless conformist. He will learn, through simulations and computerized games, to meet many of the life problems he will face. He will find it permissible to engage in fantasy and daydreams, to think creative thoughts, to capture these in words or paints or constructions. He will find that learning, even difficult learning, is fun, both as an individual activity and in cooperation with others. His discipline will be self-discipline.

His learning will not be confined to the ancient intellectual concepts and specializations. It will not be a *preparation* for living. It will be, in itself, an *experience* in living. Feelings of inadequacy, hatred, a desire for power, feelings of love and awe and respect, feelings of fear and dread, unhappiness with parents or with other children — all these will be an open part of his curriculum, as worthy of exploration as history or mathematics. In fact this openness to feelings will enable him to learn content material more readily. His will be an education in becoming a whole human being, and the learnings will involve him deeply, openly, exploringly, in an awareness of his relationship to the world of others, as well as in an awareness of the world of abstract knowledge.

Because learning has been exciting, because he has participated heavily and responsibly in choosing the directions of his learning, because he has discovered the world to be a fantastically changing place, he will wish to continue his learning into adult life. Thus communities will set up centers that are rich environments for learning, and the student will *never be graduated*. He will always be a part of a "commencement."

Persons in Industry

In view of my past prejudices I find it somewhat difficult but necessary to say that of all of the institutions of present-day American life, industry is perhaps best prepared to meet year 2000. I am not speaking of its technical ability. I am speaking of the vision it is acquiring in regard to the importance of persons, of interpersonal relationships, and of open communication. That vision, to be sure, is often unrealized but it does exist.

Let me speculate briefly on the interpersonal aspect of industrial functioning. It is becoming increasingly clear to the leaders of any complex modern industry that the old hierarchical system of boss and employees is obsolete. If a factory is turning out one simple product, such a system may still work. But if it is in the business of producing vehicles for space or elaborate electronic devices, it is definitely inadequate. What takes its place? The only road to true efficiency seems to be that of persons communicating freely with persons — from below to above, from peer to peer, from above to below, from a member of one division to a member of another division. It is only through this elaborate, individually initiated network of open human communication that the essential information and know-how can pervade the organization. No one individual can possibly "direct" such complexity.

Thus if I were to hazard a guess in regard to industry in the year 2000 it would be something different from the predictions about increasing technical skill, increasing automation, increasing management by computers, and the like. All of those predictions will doubtless come true but the interpersonal aspect is less often discussed. I see many industries, by the year 2000, giving as much attention to the quality of interpersonal relationships and the quality of communication as they currently do to the technological aspects of their business. They will come to value persons as persons, and to recognize that only out of the *communicated* knowledge of all members of the organization can innovation and progress come. They will be forced to recognize that only as they are promoting the growth and fulfillment of the individuals on the payroll will they be promoting the growth and development of the organization.

What I have said will apply, I believe, not only to persons in management but to persons classed as "labor." The distinction grows less with every technological advance. It also applies, obviously, to the increasingly direct and personal communication between persons in management and persons in the labor force, if an industry is to become and remain healthily productive.

RELIGION AS INTERPERSONAL LIVING

Historically, much of man's life has revolved around his relationship to his God or gods and around his relationship to others who share his religious views. What will be the situation three decades from now?

It is definitely conceivable that out of a deep fear of the rapidly changing world he is creating, man may seek refuge in a sure dogma, a simplistic answer to life's complexities, a religion which will serve him as security blanket. This seems unlikely, but I can imagine the circumstances under which it might occur.

The more likely possibility — or so it appears to me — is that by the year 2000, *institutionalized* religion, already on the wane as a significant factor in everyday life, will have faded to a point where it is of only slight importance in the community. Theology may still exist as a scholastic exercise, but in reality the God of authoritative answers will be not only dead but buried.

This does not mean at all that the concerns that have been the basis of religion will have vanished. The mysterious process of life, the mystery of the universe and how it came to be, the tragedy of man's alienation from himself and from others, the puzzle of the meaning of individual life — these mysteries will all be very much present. There may, indeed, be a *greater appreciation* of mystery as our knowledge increases (just as theoretical physicists now marvel at the true *mystery* of what they have discovered).

But religion, to the extent that the term is used, will consist of tentatively held hypotheses that are lived out and corrected in the interpersonal world. Groups, probably much smaller than present-day congregations, will wrestle with the ethical and moral and philosophical questions that are posed by the rapidly changing world. The individual will forge, with the support of the group, the stance he will take in the universe — a stance that he cannot regard as final because more data will continually be coming in.

In the open questioning and honest struggle to face reality which exist in such a group, it is likely that a sense of true community will develop — a community based not on a common creed nor an unchanging ritual but on the personal ties of individuals who have become deeply related to one another as they attempt to comprehend and to face, as living men, the mysteries of existence. The religion of the future will be man's existential choice of his way of living in an unknown tomorrow, a choice made more bearable because formed in a community of individuals who are like-minded, but like-minded only in their searching.

In line with the thread which runs through all of my remarks, it may well be that out of these many searching groups there may emerge a more unitary view which might bind us together. Man as a creature with ability to remember the past and foresee the future, a creature with the capacity for choosing among alternatives, a creature whose deepest urges are for harmonious and loving relationships with his fellows, a creature with the capacity to understand the reasons for his destructive behaviors, man as a person who has at least limited powers to form himself and to shape his future in the way he desires — this might be a crude sketch of the unifying view which could give us hope in a universe we cannot understand....

35

Future Shock and the Curriculum

Harold G. Shane

Harold G. Shane, whom the reader has already met in an article in Part Two on curriculum for the Seventies, calls attention to future shock. He demonstrates that "dizzying disorientation" is already upon us and suggests "preventive medicine" for educators confronted with continuing and accelerating future shock.

Mr. Shane, University Professor of Education at Indiana University, is a scholarly practitioner of future-planning.

Most Americans who have traveled in Afro-Asia or Latin America are aware of the phenomenon of *culture shock*. This is a psychosomatic reaction, often of considerable violence, that results when one becomes entangled in the invisible web of a new and partly incomprehensible way of life. Explicitly, the shock comes from a sense of confusion that arises when the customs, language, and similar elements of an alien people fail to make sense in the context of the experiences transferred from the familiar cultural landscape through which one previously has learned to thread his way.[1]

CULTURE SHOCK AND FUTURE SHOCK

Persons who grow up in other cultures simply do not see and hear things as we do, and vice versa. Concepts of time, territorial or space rights, status, and so on are not only different, they may be in conflict. In an anthropologist's words, it is no longer valid to assume ". . . when two human beings are subject to the same experience, [that] virtually the same data are being

Harold G. Shane, "Future Shock and the Curriculum," *Phi Delta Kappan*, October, 1967, 67–70. Reprinted by permission of the author and publisher.

[1] Cross-cultural misunderstandings, confusion, and "shock" are simply and clearly discussed by the anthropological linguist, Edward T. Hall. Cf. his books, *The Silent Language* (Doubleday, 1959) and *The Hidden Dimension* (Doubleday, 1966).

fed to the two control nervous systems and that the two brains record similarly."[2] To use an illustration, a Spaniard and a person from the U.S. do not see or "record" the same bullfight in the Madrid bull ring. The *Madrileño* identifies with the skilled matador and the American identifies with the doomed bull. Obviously, a similar sensory input leads to totally different reactions.

Just as many people from the U.S. are upset when residing overseas by the absence of familiar cultural clues and suffer culture shock, many Americans are beginning to suffer from *future shock*.[3] Future shock, like culture shock, is a condition marked by a decline in cognitive powers, misinterpretation of reality, and loss of the ability to communicate ideas with one's usual skill.

We have encountered the future so rapidly and with such violent changes in the ordered and familiar patterns of our way of life that we are suffering ". . . the dizzying disorientation brought on by the premature arrival of the future."[4]

Many generations of change have been compressed into the span of 10 years; so brief a period that it is scarcely a single second on the clockface of history.[5] As a result, the changed social and scientific environment in which persons find themselves today is literally as strange, in many ways, as that in which the U.S. foreign aid worker or Peace Corps volunteer finds himself in an Indian village of the Andes, a Hausa tribe in Nigeria, or a center of Moslem life in West Pakistan.

The possible consequences of future shock for education are considerable. Let us first review the sources of the dislocation that seems to threaten the composure and effectiveness of individuals involved in educational leadership, research, and service.

SOME EDUCATIONAL SOURCES OF FUTURE SHOCK

During the 1920's and 1930's the educational scene in the U.S. was a lively one. Changes were made in methods and materials, and periodical literature was full of stimulating ideas. Manuscript writing, the project method, teacher-pupil planning, social reconstruction through education, and a hundred similar proposals found strident supporters and dogged opponents.

Violent as the debates of the times became, however, no one seemed to be traumatized or even seriously upset as verbal warfare between conservative and liberal, between "subject-oriented" and "learner-oriented," forces enlivened commerce in the free market of educational ideas. Certainly,

---

[2] Edward T. Hall, *The Hidden Dimension*. New York: Doubleday & Co., Inc., 1966, p. 2.

[3] Insofar as I can determine, the term *future shock* was coined by Alvin Toffler. See his "The Future as a Way of Life," *Horizons*, Summer, 1965.

[4] *Ibid.*, p. 109.

[5] The speed and scope of change are so great as to blur vision and memory. A good review and reminder of what happened in the 25 years between 1939 and 1964 can be found in John Brook's readable social history, *The Great Leap*. New York: Harper and Row, 1966. 382 pp.

prior to the 1950's there was less uneasiness, less uncertainty, and less poorly concealed panic about the nature, the merit, and the speed of educational change than there is now.

No real future shock was experienced by educators of this era because new practices — despite the debates they generated — were rarely rapid[6] and generally were *extensions* and *refinements* of familiar ideas, methods, and procedures rather than basic *changes* or *innovations* involving heretofore unfamiliar technologies or based on concepts with little or no precedent.

What, then, has recently happened *in* education and *to* education to bring on the "dizzying disorientation" caused by a premature collision with the future? Since around 1950 many educators have found themselves confronting new educational directions to which their past learning and experience simply do not transfer. For purposes of clarity, some examples need to be given to show how, in a very few years, the jolting educational changes of a long lifetime have been compressed into a 10-year interval.

Education's casual and sometimes pious interest in the contributions of related disciplines got out of hand. Specialists outside of the teaching profession began to contribute more than the schools could readily assimilate in mathematics, cultural anthropology, linguistics, ethology,[7] sociology, biochemistry, and so on.

Long-postponed implementation of civil rights legislation created many stresses.

New interpretations of the role of higher education created issues as to its scope, purpose, and control as post-secondary education began moving toward virtual universalization.

The educational power structure began to show signs of changing, particularly at the national level. (For example, the administration of one USOE function moved from an Ed.D. in administration to a Ph.D. in anthropology, and thence to a systems engineer formerly with a major U.S. corporation.)[8]

After the future shock of Russia's sputnik in 1957 and the questioning of U.S. education which it created, there was an unprecedented increase in the funding of education. This was an unsettling experience in itself; it further disturbed administrators because local choice in the deployment of the monies did not increase in proportion to the sums available.

Both the concentration and overspill of population in U.S. cities were recognized as a conspicuous problem, as were the new inner-city–megalopolitan inequities in educational opportunities.

[6] Years ago, on the basis of a study of trends, Mort and Cornell concluded that it required from 75 to 100 years for an educational idea or theory to be translated into common practice. Cf. Paul Mort and Francis Cornell, *American Schools in Transition.* New York: Bureau of Publications, Teachers College, Columbia University, 1941. p. 49.

[7] *Ethology*, a relatively new science is not always listed in the dictionary. It is concerned with the precise, methodical study of innate, or inherited, animal behavior.

[8] Cf. Peter Schrag, "Voices in the Classroom: Is There a New Establishment?" *Saturday Review*, Oct. 15, 1966. p. 87.

The "learning business" virtually exploded as the educational and financial possibilities of technology were recognized. Among those involved in new combines and novel ventures in educational technology: Time, Inc., G.E., I.B.M., Raytheon, C.B.S., R.C.A., Minnesota Mining and Manufacturing, et al.[9]

Several years before Marshall McLuhan reported that TV was "retribalizing" U.S. children (and turning the world into a "global village"), it became apparent that there were unusual behavioral and intellectual mutations occurring among the young.[10] These inward changes seem to be one of many causes of nationwide "protest movements" among youth. The "phantom curriculum" created by mass media, the great unindexed body of data children acquire even before beginning kindergarten, has made education's clientele "different" in the span of a decade.

Cybernetics — the realm of automatic control systems in mechanical electrical communication systems — is another great generator of future shock in education. Whether reflected in individualized computer programming for pupils or in complex information retrieval, such developments as computer based instruction (CBI) and individually planned instruction (IPI), with the computer serving as a mediating agency, are an unnerving change to many teachers and create within them fears as to their downward fall into obsolescence.[11]

"New" approaches and content in such fields as mathematics, science, and English instruction have placed teachers at all levels under heavy stresses. The pressure at the moment is especially high in the field of English, where the introduction of so-called "linguistic approaches," often based on incompletely developed theories and partially tested hypotheses, has created considerable confusion and disturbance among teachers.[12]

The 10 preceding examples suffice to illustrate how educators have been thrust from yesterday into tomorrow. On the whole, the points made also show how future shock ensues when, in the face of so many rapid changes, one is deprived of familiar clues that hitherto have successfully guided his interaction with his environment.

SOME SUGGESTIONS FOR COPING WITH FUTURE SHOCK IN EDUCATION

Although the new malady of future shock is disconcerting, care has been taken to avoid labeling it as "bad." Just as recovery from culture shock after

[9] Cf. Henry Bern, "Wanted: Education Engineers," PHI DELTA KAPPAN, January, 1967, pp. 230–36.

[10] Probably the best digest of McLuhanism and the "media impact" was written by one of his colleagues at Fordham University. Cf. John M. Culkin, S.J., "A Schoolman's Guide to Marshall McLuhan," Saturday Review, March 18, 1967.

[11] Cf. John C. Flanagan, "Functional Education for the Seventies," PHI DELTA KAPPAN, September, 1967, pp. 27–31.

[12] For a recently published review and appraisal of developments, cf. Harold G. Shane, Linguistics and the Classroom Teacher. Washington, D.C.: The Association for Supervision and Curriculum Development, NEA, 1967. 120 pp.

a few disturbing months of residence in Bangkok or Cairo can herald an increase in one's wisdom and intercultural insight, so U.S. educators' exposure to a future they were not prepared to meet so soon could do a great deal to improve our schools. After all, much of the rest of the world also is meeting an even more unanticipated future head-on; why not the curricula in our schools? Consider the developing countries overseas that are attempting in 25 years to adapt certain processes of democratic government which, after nearly two centuries of experiment, remain in a condition of imperfect development even in our own land. Nor are many of these countries doing too badly in view of the odds imposed by tribal traditions, illiteracy, and myriads of similar problems.

What, specifically, promises to be good medicine with which to treat future shock in education? For one thing, it should be recognized that old and young educators vary in their need for therapy. The young ones merely need the right diet, the proper "care and feeding" that will enable them to work contributively in a newly arrived future. After all, tomorrow is not strange for those who belong to it. The beginning teacher today never knew the pre-TV world, was an infant when the day of the atom began in 1945, and hadn't finished elementary school when sputnik orbited us into the space age a decade ago.

Our problem in pre-service education and in graduate study, therefore, is to do whatever is necessary to avoid contaminating tomorrow's teachers with the future shock "fall-out" of our groundless personal fears and unfounded illusions about education. Our best, if not our only, treatment here is *preventive* medicine.

Now let us turn our thinking to the question of what can be found in the pharmacopoeia to remedy our malady. This includes treatment for philosophically blurred vision, curricular dyspepsia, and the temporary aphasia resulting from technical progress and accompanying social upheavals, which temporarily have exceeded both our grasp of change in education and our receptivity to it. Hopefully, the following prescriptions are the result of good diagnoses.

Develop In-service Education Programs that Face the Future. Educational leadership needs to bring teachers' thinking into focus with respect to their tasks in the immediate future. This is important when we realize that some of the younger ones will still be influencing educational practices in 2015 A.D. Among examples of possible in-service practices are:

Greatly liberalized leave policies to encourage teachers to re-educate and to retool themselves with respect to educational theory, content, and practice.

New relationships with higher education such as visiting professorships awarded *by public schools* to college staff members, on loan from universities, to serve in local program development and in-service classes.

Greater *informed* teacher participation in decision making that bears on rapid program change.

Provision for teachers' short-term instruction in theory, in basic maintenance, and in the use of the products of the "learning business," possibly through resident study in plants producing new media.

Experiments with salary differentials for specialized faculty assignments.

"Residencies," following pre-service education, during which beginning teachers are "phased in" to their work as part of educational teams in the schools.

Much greater use of teacher exchange, especially among U.S. schools and within large districts, but including overseas schools.

Deliberately Purchase Imagination. We need to purchase imagination, to develop a breed of professionally respectable educators who have the skills of educational navigation plus the vision of scientific soothsayers. The schools need to buy top-flight brains just as industry has done. The schools also need individuals who are skilled in *change analysis* and in developing sound educational thrust into the 1970's and 1980's.

Reverse the Traditional Emphasis on the Upper Levels of Education. From earliest times we have respected the important role of secondary and collegiate education. Available funds and status have gravitated to high schools and colleges, and elementary school faculty members have been left to wail, "But I'm only a second-grade teacher." It will help us to cope with the future if we literally reverse our educational priorities. While we have given lip service to the importance of early childhood, we have nevertheless provided a starvation diet for these formative years. We will move into the future in distinctly better order when teachers of the youngest are prepared (and rewarded) in the same manner as those who direct the work of doctoral candidates.[13]

Recognize and Alleviate the Reasons for Student Protest Movements. Vehement student protests and demonstrations in almost every type of college and university (and in some secondary schools) have been one of the unsettling developments on U.S. campuses. *We need to recognize that the protest movement itself is a manifestation of future shock hitting students.* In the 1930's humane relationships and mutual respect were encouraged in classrooms as teachers and young people alike stood bewildered by the depression and their shared misery.

World War II, the cold war, and sputnik combined to usher in the present college-level shock waves of mechanization, standardization, automation: all inadvertent but effective ways of eroding security, the stimulation of discovery-inquiry, and self-identity.[14] A re-humanization of education with greater stress on individua*lity* rather than individualization seems overdue.

[13] Also cf. G. B. Leonard, "A Hopeful Look at Education in 2000 A.D.," *Educational Services Bulletin No. 21*, Arizona State University, pp. 9–23.

[14] Biological research of a wide-ranging nature is confirming the importance of security, stimulation, and identity. Cf. the society of inward antagonism (or *noyau*) concept in J.-J. Petter, "L'Ecologie et L'Ethologie des Lémuriens Malgache," *Mémoires du Muséum National d'Histoire Naturelle*, Tome XXVII, Fascicule 1, Paris, 1962.

Conceive a Model of a "Lifetime Curriculum." It seems reasonable to conceptualize the idea of the lifetime curriculum as a useful means of diminishing future shock. The "lifetime curriculum" concept presupposes that the current rate of change will continue to crowd us, that world problems will by no means diminish, that a number of yesterday's arts and occupations will change or disappear, that the rate of knowledge accumulation will continue to increase, and that human beings will continue to fall somewhere short of perfection.

Under this set of circumstances, and assuming the continuation of trends such as those leading toward the leisure of an eight-month year for workers[15] and to the transfer of magnetic programmed tapes rather than of people to operate machines,[16] it seems reasonable for the schools to sponsor a lifetime of education. By the 1980's or 1990's this could become virtually an educational "conducted tour" or continuum of learning experience stretching from early childhood to old age for those who sought it. Let us turn in the next three topic headings to a more precise consideration of what form this proposal might take when phased into the educational environment.

Design New Comprehensive Self-realization Centers. Highly effective tonic for diminishing *future* attacks of future shock probably can be found in the form of the Self-Realization or S-R center. This may be defined as a unified educational complex providing learning services for an entire population. What is, in the 1960's, labeled "elementary," "secondary," and "higher" education doubtless will be handled on a unitary or coordinated basis in such a complex. Such elements in our social infrastructure as recreation and health services, museums, conservatories, planeteria, and aquaria also might be administered and operated in the education center — at least until such a time as their functions are superseded by multi-dimensional simulation.

Create the Kinds of School Organization Which the Future Mandates. Most discussions and proposals with direct relevance to the structure and administration of education have shown remarkably little long-range foresight. Concentration on the present is understandable and necessary.[17] At the same time, planning for the operation of schools likely to be needed in 1977 — not to mention 1997 — should not be neglected. Public schools and universities need to begin to project ways to cultivate administrators adept in new ways of thinking and acting, since the young men and women who will provide our senior leadership for administration in 1997 are just now beginning to cast a speculative eye on preparation for this vocation.

[15] Ottino Caracciolo di Forino, "Some Reflections for 1986," *Business Horizons*, Spring, 1967, pp. 31–38.

[16] *Ibid.*, p. 35. Signor di Forino anticipates that, once automated equipment (say in Africa) is installed, we will not need to send technicians to operate it. We will simply send programmed tapes which *replicate* their skills in operating the machines.

[17] As one harassed administrator put it, "I don't celebrate *arrival* of the new year; I celebrate *survival* of the last year."

Within the next few years we will need rapidly to develop the prototype for a combination scholar-scientist-senior administrator who is capable of orchestrating the activities of education centers serving clusters of people ranging from one million to 20 million or more in size and from 18 months to well over 100 years in age.[18] Such proposals are by no means science fiction. Indeed, major educational complexes already operating foreshadow this sort of emergent development. What we need is less haphazard drift and more deliberate planning of their design.

School organization likewise needs to develop a momentum that will carry it ahead. For at least a century educators have tried to devise organizational plans and structures which would facilitate instruction and temper the problem of human differences.[19] Most thinking that has been done thus far has concentrated on changes within the framework of basically *conventional* schools. The next evolutionary step in organizing schools to cope with individuality will not come in a conventional form at all.[20] Let us next examine three ideas which should help us to counter future shock. Each promises to be helpful in improving teaching methods and content.

Phase in the Cyborg Unit. A cyborg unit is a cooperative combination of machine and human *controlled by the latter*.[21] The word is derived by combining CYBernetic and ORGanic. Functionally speaking, a man with an artificial kidney is a cyborg. Within the next 10 years, as a result of meeting the future so quickly, we are almost certain to develop cyborg teams: teachers whom educational media and technology have extended almost beyond our present capacity to imagine.[22] We will begin to show signs of recovering from future shock when conventional school organization and school plant have been replaced by the S-R type of education center mentioned above: essentially one large teaching aid operated *with human values paramount* and in which man, media, and machines serve man.

Such a school would not be *centered* around media — *the school plant itself would be media* from which people of all ages and backgrounds would learn. The designing of learning, the retrieval of information, the encouragement of self-direction, the extension of experience for persons of all ages at any time of the year, and above all the consummately skillful low-pressure nurture

[18] Life spans of 200 years or more are forecast for 2100 A.D., with the "human" body quite possibly—in its later years or due to injuries—composed of its present organic equipment plus, say, a mechanical heart, leg, liver, or lung. More and more we will find old age treated like a disease rather than as an inevitable fate.

[19] A vintage article by Henry J. Otto relates in interesting retrospect the efforts made to organize schools to cope with individual differences between 1860 and 1930. Cf. references cited.

[20] Two current research reports related to grouping, broadly conceived, anticipate the future. Cf. Miriam Goldberg, Harry Passow, and Joseph Justman, *The Effects of Ability Grouping*. New York: Teachers College Press, Columbia University, 1966. 254 pp. Also cf. H. A. Thelen, *Classroom Grouping for Teachability*. New York: John Wiley & Sons, Inc., 1967. 274 pp.

[21] Cf. B. R. Joyce, *The Teacher and His Staff: Man, Media, and Machines*. Washington, D.C.: Center for the Study of Instruction, NEA, 1967.

[22] It was Marshall McLuhan who said that all media work us over completely because they function as psychic or physical extensions of some human faculty. E.g., the wheel is an extension of our feet.

and guidance of human development and questing would be the task of the cyborg-team teachers. Anything but a machine himself, such a teacher presumably would have no more than three class-contact hours during a "3-M day" in which man, media, and machine combined their input, guidance, and evaluative feedback to make learning meaningful for the individual learner in the quest for his personal goals.

The gradual phase-in of media and machines as hinted above is an excellent potential cure for future shock. Lest scoffers cry "science fiction," it is worth noting that by 1967 planning of educational resources of the sort described already had appeared in print for a proposed community of 100,000 contemplated near Phoenix, Arizona.[23]

Learn How to Annex Content From Other Fields. By the 1950's it was already clear that part of education's future shock stemmed from developments in content fields which, as in the case of the "new math" or "new science," reflected the trend toward curriculum change guided from outside the teaching profession.[24] Proper therapy to relieve this shock is self-evident. Education needs to seize the initiative and develop the brain-power and the means for methodically annexing the relevant content and tools or methods of promise created in related disciplines.

In effect this is a proposal that education not only plan to draw on materials from other fields to strengthen itself, but also that education bring into its ranks many more persons whose preparation combines educational *and* academic backgrounds.

Apply the "Culture-centric Curriculum Change" Concept. Many approaches have been made to curriculum change — so many that the literature bristles with jargon and drips with slogans. None has proved to be a final answer. A promising and largely untried approach that augurs well for easing our progress into future changes is basing curriculum coordination and change on the analysis of culture as indirectly proposed by Trager and Hall.[25] Cultural anthropology holds much promise for helping educators to realize how the cultural backgrounds of mankind create major potential misunderstandings.

Humans are not turned into stereotypes by growing up under the influence of an alien culture or under U.S. subcultural influences — but neither is the superficial assumption that "all men are alike" an intellectually defensible one. In a world rapidly becoming a crowded global space ship as it spins into the future, we need to base the curriculum on the results of study-indepth of the human clientele of the school.

THE FAR SIDE OF THE GREAT WATERSHED

There have been only a few great watersheds in history. Two of these mountainous divisions separating an outmoded past from a suddenly altered

---

[23] The learning center, one of comprehensive dimensions, proposed by G. B. Leonard, *ibid.*, p. 10 ff.

[24] Cf. John Goodlad, *The Changing School Curriculum.* New York: Fund for the Advancement of Education, 1966. 122 pp.

[25] Cf. Edward T. Hall, *ibid., et passim.*

future were the development of printing and the onset of the Industrial Revolution. Mass media and cybernetics made the mid-twentieth century a third great watershed.

In the early 1800's, in response to the shock effect of the Industrial Revolution in Great Britain, a number of unemployed factory workers went berserk. Under the exhorting of a slow-witted Leicestershire mill worker, Ned Ludd, these "Luddites" smashed the power-driven looms which they felt had robbed them of their jobs. In education, as we move over to the far side of our 20th century watershed, it is important that we avoid similar panic patterns of behavior.

Let us demonize neither change nor machinery; let us recognize reality. *We cannot change the history of education's collision with the future, but we can conceptualize and build better programs of instruction as we digest the meaning of new opportunities and responsibilities.*

In the process, let us make a more determined effort to communicate clearly. This includes acknowledging that labeling or defining problems is not solving them, and that words are no substitute for action. And let us keep and increase our confidence in the cognitive powers of ourselves and others. This involves recognizing that *the virtually untapped power of the human mind set free dwarfs the power of any machine — and that machines were created by men to serve men; not for men to serve, but for men to use in freeing that power of the mind.*

36

Future-Planning and the Curriculum

Harold G. Shane and June Grant Shane

The Shanes, collaborating in "Future-Planning and the Curriculum" recommend future-planning to "create the particular future that our beliefs recommend from among the many less desirable alternative futures in which education, by default, may find itself." Their article summarizes the high points in the history of futurism. The authors describe possible uses of ORPHIC techniques to arrive at an intellectually tested consensus with respect to proposed curriculum changes.

Harold G. Shane and June Grant Shane, "*Future*-Planning and the Curriculum," *Phi Delta Kappan*, March, 1968, 372–377. Reprinted by permission of the authors and publisher.

Collaborating with Harold G. Shane is his wife, June Grant Shane, formerly of the University of Pittsburgh and currently Pro fessor of Education at Indiana University.

During the past decade, and particularly in the last four or five years, the concept of *future*-planning has been explored in such fields as business, government, the military, and certain sciences. *Future*-planning involves a number of promising procedures *for anticipating and shaping or influencing the various possible futures which lie before mankind.*

The concept is of major importance to education, yet it is little known in educational circles. The times now seem right for educators to consider applying these challenging methodologies in the identification of acceptable educational alternatives and for developing school policies and programs.

Future-planning is proposed as a procedure for creating curricular and instructional strategies that are more than hindsight remedies for today's problems. It employs a sophisticated means for combining values as well as data from education and related disciplines. These, together with the power of controlled imagination, are deliberately employed to *create the particular educational future that our beliefs recommend from among the many less desirable alternative futures in which education, by default, may find itself.*

In this article it is our purpose to explain what *future*-planning is, and to suggest what it could mean for curriculum design, research, and development in the 1970's and 1980's.

What Future-Planning Is

Future-planning should not be confused with future *planning*. The latter has been commonplace in education for generations as teachers and administrators have endeavored to determine what current circumstances and trends suggested. In other words, much future *planning* has been passive, generally linear, and most frequently based on intuitive guesses or estimates as to the nature of tomorrow.

Future-planning, on the other hand, is active, conceives of the future as a fan-like spread of many "possibles," and assumes that the nature of our tomorrows can be mediated, even to some extent determined, through systematic conjecture based on analysis and projection of data. A few months ago Olaf Helmer of RAND Corporation phrased it this way:

> . . . in the last few years . . . a wholly new attitude toward the future has become apparent among policy planners and others concerned with the future of society. Customary planning horizons are being extended into a more distant future, and *intuitive gambles are being replaced by a systematic analysis of the opportunities the future has to offer.*[1]

---

[1] Olaf Helmer, "The Future of Science," unpublished typescript of an article prepared for October, 1967, publication in *The Science Journal*, pp. 2–4 (italics added).

Ways[2] contends that the "art of futurism" will be recognized within 10 years, both at home and abroad, as a salient American characteristic. Other interest-compelling viewpoints are abundant. Alexander[3] wrote about the procedures and developments in U.S. corporations as they strive to design tomorrow, and Kopkind[4] made a highly informative 1967 status report on the future-planners and "technopols" who are now working in the heartlands of government and industry. Bell,[5] who discusses the concept of the "post-industrial society," also suggests ways in which projected and applied theoretical knowledge have become "the matrix of innovation" by which society now lives and grows.

Since applied and informed conjecture is the fuel that feeds the art of studying the implications of probable future developments, from what is the fuel extracted? A concise statement of the background of *future*-planning and its potential contributions to curriculum change is in order.

A CAPSULE HISTORY

Voltaire (1694–1778) appears to have been one of the first men to have the idea of deliberately peering into the future. Back in the seventeenth century he proposed the term "prevoyance" for the process. But it was Louis XV — a man with an understandable uneasiness about the future — for whom the first predictive study was made. A document, subsequently found in the *armoire de fer* or strongbox of Louis XVI in the aftermath of the French Revolution, revealed that a Foreign Ministry employee, one J. L. Flavier, had made a 1773 report based on a system of "reasoned conjectures" which presented probable foreseeable changes.[6]

H. G. Wells, who was quick to foresee the impact of industry and technology on early twentieth century life, also seemed aware of the power of reasoned prediction. "Every disastrous thing that has happened in the past 20 years," he said, "was clearly foretold by a galaxy of writers and thinkers 20 years ago."[7]

Future-planning began to assume its present form in the later years of World War II. During this period operations research, with its stress on model-building based on the best available information, was first used. New techniques for planning were developed to deal with "multiple possibilities" and "alternate outcomes" in military landings, campaigns, and bombings.

During the postwar years, Olaf Helmer and T. J. Gordon[8] of the RAND

[2] Max Ways, "The Road to 1977," *Fortune*, January, 1967, p. 94.

[3] Tom Alexander, "The Wild Birds Find a Corporate Roost," *Fortune*, August, 1964, pp. 129–34; 164–68.

[4] Alexander Kopkind, "The Future-Planners," *The New Republic*, February 25, 1967, pp. 19–23.

[5] Daniel Bell, "Notes on the Post-Industrial Society (I)," *The Public Interest*, Winter, 1967, p. 29.

[6] Cf. Bertrand de Jouvenel, *Futuribles*, a paper presented at a RAND Seminar, November 30, 1964, p. 4.

[7] Cited by Edgar Dale in "What Can Literature Do?" *The Newsletter*, November, 1967, p. 3.

[8] Cf. the RAND Archives: *Report on a Long-Range Forecasting Study*, Olaf Helmer and T. J. Gordon, September, 1964.

Corporation explored some highly interesting techniques for *future*-planning. Olaf Helmer[9] in his *Social Technology*, for example, offers specific suggestions for applying operations research techniques to the social sciences. He feels that the rewards resulting from development of a social technology must not be disregarded if the gap between the physical and social sciences is to be lessened. A number of fugitive materials associated with the application of knowledge to the modulation of future "possibles" are to be found in RAND document files.[10] Henry S. Rowen, young (41) new president of the corporation, seems likely to stimulate further a scrutiny of tomorrow. Until 1965 he was a top long-range *future*-planner in the Defense Department.[11]

To conclude our capsule history, the Bell Telephone Laboratories are credited with the origin of the systems approach,[12] and by the mid-Fifties General Electric had created TEMPO for socioeconomic forecasting. Westinghouse — along with the major automotive companies — rapidly followed suit.[13] During the same period, business management consultants such as Booz, Allen, and Hamilton, Inc., began using PERT (Program Evaluation and Review Techniques — a systematic method for planning for many diverse activities) as a management information device. As a means of coping with the future, PERT was ". . . generally credited with a major contribution in making the Polaris missile operational two years ahead of the original schedule."[14]

By 1967, *future*-planning and methodical speculation had become widespread both in the U.S. and overseas. If it were not for certain "internal" or "process" complexities that served as safeguards, it might now be almost of epidemic proportions. England, France, and Germany are among the countries that now have well-developed groups and teams making intellectual forays into the future. In Paris, for example, Bertrand de Jouvenel has become a kind of intellectual dean of futurists. The Ford Foundation has sponsored a group called the *Futuribles*, a small international group of social scientists, for which de Jouvenel is chairman. Their scholarly series of essays reflecting opinions about possible future developments has awakened widespread interest, and de Jouvenel's book, *L'Art de La Conjecture*, has recently been translated into English. Further, at the initiative of Pierre Massé, a 155-page report on changes anticipated by 1985 in 16 dimensions of Franco-European living has been published.[15]

In our own country current interest in future scanning and *future*-planning, as of 1968, has become too widespread even to summarize here. A few examples:

[9] RAND Archives: *Social Technology*, Olaf Helmer, February, 1965.
[10] An example from RAND's Archive Copies: *Management Science Frontiers: 1970–1980*, E. U. Denardo and M. S. Geisler, June, 1967.
[11] Max Ways, *loc. cit.*
[12] Lawrence Lessing, "Systems Engineering Invades the City," *Fortune*, January, 1968, p. 157.
[13] Brownlee Haydon, "The Year 2000" Typescript dated March, 1967. Read at Wayne State University, March 2 and 23, 1967, p. 5.
[14] Booz, Allen, and Hamilton, Inc., *New Uses and Management Implications of PERT*. New York: Booz, Allen & Hamilton, Inc., 1964, p. 1.
[15] Cf. *Réflexions pour 1985*. Paris: La Société Industrielle d'Imprimerie, 1964, 155 pp.

The New York Times has appointed a "Committee on the Future" for editorial planning that *anticipates* news a decade hence.

In the groves of academe, the American Academy of Arts and Sciences (at Lawrence K. Frank's urging) has established a "Commission on the Year 2000" under the chairmanship of Daniel Bell. It has already (1967) devoted a 363-page issue of its 50,000 circulation magazine, *Daedalus*, to a progress report on the commission's deliberations.[16]

Resources of the Future, an organization aided by the Ford Foundation, has completed an excellent group of publications.

The RAND Corporation has sponsored a series of predictive studies under Helmer and Gordon.

The U.S. Future Society has been organized and is publishing a "Newsletter for Tomorrow's World."

A 431-page "framework for speculation on the next 33 years," a book entitled *The Year 2000,* appeared during the winter of 1967–68 and became a popular nonfiction title.

Further "historical" or "present status" data would probably extend our remarks from the verge of tedium to the border of ennui.

What Future-Planning Can Contribute to the Curriculum

Because the shaping of educational policies presumably can be improved by employing systematic conjectural techniques as has been done in science, government, business, and the military, what are some of the values suggested by a careful reading of the current literature of futurism?

At least two direct "outcome values" of future-probing are virtually self-evident. Seven "process values" based on the emerging techniques of *future-planning* also appear. Let us take them in order.

Outcome Values

The use of *future*-planning in education is supported by two highly persuasive points: 1) It can help us to avoid just plain stupid mistakes, blunders that could have been by-passed if we had only expended the effort to look ahead intelligently and systematically; and 2) it enables us to foresee dangers and problems in time to consider alternatives, preventing possible unpleasantness, lost time, faulty learning, or human maladjustment.[17]

Process Values

Bear in mind that *future*-planning of the curriculum is inherently a *process* for encouraging change to occur within an educational system. It does not

---

[16] "Toward the Year 2000: Work in Progress," *Daedalus,* Summer, 1967.

[17] Cf. Haydon, footnote 13, p. 17 ff., for examples from the field of conservation illustrating resources wasted through non-planning.

involve a body of dogmatic rules to be followed. It provides a means of changing education and its processes so that individuals may better control and influence forthcoming developments that seem likely to shape their lives. Process values are derived from the interplay of participants with the procedures and ideas that are involved. Some of these values are as follows:

1. Careful consideration is given to the identification of a wide range of possible educational developments. Thus planning is brought into sharp focus as alternative futures are suggested and explored.
2. When a spectrum of possible outcomes in education has been determined, appropriate criteria can be used to assess the means to be employed in obtaining particular ends.
3. Progress is assessed continually through such devices as PERTing, which serve to keep persons working with curriculum models from getting too far out of synchronization. Continuing evaluation also permits in-process changes (i.e., flexibility) in moving toward established ends when mitigating needs become evident.
4. *Future*-planning employs intellectually demanding but rewarding procedures as carefully derived information and referents are fed into the framework for speculation. The input of specialized knowledge or data based on "expertise" constantly validates the sequential decisions that are made in developing a model for curriculum change. The input also serves to reaffirm or to modify educational ends.
5. *Authoritarian* direction becomes subordinate to *authoritative* leadership provided by a) information input, b) the persuasive *merit* of a given idea, and c) the continuing use of research relevant to (or generated by) the processes of *future*-planning.
6. The processes of *future*-planning encourage synergistic[18] outcomes. In other words, prediction, research, process, and interaction taken together produce an outcome greater than the sum of the input. Also, in *future*-planning, we increase our potential ability to predict outcomes when several lines of thought modify one another and thus increase overall accuracy.[19]
7. In education as in the social sciences, the techniques of *future*-planning (operations research and expert judgment) offer considerable promise for developing an "interdisciplinary systems approach" to the study of curriculum problems.[20] In effect, we should be able to adapt and reconstruct some of the operational methods from the realm of physical technology to the domain of social and educational technology.[21]

[18] Webster defines "synergism" as the simultaneous action of separate agencies which, together, have a greater total effect than the sum of their individual effects.

[19] Points such as those given here have been carefully assessed by social scientists. Cf. Herman Kahn and Anthony J. Wiener, *The Year Two-Thousand*. New York: The Macmillan Co., 1967. Synergistic interrelationships are discussed on pp. 67–71.

[20] Lessing, *op. cit.*, pp. 157, 217.

[21] This point is developed in Olaf Helmer, *Prospects of Technological Progress*, RAND typescript of speech given in Tokyo, dated August, 1967, pp. 9–10.

So much for some of the promising elements which seem to support the infusion of *future*-planning in curriculum change. Let us now consider some of the conjectures about the next 50 years — years in which today's children and youth will spend most of their productive adult lifetimes. What "contextual map" can be drawn for society's educational needs? What ideas do we need to explore, test, and apply?

RAW MATERIAL FOR FUTURE-PLANNING THE CURRICULUM

At least in a general way, much of the input needed for effective *future*-planning in education is already available. Books such as Kahn and Wiener's *The Year Two-Thousand*,[22] and journals such as *Daedalus* with its issue "Toward the Year 2000,"[23] the *Futuribles*[24] essays, articles and books listed in Harrison's *Bibliography on Automation and Technological Change and the Future*,[25] and literally dozens of other sources have been appearing in increasing numbers since the early 1960's.[26]

These publications have not only made available both the general concept and design of prevoyance or future-peering; they also suggest abundant factors and developments which highly reputable specialists in the physical sciences, social sciences, and other relevant fields feel should be considered and tested as we move into the future. Kahn and Wiener provided especially interesting information when they cited 100 "likely," 25 "less likely," and 10 "radical" innovations that could occur by 2000 A.D.[27] A quick check of the 100 "likelies" indicates that as many as 40 of the forecasts either directly or indirectly relate to education, hence provide data for conjecture by the educator.

Not only do we have the prospective scientific and technical innovations needed to stimulate and develop educational *future*-planning, we also have much theoretical data, based on trend projection, suggesting that during the next 30 years: 1) five billion people will be living; 2) population increases will begin a relative decline; 3) major increases in food production will occur (e.g., through "ocean farming"); 4) the world GNP will triple and perhaps quadruple; and 5) that automated urban complexes will house most Americans, who by then will be living in a credit-card economy. Also, 6) educational technology will be much more sophisticated; 7) drugs to effect desired therapy related to personality modification will be widely used; and

[22] *Ibid., et passim.* Cf. especially Chapters I–IV.

[23] *Ibid.* Cf. footnote 15 *supra.*

[24] A series of essays by experts in different fields in which opinions about possible future developments are expressed. These are prepared by the *Futuribles* group chaired by Bertrand de Jouvenel.

[25] A listing of materials assembled for two RAND projects by A. Harrison dated March, 1967.

[26] Cf. June Grant Shane, "Contemporary Thought, with Implications for Counseling and Guidance: A Bibliography." *Bulletin of the School of Education,* Indiana University, July 1967, 106 pp.

[27] Kahn and Wiener, *ibid.,* pp. 51–57. It is significant that two of the 100 "likely" innovations forecast had become realities while this book was being published: major organ transplants and laboratory-created life forms.

8) life-spans will be appreciably increased with 9) both our leisure habits and patterns of job-retraining changed as a result.[28]

In other words, if properly developed techniques, policies, and procedures (already offering exciting possibilities) are applied to education, we now have sufficient available socio-scientific "information-input" to begin reasoned conjectures for *future*-planning. But educational planning must also be done methodically. While educational futures could be arrived at in a haphazard manner, it is an inefficient and possibly dangerous way to approach them.

AN APPROACH TO FUTURE-PLANNING THE CURRICULUM

What opportunities reside in creative educational conjecture, or "edu-conjecture," about tomorrow's schools? What techniques can be used in *future*-planning instructional programs and how do they differ from procedures ordinarily employed in planning intelligently for the next decade?[29]

The processes of *future*-planning, as reviewed here, depend on the use of the ORPHIC techniques: *a cluster of procedures based on the systematic use of coordinated expert opinion in education and in related disciplines for purposes of 1) exploring numerous possible educational futures, 2) selecting the best possible futures among them, and 3) developing models for helping achieve desired educational goals.*[30]

"ORPHIC" is an acronym for ORganized Projected Hypotheses for Innovations in Curriculum. Its dictionary meaning is "oracular." ORPHIC techniques were introduced during 1967–68 to chart educational changes for a large metropolitan school survey conducted under the auspices of the Midwest Administration Center of the University of Chicago.[31] Within the limitations imposed by space, we will attempt to review the various steps that may be used in applying ORPHIC techniques, the criteria for selecting experts for educational *future*-planning, and some means of enhancing the value of expertise in such planning.

ORPHIC PROCEDURES IN EDUCATIONAL FUTURE-PLANNING

ORPHIC procedures, in the exploratory stages they have reached thus far, bring together in an "arena for conjecture" two kinds of experts who are important in educational *future*-planning: the specialist with his data and pre-

[28] Cf. Olaf Helmer, *ibid.*, p. 2 ff.

[29] Cf. Edgar Morphet and C. O. Ryan, *Designing Education for the Future*, 1967, three volumes, published by Citation. These materials are excellent illustrations of intelligent planning for the future but are *not* based on the use of *future*-planning as described here.

[30] Recognition is due RAND, Inc., for pioneering in *future*-planning through the controlled use of expert judgment. The little-known Delphi technique, which involves the use of a panel of specialists, was used by RAND and appears in the literature as far back as the late 1950's.

[31] In an initial venture in educational future planning during January, 1968, Edward T. Hall, Robert Havighurst, and Herbert Thelen were the interdisciplinary participants. A second planning group, one meeting a few weeks later, consisted of Robert H. Anderson, Frank Estvan, and Sidney P. Marland, Jr.

dictions and the generalist who formulates, analyzes, assesses alternatives, and contributes to conceiving and building models.

The action in the arena for conjecture does not have as one of its features gladiatorial confrontation, debate, or refutation. It is concerned with creating an intellectually tested consensus with respect to ideas or hypotheses for curriculum changes that are based on the best information available. A persistent effort is made to achieve synergistic outcomes (see footnote 18) through which the product of several minds assumes a more advanced and precise form than such minds would have attained by working alone.

The arena for conjecture may be thought of as an intellectual amphitheater for *future*-planning; one in which the ideas of experts have an opportunity to prove their survival value and to sharpen the thinking of others. The interaction of the experts differs from that of a conventional panel discussion, symposium, or "bull session" in several respects:

1. Each specialist methodically prepares a preliminary résumé of possible futures in his discipline (e.g., anthropology, biochemistry) that relate to futures which fan out ahead for education. This is the *trend census*.
2. In exercising his authoritativeness a consultant is requested to pre-test his thinking and suggestions by considering such factors as a) the "half-life of validity" (valid premises and ideas age so quickly now we must allow for their possible demise and anticipate their successors), b) possible "pseudo-experimentation" (since some ideas are dangerous, others costly or difficult to attempt, how would the expert develop a hypothetical experiment, and what possible findings might result?), c) what "scenario" would he plan when conceiving of a curriculum for 1985 as he envisions it evolving day-by-day from its precursor?
3. When ORPHIC techniques are used, heed is methodically given to checking the relationship between hypotheses and evidence.[32] In other words, a continuing effort is made to insure that a possible proposed educational future has evidence supporting it. Any viable hypothesis pertaining to the curriculum also passes at least the three following tests: a) *technical* — the curriculum innovation is possible; b) *economic* — it is financially feasible; c) *operational*—it is worth doing in terms of the school's philosophy, clientele, view of learning theory, and so forth.
4. The expert places in the arena for conjecture the curricular changes (e.g., 1970–1985) his field of specialization suggests for a) substantive content, b) instructional procedures, or c) paracurricular experiences that might better permit schools to maximize human development.

The foregoing explanation of how ORPHIC planning departs from casual discussions or symposia also serves to explain the essence of the *future*-plan-

---

[32] We have based this on the Helmer-Rescher degree of confirmation concept and formula, and their "personal probability" measure. Cf. Olaf Helmer and Nicholas Rescher, "On the Epistemology of the Inexact Sciences," *Management Science* 6:25–52, 1959. Note pp. 34–36, where [dc (H, E) = m/n] is presented, E being based on m/n—P (m out of n objects having the property P.)

ning technique itself. It is a pragmatic-empirical chain-series of reasoned predictions looking at the many tomorrows that could ensue in education and following a process designed to permit a particularly acceptable educational future to have a better chance of becoming a reality through creative imagination and hard work. By its nature and processes, *future*-planning can help make our schools important and interesting educational outposts on the borders where people strive for better tomorrows.

CRITERIA FOR SELECTING EXPERTS

Future-planning inherently serves to encourage qualified persons in both education and related disciplines to work together to improve the curriculum. These experts are selected to facilitate reaching a balanced predictive consensus. At least to a considerable degree, the expert sharing in ORPHIC processes should meet all or nearly all of the following criteria:

Specialized information and skill.

Ability to apply both his expertise and evidence in the process of prediction; the power to see, in the absence of data, the main alternatives or future developments on which education should hinge.

A high "reliability quotient"; when previously confronted with hypotheses, he generally has identified the ones which proved to be sound.

A past record marked by stable and sustained expertise, including that of making pronouncements which subsequently earned acceptance among his peers.

Breadth within his discipline.

Intra- and multidisciplinary understandings and insights.

Imagination with respect to both theory and its applications, and well-developed idea exchange skills.

A grasp of educational realities.

A willingness to support socioeconomic equalitarianism created by opportunities made available through the schools.

ENHANCING THE EFFICIENCY AND INTELLECTUAL POWER OF THE EXPERT

Once a team of highly qualified persons has been assembled to study possible educational futures, what are some of the common-sense things that can be done to facilitate their communication? Here are several useful suggestions.

For one thing, easy and rapid access to a wide range of educational and other types of information is of great importance when specialists meet. Also, the construction of models[33] can be very helpful in explaining problems,

---

[33] As used here, "model" refers to a graphic-visual concept portrayal of relevant elements and their relationships in a situation. There are three-dimensional, pencil and paper, and mathematical models. Each type should provide the best data and perceptions available on a given situation or problem when properly constructed.

clarifying concepts, and avoiding misinterpretations. An actual 3-D model could be of value, for instance, to a team planning for space use on the campus thus simulated. Likewise, a model of a school's administrative structure could be valuable to a team of consultants about to begin studying data prior to engaging in forecasts regarding a "best" future.

Finally, a carefully nurtured series of opportunities to interact with others also is vital. What is sought here is the synergistic outcome which the combined efforts of experts from related disciplines and education hopefully will produce; an outcome which proves to be greater or more effective than the sum of its individual or isolated parts.

Caveats for Educational Future-Planners

Future-planning of curricula should be undertaken with several cautions in mind as educators use the available "raw materials" extracted from interdisciplinary sources to channel the fan-shaped multiple futures that lie before the schools into emergent "good" futures consistent with sound societal values. To illustrate, many technical innovations have proved to be mixed blessings. It is important to remember that an automobile, for example, when driven 25 miles, consumes the breathable air that seven million people use during a 30-minute interval. Nuclear technology used commercially also creates a plutonium by-product that could increase the ownership of nuclear weapons. Weather control could throw entire areas out of balance. To cite one more illustration, the use of insecticides and weed killers is becoming one of our greater long-term causes of dangerous chemical pollution of the environment.

In educational conjecture, therefore, prudence must be mingled with foresight so as to avoid inadvertent "pollution" also, be it from education itself or from inept efforts of its well-meaning friends in other disciplines. Obvious caveats in curriculum planning include the danger of subordinating human values to technological ones; random tinkering with human personality; diminishing the importance and significance of individuality; and clothing obsolete goals, content, and procedures with computer-assisted techniques that only serve to help children and youth learn the wrong things more rapidly than they do now.

Another danger could be that of a small, powerful, and autocratic group appointing itself to mastermind the content and procedures of education for 1980 or 1990. A more disastrous "victory" for either physical or social technology would be difficult to imagine than one that led to a system in which a few central *future*-planners — no matter what their field of specialization — superimposed only their values on the schools and on the brain banks of the computers which seem certain to gain in educational importance.

The Future Belongs to Those Who Plan It

It has been evident for some time now that education is beginning to be recognized for what it is: a force of such social and political importance that it cannot remain laggard, obsolescent, or inefficient. In fine, *someone* is going to determine the shape of our emergent educational futures because they are too portentous to be left to chance.

The future belongs not to those who plan to *meet* it, but to those who actively *plan* it. In education we are placed on our mettle not to do battle against persons in other disciplines who are also concerned with creating a better world of teaching and learning. Rather, we are challenged to encourage leadership within our own ranks — a leadership based on the merits of creative ideas and their implications for more adequate educational tomorrows. Thus we undertake to do *future*-planning *along with* rather than *against* those who strive, in their respective specialties, to sharpen the directions, improve the methods, and enhance the power of education's tomorrows.

B. The Technological Revolution and the Future

37

Computer Technology and the Future of Education

Patrick Suppes

Patrick Suppes is a pioneer in computer-assisted instruction. He here describes how computers can be used to provide individualized instruction and distinguishes among drill-and-practice systems, tutorial systems, and dialogue systems. Suppes predicts "that within the next decade many children will use individualized drill-and-practice systems in elementary school; and by the time they reach high school, tutorial systems will be available on a broad basis. Their children may use dialogue systems throughout their school experience."

Mr. Suppes' remarkable versatility is demonstrated by his positions at Stanford University, where he is director of the Institute of Mathematical Studies in the Social Sciences and a professor in the Departments of Philosophy, Statistics, and Education.

Current applications of computers and related information-processing techniques run the gamut in our society from the automatic control of factories to the scrutiny of tax returns. I have not seen any recent data, but we are certainly reaching the point at which a high percentage of regular employees in this country are paid by computerized payroll systems. As another example, every kind of complex experiment is beginning to be subject to computer assistance either in terms of the actual experimentation or in terms of extensive computations integral to the analysis of the experiment. These applications range from bubble-chamber data on elementary particles to the crystallography of protein molecules.

As yet, the use of computer technology in administration and management

Patrick Suppes, "Computer Technology and the Future of Education," *Phi Delta Kappan*, April, 1968, 420–423. Reprinted by permission of the publisher.

on the one hand, and scientific and engineering applications on the other, far exceed direct applications in education. However, if potentials are properly realized, the character and nature of education during the course of our lifetimes will be radically changed. Perhaps the most important aspect of computerized instructional devices is that the kind of individualized instruction once possible only for a few members of the aristocracy can be made available to all students at all levels of abilities.

Because some may not be familiar with how computers can be used to provide individualized instruction, let me briefly review the mode of operation. In the first place, because of its great speed of operation, a computer can handle simultaneously a large number of students — for instance, 200 or more, and each of the 200 can be at a different point in the curriculum. In the simplest mode of operation, the terminal device at which the student sits is something like an electric typewriter. Messages can be typed out by the computer and the student in turn can enter his responses on the keyboard. The first and most important feature to add is the delivery of audio messages under computer control to the student. Not only children, but students of all ages learn by ear as much as by eye, and for tutorial ventures in individualized instruction it is essential that the computer system be able to talk to the student.

A simple example may make this idea more concrete. Practically no one learns mathematics simply by reading a book, except at a relatively advanced level. Hearing lectures and listening to someone else's talk seem to be almost psychologically essential to learning complex subjects, at least as far as ordinary learners are concerned. In addition to the typewriter and the earphones for audio messages, the next desirable feature is that graphical and pictorial displays be available under computer control. Such displays can be provided in a variety of formats. The simplest mode is to have color slides that may be selected by computer control. More flexible, and therefore more desirable, devices are cathode-ray tubes that look very much like television sets. The beauty of cathode-ray tubes is that a graphical display may be shown to the student and then his own response, entered on a keyboard, can be made an integral part of the display itself.

This is not the place to review these matters in detail; but I mean to convey a visual image of a student sitting at a variety of terminal gear — as it is called in the computer world. These terminals are used to provide the student with individualized instruction. He receives information from audio messages, from typewritten messages, and also from visual displays ranging from graphics to complex photographs. In turn, he may respond to the system and give his own answers by using the keyboard on the typewriter. Other devices for student response are also available, but I shall not go into them now.

So, with such devices available, individualized instruction in a wide variety of subject matters may be offered students of all ages. The technology is already available, although it will continue to be improved. There are two main factors standing in our way. One is that currently it is expensive to prepare an individualized curriculum. The second factor, and even more important, is that as yet we have little operational experience in precisely how this should best be done. For some time to come, individualized instruction will have to depend on a basis of practical judgment and pedagogical intuition of the sort now used in constructing textbook materials for ordinary courses. One of the exciting potentialities of computer-assisted instruction is that for the first time we shall be able to get hard data to use as a basis for a more serious scientific investigation and evaluation of any given instructional program.

To give a more concrete sense of the possibilities of individualized instruction, I would like to describe briefly three possible levels of interaction between the student and computer program. Following a current usage, I shall refer to each of the instructional programs as a particular system of instruction. At the simplest level there are *individualized drill-and-practice systems*, which are meant to supplement the regular curriculum taught by the teacher. The introduction of concepts and new ideas is handled in conventional fashion by the teacher. The role of the computer is to provide regular review and practice on basic concepts and skills. In the case of elementary mathematics, for example, each student would receive daily a certain number of exercises, which would be automatically presented, evaluated, and scored by the computer program without any effort by the classroom teacher. Moreover, these exercises can be presented on an individualized basis, with the brighter students receiving exercises that are harder than the average, and the slower students receiving easier problems.

One important aspect of this kind of individualization should be emphasized. In using a computer in this fashion, it is not necessary to decide at the beginning of the school year in which track a student should be placed; for example, a student need not be classified as a slow student for the entire year. Individualized drill-and-practice work is suitable to all the elementary subjects which occupy a good part of the curriculum. Elementary mathematics, elementary science, and the beginning work in foreign language are typical parts of the curriculum which benefit from standardized and regularly presented drill-and-practice exercises. A large computer with 200 terminals can handle as many as 6,000 students on a daily basis in this instructional mode. In all likelihood, it will soon be feasible to increase these numbers to a thousand terminals and 30,000 students. Operational details of our 1965–66 drill-and-practice program at Stanford are to be found in the forthcoming book by Suppes, Jerman, and Brian.[1]

At the second and deeper level of interaction between student and computer program there are *tutorial systems*, which take over the main responsibility both for presenting a concept and for developing skill in its use. The intention is to approximate the interaction a patient tutor would have with an individual student. An important aspect of the tutorial programs in reading and elementary mathematics with which we have been concerned at Stanford in the past three years is that every effort is made to avoid an initial experience of failure on the part of the slower children. On the

---

[1] P. Suppes, M. Jerman, and D. Brian, *Computer-assisted Instruction at Stanford: The 1965–66 Arithmetic Drill-and-Practice Program.* New York: Academic Press, 1968.

other hand, the program has enough flexibility to avoid boring the brighter children with endlessly repetitive exercises. As soon as the student manifests a clear understanding of a concept on the basis of his handling of a number of exercises, he is moved on to a new concept and new exercises. (A detailed evaluation of the Stanford reading program, which is under the direction of Professor Richard C. Atkinson, may be found in the report by Wilson and Atkinson.[2] A report on the tutorial mathematics program will soon be available. The data show that the computer-based curriculum was particularly beneficial for the slower students.)

At the third and deepest level of interaction there are *dialogue systems* aimed at permitting the student to conduct a genuine dialogue with the computer. The dialogue systems at the present time exist primarily at the conceptual rather than the operational level, and I do want to emphasize that in the case of dialogue systems a number of difficult technical problems must first be solved. One problem is that of recognizing spoken speech. Especially in the case of young children, we would like the child to be able simply to ask the computer program a question. To permit this interaction, we must be able to recognize the spoken speech of the child and also to recognize the meaning of the question he is asking. The problem of recognizing meaning is at least as difficult as that of recognizing the spoken speech. It will be some time before we will be able to do either one of these things with any efficiency and economy.

I would predict that within the next decade many children will use individualized drill-and-practice systems in elementary school; and by the time they reach high school, tutorial systems will be available on a broad basis. Their children may use dialogue systems throughout their school experience.

If these predictions are even approximately correct, they have far-reaching implications for education and society. As has been pointed out repeatedly by many people in many different ways, the role of education in our society is not simply the transmission of knowledge but also the transmission of culture, including the entire range of individual, political, and social values. Some recent studies — for example, the Coleman report — have attempted to show that the schools are not as effective in transmitting this culture as we might hope; but still there is little doubt that the schools play a major role, and the directions they take have serious implications for the character of our society in the future. Now I hope it is evident from the very brief descriptions I have given that the widespread use of computer technology in education has an enormous potential for improving the quality of education, because the possibility of individualizing instruction at ever deeper levels of interaction can be realized in an economically feasible fashion. I take it that this potentiality is evident enough, and I would like to examine some of the problems it raises, problems now beginning to be widely discussed.

Three rather closely related issues are particularly prominent in this dis-

[2] H. A. Wilson and R. C. Atkinson, *Computer-based Instruction in Initial Reading: A Progress Report on the Stanford Project.* Technical Report No. 119, August 25, 1967, Institute for Mathematical Studies in the Social Sciences, Stanford University.

cussion. The first centers around the claim that the deep use of technology, especially computer technology, will impose a rigid regime of impersonalized teaching. In considering such a claim, it is important to say at once that indeed this is a possibility. Computer technology could be used this way, and in some instances it probably will. This is no different from saying that there are many kinds of teaching, some good and some bad. The important point to insist upon, however, is that it is certainly not a *necessary* aspect of the use of the technology. In fact, contrary to the expectations sometimes expressed in the popular press, I would claim that one of the computer's most important potentials is in making learning and teaching more personalized, rather than less so. Students will be subject to less regimentation and lockstepping, because computer systems will be able to offer highly individualized instruction. The routine that occupies a good part of the teacher's day can be taken over by the computer.

It is worth noting in this connection that the amount of paper work required of teachers is very much on the increase. The computer seems to offer the only possibility of decreasing the time spent in administrative routine by ordinary teachers. Let us examine briefly one or two aspects of instruction ranging from the elementary school to the college. At the elementary level, no one anticipates that students will spend most of their time at computer consoles. Only 20 to 30 percent of the student's time would be spent in this fashion. Teachers would be able to work with classes reduced in size. Also, they could work more intensely with individual students, because some of the students will be at the console and, more importantly, because routine aspects of teaching will be handled by the computer system.

At the college level, the situation is somewhat different. At most colleges and universities, students do not now receive a great deal of individual attention from instructors. I think we can all recognize that the degree of personal attention is certainly not less in a computer program designed to accommodate itself to the individual student's progress than in the lecture course that has more than 200 students in daily attendance. (In our tutorial Russian program at Stanford, under the direction of Joseph Van Campen, all regular classroom instruction has been eliminated. Students receive 50 minutes daily of individualized instruction at a computer terminal consisting of a teletype with Cyrillic keyboard and earphones; the audio tapes are controlled by the computer.)

A second common claim is that the widespread use of computer technology will lead to excessive standardization of education. Again, it is important to admit at once that this is indeed a possibility. The sterility of standardization and what it implies for teaching used to be illustrated by a story about the French educational system. It was claimed that the French minister of education could look at his watch at any time of the school day and say at once what subject was being taught at each grade level throughout the country. The claim was not true, but such a situation could be brought about in the organization of computer-based instruction. It would technically be possible for a state department of education, for example, to require every fifth-grader at 11:03 in the morning to be subtracting one-fifth from three-tenths, or for every senior in high school to be reciting the virtues of a democratic society. The danger of the technology is that edicts can be enforced as well as issued, and many persons are rightly concerned at the spectre of the rigid standardization that could be imposed.

On the other hand, there is another meaning of standardization that holds great potential. This is the imposition of educational standards on schools and colleges throughout the land. Let me give one example of what I mean. A couple of years ago I consulted with one of the large city school systems in this country in connection with its mathematics program. The curriculum outline of the mathematics program running from kindergarten to high school was excellent. The curriculum as specified in the outline was about as good as any in the country. The real source of difficulty was the magnitude of the discrepancy between the actual performance of the students and the specified curriculum. At almost every grade level, students were performing far below the standard set in the curriculum guide. I do not mean to suggest that computer technology will, in one fell stroke, provide a solution to the difficult and complicated problems of raising the educational standards that now obtain among the poor and culturally deprived. I do say that the technology will provide us with unparalleled insight into the actual performance of students.

Yet I do not mean to suggest that this problem of standardization is not serious. It is, and it will take much wisdom to avoid its grosser aspects. But the point I would like to emphasize is that the wide use of computers permits the introduction of an almost unlimited diversity of curriculum and teaching. The very opposite of standardization *can* be achieved. I think we would all agree that the ever-increasing use of books from the sixteenth century to the present has deepened the varieties of educational and intellectual experience generally available. There is every reason to believe that the appropriate development of instructional programs for computer systems will increase rather than decrease this variety of intellectual experience. The potential is there.

The real problem is that as yet we do not understand very well how to take advantage of this potential. If we examine the teaching of any subject in the curriculum, ranging from elementary mathematics to ancient history, what is striking is the great similarity between teachers and between textbooks dealing with the same subject, not the vast differences between them. It can even be argued that it is a subtle philosophical question of social policy to determine the extent to which we want to emphasize diversity in our teaching of standard subjects. Do we want a "cool" presentation of American history for some students and a fervent one for others? Do we want to emphasize geometric and perceptual aspects of mathematics more for some students, and symbolic and algebraic aspects more for others? Do we want to make the learning of language more oriented toward the ear for some students and more toward the eye for those who have a poor sense of auditory discrimination? These are issues that have as yet scarcely been explored in educational philosophy or in discussions of educational policy. With the advent of the new technology they will become practical questions of considerable moment.

The third and final issue I wish to discuss is the place of individuality and human freedom in the modern technology. The crudest form of opposition to widespread use of technology in education and in other parts of our society is to claim that we face the real danger of men becoming slaves of machines. I feel strongly that the threat to human individuality and freedom in our society does not come from technology at all, but from another source that was well described by John Stuart Mill more than a hundred years ago. In discussing precisely this matter in his famous essay *On Liberty,* he said,

> the greatest difficulty to be encountered does not lie in the appreciation of means towards an acknowledged end, but in the indifference of persons in general to the end itself. If it were felt that the free development of individuality is one of the leading essentials of well-being; that it is not only a co-ordinate element with all that is designated by the terms civilization, instruction, education, culture, but is itself a necessary part and condition of all those things; there would be no danger that liberty should be undervalued, and the adjustment of the boundaries between it and social control would present no extraordinary difficulty.

Just as books freed serious students from the tyranny of overly simple methods of oral recitation, so computers can free students from the drudgery of doing exactly similar tasks unadjusted and untailored to their individual needs. As in the case of other parts of our society, our new and wondrous technology is there for beneficial use. It is our problem to learn how to use it well. When a child of six begins to learn in school under the direction of a teacher, he hardly has a concept of a free intelligence able to reach objective knowledge of the world. He depends heavily upon every word and gesture of the teacher to guide his own reactions and responses. This intellectual weaning of children is a complicated process that we do not yet manage or understand very well. There are too many adults among us who are not able to express their own feelings or to reach their own judgments. I would claim that the wise use of technology and science, particularly in education, presents a major opportunity and challenge. I do not want to claim that we know very much yet about how to realize the full potential of human beings; but I do not doubt that we can use our modern instruments to reduce the personal tyranny of one individual over another, wherever that tyranny depends upon ignorance.

38

The IMPENDING
Instruction Revolution

Harold E. Mitzel

Stanley Elam, editor of Kappan, *the liveliest of today's educational journals, calls this article "one of the best summaries we have seen of the early stages of a revolution which, Mr. Mitzel believes, will be completed by the turn of the century." Mitzel describes different concepts of individualized instruction and calls for adaptive instruction, "the tailoring of subject matter presentation to fit the special requirements and capabilities of each learner."*

Harold E. Mitzel is professor of educational psychology at Pennsylvania State University. His article is a version of a paper he presented to the American Society for Engineering Education.

First, let me explain my choice of the above title. It is fashionable in these days of rhetorical excess to describe change as revolutionary in scope. The mass media remind us daily that revolutions are occurring right under our noses. We hear of (and see) the Social Revolution, the Sexual Revolution, the Technology Revolution, the Student Revolt, the Faculty Revolt, and so on. Apparently any complete or sudden change in the conduct of human affairs, with or without a violent confrontation or an exchange of power, may properly be called a revolution.

It is my thesis that the last three decades of the twentieth century will witness a drastic change in the business of providing instruction in schools and colleges. Change by the year 2000 will be so thoroughgoing that historians will have no difficulty in agreeing that it was a revolution. You will note the omission of words like "teaching" and "learning" in describing the coming revolution. Teaching connotes for most of us an inherently person-mediated activity and the vision of the "stand-up" lecturer comes most immediately to mind. One of the concomitants of the impending change is a major modification of the role of teacher. It is likely that future terms

Harold E. Mitzel, "The IMPENDING Instruction Revolution," *Phi Delta Kappan*, April, 1970, 434–439. Reprinted from *Engineering Education*, Vol. 60, No. 7, (March, 1970), 749–754. © 1970 American Society for Engineering Education.

for teacher may be "instructional agent" or "lesson designer" or "instructional programmer." As for learning, we take the position that the word is not a way of describing an *activity* of the student, but rather a way of characterizing change in the student's behavior in some desired direction between two definite time markers. Pask[1] has pointed out that teaching is "exercising control of the instructional environment by arranging scope, sequence, materials, evaluation, and content for students." In other words, instruction is the general term for the process and learning is the product.

My objective is to challenge you with the shape of the instruction revolution, to point out how you as a teacher or administrator can cooperate and cope with it, and to suggest some of the social changes which are currently fueling this revolution.

Individualized Instruction

At the secondary school level, American educators, beginning with Preston W. Search[2] in the late nineteenth century, have been interested in the goal of individualization. Between 1900 and 1930, disciples of Frederick Burk (see Brubacher[3] and Parkhurst[4]) devised and implemented several laboratory-type plans for self-instruction in the lower schools. These were self-pacing plans for the learner and demanded a great deal of versatility on the part of the teacher. Additional impetus for the theoretical interest of educators in individualization stemmed from the mental testing movement, beginning with the seminal work of Binet[5] about 60 years ago. Early intelligence tests clearly showed differences in speed of task completion among pupils, and these differences were easily confirmed by a teacher's own observations of mental agility. At the practical level, a great deal of individualization took place in rural America's one-room schools. Fifteen to 25 children spread unevenly through ages 6 to 14 necessarily committed the teacher to large doses of individual pupil direction, recitation, and evaluation. With population increases and school consolidations, most village and rural schools began to look like rigidly graded city schools. Teachers found themselves responsible for larger and larger groups of children of approximately the same age and about the same physical size. It is little wonder that some of the zest, enthusiasm, and obviousness of need for individualized teaching was lost. When teachers complained about too-large classes, the lack of time to spend with individual pupils, the wide diversity in pupil ability levels, many not-so-smart administrators introduced "track-

[1] G. Pask, "Computer-Assisted Learning and Teaching," paper presented at Seminar on Computer-Based Learning, Leeds University, September 9–12, 1969.

[2] P. W. Search, "Individual Teaching: The Pueblo Plan," *Education Review*, February, 1894, pp. 154–70.

[3] J. S. Brubacher, A *History of the Problems of Education*, 2nd ed. New York: McGraw-Hill, 1966.

[4] H. H. Parkhurst, *Education on the Dalton Plan*. New York: E. P. Dutton & Co., 1922.

[5] A. Binet and T. Simon, *The Development of Intelligence in Children*, trans. Elizabeth S. Kite. Vineland, N.J.: The Training School, 1916.

ing" or "streaming" strategies. Separating children into homogeneous classes according to measured mental ability within age groups has been shown conclusively to fail to increase the achievement level of groups as a whole.[6] Homogeneous ability grouping has, on the other hand, seriously exacerbated social problems connected with race and economic levels by "ghettoizing" classrooms within the schools, even though the schools served racially and economically mixed neighborhoods.

Whereas the common schools have *some* history of experimentation with individualized instruction methods, higher education, led by the large state universities, has pushed the development of mass communication methods in instruction. The large-group lecture and the adaptation of closed-circuit television are examples of higher education's trend away from individualized instruction. Of course, the outstanding accomplishments of American university graduate schools could never have been achieved without the cost-savings introduced by mass communications techniques in their undergraduate colleges.

Interest in individualized instruction had a surge about 15 years ago when Harvard's B. F. Skinner[7,8] advocated an education technology built around the use of rather crude teaching machines. It soon became apparent that there was no particular magic in the machines themselves, since they contained only short linear series of questions and answers to word problems called "frames." These programs were quickly put into book form and the programmed text was born. Although it enjoyed initial success with some highly motivated learners, the programmed text has not caught on in either the lower schools or in higher education as a major instructional device. Industry and the military forces seem to have made the best use of programmed texts, perhaps because of a high degree of motivation on the part of many learners in those situations.

Most recently, an educational technique for the lower schools has been developed out of the work of the Learning Research and Development Center at the University of Pittsburgh. The method, called "individually prescribed instruction" or IPI, is described by Lindvall and Bolvin,[9] by Glaser,[10] and by Cooley and Glaser.[11] Behind the method lies the careful development of a technology based on precise specification and delineation

---

[6] J. I. Goodlad in *Encyclopedia of Educational Research*, 3rd ed., ed. C. Harris. New York: Macmillan, 1960.

[7] B. F. Skinner, "The Science of Learning and the Art of Teaching," *Harvard Educational Review*, Spring, 1954, pp. 86–97.

[8] B. F. Skinner, "Teaching Machines," *Science*, 128, 1958, pp. 969–77.

[9] C. M. Lindvall and J. O. Bolvin, "Programed Instruction in the Schools: An Application of Programing Principles in Individually Prescribed Instruction," in *Programed Instruction*, ed. P. C. Lange. The Sixty-Sixth Yearbook of the National Society for the Study of Education, Part II. Chicago: The University of Chicago Press, 1967, pp. 217–54.

[10] R. Glaser, *The Education of Individuals*. Pittsburgh, Pa.: Learning Research and Development Center, University of Pittsburgh, 1966.

[11] W. W. Cooley and R. Glaser, "An Information Management System for Individually Prescribed Instruction," Working Paper No. 44, Learning Research and Development Center, University of Pittsburgh, mimeographed, 1968.

of educational objectives in behavioral terms. Pupils work individually on a precisely scaled set of materials with frequent interspersed diagnostic quizzes.

It must be clear, even after this sketchy review of the history of individualized instruction, that the concept has been pursued in a desultory fashion. I have heard hour-long conversations on individualization by educators who have only the vaguest notion of what is encompassed by the concept. Let me review five *different* concepts of individualization and acknowledge that I am indebted to Tyler[12] for some of these distinctions.

First, most educators agree that instruction is "individual" when the learner is allowed to proceed through content materials *at a self-determined pace that is comfortable for him.* This concept of self-paced instruction is incorporated into all programmed texts and is perhaps easiest to achieve with reading material and hardest to achieve in a setting that presents content by means of lectures, films, and television. Oettinger,[13] in his witty but infuriating little book, *Run, Computer, Run,* refers to this self-pacing concept of individualization as "rate tailoring."

A second concept of individualized instruction is that the learner should be able *to work at times convenient to him.* The hard realities of academic bookkeeping with the associated paraphernalia of credits, marks, and time-serving schedules make this concept difficult to implement in colleges or in the common schools.

That a learner should *begin instruction in a given subject at a point appropriate to his past achievement* is a third way of looking at individualization. This concept makes the assumption that progress in learning is linear and that the main task is to locate the learner's present position on a universal continuum. Once properly located, he can then continue to the goal. These notions seem to have their optimum validity for well-ordered content like mathematics or foreign languages. In fact, the advanced placement program, which provides college credit for tested subject matter achievement during secondary school, is a gross attempt to get at this kind of individualization.

A fourth concept of individualizatior is the idea that *learners are inhibited by a small number of easily identifiable skills or knowledges.* The assumption is that the absence of these skills is diagnosable and that remedial efforts through special instructional units can eliminate the difficulty. Colleges and universities seeking to enroll a higher proportion of their students from among the culturally disadvantaged and the economically deprived will be forced to bring this concept to bear if they wish to maintain current academic standards.

A fifth concept is that individualization can be achieved by *furnishing the learner with a wealth of instructional media from which to choose.*

[12] R. W. Tyler, "New Directions in Individualizing Instruction," in *The Abington Conference '67 on New Directions in Individualizing Instruction.* Abington, Pa.: The Conference, 1967.
[13] A. G. Oettinger and S. Marks, *Run, Computer, Run.* Cambridge, Mass.: Harvard University Press, 1969.

Lectures, audio tapes, films, books, etc., all with the same intellectual content, could theoretically be made available to the learner. The underlying notion is that the learner will instinctively choose the communication medium or combination of media that enable him to do his best work. The research evidence to support this viewpoint and practice is not at all strong.[14] Perhaps even more persuasive than the lack of evidence is the vanity of instructors who cannot understand why a student would choose a film or an audio tape in preference to the instructor's own lively, stimulating, and informative lectures.[15]

I have reviewed five concepts of individualization which have some credence in education, but by far the most prevalent interpretation is the one of self-pacing, or rate tailoring. These notions lead us directly to the idea of adaptive education in responsive environments, which I want to discuss shortly. But first, one more distinction. "Individual instruction," where one studies in isolation from other learners, should probably be distinguished from "individualized instruction," where the scope, sequence, and time of instruction are tailored in one or more of the five ways I have just described. "Individualized instruction" can still be in a group setting and, in fact, was commonly practiced in rural one-room schools, as mentioned earlier. On the other hand, "individual instruction" can be singularly rigid, monotonous, and unresponsive to the needs of the learner. You could, for instance, take programmed text material which is designed for individualized instruction and put it into an educational television format. Each frame could be shown to a large group of students for a short time, allowing the students to pick a correct option and then going on to another frame. This procedure would be individual instruction with a vengeance. But it forces a kind of lockstep on students of varying abilities and interests that is the antithesis of "individualized instruction."

ADAPTIVE EDUCATION

I predict that the impending instruction revolution will shortly bypass the simple idea of individualizing instruction and move ahead to the more sophisticated notion of providing *adaptive education* for school and college learners. By adaptive education we mean the tailoring of subject matter presentations to fit the special requirements and capabilities of each learner. The ideal is that no learner should stop short of his ultimate achievement in an area of content because of idiosyncratic hang-ups in his particular study strategies.

We have seen how the concept of individualized instruction has been pretty well arrested at the level of encouraging the learner to vary and con-

14 S. N. Postlethwait, "Planning for Better Learning," in *In Search of Leaders*, ed. G. K. Smith, Washington, D.C.: American Association for Higher Education, NEA, 1967, pp. 110–13.
15 D. T. Tosti and J. T. Ball, A *Behavioral Approach to Instructional Design and Media Selection*, BSD Paper Number 1, Observations in Behavioral Technology, Albuquerque, N.M.: The Behavior Systems Division, Westinghouse Learning Corporation, 1969.

trol his task completion time. Many additional, more psychologically oriented variables will have to be brought into play to achieve the goals of adaptive education, as well as the adoption of individualizing techniques. We know a great deal about individual differences among people in regard to their sensory inputs, their reaction times, their interests, their values and preferences, and their organizational strategies in "mapping" the cognitive world. What we do not know very much about is the extent to which, or how, these easily tested, individual difference variables affect the acquisition and retention of new knowledge. Psychological learning theory has been preoccupied with the study of variables in extremely simple stimulus-response situations, and investigations of meaningful learning phenomena have clearly dealt with human subjects as if they were all cut from the same bolt. The exception to this observation is, of course, the variable of measured mental ability, which has been shown to be related to achievement in conventionally presented instruction and has been carefully controlled in many learning experiments involving human subjects.

Essential to the idea of adaptive education is the means of utilizing new knowledge about individual differences among learners to bring a highly tailored instructional product to the student. As long as we are dealing with static or canned linear presentations such as those contained in books, films, video tapes, and some lectures, there seems to be little incentive to try to discover what modifications in instructional materials would optimize learning for each student. To plug this important gap in the drive toward vastly improved learning, the modern digital computer seems to have great promise. About a decade ago, Rath, Anderson, and Brainerd[16] suggested the application of the computer to teaching tasks and actually programmed some associative learning material. In the intervening decade, a number of major universities, medical schools, industries, and military establishments have been exploring the use of the computer in instruction. Five years ago we instituted a computer-assisted instruction laboratory at Penn State and have been trying to perfect new instructional techniques within the constraints of available hardware and computer operating systems.[17,18,19,20] There are, according to my estimate, some 35 to 40 active computer-assisted

[16] G. J. Rath, N. S. Anderson, and R. C. Brainerd, "The IBM Research Center Teaching Machine Project," in *Automatic Teaching: The State of the Art*, ed. E. H. Galanter, New York: Wiley, 1959, pp. 117–30.

[17] H. E. Mitzel, *The Development and Presentation of Four College Courses by Computer Teleprocessing*. Final Report, Computer-Assisted Instruction Laboratory, The Pennsylvania State University, June 30, 1967. Contract No. OE-4-16-010, New Project No. 5-1194, U.S. Office of Education.

[18] H. E. Mitzel, B. R. Brown, and R. Igo, *The Development and Evaluation of a Teleprocessed Computer-Assisted Instruction Course in the Recognition of Malarial Parasites*. Final Report No. R-17, Computer-Assisted Instruction Laboratory, The Pennsylvania State University, June 30, 1968. Contract No. N00014-67-A-0385-0003, Office of Naval Research.

[19] H. E. Mitzel, *Experimentation with Computer-Assisted Instruction in Technical Education*. Semi-annual progress report, R-18, Computer-Assisted Instruction Laboratory, The Pennsylvania State University, December 31, 1968.

[20] "Inquiry," Research Report published by Office of the Vice President for Research, Penn State.

instruction (CAI) installations operating in the world today, and fewer than 100 completed, semester-length courses or their equivalent. Almost none of these courses have been constructed according to the ideals I mentioned for adaptive education. Indeed, many of them look like crude, made-over versions of programmed textbooks, but this does not disturb me when I recall that the earliest automobiles were designed to look like carriages without the horses. The fact is that the modern computer's information storage capacity and decision logic have given us a glimpse of what a dynamic, individualized instruction procedure could be, and some insight into how this tool might be brought to bear to achieve an adaptive quality education for every student. We do not claim that the achievement of this goal is just around the corner or that every school and college can implement it by the turn of the century. We do believe that progress toward a program of adaptive education will be the big difference between our best schools and our mediocre ones at the end of the next three decades.

What individual difference variables look most promising for adapting instruction to the individual student via CAI? At Penn State we are testing the idea that a person learns best if he is rewarded for correctness with his most preferred type of reinforcement.[21] Thus some students will, we believe, learn more rapidly if they receive encouragement in the form of adult approval. Others will perform better if they receive actual tokens for excellence at significant places in the program, the tokens being exchangeable for candy, cokes, or other wanted objects. Still others respond to competitive situations in which they are given evidence of the superiority or inferiority of their performance compared to that of their peers. It is a fairly simple matter to determine a learner's reward preference in advance of instruction and to provide him with a computer-based program in which the information feedback is tailored to his psychological preference.

Perhaps the most dynamic and relevant variable on which to base an adaptive program of instruction is the learner's immediate past history of responses. By programming the computer to count and evaluate the correctness of the 10 most recent responses, it is possible to determine what comes next for each learner according to a prearranged schedule. For example, four or fewer correct out of the most recent 10 might dictate branching into shorter teaching steps with heavy prompting and large amounts of practice material. A score of five to seven might indicate the need for just a little more practice material, and eight or more correct out of the 10 most recent problems would suggest movement onto a fast "track" with long strides through the computer-presented content. The dynamic part of this adaptive mechanism is that the computer constantly updates its performance information about each learner by dropping off the learner's response to the tenth problem back as it adds on new performance information from a just-completed problem.

[21] C. A. Cartwright and G. P. Cartwright, *Reward Preference Profiles of Elementary School Children,* mimeographed, Computer-Assisted Instruction Laboratory, The Pennsylvania State University, 1969. Paper presented at the meeting of the American Educational Research Association, Los Angeles, February, 1969.

There are two rather distinct strategies for presenting subject matter to learners. One is *deductive*, in which a rule, principle, or generalization is presented, followed by examples. The other strategy is *inductive* and seeks, by means of a careful choice of illustrative examples, to lead the learner into formulating principles and generalizations on his own initiative. In the lower schools, inductive method is called "guided discovery" and has been found useful by many teachers. Our belief at the Penn State CAI Laboratory is that these two presentation strategies have their corollaries in an individual differences variable and that, for some students, learning will be facilitated by the deductive approach; others will learn more rapidly and with better retention if an inductive mode is adopted. A strong program of adaptive education would take these and other identifiable learner variables into account in the instructional process.

EVALUATION AND STUDENT APPRAISAL

One of the important concomitants of the instruction revolution will be a drastic revision in the approach to learner evaluation and grading practices by faculty. Even the moderate students on campus are saying that letter grades are anachronistic. On many campuses, including our own, students have petitioned for, and won, the right to receive "satisfactory" and "unsatisfactory" evaluations of their work in certain non-major courses. Other students have attacked all grades as a manifestation of a coercive, competitive, materialistic society. Without admitting to being a tool of a sick society, we should change this part of the business of higher education as rapidly as possible.

It seems to me that most formal instruction has been predicated on the notion that a course is offered between two relatively fixed points in time. In addition, the tools of instruction, such as lectures, textbooks, references, and computer services, are all relatively fixed and are the same for all learners. To be sure, the students do vary the amount of time they spend with these tools. Even there, the college catalogue tells the students that they should all study three hours outside of class for every hour in class. At the close of the period of instruction or end of the course, usually the end of the term, we give the students an achievement test that is constructed in a way that will maximize the *differences* among their scores. To get this seemingly important differentiation between our students in achievement, we have to ask extremely difficult questions. Sometimes we even go so far as to ask questions about footnotes in the text. In fact, we often have to ask questions on topics or objectives that we have made no attempt to teach. Our rationalization for this tactic is that we want the students to be able to *transfer* their knowledge. After obtaining the achievement examination results, we consult the trusty "normal curve" and assign A's, B's, C's, D's, and F's according to our interpretation of the grading mores of the institution. With time and materials fixed, we are essentially capitalizing upon the same human abilities that are measured by intelligence tests. Thus it is not surprising that intelligence and teacher-assigned grades tend to be highly correlated.

We could, as collegiate educators, do society and ourselves a big favor by making a fundamental shift in our approach to teaching and examining. (Incidentally, we might generate some relevance "points" with our students.) First, we should say (and mean) that our job is helping each of our students to achieve *mastery* over some operationally defined portion of subject matter.[22] Furthermore, failure by any student putting forth an effort is a failure on our part as teachers, or a breakdown of the selection system. Now, to do this job we will have to get rid of a lot of the present practices and irrelevancies of higher education. There is no point in maintaining an *adversary* system in the classroom, with the students against the instructor and each of the students against each other. Society may think that it wants us to mark our students on a competitive scale, but how much more sensible it would be if we could say, on the basis of accumulated examination evidence, that John Jones has achieved 85 percent of the objectives in Engineering 101, rather than say that he got a "B." If our job is to help the student master the subject matter or come close — say, achieve 90 percent or greater of the objectives — then we are going to have to adapt our instruction to him. As a starter, we could individualize by letting the student pace his own instruction. We know, for example, from preliminary work with class-sized groups in computer-assisted instruction, that the slowest student will take from three to five times as long as the fastest student in a rich environment of individualized teaching material. During a recent computer-mediated in-service teacher education course presented by Penn State in Dryden, Virginia, to 129 elementary school teachers, the average completion time was 21 clock hours. The fastest student finished in 12 hours and the slowest took 58 hours.[23]

Student evaluations should also be based on the concept that an achievable mastery criterion exists for each course. We should no longer engage in the sophistry of classical psychometrics, in which we prepare a test or examination deliberately designed to make half the students get half the items wrong. It is true that such a test optimally discriminates among the learners, which we justify by claiming need for competitive marking information. If, however, 50 percent of the students get 50 percent of the items wrong, then either we are asking the wrong questions or there is something seriously wrong with our non-adaptive instructional program.

Under optimum circumstances, we might get an enlightened view of the faculty's need to adopt mastery-type student evaluation procedures and we might get professors to talk less, but we would still be faced with the psychological problem of instructor dominance or instructor power. The power over students which the "giving" of grades confers on professors would not be yielded easily by many in college teaching today. As Pogo says, "We have met the enemy and he is us."

If we, as faculty and administrators in higher education, embraced the

[22] B. Bloom, "Learning for Mastery," *UCLA Evaluation Comment*, 1968.
[23] K. H. Hall, *et al.*, *Inservice Mathematics Education for Elementary School Teachers via Computer-Assisted Instruction*. Interim Report, No. R-19, Computer-Assisted Instruction Laboratory, The Pennsylvania State University, June 1, 1969.

notion of teaching for student mastery by means of individually adaptive programs, then these are some of the concomitants:

1. Instructors would have to state their course objectives in behavioral terms.
2. Achievement tests keyed to course objectives would have to be constructed and used as both diagnostic placement and end-of-course determiners.
3. The bachelor's degree might take from two to eight years instead of the traditional four, because of the wide variability in mastery achievement.
4. Instead of telling three times a week, instructors might have to spend their time listening to students individually and in small groups where progress toward subject mastery required careful monitoring.
5. Instead of being primarily concerned with a discipline or with a specialization, those who profess for undergraduates would have to make the student and his knowledge their first concern.
6. Evaluation for promotion and salary increments for college teachers would be based on measured amounts of growth exhibited by their students and on numbers of students who achieved a specific mastery criterion.

If professors and deans ignore the reasoned demands for reforms of undergraduate instruction which come from the students, the government, and a concerned citizenry, then the revolution will be ugly and wrenching. The so-called "free universities," with their obvious shortcomings, are already harbingers of the chaos into which traditional higher education could slip if there is no responsiveness on the part of a majority of academicians to the need for change.

In the current wave of student unrest, many of the best articulated issues are local in nature, like the quality of food in the cafeteria or the relaxation of dormitory visiting rules for members of the opposite sex. Underneath these surface issues, however, lies the *one big issue*, which the students themselves haven't spelled out clearly. This is the issue of the relevance of contemporary collegiate instruction for students' lives. It seems to me students are saying, albeit not very clearly, that they want some wise adult to care about them, to pay attention to them, to listen and to guide them. We sit on our status quo's and ignore their cry for help at our peril.

Increasing Heterogeneity

Part of the fuel breeding the revolution in instruction is the increasing heterogeneity in mental ability and scholastic preparation among college students. The combined power of the teaching faculty, regional accrediting agencies, and shortage of spaces for students has, until recently, enabled many public universities to become increasingly selective. In fact, prestige among higher education institutions has been closely correlated with the height of the norms for entrance test scores. Even the great state universities, which began under the land-grant aegis as people's colleges, have a kind of "elitist" aura about them. The Rising aspirations of minority groups, particularly blacks, have pointed up the fact that the poor, the disadvantaged, and the dark-skinned of our society do not share equally in whatever benefits a post-secondary college experience confers. A recent study and report by John Egerton for the National Association of State Universities and Land-Grant Colleges[24] was based on 80 public universities which enroll almost one-third of the nation's college students. He found that less than two percent of the graduate and undergraduate students were Negro in these institutions and that less than one percent of the faculty were black. Yet approximately 11 percent of the total U.S. population is black. It seems irrefutable that, with society's new awareness of the inequality in higher education, university entrance standards will have to be lowered for sizeable groups of blacks who have been poorly educated in the nation's secondary schools. Accounts of City University of New York's open admissions plan for fall, 1970, provide ample proof of the beginning of this trend, and Healy's[25] recent article firms up the humanitarian and social theory for the change in this great university. The lowering of entrance requirements will inevitably increase the heterogeneity of scholastic skills which makes the conventional teaching job so difficult.

Another source for increasing individual differences among college undergraduates is their stiffening resistance to required courses. Students clearly want more freedom of choice in devising their education programs. They want to determine what subjects are relevant to their lives and are increasingly impatient with elaborate prerequisites and multi-course sequences. Although the activists are not likely to win a complete victory on this score, the pressure which they generate will serve to breach the walls and gates around courses that have carefully been built by faculty over the years in order to make the conventional job of teaching somewhat more manageable. In addition to the student rejection of required courses, there is a corresponding need for the teaching of interdisciplinary subjects. Students see, perhaps more clearly than the faculty, that solution of the nation's problems such as urban decay, congestion, air and water pollution, and war and peace are not going to be solved by the unitary application of knowledge from traditional disciplines. For purposes of this discussion, the drive toward more interdisciplinary courses of study can only increase the heterogeneity among students which the faculty has labored to minimize.

CONCLUSION

I have argued that we are now living with the early stages of a revolution in instruction which will be more or less complete by the turn of the century. The major changes will be primarily characterized by individualization of

---

[24] B. Nelson, "State Universities: Report Terms Desegregation 'Largely Token,'" *Science*, June 6, 1969, pp. 1155–56.

[25] T. S. Healy, "Will Everyman Destroy the University?" *Saturday Review*, December 20, 1969, pp. 54–56+.

instruction leading to sophisticated systems of adaptive education. Two concomitants of the revolution which seriously concern college faculty and administrators are the need for new fundamental concepts of student appraisal and adaptation to increasing heterogeneity among the students in our charge.

39

The Knowledge Machine

Elizabeth C. Wilson

Elizabeth C. Wilson wrote this article after participating in a George Washington University traveling seminar through which she visited Palo Alto, Pittsburgh, Cambridge, and other centers of computer-assisted instruction. Miss Wilson presents a thoughtful and comprehensive appraisal of "the knowledge machine" and asks for dialogue on the role of the school in tomorrow's society and on the issue of which authorities are to have responsibility for control and regulation of education and of the knowledge machine.

Elizabeth C. Wilson is an active curriculum worker. She is director of the Department of Supervision and Curriculum Development in the constantly-innovating Montgomery County Public Schools in Maryland.

Marshall McLuhan and George B. Leonard (in a recent issue of *Look* magazine)[1] visualize an educational Utopia as a result of technological advances. According to these prophets, "schooling as we now know it may be only a memory." They foresee computers with the capacity to understand both speech and writing, making "all of mankind's factual knowledge available to students everywhere in a matter of minutes or seconds." Computers as part of electronic learning systems containing television and sophisticated programed materials will help tomorrow's student become "an explorer, a researcher, a huntsman who ranges through the new educational world of

Elizabeth C. Wilson, "The Knowledge Machine," *Teachers College Record*, 70 (November, 1968), pp. 109–119. Reprinted by permission of the author and publisher.

[1] Marshall McLuhan and George B. Leonard, "The Future of Education: The Class of 1989," *Look*, February 21, 1967.

electronic circuitry and heightened human interaction just as the tribal huntsman ranged the wilds.

The McLuhan-Leonard vision assumes that standardized mass education
will be a thing of the past, discarded along with the material mass-production
line with which it has run parallel. It takes for granted that tomorrow's
teachers will have adjusted to a new role in a schoolroom which is literally
the world. It expects that "fragmentation, specialization and sameness will be
replaced by wholeness, diversity and, above all, a deep involvement." Mankind can then truly be "educated by possibility . . . in accordance with his
infinity," as Soren Kierkegaard had hoped.[2]

But Kierkegaard, we remember, linked educational possibility with dread.
And dread is the mood we tend to associate with other distinguished contemporary prophets like Aldous Huxley, George Orwell, and more recently
Leo Szilard.[3] These men were equally fascinated by the future and, if not
by computers per se, at least by technology and by communication. They
were, however, painfully aware of the sombre possibilities of the political
control of education and of the slow death of the humane values we now
cherish. They had a healthy fear of man's lack of self-control and ability to
misuse his technological advances.

The predictions of these two sets of prophets are poles apart. Which of
them has more validity for the future? Which is more probable?

I would like to believe that McLuhan and Leonard are *not* dealing with
dreams — that future educational patterns can break out of old molds — that
the school of tomorrow can in fact be "more concerned with training the
senses and perceptions than with stuffing brains."[4] But I have lived a long
time with education, both in its formal existence in places called schools, and
in its informal manifestations in the socialization process. This experience
documents the layers of conservatism which exist within the educative establishment, within the local communities whose values the schools reflect, and
within the local and national political structure. Conventional wisdom regarding the task of the school dies hard.

THE MAKING OF THE MOLD

We must remember that the function of the school has evolved slowly
over literally thousands of years. In simple societies, where learning to become adult members of the society was relatively uncomplicated, educational
arrangements tended to be informal. They were handled by the family, by
elders and chief priests, and by peer groups, through ceremonies, rituals, and
participation in the economic work of the groups. When a society became
more complex, and especially when there grew up a heritage of written
symbols, specialized agencies or schools appeared. A particular group of people known as teachers were given the task of transmitting the more com-

[2] Soren Kierkegaard, *The Concept of Dread.* Translated by Walter Lowrie. Princeton
University Press, 1944.
[3] Leo Szilard, *The Voice of the Dolphins.* New York: Simon and Schuster, 1961.
[4] McLuhan and Leonard, *op. cit.*

plicated, symbolic, and abstract aspects of the culture. Thus the schools became the formal institutions which augmented and supplemented the educational function of the family and of the religious and economic institutions of the society. As I. L. Kandel once wrote:

> When a formal system of education is organized, society selects from all those cultural experiences to which the child is exposed those aspects of its culture which it regards as most valuable for its own coherence and survival.[5]

In our society, the conscious task of the schools has traditionally been an intellectual one. The "major" subjects of the curriculum have been related to the learning of symbols, i.e., language (native and foreign, written and spoken) and mathematics, and to "factual," data-collecting subjects, i.e., history and the social sciences and science. By and large, these subjects were taught and learned by rote. The progressive education movement of the twenties and thirties abortively attempted to bring higher levels of cognition into the process. The current Curriculum Reform Movement with its emphasis upon the "structure of the disciplines" and the "scholar's method of inquiry" is the second thrust of this century to help the schools breed inquiring minds and to help students learn how to learn.

The idea that the primary function of the school is to teach the basic skills and to acquaint the student with the funded knowledge of mankind has a long history both in theory and in practice. It is one which I have espoused since the beginning of my career and one which I will abandon with reluctance. But if McLuhan and other experts[6] are correct about the scope and speed of the electronic revolution already on our doorsteps, then the whole concept of the function of the school in our society needs massive reexamination.

REEXAMINATIONS

According to my best judgment, the first section of the "standard" curriculum to be absorbed by electronic multimedia will be the skills of language and mathematics — those subjects which can be logically and sequentially programed. Next will come what one scholar has called the "empirics," that is, science and the social sciences.

When that curricular absorption happens, what then will be the function of the school? To prepare students for vocations? To concentrate on the "soft" subjects like the fine arts, recreation, social and moral education? To use the knowledge acquired? To become a baby sitter?

The vocational function of the school seems less and less likely to be prominent in the year 1985. The first reason for this phenomenon has to do with swift and widespread change in the world of work. Specific vocational prep-

[5] I. L. Kandel, "The Transmission of Culture: Education as an Instrument of National Policy," in *Conflicts of Power in Modern Culture*, Symposium of the Conference on Science, Philosophy and Religion. New York: Harpers, 1948.

[6] See "The Electronic Revolution," a special issue of *The American Scholar*, Spring 1966, Vol. 35, No. 2.

aration will need to be done on the job, if at all. Actually, this situation already obtains. A second reason relates to the need of tomorrow's worker to be flexible, and hence to concentrate on the basic skills and concepts which will help him learn how to learn. A third reason suggests a revolutionary change in attitudes toward work — the death of the Protestant work ethic, if you will, and concurrently a shift from concentration on products to a concentration on services and leisure time activities.

If vocational and professional training are increasingly accomplished through internships in the "real" world, the "school," if it continues to exist at all, is left with what are now considered "minor subjects" in the explicit curriculum, and with a great deal of what we educators call the implicit and affective curriculum. By implicit curriculum here we mean the social system of the institution — those potent and seldom conscious factors by which institutions mold the young. For example, look at the Americanization of hordes of first and second generation immigrant children, or more recently, at the enhancement of adolescent peer culture by the schools. By the affective curriculum, we mean the values and attitudes that are absorbed from the climate and the person-to-person contacts created by an institution. And we also mean the "soft" and controversial elements of curriculum which historically were assumed by the family or by religious and social agencies. Examples of this kind of "soft" curriculum are sex education, driver training, race relations, and guidance in self-understanding.

Another possibility is that the school as an institution will cease to exist. If its primary intellectual functions can be performed by electronic media, then there is little need for the institution in its traditional sense. Rather, other social agencies could divide up the "frill" curricula left, and the schools as we know them could be dissolved.

This possibility, however, seems unlikely. In the first place, despite the press of the basic education movement for the schools to go back to the three R's and cut out frills, and despite the return to the scholarly disciplines characterized by this decade's Curriculum Reform Movement, the public has more and more looked to the schools to solve its social as well as its intellectual problems. Thus the schools have been asked to take on the race and poverty problems of Inner City and the sex and delinquency problems of Suburbia. The school is seen more and more *in loco parentis* — a place that is really responsible for the socialization process of the young and for the transmission of middle class morality.

New Models

It is probably time that the public faced up to what it has been asking of the schools. Perhaps the school of tomorrow should model itself upon the Israeli kibbutz, assuming the basic affective educative function of the family, when that does not exist, and assisting parents in a modern version of the extended family of simple times and cultures. The school might also serve as the coordinator and integrator of a variety of educational agencies outside the school like fine arts centers, or laboratory-work centers sponsored and manned by industry and the professions, or recreational centers and camps, or multi-media centers where the "knowledge machine" would be available.

This version of the school of 1985 has elements in common with that of McLuhan and Leonard, with that of two young Harvard professors Fred Newmann and Donald Oliver,[7] and with that of Peter Peterson, President of Bell and Howell Company.[8] There are many others. The point is not how many versions but how radical. For radical the future schools will need to be if they are to absorb rather than be absorbed by the computer.

Any of these projections are light years ahead of present day conventional wisdom about the education process, whether that wisdom is housed within the educational establishment or within the public-political domain. The projections, furthermore, are based not only upon the electronic revolution, but also upon some educated guesses about the effects of such phenomena as the "pill," megalopolis, and growing leisure time upon institutions like the family, the church, and the government. All these subjects are emotional dynamite. The public would prefer not to examine them too closely. Yet, they are all part of the whole, as is an embryonic new morality which is now only a small cloud on the horizon. The task ahead will be far more simple. We will do well to keep in mind Toynbee's comment that:

> . . . every historical-culture pattern is an organic whole in which all the parts are interdependent, so that if any part is prised out of its setting, both the isolated part and the mutilated whole behave differently from their behavior when the pattern is intact.[9]

POLICY-MAKING AND PLANNING

The electronic revolution is hard on us. If its social accomplishment is to move without major disasters, particularly in the moral and political realms, policy planning of the first order of magnitude is required. The impact of the knowledge machine may well be greater than that of the atomic bomb upon warfare. Task-forces of the best minds in the country should open continuing debates upon the issues involved. Long range studies must be mounted to conceptualize and document the problems and issues. The five new research centers just announced by the United States Office of Education are a step in the right direction.[10] Let us hope they will consider at length the privacy and the control issues — in my mind the most serious of the moral and political questions raised by computer technology. They should also consider the changing role of the school in the total educative process.

These tasks will require Renaissance men — mature, humane philosophers of a kind not much in demand earlier this century. These wise men must

---

[7] Fred Newmann and Donald Oliver, "Education and Community," *Harvard Educational Review*, Volume 37, Number 1, 1967.

[8] Peter G. Peterson, "The Class of 1984 . . . Where Is It Going?" Keynote Address National Conference of State Legislators, December 4, 1966.

[9] Arnold Toynbee, *The World and the West*. London: Oxford University Press, 1963.

[10] *Education USA: Washington Monitor*, June 19, 1967.

not permit themselves to be seduced by big money or by the cyberneticians
— a self-confident group with a private in-group language. Rather, they need
to address themselves to the problem stated in the following paragraph:

> In the field of computer design the most severe lack of knowledge is not how
> to design and build bigger and faster machines, but how to make them func-
> tion, how to integrate them into the human world, and how to make them
> do what we want them to do. Norbert Wiener's later writing harped upon
> the danger we risk by building machines to perform functions that we do
> not adequately understand. The dangers are real because our ability to de-
> sign machines is more fully developed than is our ability to understand the
> purposes to which they might be put; and we could end by putting elec-
> tronic machines to uses we would not want to put them if we really un-
> derstood what the uses were.[11]

Further, these task forces and scholars need to think long and hard about
the kinds of people and the kinds of society seen as desired and desirable by
the end of the century, and about how computer technology can help and
how it can hinder such growth and development. Value questions will be
paramount.

These discussions and arguments should not be held within ivied walls.
They need wide dissemination and involvement by every imaginable variety
of citizen, business, government, and professional groups. The continuing
dialogue should become part of the atmosphere, just as is continuing discussion about the control and use of the atomic bomb.

Such thrashing out of direction needs to be based upon scientific and
technological literacy on the part of participants — a cross-fertilization of C. P.
Snow's two cultures. Such literacy presupposes adult education — for teachers
as well as for interested citizens. Indeed, the impact of technology upon society should be a persistent theme which pervades the entire curriculum at all
levels from the kindergarten through graduate school. An immediate step
in this direction could well be the sponsoring of a well-planned curriculum
project of this nature. Then, at the least, we might start to build a reservoir
of informed citizenry, who have more than a nodding acquaintance with the
space age, and with the astonishing new developments in the biological sciences, as well as with the computer. Designed for both young people and
their elders, such a curriculum might help to narrow an otherwise ever widen-
ing generation gap.

CURRICULUM DEVELOPMENT

Consideration of the need for building substantive curriculum on the effect
of technology on society initiates the whole subject of future curricular im-
peratives. They are multiple. Let us start from the premise that tomorrow's
educated citizen will need more liberal education in the Greek sense of the
word liberal than ever before. The reasons are obvious. In the first place, the

[11] Robert McClintock, "Machines and Vitalists: Reflections on the Ideology of Cybernetics," *American Scholar*, Spring, 1966, Vol. 35, Number 2, pp. 254–255.

Greek citizen's education will soon be a possibility for every man. Secondly, every man will have the leisure to cultivate grace and beauty, to contemplate the good life, and to wonder about the unknown. Thirdly, tomorrow's citizen will need more direct sensory contact with reality than ever before to counteract the potent artificial environment created by electronic media systems.

Increasingly important, therefore, are the arts — particularly the performing and the applied arts. Physical education should regain the place it had in the Greek curriculum. Outdoor education, camping, and home arts take on new meaning in this context. (Even today we are recognizing that "roughing it" in natural surroundings is now only possible for the privileged few.) Much of tomorrow's curriculum must take place in studios, in laboratories, on trips. Thus children may cultivate their perceptions and delight in the singular — in the concreteness of everyday contact with the natural world — in the stuff which makes artists out of people.

Similarly, deep and lasting personal contacts must be an integral part of this new educative process. The warmth of individual for individual and the intimacy of a stable caring community must offset the cool objectivity and impersonality of the machine, as well as provide an important motivational base for further learning. As Gerald Johnson puts it:

> The knower and the known are not a pair. They are two thirds of a trio. There remains the relation between them, a third factor as important as either of the others.[12]

This relationship must be as much a part of the new curriculum as the direct aesthetic experience itself. Indeed this new curriculum should be concerned equally with process and with product.

This person-to-person contact needs also to be an essential ingredient of the part of curriculum which deals with application and synthesis of knowledge. The community seminar described by Fred Newman and Donald Oliver[13] suggests this kind of affective background for the probing of intellectual issues. But until such natural forums become part of ordinary practice, the task can be done by the schools, providing they can be backed up with curriculum and instructional materials centering around such vital issues as urban slums, the generation gap, and pollution. The new courses on technology and society mentioned earlier could provide some of the substance for these dialogues.

This call for non-computerized sections of an increasingly humane curriculum does not imply lack of attention to the crying need for more curriculum software for computers. What exists now is pathetically thin. I suspect, however, that we have put the cart before the horse. Surely, except for experimental purposes, we don't want to develop curriculum simply because it lends itself to computer programing. Good curriculum comes first. Then the job is to see what subject matter and approaches can be best

---

[12] Gerald Johnson, "Some Cold Comfort," *American Scholar*, Spring 1966, Vol. 35, Number 2, p. 194.

[13] Fred Newmann and Donald Oliver, *op. cit.*

handled by the computer. For example, as stated earlier, logical sequences of symbolic learning seem particularly well suited to computer programing. So also are all kinds of informational retrieval systems in all subjects from science to histories of art and music. Games and simulation schemes also seem easily adapted for computer use. But in all curriculum building, the first question to ask is why? Unimportant or mediocre ends will produce unimportant and mediocre means whether the teacher is alive or is a mechanical monster.

To summarize, policy makers need to provide for the full range of a rich and varied curriculum for all sorts and conditions of learners, modes of learning, and subject matters. Whether or not it is to be computerized is a second order of priority. Let us, of course, continue to experiment with computer programs which treat the logical, the symbolic, and the empirical. But let us remember that the better these programs deal adequately with the funded knowledge of mankind, the more important will be the "soft-soft" sides of the present day curriculum, i.e., philosophy, the humanities, and the arts, both fine and practical.

Studying Institutional Change

Dreaming about the educational process of tomorrow and developing new curriculum tailored to the future can be empty exercises if these ideas and materials are not accepted and used. And to date, the schools have been the despair of innovators. During the last decade a brave new world in the schools was to have been ushered in by the Curriculum Reform Movement, with the advent of new organizational patterns like team teaching and non-graded schools, and with the development and promotion of new instructional media like television, language laboratories, and programed materials, including computers. Yet despite the amount of publicity given to these innovations and to the examples of a few schools and school districts given national visibility, not much basic change has occurred in the rank and file of classrooms in the nation. Very little has happened of an organic nature or of the proportions required by projections for 1985.

Given this background of experience, what strategies are in order? Is it hopeless to attempt to move the Leviathan that is the public school? Or should the government continue the strategy it has employed within the last few years, namely, to by-pass the educational establishment?

Probably both strategies will be needed for some time to come, particularly if the policy makers feel any responsibility toward the current generation of students and teachers now in the schools. In this connection we note that the great mass of public school teachers and administrators and the faculties of teacher-training institutions have not been involved in the excitement of the sixties. Nor will they be in the seventies and eighties if the problems of massive change of a conservative social institution are not faced head on. Attempts to get at this problem have been flying blind much of the time. This blind spot has several causes. One has to do with the lack of real school knowledge and experience on the part of the innovators of the last decade.

Another relates to the lack of articulate non-defensive leadership within the schools. A third suggests that the major energies of the Great Society leaders have been more directed toward social problems than toward educational ones. But, for whatever reasons, the fact remains that the task is huge, that a bits-and-pieces approach has been singularly unproductive, and that the full complexities of institutional change have been to date ignored.

At the same time, there *are* some attacks which hold promise, even though far from fool-proof. One of these relates to applications of systems analysis to the complex problems faced by school systems. Such applications will require conceptualization of the relationships of administrative and managerial decision-making with models of rational planning for curriculum and instruction. Field testing of such models and conceptual schemes is essential to their development and use, and there is a body of theory and experience upon which to build. Furthermore, school systems, whatever their fate, could profit from the self study and long-range planning required by full scale adaptation of systems analysis to their problems. Computers, incidentally, could greatly enhance the proper study of a school system either by itself or by outsiders.

SYSTEMS APPROACHES

Similarly, a systems approach to the computer as one of many instructional tools is badly needed. Such studies would place the computer in a multi-media context and would examine what learning modes, media, and material seem to work best with what curriculum and with what learners. We suspect, for instance, that there are many less sophisticated devices for enhancing learning (such as the book) which will continue on occasion to be an effective means to an educational end. Systems approach studies could give perspective to the potential of the computer as an instructional aid, refine its contributions, and speed its acceptance by the profession and by the public.

Another complex which requires long-range study is the whole teacher-education-leadership-training continuum. This is an arena which must be entered if change in the school system is a desired aim. Again there is need for conceptualization of the problem and for a systems approach to its administration and management. This approach hopefully would be intimately related both to the multimedia materials approach and to the curriculum and institutional schemes discussed earlier. Only as all the dimensions of the problems are defined can the issue be attacked in any rational fashion. Only against such a background can predictions about changes in the role of the teacher make much sense. Thus action research into such issues as the effects of computer-assisted instruction upon teacher percepts of their roles or as the impact of various staffing and organizational patterns somehow must tie into a larger whole. Only under such conditions can we take into account Toynbee's observation that the "isolated part and the mutilated whole behave differently" when they are removed from their natural setting.

Other obvious large long-range studies relate to the school and community structure, to the political decision-making process outside the school system, to the whole psychology of learning and child-rearing, as well as to the future functions of the family. These studies are undoubtedly under way now in several universities. They need continued governmental or foundation support. Equally important, however, is the building of a cadre of educational engineers or change agents who can translate the results of such studies into ongoing operational school programs.

CIRCUMVENTING ESTABLISHMENTS

In addition to all these studies of change within the school system, strategies which circumvent the school establishment need to be explored and their consequences studied. There seems little doubt that some products of this strategy, for example, the Head Start program, promise to have remarkable impacts and staying powers. There is much to be said for the generation of ideas and practice *outside* the body politic and for the creation of new institutions or agencies designed to assume functions traditionally belonging to the older institutions. These strategies, however, are only successful part of the time. The federal government, we know, has buried countless numbers of task force reports and has often built new agencies on new agencies in the vain hope of breathing life into important governmental functions. Despite this history, it would be interesting to follow experiments with the studio-workshop-laboratory idea outside of the school, or with local adaptations of the kibbutz, or with computer or multimedia learning centers, community based and separated from the school. And surely business enterprises should be encouraged to be partners in the process, providing authorities recognize that they are not infallible either, despite their sophisticated talk and smooth exterior charisma.

Of note is the fact that I have omitted any references to research and development in computer hardware. This omission is on purpose. I have confidence that the hardware will continue to be developed and be adapted to instructional uses without outside assistance. Rather, my plea is for software, software, and more software. Perhaps this is an incorrect use of this term, but my definition relates to the *messages* the computers will carry, such as sequential skill development in mathematics or retrieval systems for topics in the social sciences. My definition of software also includes the promotion of programs, like the development of small, family-like, outdoor camps, designed to offset the environment created by the computer and to balance the "new" curriculum. In addition, my "soft-ware" encompasses public examination of the emerging new roles for schools in our society, and searching appraisals of the political and moral issues relating to control of the knowledge machine.

CONCLUSION

All the studies and researches and programs related to the school and the computer are important. Were I a maker of policy, however, I would give first priority to the establishment and maintenance of dialogues about education in every forum and marketplace in the land. The major topics would be:

1. What should be the role of the school in tomorrow's society?
2. What authorities are to have the responsibility for control and regulation of education, in or out of school?
3. Who will control the knowledge machine?

Again, were I a policy maker, I would approach the task with fear and trembling. Tampering with the functions of a major social institution is a risky business. Yet the electronic revolution leaves us very little choice. Either we consciously take on the job or the knowledge machine will do it for us.

40

Educational Technology and Professional Practice

William Van Til

"Educational Technology and Professional Practice"grew out of the interest of an educational organization in the meaning of technology for contemporary educational practice. The John Dewey Society for the Study of Education and Culture, composed largely of philosophers of education and progressive-minded curriculum workers, authorized a commission to report to its membership. The editor served as chairman of the commission and developed this working paper which was shared with the members and other interested groups. The paper examines the promise and dangers inherent in future use of educational technology.

THE WAVE OF EDUCATIONAL TECHNOLOGY

A new wave of educational technology is moving swiftly toward the land of professional practice. Throughout the land, the products carried ashore by

William Van Til, "Educational Technology and Professional Practice," *Insights*, 4 (June, 1967), 2–5. Reprinted by permission of the author and publisher.

a recent earlier wave are clearly visible. Television and language laboratories are found in many schoolhouses, sometimes well-used, sometimes neglected except for the TV set in the faculty lounge. The wreckage of early models of teaching machines speckle the beaches, but programmed learning in book form has been salvaged by some. Cargo brought by an even earlier wave is well established in most of the schoolhouses of the land — cumbersome movie projectors, versatile tape recorders; overhead projectors. In every schoolhouse the products borne in centuries before by the greatest flood in history is in evidence; the Gutenberg wave washed books not only into every schoolhouse but into the hands of every learner. Some teachers believe that no other software than books should be used in schoolhouses.

The new wave of educational technology is off the shore and swiftly approaching. As its cargo, the wave carries computers, talking typewriters, total packages of learning materials, systems analysis and management. Glimpses of the hardware can be seen from the shore; some of the machines beep, bleat, and click. The software is less apparent; it may be missing.

Again, alarums and confusions sweep the land of professional practice. Some prophesy that the new wave will sweep away the teachers, some predict that it will damage the learners. Some prognosticate that the new wave will crest, break, and ebb harmlessly, leaving the schoolhouses scarcely touched. Some welcome the new wave and its cargo of technology. Others put up storm windows and board the doors of the schoolhouses.

Urgently, the mass media of the land issue an epidemic of reports on the coming flood. Large or small, public or professional, the periodicals report and speculate. Take January, 1967, alone. *Life's,* "The Computer as a Tutor"; *Time's,* "Colleges: A Satellite Built for TV"; *Saturday Review's,* "Changing Directions in American Education"; *Childhood Education's,* "Educational Technology and the Classroom Teacher"; *Phi Delta Kappan's,* "Big Business Discovers the Education Market"; *American Educational Research Journal's,* "An Approach to the Use of Computers in the Instructional Process and an Evaluation"; *N.J.E.A. Review's,* "Big Business in the Schools"; *Insights',* "Educational Technology and Professional Practice"; *Social Education's,* "Teachers, Computers and Games"; *CBS',* "The Communications Revolution"; *NET's,* "The Computer Tutor."

Mankind has long been ambivalent about science and its application, technology. Science has been eulogized as the road to knowledge, and the way to improve man's environment and his life. Technology has been embraced as the dispenser of comfort, the source of high living standards. Yet, simultaneously, science and technology have been feared by mankind as Frankenstein's monster, as the automaton-like golem of medieval Jewish legend, as the path leading from the serenity of *Walden* in 1854 to the sterility of *Brave New World* in 1984.

American educators have shared this ambivalence. No stouter defender of science could be found than John Dewey with his steady support of the scientific method and of scientific inquiry. Yet today among the exponents of the Dewey tradition apprehension is widespread concerning potential abuses of science's application, technology. Have we rubbed Aladdin's lamp of science only to have the genii of technology appear with mind control, domination by industrial-business-educational complexes, reduction of educators to robot-like roles?

Computer-aided instruction, talking typewriters, total packages of learning materials, systems analysis and management surge closer to the shores of professional practice. What is predictable as to the new wave? What problems confront the creators of the new technology? What promise comes with the new wave? What dangers? What is the role and responsibility of the modern educator? To such questions this working paper addresses itself.

WHAT IS PREDICTABLE?

Some things seem clear.

Educational technology will not go away. It is here to stay. In the last half of the twentieth century an industrial revolution which was long overdue has finally reached education. As Lewis Mumford has repeatedly reminded us, no trend in the modern world has been as inexorable as the onward movement of the industrial revolution, constantly utilizing new sources of power.

Wooden shoes thrown into the machinery did not sabotage the original industrial revolution. Nor will any educator's version of sabotage stop the application of the industrial revolution to the educational enterprise. No King Canute can sweep back the tides of technology and none should apply for the role unless he enjoys exercises in futility. Unlike Anne Lindbergh's "Wave of the Future," which was a temporary political abberation mistaken for an irresistible force, the power of the trend toward greater industrialization is strong. While trends are reversible by man, the onward march of machines seems an unlikely candidate for any about-face, short of a nuclear war reducing its survivors to savagery. Mankind has too much riding on his bet on science and technology.

John R. Stark of the Joint Economic Committee points out, "Educational technology has become an important source of investment for many U.S. corporations, and it is estimated that expenditures on educational hardware now exceed one billion dollars a year. A brief review of the companies now involved in its manufacture looks like a 'Who's Who' of the corporate world."[1] Thus, big business is entering aggressively into a market in which expenditures for education on the elementary, secondary and college levels have risen from eighteen billion dollars in 1955 to forty billion dollars today with the prospect of reaching sixty billion dollars ten years from now. Whatever one's attitude toward big business in the United States of America, any realistic analysis must admit its power.

Equally predictable is that the oncoming of the new wave of technology, though forceful, will be gradual, rather than immediately overwhelming. The present beginning point is largely with skills, drills, and excesses. For instance, spelling, reading, and arithmetic are characteristic current fields of

---

[1] Stark, John R., "Educational Technology: A Communications Problem," *Phi Delta Kappan*, January 1967, p. 196.

endeavor for the new machines. This is due, in part, to the state of the art of technology. But it is also due to the state of the art of education.

There are formidable problems of cost too, as Charles Silberman points out concerning the automation process as a whole in *The Myths of Automation*. Patrick Suppes has recognized the problem of costs in connection with his computer instruction in arithmetic at Stanford in California. The history of technology indicates that cost factors in time can be overcome. But they add force to the contention that the development of the new technology will be gradual rather than an overnight phenomenon.

WHAT PROBLEMS CONFRONT THE CREATORS OF THE NEW TECHNOLOGY?

It is likely that the most formidable problem for the new industrial-educa-tional technology will not be the hardware, but will instead be the software, particularly in its relationships to ends of education. The American experience advises that engineering ingenuity will conquer the problem of hardware, the physical equipment. The persistent difficulty will be the software, in effect, what goes into the machine. Here the problem is the ends of education.

Hardware can be neutral as to the ends of education. Software cannot; it is inextricably involved with questions of purposes, of philosophy, of objectives, of goals, of sources of curricular content.

Already the problem of the ends of education is bedevilling the creators of technologies as they move beyond the simpler tasks of teaching skills. Some hope for a definitive statement from the educational profession. They ask not only for the comprehensive goals of American education but also for detailing the specific objectives, somewhat in the tradition of the scientific curriculum movement developed in the early twentieth century by Bobbitt and Charters. (And what happens to Dewey's goal of growth? What happens to social reconstruction?) Others assume the insolubility of the problems of agreed-upon ends in a pluralistic society. They ask only for specificity in objectives related to separate and discrete parts of the educational enterprise, such as a single discipline, even a single task.

The problem of ends of education is particularly vexing for the exponents of applying the systems approach to education. "Systems studies," says Donald W. Meals of Raytheon, "trace out and assess the new impact of a new policy on related activities in order to predict how effective the total set of interacting elements (a system) will be in performing its mission." As applied to education, he points out that "systems analysis calls upon the educator today to see his activity as a whole — not only the whole child but also the curriculum *and* the media *and* the teacher *and* the management system for putting these *and* other resources together in a functional system."[2] The kinship of the systems approach to the concern of modern educators for the *total* curriculum in a world in which the curriculum is revised subject matter by subject matter with none responsible for the whole, is both strik-

[2] Meals, Donald W., "Heuristic Models for Systems Planning," *Phi Delta Kappan*, January, 1967, pp. 199–200.

ing and obvious. Yet both enterprises, systems analysis and concern for the total curriculum as a whole, frequently falter on the rock of disagreement, characteristic today and prevalent through the ages, as to the proper ends of education and as to the kind of human being to be developed through the educational enterprise.

Another central question for educational technology and professional practice is a human one. As a matter of fact, it is two million questions — the teachers of the land. As the new technology develops, the teacher's role will change. But in what direction?

A first alternative contemplates an educational world in which engineers design the hardware and experts employed by mammoth corporations design the software. The software is inserted in the hardware and the teacher becomes a machine tender, a button presser, a mechanic, a robot.

No one in the industry-business-education complex or in professional practice will admit to advocacy of such a role for the teacher. Yet the nightmare possibility is inherent in some unstated and thus uncriticized assumptions.

A second alternative conceives the teacher as a person who modifies the software and even the hardware. His (or her) perceptions and insights get embodied in the materials used. He becomes "master of the mix," "a master teacher," "a laboratory supervisor." Some exponents of the new technology claim that till now he has been a presentation device through exercise of his vocal cords and chalk, a good actor dramatizing materials before the class. Now, they say, he will assume an executive role as a manager, a chooser of resources, a diagnostician, a coordinator. Away from his materials laboratory and from his students he may become a course writer, a curriculum creator.

Alternative two is a role which the present teacher partially represents through use of movies, tape recorders, paperbacks, individualized learning materials for students. In the new world of technology, this type of professional practice would be maximized. Some regard the new role as characteristic of the upgrading which is said to accompany the development of technology.

A third alternative is the teacher who is truly freed by machines and materials which provide individualized instruction. The key claim of the new technology is that individualized instruction only now can be truly achieved. The chores of drill, exercises, skill development will be taken over by the computers and the talking typewriters. Total packages of books tied to films, filmstrips, tapes, et cetera, will replace dramatized presentations. The teacher will be freed for human interaction. He has opportunities for the kinds of open discussion that seem unlikely to become characteristic of machines. He can become a person who is related to other human beings, a guide and a problem sharer with the young. He can foster creativity and problem-solving based on facts assembled by machine sources. He can live up to the conception of the teacher implied in the comment, "Any teacher who can be replaced by a machine should be."

Alternative three goes beyond the type of individualization commonly urged as a philosophic rationale by the exponents of the new technology as they describe potentialities for individualization inherent in their endeavors.

What is inherent in the third alternative is a step beyond individualization, namely, humanization and personalization of education. Since the role is, by definition, unrelated to the techniques of the new technology, some developers of technological devices are either blind to its importance or regard it as irrelevant to their concerns. But it can never be irrelevant to educators who, with John Dewey, would combine scientific inquiry with democratic value orientation.

WHAT PROMISE AND DANGER COME WITH THE NEW WAVE?

The promise of the new technology is apparent.

Computer-aided instruction may eliminate skill drudgery even as mechanization in industry has sharply reduced manual labor. But this is not all. Enthusiasts are confident that the computer can go far beyond its present modest beginnings. They visualize the computer as a way of developing problem-solving ability. They point out its potentiality for interaction with the child of a generation, unlike our older generation, which is accustomed to machines that talk to one (having been brought up with radio, TV, tape recorder), which is ready to accept machines with which they can interact (having known language labs).

The talking typewriter is regarded by its sponsors as but one part of a design of a whole environment for learning. Data to be fed into the talking typewriter can be derived from the learner himself and can also be based on teacher experience. So high a degree of individualization is possible, say the exponents, that the individual learner's experience can be child-centered far beyond the dreams of an early version of progressive education. The child interacts with the typewriter on the interests of that particular child.

Those who prepare total packages of learning materials predict a richness and depth of materials never before achieved. Rather than simply read or talk of past history, students would be immersed in it through films, videotapes, dioramas, "wrap-around environments." All of his senses would be brought into play as the richest resources derived from radio, movies, television, books, demonstrations, fact banks would be called upon.

The systems analysts tell us that their approaches are kin to the persistent concern of curriculum workers for the total curriculum. Within a systems approach, construction of the curriculum through reconstruction of bits and pieces of the total curriculum, in the manner of PSSC physics or SMSG math, would be obsolete. The systems approach demands consideration of the total encompassing picture.

WHAT DANGERS COME WITH THE NEW WAVE?

Yet with the promise come dangers. There is the danger of the new technology being sold under the slogans of creativity, high individualization, and problem-solving, yet delivering mechanical and packaged traditional rote education more meaningless than that of the most inept traditionalist. There is the danger of attributing to machine instruction what can only be done by man in a humanistic setting. There is the danger that, in a world where educators either cannot or will not indicate comprehensive ends along with specific objectives of education, the initiative will be seized by a business-industrial-education complex with little knowledge of the complexities of professional practice.

Of all the dangers, the greatest besetting the visionaries who are developing the new technology is that in the profit economy in which they operate some will go too fast. Ironically, in light of the long-standing American disapproval of bigness in business, the possibility is that premature production would be characteristic of the smaller companies, the wild-catters lacking the resources and staying power of the industrial giants who can afford to wait. Only the giants (say the giants) can take a long time, accepting perhaps ten years of not making profit. Yet even the giants can't and won't wait forever — big business executives too live under the whip of profits. Sometimes the visionaries, those excited by the new possibilities, move on to new ideas. A tough-minded profit-oriented management may stay on and plunge ahead, damning the torpedoes.

If the universities and the regional laboratories do not set up yardstick schools in which the new technology may be tried, big business may take the bull by the horns, setting up profit-making schools. There is even talk of buying school systems from communities, assuming the community's taxes, and specifying the content for the model school. Those who think the latter a remote Orwellian possibility might study present relationships of big business to schools as services are contracted under the auspices of a cooperative federal government.

WHAT IS THE ROLE AND RESPONSIBILITY OF THE MODERN EDUCATOR?

At this stage of the development of the new technology, no possibility should be ruled out. Much depends on the willingess and ability of educators to interact with the new industrial-business-education complex.

Minor suggestions include occasional exchange of posts with educators in professional practice taking posts in technological developments: conversely, with creators of the new technology teaching in schools and universities. Also suggested is a small congress of philosophers of education, educational psychologists, curriculum workers, and other theorists in education interacting as advisory consortiums with members of the industrial-business-education complexes willing to share ideas.

Major suggestions involve a new conception of the laboratory school, sponsored by universities and regional laboratories. Laboratory schools might become, in part, demonstration centers testing hardware, software, whole environments, learning resources, systems.

Another major suggestion involves cooperation with management on the establishment of standards and yardsticks to guide and control the development of the proliferating materials. Costly choices by schools will be made perhaps within the next five years and school boards are unequipped to make decisions alone. Objectivity is hard to achieve. Even now educators in government and universities have their loyalties to corporate bodies through past, sometimes present, and always potential relationships to the industrial giants. That yardsticks and standards must come is likely, given the experience of industry with self- and government regulation and of education with certification. The question appears to be whether such standards will be developed by the industry-business-education complex alone (and then be criticized by the profession), by the profession independently (and then perhaps be ignored), or by both jointly.

Steadily the new wave of technology comes nearer the shores of professional practice. The responsibility of the professional educator is to think through the relationship of educational technology and professional practice and to act decisively and effectively before it is too late to make an impact on events.

Both promise and dangers exist in the potential development of the new technology. The creators face problems which cannot be well solved without educational theorists and practitioners such as members of the John Dewey Society. Characteristically, the John Dewey Society members combine reliance on scientific inquiry and method with concern for democratic values as they consider the proper ends of education. Characteristically, the John Dewey Society members exert significant influence on matters of professional practice, such as the role of teachers. Members, and the Society as a whole, should play an important role and assume significant responsibility now with respect to educational technology and professional practice. If this be so, how should the members and the Society best proceed?

C. Aspects of the Curriculum of the Future

41

Science Education in 1991[1]

Leopold E. Klopfer

"Science Education in 1991" is a vivid and imaginative extrapola-
tion of current trends in science education. The reader may wish
to compare Klopfer's ideas on science education for the future with
those of Tanner on science education for the Seventies in Part Two
of this anthology.

Leonard Klopfer is Associate Professor of Education and a re-
search associate in the Learning Research and Development Center
at the University of Pittsburgh. His views, like those of the authors
of the two articles which follow, were presented to a University of
Chicago audience as part of a series of discussions of American
education as it might be in 1991.

> There is indeed much in what you say, . . .
> One can look back a thousand years easier
> than forward fifty.
> —EDWARD BELLAMY (*Looking Backward,* 1888)

Science education in the last decade of the twentieth century will differ
importantly from science education today. This will be so because by 1991
science teachers and educators generally will have adopted and adapted the
worthwhile innovations originated in our own time, and because the basic
dilemma which now underlies the teaching and learning of science cannot
remain unresolved. In the past decade, the teaching of science in America

Reprinted from "Science Education in 1991," by Leopold Klopfer by permission of
The University of Chicago Press. *The School Review* (Sept.–Dec., 1969), 199–208,
210–214, 216–217.

[1] The year 1991 in the title of this paper is used as a convenient indicator for the
last decade of the twentieth century. Thus, the title should not be interpreted to imply
pinpoint predictions for a particular year in the future. Based in part on a presentation
in the "Teaching and Learning, 1991" lecture series at The University of Chicago, this
paper seeks merely to assess key aspects of science education today and to suggest productive directions for the teaching and learning of science during the next quarter of
this century.

has been the focus of countless changes as curriculum revisions on an un-precedented scale have swept over the science courses of the high schools and, more recently, the science offerings in the elementary and junior high schools and in the colleges. Much has been accomplished and will continue to be accomplished in the years to come. However, despite the great flurry of new science courses, new curricula, new materials, and new approaches, the basic dilemma confronting science education has been largely ignored. The numerous course and curriculum improvement projects, rightly concerned with attaining their own objectives and not with matters of policy, have con-tributed little to the resolution of the dilemma; they have highlighted its urgency.

The dilemma at every level of science education has its roots in the discrepancy among the goals of science education appropriate for different groups of learners. The goals of science education appropriate for those students who will enter careers in science and in fields closely related to science are quite different from the goals of science education for the much larger proportion of students who will not pursue such careers. Our dilemma arises from the fact that both sets of goals have legitimate claims on the education in science offered in schools and colleges. This is true today, and it will also be true in the last decade of this century.

There is little question today about society's need for research scientists in reasonably large numbers and of high competence. Not only is the still-accelerating development of scientific understanding the primary hallmark of man's intellectual adventure in our times, but the continually renewed fundamental knowledge won through the efforts of scientists provides the essential base for the growth and survival of all advanced, technologically oriented nations in the second half of the twentieth century. Concomitant with the need of society for talented men and women to develop our under-standing of the natural world, there is an equally important need for strong corps of imaginative people who will fashion the means of design, develop-ment, and production that make possible the application of scientific ad-vances for the benefit of man. These are the applied scientists and engineers in industries and in large-scale, government-sponsored projects who serve as the vital articulating backbone of our technological progress. While it is true that in many fields the distinction between fundamental science and the applications of science is rapidly becoming more hazy and may even be artificial, it still seems useful to distinguish the scientist, acting as scholar (the historical term "natural philosopher" is particularly apt), from the engineer, acting as implementer, in terms of the different functions which each performs in society today and will perform in the society of 1991.

Another professional whose effective services to society and to man are closely related to the growing understandings of science is the physician. The practice of medicine, already mightily influenced by the scientific understanding of living processes and interactions on various levels of biologi-cal organization, will surely become immeasurably enriched and increasingly sophisticated as a result of the imminent discoveries and breakthroughs in the biomedical areas of science that the next quarter century will witness.

As he ministers to the sick and promotes the cure and prevention of diseases of the human body and mind, the modern physician of 1991 will be the implementer par excellence in applying the advances of science to the benefit of man.

These three types of professionals — scientists, engineers, and physicians — all play decisive roles in the dynamic twentieth-century society of today and of the decades to come. Although science and technology are expanding rapidly in this country today, the rate of expansion will not diminish, according to most forecasters, in the immediately ensuing years.[2] Thus, the number of scientists and engineers required will be larger in the future. At the same time, since the population of the United States is expected to grow in the coming decades, the number of physicians needed will increase, assuming that the present physician-to-persons ratio is maintained or improved. Nevertheless, though the number of scientists, engineers, and physicians in our society will be larger, the proportion of people in the population who are engaged in these professions will probably not increase greatly. Sensible estimates suggest that scientists, engineers, and physicians will in the future, as they do today, constitute somewhere between 5 and 10 percent of the total labor force in the United States.

For the prospective scientists, physicians, and engineers, the primary goal of their science studies up to the bachelor's degree in college is to obtain the basic preparation for their further professional studies and experiences, in which a sound understanding of science is central. For this reason, the competencies of these students in science must be developed as broadly and as deeply as possible in the course of their secondary school and undergraduate college years. This goal cannot be attained easily, for the domains of scientific knowledge are already vast, and the regular increments to science in new discoveries and ideas sally forth in relentless flood. Since the time available in college alone is not sufficient to encompass all the preparation in science required by the aspiring scientist, physician, or engineer, the secondary school was enlisted many years ago in this task. The secondary school sought to respond, and the preparation of students for college science courses became one of the accepted aims of high school science teaching. Numerous high school science teachers now consider this preparation for later science courses to be the principal or only aim of science instruction in the secondary school. It is clear that the goals relating to preprofessional preparation in science are very much in evidence in science education today. The same set of goals will also be evident in science education in 1991.

Yet, there is another important set of goals, in conflict with the goals discussed thus far, that has at least an equal claim on giving direction to the teaching and learning of science. While the goals relating to preprofessional preparation in science are appropriate for students planning to become scientists, physicians, and engineers, only a small minority of the total population is engaged in these professions. Well in excess of 90 percent of all

---

[2] Numerous projections of trends in the closing third of the twentieth century have been published recently. One of the most interesting of these studies is reported in Herman Kahn and Anthony J. Wiener, *The Year 2000* (New York: Macmillan Co., 1967).

working people are engaged in occupations that are *not* directly related to science. This proportion for today will remain essentially the same in 1991. To this must be added the proportion of women who are housewives and mothers, but who are unaccountably designated as "unemployed," and it becomes clear that almost everyone is a nonscientist. For the nonscientist, the goals of his education in science cannot be the same as for the prospective scientist, physician, or engineer.

The goals of science education appropriate for everyone in schools and colleges are those which will contribute to the individual's scientific literacy. Literacy in science is essential for every man and woman who hopes to function effectively in our twentieth-century society. It will enable the individual in a rapidly changing environment to make intelligent choices about his personal well-being. It will provide him with a basis for judging and taking action on issues related to science that affect every citizen. It will enable him to better understand and appreciate the functions of science and technology in a transformed world. Indeed, there is a great deal to be accomplished in developing each student's scientific literacy through his science studies in school and college.

One component of scientific literacy is the understanding of key concepts and principles of science. Even though an individual is not personally engaged in a scientific or science-related occupation, he needs some basic understanding of scientific ideas to be able to comprehend the phenomena and the changes in the natural world in which he lives. Certain commentators have labeled such basic knowledge "survival science." It includes both the functional understanding of key concepts and the recognition of how these concepts apply to the practical affairs of life. "Survival science" consists of the essential knowledge and understanding every individual needs in an age of technology derived from science. Through his understanding of key science concepts and principles, the scientifically literate person is able to choose courses of action which will help him to live in safety and in health.

More important than the understanding of scientific concepts, however, is the component of scientific literacy related to how scientific ideas are developed. George Sarton wrote:

> It is not at all necessary that the average man should be acquainted with the latest theory of the universe or the newest hormone, but it is very necessary that he should understand as clearly as possible the purpose and method of science. This is the business of the schools, not simply of the colleges but of all the schools from kindergarten up.[3]

This comment suggests that a major emphasis in education for scientific literacy must be placed on the process of scientific inquiry. Every student should come to fully comprehend and appreciate what scientists do as they seek understanding of the natural world through the construction of networks of ideas. He must learn how scientific ideas are formulated, tested, and inevitably, revised, and he must learn what impels scientists to engage

[3] Quoted in Bentley Glass, "Renascent Biology," *School Review* 70 (Spring 1962): 19.

in this activity. Only if he thoroughly understands the aims and the processes of scientific inquiry will a person's confidence in science and scientists not be undermined when he learns of newly proposed scientific concepts and ideas that flatly contradict the concepts he previously studied in school. The scientifically literate person, with his understanding of scientific inquiry, will be able to accept such reformulations of scientific ideas and will remain unperturbed.

A further crucial component of scientific literacy is an understanding of the interactions between science and the general culture. The understanding of scientific concepts and of scientific inquiry are without substance if the student, who will be the citizen of tomorrow, is unaware of the impact of science and related technologies on contemporary society. Commenting on the need to develop a citizenry properly educated in science, Paul Hurd said that the major goal for science teaching is first

> to have students develop something more than a commonsense understanding of the natural world and, secondly, to understand science as a cultural asset, both with reference to its intellectual value and its social import. If young people are to take an active part in the affairs of our country and behave as rational citizens, they will need to understand not only the scientific enterprise, but its role in technology; and the place of both science and technology in the advancement of mankind.[4]

Perhaps the two most salient features of civilized life in the twentieth century have been the progress made possible by technology in reducing man's physical labor, in communication, in transportation, in increasing material comforts; and the transformations engendered by science in man's thinking and beliefs. A person who is scientifically literate would be cognizant of the multiple interactions between science and the general culture, and would incorporate aspects of his understanding into his personal planning, into his political decisions, and into his view of the world.

It is certainly quite obvious that the goals related to the development of scientific literacy are greatly different from the goals related to preprofessional science preparation. Good arguments have been advanced for the importance of both sets of goals in science education. However, scientists, teachers, and educators alike have been constantly confused about which set of goals their science programs and science courses were supposed to achieve. Many are still confused, for both sets of goals are worthy; but both cannot be achieved effectively at the same time in the same classroom as it is presently organized. This is the basic dilemma in science education today.

By 1991, a pattern of science education will have emerged which provides a resolution of our current dilemma. In common with other schemes of educational organization, this pattern will have evolved from its predecessors and will reflect the adjustments that a society inevitably makes

---

[4] Paul DeHart Hurd, "The Scientific Enterprise and the Educated Citizen" (paper presented at the National Science Teachers Association Regional Conference, San Diego, Calif., November 17, 1966), p. 2.

in its educational system in order to accomplish its aims of perpetuation and growth.[5] This pattern is a projection of current trends in science education and of current capabilities in American society for making adjustments in its educational system. Moreover, the projected pattern and the details of the programs within it take account of the best of the innovations already evident today in the teaching and learning of science.

The key feature in the science education pattern of 1991 will be the clear distinction of two curricular streams through the secondary schools and colleges. One curricular stream will be designed for students planning to enter careers as scientists, physicians, and engineers. We shall call this the Prospective Scientists stream, or PS stream. The other curricular stream will be designed for students who will become the nonscientist citizenry in all strata of the society, that is, people who will have careers as housewives, service workers, salesmen, business managers, artists, accountants, government officials, history professors, clergymen, etc. We shall call this the Scientific Literacy stream, or SL stream. Differentiation of students into the PS stream or the SL stream will begin at about age fourteen when they choose the high school they will attend.

In contrast with the usual instructional practices of today, the study of science in 1991, at all educational levels and in both the PS and SL curricular streams, will be characterized by individualized learning. Individualization of instruction will very likely be characteristic not only of science education, but of all areas of study in the schools and colleges of the last decade of the twentieth century. Whereas the customary unit for arranging instruction today is a group of students organized as a class or a course, the focus in 1991 will be on the individual student and his progress through sequences of learning experiences. For the learning of science, varied resources and materials that are maximally adapted to individual needs and learning styles will be provided, so that the student may have available numerous alternative pathways for attaining the successive proficiency levels. By 1991, the establishment of proficiency levels, each based on progress normally anticipated during one year of science study, and the setting of similar proficiency levels for other learning areas, will have made it possible to discard the present system of elementary and high school grade levels, based on the number of years the child has attended school. In a nongraded school, every student will be able to pursue his study of science at a rate best suited to his individual capacities. To plan and operate such an individualized learning system, the science teacher of 1991 will require assistance both in management and instruction, and this support will be provided through the necessary and appropriate electronic computer installations serving the schools.

Beginning in the kindergarten of the elementary schools of 1991, all students will study in a basic science education program, running through

[5] For an illuminating analysis of this process, see Francis S. Chase, "School Change in Perspective," in *The Changing American School*, ed. John I. Goodlad, 65th Yearbook of the National Society for the Study of Education, part 2 (Chicago: University of Chicago Press, 1966), pp. 271–306.

nine proficiency levels. The science program will be comprehensive and will be designed, in part, to provide each student with some basis in experience for deciding whether or not he should choose to go into the PS stream. However, more objective information for making this decision will be provided by the student's performance on the Career Prediction Test Battery, taken by every boy and girl during his final year in the elementary school. In consultation with career guidance counselors, the student and his parents will be able to choose either a high school in the PS stream or a high school in the SL stream.

The high schools in the SL stream will accommodate approximately 85 percent of all the students. Approximately 15 percent of all students will attend the high schools in the PS stream. Since the curriculum of the high schools in the PS stream will be highly specialized and demanding, attendance at these special schools will be determined by a student's strong interests and high predicted probability for a career in science, medicine, or engineering, not by the prestige of the school's selectivity. The high schools in the PS stream will be associated with, and may be located near, a college, university, or industrial organization which has a direct interest in the careers of the students who attend these schools. Appropriate cooperative arrangements and programs will be established between each school in the PS stream and its associated collegiate or industrial institution. When this pattern of science education is fully implemented, there will be perhaps 3,000 special high schools in the PS stream throughout the country. By using regional attendance districts as the basis for the geographical areas to be served by particular schools, no child who has the interest and the potential to succeed in the PS stream will be denied the opportunity to attend one of these special high schools.

The high schools in the SL stream in 1991 will be organized somewhat like the comprehensive high schools of today, but they will not serve those students who are heading toward careers as scientists, physicians, or engineers. A broad variety of curricular offerings will be available to the students in schools in the SL stream, since these students represent a great range of aptitudes and interests and are headed toward many different future careers. One element, however, will be common in the learning program of every student in these high schools: He will study science in each year of his secondary school experience. His program of science studies will be quite different from that offered in the schools in the PS stream, but the required study of science will be just as vital to his education as the required study of English. Opportunities for additional science study beyond the basic requirement may also be offered in the high schools in the SL stream as need and demand may dictate. Yet, the science offerings in these schools will not be nearly so ample or diverse as those in high schools in the PS stream. Here the learning program of each student will call for the study of science and related mathematics during one-half to three-fifths of the total time of his high school education.

With this background of the pattern of science education that can be expected in American elementary and secondary schools in the last decade of this century, it may be enlightening to take a tour, in imagination, of several educational locales in that future time.

ELEMENTARY SCHOOL SCIENCE, 1991

Miss Edwards is a science teacher in the intermediate unit of the Skylark School. (The school, incidentally, is not brand-new, but was built seven years ago in 1984. Like most elementary schools constructed in the past decade, the Skylark School contains both a primary unit for the younger children and an intermediate unit for the children who are studying toward proficiency levels six through nine in the several areas.) Miss Edwards is young, fairly new to teaching, and perhaps a little more glib in talking about the elementary science curriculum than some of the other teachers on the science staff of the intermediate unit.

"Most of these children have passed the sixth proficiency level," she replies to our question. "They're progressing at about an average rate, though two of the girls seem to have a real aptitude for science and are working on some very original projects. All the children are excited about their science investigations, I'm happy to say, and they're coming around to seeing for themselves the value of science in this modern age. And, after all, I think those are the main aims of science instruction in the elementary school — to generate in every child the excitement and joy of investigating the natural world and to build up a wholesome appreciation of the importance of science in society today.

"At Skylark School," continues Miss Edwards, "the children have science every day beginning in the kindergarten. I believe that all elementary schools in the country today give some time to science every day for all children. Besides this, of course, science reading materials and stories about scientists have a large part in the reading development program in our school's primary unit. Our primary unit and this intermediate unit are organized on the nongraded principle, which was pioneered in American elementary schools in the 1950s, so that each child may progress at his own learning rate in each area of the curriculum. In science, for example, this means that some children enter the science program of the intermediate unit during their fourth school year after kindergarten, most of the children enter in their fifth year, and a few start the intermediate unit's science program during their sixth year. Of course, our school's total science curriculum from the kindergarten on up is built around an integrated sequence of learning experiences for the children. The plan for our total science curriculum was brought up to date by the Skylark School staff only two or three years ago."

Miss Edwards deftly punches a code number on the console of the televiewer next to her desk, and we obtain a display of the school's current science curriculum plan. We note that this plan follows rather closely the Revised Recommendations for Elementary School Science, published by the National Science Teachers Association in 1987.

"Our science curriculum is individualized and reflects our belief that every child must obtain a basic literacy in science by the time he leaves the elementary school, just as every boy and girl must develop competence in using the English language and obtain a functional understanding of mathematics. The science curriculum has two principal emphases: the processes of scientific investigation and the major conceptual schemes of science. From what I learned at the university about the history of science education, I understand that these same emphases for science curriculum planning were already being recommended nearly thirty years ago, for instance in the 1964 publication of the National Science Teachers Association, *Theory into Action*. Well, the intervening years have certainly put these ideas into action in elementary school science.

"One of the starting points for the planning of our science curriculum was the recent insights obtained by behavioral scientists into the child's physical, emotional, and intellectual development. This information was used to help us decide which scientific processes and concepts would be placed at different stages of the curriculum, and also to help decide which activities and investigations children could carry out most profitably at different times. Naturally, since each child is an individual who learns best in his own unique way, no decision we make about ordering of learning experiences is infallible, but we can make better judgments today than we could have in the past. At the same time, our science staff still believes that we should have on hand at least two or three alternative ways that the student can use to learn every important idea and skill in the science curriculum. In working with children, I've found that the processes of scientific investigation are widely applicable to all disciplined mental activity, not only to science. This suggests to me that, by emphasizing such processes as observation, classification, measurement, communication, hypothesizing, and theory-building, we have the opportunity to coordinate the children's learning across several curriculum areas in the total program of the Skylark School."

Miss Edwards interrupts our conversation now, since several students have signaled her for help. Walking around the large laboratory-classroom to the various student stations, we see the children, individually and in small groups, busily working on a number of different investigations. Each child seems to be following a plan of study that interests him and that he has worked out for himself, with Miss Edwards' help. The laboratory-classroom is quite fully equipped and has ample space for each student to set up his experiments so that they will not be disturbed. Miss Edwards points out several original investigations that were suggested and designed by the students carrying them out, but she admits that most of the children are doing experiments that arose from problems discussed in the students' study guide. Returning to our previous conversation, Miss Edwards continues:

"As you see, the children get a good deal of experience, when doing their own investigations, with processes that are the same as those scientists use to advance science. This is how we make real our emphasis on the processes of scientific investigation. The second emphasis in our curriculum, as I've already mentioned, is on the major conceptual schemes of science today. These major concepts now held by scientists have some permanence over time, even in the face of the continuous changes in science with its rapid accumulation of new information and constantly shifting ideas. In our curriculum plan, the concepts, subconcepts, and topics which the children study are all a part of a development leading to the several major conceptual schemes of today's science. It's very interesting, you know, that forward-looking science educators of twenty-five years ago argued that major conceptual schemes of science could be used to structure the subject content of the school science curriculum, and this idea has persisted until today.

"I think it's also quite interesting that the major concepts proposed in the 1960s for organizing the elementary school science curriculum were so limited. Science has certainly grown tremendously since those days. Some of the old conceptual schemes can still be recognized in those we use today, but they've all been expanded and modified by new scientific understanding. The major conceptual schemes emphasized in the development of our science curriculum includes these ideas: intergalactic relativity and complementarity, interactions of force fields, organizational levels of living and nonliving systems, physical and biological interactions in ecosystems, functional evolution of living and nonliving forms. Naturally, the full development of these conceptual schemes through all the levels of our science curriculum also includes the applications of the various concepts and ideas to the practical affairs of everyday life. And that's another way in which the major concepts used in the 1960s were limited; it seems that most people then thought of science only as some form of pure knowledge. I understand that the application of science to the benefit of man used to be considered as something separate from science even as recently as fifteen years ago. Don't you think that's strange?" . . .

A HIGH SCHOOL IN THE PS STREAM

Just published is the new *Student Handbook* of the Paul Sabatier High School for the school year 1991–92. The prose in a student handbook can appear pretty dreary. But not to Frank. He is a freshman in the school, and he's reading his copy of the *Student Handbook* with rapt attention.

On the opening page is the principal's message, which contains, as in every previous edition of the handbook, a brief review of the school's founding. Paul Sabatier High School was founded in 1981 and was the first high school in the country to serve students in the PS stream. Paul Sabatier (1854–1941) was a French scientist, winner of the Nobel Prize for chemistry for his work on catalytic hydrogenation, and his name was chosen for the school to call attention both to the international character of science and to the interdependence of science and technology. (Applications of Sabatier's work on catalysis made possible the economical manufacture of edible fats from plant oils.) Next in the *Student Handbook* is a statement from the president of the university associated with Paul Sabatier High. The president's message mentions the cooperative arrangements for advanced study and for laboratory work experiences on the university's campus and also cites the extensive program of supplementary seminars given in the high school by visiting university scientists and other faculty members. With a calculated flourish, the president ends his statement with a quotation from Pascal. "That which is known is like a circle pushing against the unknown. The larger the circle of knowledge the greater the awareness of the unknown."

Frank flips the page of his *Student Handbook* to the section which describes the required core program of the school. He quickly discovers that every student is required to study communication during every year. (Communication studies are roughly equivalent to what was taught in courses called English in former times.) In addition, every student must study social sciences, mathematics, and a foreign language until he attains the twelfth proficiency level in each area. Attainment of the twelfth proficiency level, both in physical science and in life science, is also required of every student. But, Frank learns, before beginning physical science and life science, he must study the Science Alpha sequence. Frank turns to the description of this sequence and reads:

> Science Alpha is an exploration of fundamental ideas in science. The student reexamines what he has learned about these ideas in his previous study of science, and he is confronted with questions concerning what knowledge is and what can be known. Ideas explored in Science Alpha include: length, mass, force, time, growth, life, mind, man. Science Alpha raises many questions, but does not provide final answers.

Confronted with this summary of the beginning science sequence, Frank gains the impression that his study of science at Paul Sabatier High School will not be superficial. This impression is not dispelled as he reads the description of the required program of study in science.

> The core program consists of the sequential study of the disciplines in physical science and in life science. Students study in both areas in parallel, and several alternative learning experiences are always provided. The study of each discipline emphasizes the structure of that discipline and its relationships to other disciplines in physical science and life science. (The study of the structure of a science discipline includes the delineation of its subject matter, the principles of inquiry appropriate to the subject matter, and the development of the key concepts used to organize the subject matter.) In the main, the several disciplines are introduced in the approximate order of their historical appearance in modern science. This order helps each student to develop some notion of the evolution of scientific thought. Once a discipline is introduced into the sequence and its historical development is reviewed, the treatment of the subject matter is in the terms of the present-day structure of the discipline. In physical science, the sequence of disciplines studied begins with astronomy; in life science, the sequence begins with human biology. The subject matter of each of these disciplines early engaged man's attention for investigation by processes of observation and reasoning. In the initial study of astronomy and human biology, however, only the

data and the problems of each discipline are developed, since the present-day structure of both these disciplines incorporates much of the structure of all the other disciplines in physical science and in life science, respectively. For this reason, the sequence of studies in physical science returns in the end to the discipline of astronomy, and the sequence in life science culminates with a return to the discipline of human biology. These disciplines are now thoroughly treated, completing the sequence of studies in physical science and in life science to the twelfth proficiency level.

Once again, there's that phrase, "twelfth proficiency level." Frank is not sure he knows exactly what it means. Julie knows. Julie is a junior at Paul Sabatier High, and she's happy to share her wisdom with a puzzled freshman.

Julie explains to Frank that the school has clearly specified objectives for every area of study. In physical science and in life science, these objectives specify the understandings of concepts, the competencies in investigative procedures, and the interdisciplinary syntheses that every student is expected to master. In addition to the statement of objectives, the standard of proficiency in each objective is also specified. Students at Paul Sabatier High generally attain this level of proficiency in most curriculum areas sometime during their junior year, that is, the twelfth year of school, counting from the beginning of kindergarten. Hence, the name "twelfth proficiency level," though some students may attain the specified level of proficiency in some curricular areas before their twelfth year.

This acceleration is possible because so much of each student's learning is on an autoinstructional basis. The school's learning centers have full facilities to give students ready access to various autoinstruction media, including books, films, videotapes, data files, and computer-programmed lessons. At least one science teacher is always available in each learning center for conferences with students. The science teachers also organize regular discussion groups, give guidance to students in their laboratory investigations, and help each student to evaluate his own progress. Together with the student, the teachers certify when he has achieved the twelfth proficiency level in physical science and in life science.

"Wait until you become a junior!" exults Julie for Frank's benefit. "After you've gotten your proficiency certification, you can choose all kinds of exciting science electives. There are advanced sequences offered here at the school in most science disciplines, and you can also go across to the university if you want. The second half of junior year and most of senior year is wide open for science electives, so you can really concentrate on a special field that interests you. Most kids take four or five sequences in their special science field before they graduate from high school. Some take as many as eight."

A HIGH SCHOOL IN THE SL STREAM

As on every Tuesday afternoon, a vigorous discussion animates the meeting of the science department of the Samuel Langley High School.

"We're being old-fashioned with our present science program," Don

Baker is saying. "All of our students now study basically the same science sequence. Even though all students in this school are in the SL stream, there's great variation in their aptitudes, interests, and future career plans. Sure, every student can progress at his own rate and can choose alternative learning materials, but I think we need to set up different science sequences for different students to match the careers they're heading toward."

"I can't agree with that," puts in Betty West, who teaches freshmen and sophomores. "You see the kids, Don, when they're juniors and seniors. Their future plans are pretty well jelled by then. That isn't so for many of them in the first two years of high school. We can't plan several different science sequences without having more definite information."

Jim Howard comments, "I think that different science sequences would be very hard to administer."

"Administrative problems shouldn't keep us from having a good program," counters Don Baker. "We have enough experts in administration at this school who can worry about these things. Besides, our computer system could manage four sequences as readily as it does one. It's up to us to decide on what's most appropriate for different students to learn in their required science studies. Broadly speaking, there are four groups of students, according to their future career plans, at Samuel Langley High. It makes sense that there should be a definite science sequence matched to each group of students. In other words, we should have four different science sequences, at least for the juniors and seniors."

"What a complicated mess that could be!" exclaims Jim Howard.

Betty West nods her head in agreement. "I think we should be careful about rushing in and making changes we might regret later on. After all, the science program we have now takes care of kids with different aptitudes and interests. First, there's the basic sequence with its three underlying themes: the interrelationships among the science disciplines, the historical development of scientific ideas, the interrelationships between science and the general culture. Study of the units of the basic sequence normally takes a student only about half of each year. For the rest of the time, he chooses and studies some of the optional units that interest him. The optional units extend particular topics in the basic sequence, and they vary in difficulty. We now have more than seventy optional units available, and we're developing additional units all the time, as students want and need them. Honestly, I really don't see anything wrong with our present science program."

"But why should we be so antiquated?" mutters Don Baker. "The pattern we're using in our science program is very much like the pattern used in the old Project Physics course of twenty years ago. After all these years, we ought to be able to do better. And we could too, if we weren't held back by a lot of antediluvian thinking."

The chairman hastens to say, "Now, Don, I'm sure no teacher here is backward in his or her thinking. We all want to have a science program that's best for the youngsters. Our present program may not be the best, but it has some strong points in its favor. A high school science program is supposed to build up from the children's elementary school science experiences. I think our program does that. A high school science program in the SL stream is supposed to give each youngster a view of the unity of science. I think ours does. A high school science program ought to include some study of current scientific developments and how they affect the society. Our program does. And our program provides individualization by letting each student progress at his optimum learning rate and through alternative materials designed for different learning styles. I agree that it's always possible to improve, but we must keep in mind that our main purpose is to develop scientifically literate young men and women. There's no one way that's necessarily the best way to accomplish this. The important thing is that we keep on thinking and keep on planning, so that we may come up with what's best for the youngsters at Samuel Langley High School. Now, Betty, would you like to carry on with the discussion?" . . .

One other general feature of the science education pattern of 1991 should be noted. It may appear that the differentiation of all students into the distinct PS and SL streams is too rigid and that, on the basis of a person's decision at age fourteen, his destiny is sealed. Actually, this is not so. Opportunities for a student to switch from one curricular stream to the other will be built into the pattern. Predictions of probable adult occupational group membership on the basis of elementary school data are not infallible (though by 1991 those predictions will be quite reliable), and a student's interests change with time. Thus, some changes across curricular streams are expected. One anticipated change is that more students will move out of the PS stream than move into it, so that a contraction of the proportion of students in this curricular stream will be observed over the years. (In fact, the approximately 15 percent of all students who start in the PS stream at the beginning of high school is about twice as large as the proportion expected to eventually complete professional training as scientists, physicians, and engineers.) At least two principal stream transfer points will be available where career decisions may be reevaluated. In the junior year of high school, transfer from the PS stream to the SL stream or vice versa may be effected with an additional six to twelve months of intensive study to compensate for the difference in the program the student has taken up to that point. Similarly, in the sophomore year of college, additional intensive study for nine to eighteen months will make it possible for a student to move from either curricular stream into the other. In this way, then, some modicum of flexibility is provided for in the pattern of science education of 1991.

Will these predictions about the science education of the future be fulfilled? Only the passage of time and events will tell us. Yet, educators with convictions and commitment can mightily influence the course of events. This paper has attempted to extrapolate through time some present-day trends in science education and to balance these trends against the demands of society and the needs of people in it. By looking to the future, we may be able to shed some light on how to proceed in the present.

42

Teaching and Learning Mathematics: 1991

Max S. Bell

"Teaching and Learning Mathematics: 1991" is devoted to the results of recent reforms in mathematics teaching and to the positive implications of the extension of these beginnings into the years ahead. Max S. Bell believes that substantial changes must be made if his positive vision is to become an actuality.

Bell is Assistant Professor in the Graduate School of Education and coordinator of the Master of Arts in Teaching program in mathematics at the University of Chicago.

My prophesying can be briefly summarized as follows: (1) I will claim that the very conservative but decidedly nontrivial reforms of the past decade in mathematics curricula — familiar to you all as the so-called new mathematics — constitutes an existence proof for the proposition that productive reform in education, and especially mathematics education, is possible. (2) I will claim that there is nevertheless a great deal left to do in extending these reforms. I will summarize those things in the present situation which will make such extensions difficult as well as certain hopeful aspects of the existing situation. (3) Based on the positive aspects of the existing situation, I will present an optimistic vision of teaching and learning mathematics in 1991 that could be made real given very substantial effort. (4) I will then present a quite different vision of 1991 based on an extrapolation from the negative aspects of today's situation. (5) I will claim that we still have a clear choice between these two visions and, in closing, will be as blunt and explicit as I can in specifying the sort of repentance we would all have to undergo if the more favorable one is to have any chance of being reality in 1991.

The proposition that genuine reform in (mathematics) education is possible was very much in doubt only ten years ago. At least four times between 1900 and 1950, campaigns had been mounted for such reform with such singular lack of success that John Gardner in 1956 described mathematics education as "A National Weakness" in the following words:

Concern over the mathematical incompetence of the average — and even above-average — American has become almost a national preoccupation. Sci-

Reprinted from "Teaching and Learning Mathematics: 1991" by Max S. Bell by permission of The University of Chicago Press. *The School Review* (Sept.–Dec., 1969), 218–228.

ence and industry cry in vain for more and better mathematicians. Ordinary businesses ask only that their employees be able to do simple arithmetic. Neither the extravagant nor the modest demands of society for mathematicians — or arithmeticians even — are being met. And public concern grows. . . . An observer who visited 60 representative mathematics classrooms in different regions of the country came to the conclusion that genuine and efficient mathematical learning was going on in only eight of them. . . . As for the curriculum, little change has occurred in it despite the fact that since 1894 many authorities have been recommending changes. The result is that the curriculum is out of touch with the real needs for mathematics in the world today, and also out of touch with the interests of the pupils.[1]

We all know from the furor in the popular press about the so-called new mathematics that *something* has gone on since 1956. There is not space to describe in detail what this something is or how it was accomplished. What can be said is that it was primarily a curriculum reform (to the extent that curriculum is expressed in school textbooks) and that the net positive effect is that there is pretty general agreement now on the substantive mathematical content that can form the basis for school instruction in mathematics. To be sure, there is still an enormous amount to be done, but by getting a grip on the single restricted variable of curriculum *content* we have established a solid base from which to work.

On the negative side, we must admit that the books produced by the reform have been frankly aimed at "college-capable" youngsters and that implementation of the reforms has been much more widespread in schools that serve the relatively privileged segment of our society than in schools that serve the less privileged and much more widespread in secondary schools than in elementary schools. It must also be observed that the recent reforms have produced only bookish materials — we have scarcely begun to direct our efforts to producing the variety in methods and materials that is required. We must also observe that the new curricula have done no more than the old in acquainting youngsters with applications of mathematics and with the fruitful uses of so-called mathematical models that have transformed many fields of study in recent years, including some parts of the humanities and social sciences. Hence, if we were to stop with what we have so far, the impact of curriculum reforms would be restricted to a narrow population and would support the sort of restrictions on opportunity to learn mathematics that will be a feature of one of my two visions for 1991.

In continuing our review of the present-day situation, let us ask what research results exist to guide and support extension of the reforms that have been achieved to date. On the positive side we observe that a large number of isolated experiments have demonstrated that with the right approach youngsters of all ages can absorb and find pleasure in an astonishing range of mathematical ideas — many of them previously reserved for graduate schools. But we must immediately make the negative comment that demonstrating that a given isolated idea *can* be taught to at least

[1] John Gardner, "A National Weakness," *American Mathematical Monthly* 63 (June 1956): 396–99.

some youngsters by at least some person is a far cry from demonstrating that it should be taught or specifying where it should be taught and what should precede and follow it.

The status of this sort of feasibility research, as well as the status of research aimed at certain larger issues, has been neatly summarized recently by E. G. Begle of the School Mathematics Study Group (SMSG):

> A glance at these reports [summarizing research efforts in mathematics education] indicates that a considerable amount of research has been done in the past and also that the volume of research is increasing rapidly. A more careful look, however, provides the melancholy information that this large number of research efforts yields very little that can be used to improve mathematics education. This is not to say that all these efforts have been wasted. There are in fact many ingenious ideas and suggestions which ought to be followed up. In general, though, the results are too special or incomplete to be of wide use.[2]

But Begle claims, and I agree, that with the progress of the past decade we can leave the substantive content variable fixed for a while and attack other aspects of research in mathematics education. With such a base to work from, genuine and productive theories of mathematics teaching and learning may be within our reach. We may get a boost here from translations of Russian research reports in this area soon to be published jointly by SMSG and the Survey of Recent East European Mathematical Literature at the University of Chicago.

What now of the present status of mathematics teachers and teacher training? On the positive side, in the past decade institutes sponsored by the National Science Foundation and industry, efforts on behalf of the teacher by the reform groups, and the use of the new materials themselves have undoubtedly raised the average level of high school mathematics teaching and, to a much lesser extent, that of junior high and elementary school mathematics teaching. With much larger numbers of college mathematics students and with the increased attractiveness of mathematics teaching generated by the excitement of the reform movements, by improved school salaries and conditions (at least in the suburbs), and by a sort of Peace Corps service syndrome, we are getting more and better candidates for secondary school mathematics teaching. On the negative side, we see that increased enrollments in high school mathematics and normal replacement needs quickly gobble up this increased supply, so that no more than two-thirds of those who now begin teaching secondary school mathematics each year are adequately trained in mathematics. When we turn to the mathematical training of elementary school teachers, the situation seems so hopeless that we have a very marked tendency simply to throw up our hands in despair. There are over a million elementary school teachers in the United States, and nearly all of these are obliged to teach mathemat-

[2] E. G. Begle, "Curriculum Research in Mathematics" (mimeographed paper, based on a talk to the Research and Development Center for Learning and Reeducation at the University of Wisconsin, November 10, 1966).

ics. But study after study shows that many, if not most, of these teachers have been so cheated in their own education that they have virtually no understanding of mathematics and openly express fear and hostility toward it. Obviously, even with the best will in the world this ignorance, fear, and hostility must be communicated to millions of youngsters in hundreds of thousands of classrooms every school day, with consequences that are easily imagined — in fact, easily observed. Yet nearly every thoughtful observer predicts that a very good grip on mathematical skills and concepts will be essential for coping with the complicated world in which children now in school will be obliged to live. Furthermore, we are pretty sure by now that many of the most durable and important of these concepts take root most easily, and perhaps only, during the early childhood years. The contradictions between these apparent facts and the sort of instruction now given in early school mathematics should be fairly obvious. "The real obstacle," says Marshall Stone, "lies not in our knowledge of mathematics or our knowledge of pedagogy but in the outmoded and inadequate preparation we are still giving . . . teachers. It is high time that we stop prating about this obstacle and take counsel as to how we can remove it."[3]

Let us conclude this examination of the present state of teaching and learning of mathematics by looking at the conditions of teaching. For this, my list of positive aspects will be a short one and my list of negative aspects rather long — though not nearly as long as it could be. In a few city schools and in some suburbs the present conditions of teaching are fairly tolerable. While teachers still have too many students, for too many hours per week, with too little subprofessional assistance, many of the ills I shall outline next are not present. But in the majority of school settings the situation is rather bleak. To consider only instructional tasks, we note that in most high schools teachers will teach five classes (150–75 students) covering two or three different subjects five days per week. If a teacher were to be so ambitious as to average one *minute* per pupil per day in checking homework, personal consultation outside of class, and other follow-up of class activity, two or three hours would be added to his five-hour teaching day. If he were to take seriously the need to devise diagnostic, remedial, and evaluation procedures and if he spent no more than one-half hour per day preparing for each of his two or three subjects, another few hours would be added. Now suppose he is interested in keeping up on new developments in mathematics, curriculum, pedagogy, and methods and perhaps in inventing new materials himself. Can he find the time for these things as well? Obviously something must give way — more for some teachers than for others. The plight of the usual elementary school teacher, with up to forty-five youngsters in many classrooms and with the expectation of expert teaching in at least language arts and reading, social studies, and mathematics is surely not less discouraging. Now add to this heavy teaching load the probable expectation that a teacher will in addition supervise a so-called study hall, keep the student records for a homeroom or divi-

3 Marshall Stone, book review, *Mathematics Teacher* 58 (April 1965): 360.

sion, and police the halls, cafeteria, restrooms, playgrounds, and parking lot during his nonteaching hours. What of crowded and dreary classrooms? What of having no place to work when not in class — even if a teacher does not have hall duty? What of state laws and local regulations that dictate that once a textbook is adopted it must be used for five or eight or ten years regardless of how bad it is or how the curriculum changes? What of compulsory attendance laws that make schools the custodians of all youngsters up to an arbitrary age, no matter how inappropriate this custodianship may be in individual cases? What of the petty and demeaning administrative nonsense that curdles the soul unless one happens to have a good sense of humor and a good eye for the ridiculous — and perhaps the courage to tell the worst administrative despots to go to the devil? Finally, what about the fact that teachers almost everywhere must do without secretarial or clerical help of any sort? There are obvious contradictions in all of the above demands on teachers to do nonteaching tasks, but permit me a digression on this last one — the lack of clerical help for teachers:

Nearly every vision of the future of education includes the use of such things as programmed learning, computer-assisted instruction, television, film clips, and the like. There will be some reliance on such devices, but the problem is obviously one of figuring out what can safely be delegated by teachers without loss to the students. Here is the contradiction: at present teachers cannot delegate even the most trivial tasks to human helpers, and they are so used to this state of affairs that it will be very difficult for them to delegate even if given the chance. If trivial tasks cannot be delegated to human helpers, how are teachers to learn to delegate important tasks to non-human helpers?

TWO VISIONS OF 1991

To sum up the present situation, we have on the positive side: (1) a solid base in curriculum materials produced by the collaborative efforts of mathematicians and schoolteachers over the past decade; (2) a large number of suggestive experiments in curriculum content and in the deeper issues of how and when children learn mathematics; (3) the beginning of understanding of the crucial importance of the early childhood years in the formation of fruitful and durable mathematics concepts; (4) a large number of high school teachers with recent training or retraining in modern mathematics and experience with new curricula; (5) a large pool of mathematics undergraduates, better trained in mathematics than ever before, from which to recruit new teachers; (6) a number of school districts where teaching conditions are tolerable and which have demonstrated that giving teachers substantial trust and resources pays off quite handsomely; (7) more and more people who are at least giving lip service to the proposition that mathematics education must be very substantially improved.

Suppose we were to assume that these positive beginnings could be extended over approximately the next twenty-five years. What sort of vision would this give us?

I see preschool youngsters playing with toys and materials designed to build rock-bottom intuition about mathematical relationships while preserving the child's right to unstructured imaginative play. These are made available not merely to children of privileged and well-informed parents but to *every* child through the intervention of community social workers and by the fact that in every neighborhood the school buildings house (but the schools do not staff or control) a second shift of volunteer and professional people who have solid connections with that particular neighborhood. The school building has become a genuine community center where people can drop in for relaxation or help, with tutoring and favorable study conditions for schoolwork or for the efforts of adults to improve their lot. Not least, there are available to parents advice and materials and toys to help the preschool youngster gain in a natural way the experience that will help him form basic mathematical concepts.

In the early school years there will be a well-organized and imaginatively implemented set of mathematical experiences based on the principle stated by Marshall Stone in his sharply critical review of the so-called Cambridge Report: "There is good reason to be quite explicit and emphatic in proclaiming that the early years of school mathematics must be as close to pure fun as the teacher can make them. The verbalization and drill can come later, when the child feels the need for them, as he will surely do if the teacher creates the right conditions in the classroom."[4] This will *not* be the fuzzy-headed random activity that helped destroy the Progressive movement but a portion of the school day spent under teachers who are themselves so relaxed and confident in their understanding of fundamental mathematical concepts that they are able to exploit the opportunities given them by the youngsters as they respond to a loosely structured exposure to mathematics. In this way youngsters will have experience with such durable and important mathematical things as counting, approximation and estimation, classification, idealization, building of rudimentary mathematical models, fundamental measure concepts, fundamental set theoretic concepts and operations, transformations, functions, correspondences, equivalence and equivalence classes, order of magnitude, guess-and-verify procedures, recursive processes, rudimentary logical operations, quantifiers, arbitrariness of definition, axiomatic structuring (via rules of games) and the consequences of altering axioms (rules), and geometric relationships. Anyone at home with these concepts can imagine how they could indeed be "pure fun" to youngsters in the early elementary grades, and it would be easy to extend the list.

Incidentally, I do not see this exposure necessarily provided exclusively or even largely by specialists in mathematics. For one thing, there are persuasive arguments for self-contained classrooms in the early school years. For another, there is not a realistic possibility of training enough specialists to do such a job in all schools — and this vision includes all schools. Finally, I think it is quite feasible to make every elementary school teacher sufficiently competent to manage such experiences, especially if specialists are available for consultation and help.

I see the teacher guiding youngsters, as they show their readiness, into

[4] *Ibid.*, p. 357.

other experiences such as verbalization of concepts, the learning of algorithms, memorization of "arithmetic facts," application of mathematics to genuine real-world problems, pursuing of consequences and building of small mathematical theories. Again, these experiences will not be random but will have a structure based on consistent theories of mathematical learning, which in turn will be based on a considerable research effort. They will be ungraded but *not* completely individualized in the sense of having each child working completely on his own, for I am willing to predict that research will show that many mathematical learnings take place best in the interplay of group discussion and inquiry. The methodological approaches will be designed to develop inquiring youngsters — youngsters who feel in their bones that they can learn, that they can find answers and solve problems if they are persistent enough, that mathematics is under their control and not a mysterious something or other imposed on them by various authority figures.

All normal youngsters would make their way through an ungraded sequence that includes those mathematical ideas and skills that can form the basis for intelligent citizenship and effective functioning in a complicated technological society. It should not be difficult to agree on such a body of content and ideas; in fact, a new SMSG project has already produced a first approximation to an outline of such a body of content and is considering how to put together the curriculum resources to implement it.[5]

I see pleasant school buildings with a number of people working cooperatively at a wide variety of professional competence levels and with a variety of machine-type devices. In other words, I see that the problems of delegation of function have been thoughtfully considered and solved. Solving these problems has not only made it easier to recruit enough teachers with sufficient mathematical understanding to manage the experiences I have described, but by using local community residents in subprofessional roles it has strengthened school-community bonds. Principals are again, as they once were, the principal *teachers* in the schools, that is, genuine leaders of the professional staff. Chief administrative officers operate vis-à-vis school staffs much as hospital administrators do vis-à-vis hospital staffs; that is, they provide and manage the resources needed by the professional staff.

Teachers of mathematics will routinely take paid leaves (days or months long) every few years to pursue research interests in mathematics or pedagogy or to add to their basic training in mathematics. These leaves will be spent either at special centers set up at universities or at science education centers existing in each large district, patterned after the centers that now exist in Japan.[6]

I see professional mathematicians, including some first-rank research scholars, allocating a certain part of their energies to the needs of mathematics education. I see them making the substantial effort required to write expositions and give classes, lectures, and courses that will communicate their sci-

[5] For a description of this project see SMSG Newsletter no. 24, available from SMSG, Cedar Hall, Stanford University, Stanford, California 94305.

[6] Bentley Glass, "The Japanese Science Education Centers," *Science* 154 (October 14, 1966): 221–24.

ence to teachers and to youngsters. A precedent for what we might conceivably have by 1991 is the involvement of top-ranked Russian mathematical scholars in the schooling of Russian children.

I see a teacher corps that consists in part of imaginative and innovative producers of curriculum materials and new teaching methods who are also imaginative and sensitive *consumers* of such materials. I also see in the teacher corps a number of people who possess one but not both of these producer-versus-consumer capability patterns. I see teacher training programs aimed at training all three categories of teachers.

You will note that this vision has something to say about preschool and early school experiences and about an ungraded elementary sequence, but I have said nothing yet about secondary schooling. What is obvious is that not everyone would complete the elementary program in the same time and that not everyone would want to proceed beyond it. But if such a program existed, the number of options possible as extensions of it are numerous indeed. For a substantial number it is not in the least unlikely that what now constitutes an undergraduate major in mathematics could be completed by the end of what is now the twelfth grade. It is also not unlikely that some students — because of ability or preference — will still be working with pleasure and profit at getting a solid grip on the basic sequence until well into the secondary school years. It is for this latter group that an enormously varied collection of curriculum materials and pedagogical techniques will exist. Hence, as far as the basic sequence of mathematical learnings go, failure will be virtually unknown among children in the normal intelligence range. The extensions of this basic sequence will be quite varied and for some people will extend to considerable mathematical knowledge and sophistication.

This vision could well include much greater articulation of school mathematics with other school subject matters by 1991, but it would take us too far afield now to speculate on the form this effort would take. In any case, the vision already includes more complications in implementation than we will find easy to cope with.

As a thoroughgoing pragmatist I have included nothing whatever in this optimistic projection that I do not see as possible to begin to implement tomorrow at the level of a first, rough approximation. The basic material for such a revolution does in fact exist. We need only pick out and exploit the most favorable aspects of our present situation. The question is, do we have the will to do this?

Do I believe that even such a modest vision will be a reality by 1991, or ever? Not in the least. A much more likely vision of 1991 can be specified by looking at the unfavorable aspects of the existing situation. According to this vision, 1991 will see an increasing stratification of schools and of mathematics education. Elementary schools in the suburbs will be much better than those in the cities, but even in the suburbs elementary mathematics instruction will be carried on by teachers who fear and despise the subject and who avoid it when possible. The better secondary schools will take those students who have survived the elementary school with some mathematical motivation and intuition still alive and will produce from them an elite that will cover a substantial amount of mathematics during the secondary school years. We will salvage for mathematics about 20 percent of our population in order to feed into the technological society of 1991 the trained people required for perpetuation and survival. Those relatively rich in home background *and* mathematical ability *and* intelligence *and* ability to adapt to school routines *and* the luck that awards a student a few good mathematics teachers — these students will get mathematically richer; those poor in any one of these things will get mathematically poorer. Conditions of teaching and learning will be improved somewhat in the schools serving up to one-half of society but will be as bad or worse than now for the rest of our society. There will still be fine talk and theories and reform movements, and mathematics will be better than ever; but the filtering down of mathematical knowledge into schools will be as ineffective as ever.

A CALL TO REPENTANCE

We have been incredibly stupid in our allocation of national resources up to now. We in education have been incredibly irresponsible in accepting this allocation virtually without protest. I see no compelling reason to believe that we will suddenly become smart or responsible. Hence, the future in 1991 seems likely to resemble my second vision rather than my first. But since, as the joke has it, only the optimist believes that the future is uncertain, let me play the optimist for a while longer. If we do indeed have a choice between these two visions, then let me be quite explicit in specifying what sort of repentances will be necessary if the better rather than the worse version is to become actual.

If you are a teacher, you must announce that after a certain reasonable time — say five years hence — you will absolutely not be responsible for trivial and degrading and time-consuming tasks that are not directly related to the instruction of the youngsters. You must see which of the tasks that sap your time and energy can be delegated to human and machine helpers. You must *not* insist that all teachers do the same things for the same number of hours per day. You must insist upon and must take periodic salaried leaves for further study and reflection. You must cooperate in research aimed at better theoretical models and must conscientiously try to implement the resulting theories.

If you are a university or college professor of mathematics, you must not sneer when a good student of yours expresses an interest in school teaching. On the contrary, you must encourage such people to make of education the exciting and rewarding career it can be. You must not be condescending to mathematics teachers now in service. Not all of us are great, but some of us are pretty good. In any case, help, not disdain, is what is called for. Some of the best of you must take an active and continuing interest in efforts at curriculum reform and in the designing of research studies that may lead to better theories of mathematics learning and teaching. You must provide expositions of significant mathematics for out-of-school study by interested youngsters and laymen. You must take Marshall Stone's advice to stop prating about the poor education of teachers and take counsel as to how to remove this obstacle. Above all, you must not weary in well-doing lest the progress of the past decade settle into a new and even more stultifying orthodoxy than what we had ten years ago.

The necessary repentance for administrators is clear cut. They must join with the teachers in implementing the repentance I first prescribed; that is, they must help make possible within the next decade the removal of trivial and degrading nonteaching tasks from the backs of teachers. Administrators must cease to conceal the effects of public niggardliness toward schools. They must resist the blandishments of the hucksters of various panaceas and must recognize the hard fact that progress will be expensive and difficult, requiring the patient and continuing efforts of us all.

The substantial progress of the past decade would have been impossible without substantial amounts of money — much of it from the National Science Foundation. This amount is just a drop in the bucket compared with what will be required to support the sort of repentance outlined above. The public must not only provide the money; it must insist on getting its money's worth, for it would be easy to triple the amount spent on schools without their changing in fundamental ways at all. (On the other hand, since any thoroughgoing reform will inevitably have some waste motion in it, some of the increased money will be wasted.) Any country that can support an effort to place men on the moon or can spend as much on Southeast Asia in a year as is spent that same year on all public secondary and elementary schooling in the entire United States can obviously afford better schooling.

To sum up, we have done a lot in curriculum reform in the past ten years, but there is an enormous amount of unfinished business. This unfinished business will not be transacted nearly so easily as the relatively conservative reforms to date. Progress will demand more effort and dislocation of existing patterns than we have ever been willing to consider up to now. Nevertheless, the decade of 1991 holds great promise only if we are courageous enough to face up to these necessities and demand that others do so as well.

43

Teaching of Social Sciences, 1991[*]

Mark M. Krug

I assume that it would be quite a perilous undertaking to talk about the teaching of physics or mathematics or biochemistry in 1991. The changes and advances in these disciplines are so rapid, so revolutionary, that projection in advance for two decades may indeed border on sheer speculation.

Fortunately, my task is to write about the teaching of the social sciences, and primarily of history, in the more or less foreseeable future. There is little doubt, if the last two decades are any guide, that, while there will be truly important or revolutionary changes in the history of the human race, and many things and events will take place which none can foresee, the changes in the teaching of the social sciences and of history on the high school and college level can be foretold and analyzed with some degree of assurance.

The basic difference, I would cautiously submit, is that, while our understanding of the earth's environment, of the cosmos, of physical phenomena, of the forces that shape our natural environment is still almost in its begin-

> The future of history teaching in American schools is the focus of the section of "Teaching of Social Sciences, 1991" selected for this anthology. Mark M. Krug discusses the alternatives open to historians at a time when structuralist ideas are being widely applied to the teaching of history. Krug has distinct reservations about the desirability of analyzing history to determine its structure as a discipline and foresees the growth of a humanistic history in the future.
>
> Krug is Professor of Education at the University of Chicago.

ning stages, our knowledge of the human personality, of social groups, of interrelationships of peoples and nations, while showing some advancement, points to few elements of stability and repetitive behavior.

Rather cynically, but with a large dose of common sense, we assume that the younger generation will always rebel and have contempt for older generations, that all revolutions will degenerate in time from the peak of idealism

Reprinted from "Teaching of Social Sciences, 1991" by Mark M. Krug, by permission of The University of Chicago Press. *The School Review* (Sept.–Dec., 1969), 165–174.

[*] Most of this material has since appeared in the book by Mark M. Krug, *History and the Social Sciences — New Approaches to the Social Studies*, Blaisdell Publishing Co., Waltham, Mass., 1966.

to the use of terror and oppression or at least cynicism, that Wilson's dream of a war that would end all war was a deception and an illusion. It has always seemed to me a wonder, not that we know so little about the behavior of man, but that, in view of the complex nature of man and the almost unaccountable variables that govern group and nation interrelationships, that we know so much.

Carleton Washburne, in a very perceptive paper entitled, "An Eighty-Year Perspective on Education," attempted to analyze the trends in education in the period between 1880 and 1960. He wrote: "During the period 1880 to 1900 we see greatly increased emphasis on the learner. From 1900 to 1920 the emphasis shifts to what is learned. From 1920 to 1940 the light turns mainly (never exclusively) on the learner again. Then from 1940 to 1960 it shifts back to what is learned. Now we are at the beginning of the shift to the learner."[1]

This may be a bit oversimplified, but the significant fact remains that, in the view of this distinguished educator, the periods of new emphasis in education last about two decades and, even more significantly, that the emphases repeat themselves. In retrospect, Washburne saw a tendency for alternating foci on the learner and on what is to be learned.

In the teaching of history one can, with some assurance, point to two major, often alternating, sometimes coexisting tendencies. One is on the content of historical knowledge and the other on the skills in historical inquiry. Since "history," as the term was first used by Herodotus, means "inquiry," therefore, it would not be correct to see these two tendencies as contradictory or exclusive of one another.

It would seem that we are now in a relatively new period in American education. The emphasis seems to be shifting more and more to how the learner learns. What is emphasized with increasing vigor is the acquisition of skills of inquiry and of the aptitudes for critical and reflective thinking. There is a widespread assumption that it would be too tedious, too time wasting to teach the students about the American Revolution, the English Civil War, the Bolshevik Revolution, or the Mexican Revolution. What the student needs is to understand some basic concepts, broad governing generalizations, and the general structure of a revolution. After acquiring this skill and these understandings, he could study any past or future revolution as the need arises and as his interest impels him to do.

Those who wish to revise the teaching of the social studies by introducing a major emphasis on structure, concepts, generalizations, and skills draw their inspiration from the work of Jerome Bruner. How do Bruner's ideas apply to history and the social sciences? Bruner maintains that each discipline can best be mastered by teaching the basic organizing principles which, according to his view, form the structure of every natural and social science. These generalizations and broad ideas help scholars who have invented them to organize their facts and their respective bodies of knowledge into meaningful and connected patterns. Students who study any discipline by looking at

---

[1] Carleton Washburne, "An Eighty-Year Perspective on Education," *Phi Delta Kappan* (May 1963), p. 72.

its structure are bound to find the interconnecting spiraling logic of these sets of broad organizing principles.

The new curriculum is to be based on Bruner's contention that "the structure of knowledge — its connectedness and its derivations that make one idea follow another — is the proper emphasis in education. For it is structure, the great conceptual inventions that bring order to the congeries of disconnected observation, that give meaning to what we may learn and makes possible the opening up of new realms of experience."[2] The implication is that the learning of one set of broad concepts will logically lead to the learning of a more complex set of conceptual frameworks. Have Bruner's theories contributed to the growing collaboration between history and the social sciences?

It may be of significance to note that, in explicating his theory of the structure of disciplines, Bruner uses, almost without exception, examples from mathematics or from the natural sciences. His interpretation of the role and power of the organizing concepts seems to be best understood and related to the function and objectives of the natural sciences — for instance, the statement of Bruner that "Knowledge is a model we construct to give meaning and structure to regularities in experience. The organizing ideas of any body of knowledge are inventions for rendering experience economical and connected. . . . The power of great organizing concepts is in large part that they permit us to understand, sometimes to predict or change the world in which we live."[3] This statement has an obvious relevance to mathematics, to physics and chemistry. The question is whether Bruner in his work on the social studies curriculum will be able to isolate some great organizing ideas in history or the social sciences which help the students "to understand and sometimes predict or change the world." Once this is done it remains to be seen whether historians will be ready to accept the structure of history as finally defined by Bruner.

Bruner cannot escape the task of defining the structure of history and of other social sciences because, according to his own conception, curriculum revision calls for two initial steps: the definition of the structure of the discipline by the scholars themselves and the organization of the discovered structure into meaningful patterns of relationships for purposes of classroom instruction. This means that Bruner would have to ask historians to define the structure of their discipline. The few historians who have tried to find some order, rhythm, or structure in history have done so with limited success and usually without the endorsement of the historical profession. Whether this task can be done by Bruner with the help of several historians who are working with him is very doubtful. The task of identifying even a small number of fundamental ideas in world history and of finding their spiraling relatedness may prove to be formidable, if not forbidding. An example of a great idea in history, cited by Bruner, "A nation must trade in order to live," is so broad and so full of fuzzy implications that its value for classroom instruction may prove to be as useless as the generalization "in war there is no substitute for victory" or "appeasement of aggressors does not pay."

[2] Jerome Bruner, *On Knowing* (Cambridge, Mass.: Harvard University Press, 1962), p. 120.
[3] *Ibid.*

Suppose that some historians, even as respectable and distinguished as those who serve as advisers to Bruner at the E.S.I. project, would conclude that they have discovered the "pre-existing" structure of history. Would their discovery be accepted by their colleagues? Is it probable that an interlocking, logically connected, progressively complex system of fundamental ideas in history, or for that matter in sociology or in political science, could ever be identified? The basic obstacle, which apparently does not exist or has been overcome in mathematics and in the natural sciences, is the lack of any logical ladder of progression in the study of sociology or history. It is not absolutely essential for a high school student to have had a course in the American Revolution in order to study the Civil War. Children do learn about the Napoleonic Wars without ever having heard of the invasions and conquests of Alexander the Great. It would be rather difficult to formulate a generalization from the Napoleonic Wars which would have a logical relationship to the wars of Alexander or the conquests of Genghis Khan.

Even granting for a moment the legitimacy of the contention that the teaching of the structure of the disciplines is the proper emphasis in education, there is a question which would naturally occur to those who have taught social studies on a high school level. Would not the teaching of the broad concepts and generalizing principles, even if taught by inventive teachers by the inductive "discovery" method recommended by Bruner, prove to be boring for students during the long stretch of the school year? Granting that some students will, after engaging in an inquiry, by imitating the ways of research of sociologists, political scientists, and historians, experience the "thrill of discovery," is it not sensible to assume that many other students would find this intellectual exercise boring and wasteful? While there is no question that in the search for structure, Bruner's discovery approach is valuable and should have a place in the social studies curriculum and in the lively, dramatic study of history and the social sciences, to build the entire social studies curriculum on the structure theory is fraught with grave dangers. Much in history and in the study of human personality and group interrelationships which cannot and should not be fitted into a structure or even related to something else is eminently worthy of teaching to our children.

If the next twenty years will indeed see in the field of social studies, a cautious, intelligent application of Bruner's valuable new insights into the theory of learning and instruction and to the essential nature of the disciplines, this will be all to the good. History teaching as it is now practiced in many schools, without imagination and with little attention to new historical research, can only benefit from careful and controlled experimentation and innovation.

If, on the other hand, we shall embrace the structural approach, without scholarly caution and reserve, without the benefit of limited experimentation and testing, and if we most unwisely eliminate the teaching of history in our elementary schools and high schools, a pall of boredom will descend upon the social studies classrooms, and we shall deserve the outcries of anguish and protest which will be forthcoming from the parents and the community at large.

But there are even more important questions. Is there such a thing as an Educated Man, a Cultured Individual, and do we assume that an educated man does possess a certain amount of well-digested and well-integrated knowledge? Is it or is it not the responsibility of each generation to transmit to the next one at least a part of its own cultural inheritance? Does a nation have a stake in teaching its young the nation's history? I believe that the answer to all these questions must be in the affirmative, although I realize the complexity of the task of marshaling cogent evidence to support these statements.

Bruner has recently made clear his position on the place of history in the social studies curriculum in elementary schools and high schools. We should be grateful to him for his candor, and if he and his supporters succeed in emasculating or eliminating the study of history from schools' curricula, no one will be able to say that this was done surreptitiously or without proper warning.

In an article in the *Saturday Review*, which the editors described as a preview of his latest book, *Toward a Theory of Instruction*, Bruner related that his work on a new social studies curriculum has led him to the conclusion that "we are bound to move toward instruction in the sciences of behavior and away from the study of history."[4] The basic reason for the need to shift from history to the behavioral sciences is that history looks to the past, the recent past, while the behavioral sciences prepare the young to grasp and to adjust to the changing human conditions. "Recorded history," says Bruner, "is only about five thousand years old, as we saw. Most of what we teach is within the last few centuries, for the records before are minimal, while the records after are relatively rich." However, Bruner continues, modern methods of retrieving and storing of information will make it possible to store masses of information and consequently, "a thousand years from now we will be swamped." Because of this specter, if I understand Bruner correctly, we ought to stop the study of history right now because, as he tells us, at that future time there would be little sense "to dwell with such loving care over the details of Brumaire or the Long Parliament or the Louisiana Purchase."

It is quite obvious that Bruner never really enjoyed the study of the dramatic record of the Long Parliament, which had a decisive influence on British political institutions and British democracy, or the study of the brilliant and dramatic exercise of presidential powers by Thomas Jefferson, whose decision made it possible, in a large measure, for the United States to be the great power it is today. Bruner is disdainful of the record of history which includes only the recent 5,000 years; he seems to be much more interested, as his anthropologically centered curriculum clearly indicates, in teaching about the 50 million-year-old history of the evolution of mammals and man. Without in any way belittling the importance of such study, the understanding of those "mere" 5,000 years is of crucial importance for our young generations if they are to live intelligent and useful lives, and if they are to be expected to make an effort to prevent the destruction of the human race in an atomic holocaust.

[4] Jerome Bruner, "Education or Social Invention," *Saturday Review*, February 19, 1966, p. 103.

John Dewey, in his interesting lectures on history given at the University of Chicago in 1899 and which were published for the first time in 1966, speaks of the obligation of one generation to transmit the accumulated experience to the next one:

> There is one point which without controversy is desirable: that the child should recapitulate the progress of the race, that he should go back of present conditions where everything seems to be given, almost without the exercise of intelligence . . . should get himself back in his imagination to the primitive condition of man . . . and then follow in his constructive imagination the typical steps by which man has seized the salient points in the situation . . . and has evolved devices . . . which have given . . . momentum onward in civilization. . . . It requires the child to recapitulate in himself the occasions which have made the race think, and makes him appreciate in terms of his own experience, the sort of thinking that had actually to be done . . . and the results that were reached by it.[5]

Bruner's ideas on structure and great organizing generalization seem to represent a wave of the future in the teaching of history and the social sciences. And yet it seems to me safe to predict that the Brunerian school will be just another passing phase which will leave in its wake, and partly as a result of its stimulation and irritation, enriched and more effective courses of study in history, geography, and a few selected social sciences. These courses will be taught more effectively, in part because of the sharpened insights that Bruner and others have discovered in the teaching-learning process.

As we have said, the structuralists, who constitute an influential group in the field of social studies, seem to be convinced that, since Bruner's ideas on the teaching of the structure of disciplines constitute the proper emphasis of education and worked for mathematics and the natural sciences, they would work as well for the social sciences and through them for the social studies.

The question which causes me concern because it is intrinsically bound with the degree of validity of the above statement is the common assumption of Bruner and of his collaborators that history is a social science, that one may include history in the social sciences when one talks about the objectives, the content, and the methods in the new social studies curricula. This seems to me to be a wholly erroneous assumption.

History, the imaginative reconstruction of the past experience of men, is much more a humanity than a science. At best it can be said that history is both an art and a science. A historian is a social scientist because he uses the scientific method of inquiry. He methodically collects his data, analyzes them systematically, looks for an inner logic in his accumulated evidence, and subjects his data to thorough testing and scrutiny by comparing the evidence from source materials of many varieties. By the use of inductive logic, the historian then develops his hypotheses and provisional and limited generalizations. After further tests and additional scrutiny of his evidence, the historian is ready to commit his findings to paper.

Up to that moment the historian was in a way a social scientist, although

[5] John Dewey, *Lectures in the Philosophy of Education: 1899* (New York: Random House, 1966), p. 258.

his testing, because of the nature of his evidence, the testimony of men long dead, and the usually fragmentary nature of the relics of the past, was neither empirical nor similar to the usual laboratory investigations. However, in the most important phase of his work, in the stage of reconstructing in writing some fragment of the past, the historian then becomes an artist who uses artistic imagination. Leopold Ranke's injunction that a historian ought to describe "Dinge wie sie eigentlich waren" ("things as they really were") was a worthy but an unrealistic slogan because we never know how things *really* were in the past. In the end, the most painstaking reconstruction of the murder of Julius Caesar is a combination of the historian's interpretation of the evidence available, his artistic imagination, and his literary ability. There is indeed little in this enterprise that is "scientific" in the accepted term of that word.

A historical work, if it is to survive and become a classic to be read by generations of schoolchildren and adults, must also be a work of great literature. The historical inquiry is based on the scientific approach and method, but the final conclusions are intuitive, highly individual; they belong to the world of art. When history is written in the grand tradition of a literary narrative, it becomes important, not only as a scientific record of a segment of the past, but also as an artistic and aesthetic experience. Thus, history is also a branch of literature and belongs not only to the social sciences but to the humanities. The *History of the Peloponnesian War* by Thucydides, *The Annals* of Tacitus, *The Decline and Fall of the Roman Empire* by Edward Gibbon, and the *History of England* by Thomas Babington Macaulay are not only great history but also masterpieces of literature. They are both artistic and scientific achievements.

In addition, history differs from social sciences in other important respects. While social scientists concentrate their efforts on the formulation of the general concepts and general rules and laws, historians, while not ignoring "lower" and "higher" generalizations, are at least as interested in the singular, the concrete, and the unique. The combination of the jingo-imperialist and the pacific president and recipient of the Nobel Peace Prize in the person of Theodore Roosevelt is as important to a historian as the discovery of a sound generalization on the basic pattern of revolutions. The human drama involved in the dismissal of Douglas MacArthur by President Truman is as important to a historian as the possible discovery of a plausible generalization explaining the recurrent economic depressions in Germany after World War I. In general, while history is interested in the study of the uniqueness of cultures and civilizations, the social sciences prefer to look for the common elements and for the common processes in all cultures. A. L. Rowse explained this difference between history and the social sciences in a particularly felicitous way:

> The study of mankind does not resemble the study of the physical properties of atoms, or the life history of animals. If you find out about one atom, you have found out about all atoms and what is true of the habits of one robin is roughly true of the habits of all robins. But the life history of one man, or

even of many individual men will not tell you the life history of other men.
. . . Men are too complicated, too spiritual, too various for a scientific analysis.[6]

The historian keeps in mind that "fifty men do not make a centipede." It would be wrong to assume that historians do not use and value broad concepts and generalizations. They do, but they prefer what Morton White in his brilliant volume *Foundations of Historical Knowledge*[7] calls "existential regularities," which are in fact rather simple lower-case generalizations or patterns of regularity.

History, unlike the social sciences, is vitally interested in the realm of values, attitudes, moods, and motives. It is not only a scientific enterprise but also a moral one. In its study of human beings involved in the great story of human drama, it is directly related to moral values inherent in life in all its manifestations. The anthropologist who lives in an Indian or Mexican village or in a tribal village in Africa, observing daily the mores and customs of the villagers, can and does abstain from any value judgment. He is no concerned whether a particular custom, however alien to his own scale of values, is "good" or "bad," "right" or "wrong." Not so a historian. He is constantly involved in value judgment and in the assessment of motives. Thucydides expressed strong views and preferences between the Athenian and the Spartan modes of government, and Gibbon made no bones about his conviction that Christianity was the main cause of the downfall of the splendid ancient civilization. Historians have probed deeply and differed sharply on the question of whether Oliver Cromwell was a truly religious man or a hypocritical autocrat. Parkman made clear his conviction that English civilization was superior to French civilization and that the Protestant religion was more amenable to free institutions than was the Catholic faith. Most American historians would agree with their distinguished colleague, Samuel E. Morison, who said in his presidential address to the American Historical Association in 1951: "Unless it be the dull pedantry of the average doctoral dissertation in history, there is no quality more repugnant to readers than chilly impartiality."[8]

The historian, unlike his colleagues in the social sciences, doubts whether many important questions and problems in history can be understood by a quantitative empirical analysis, which is the preferred method of inquiry of social scientists. The historian is increasingly impressed with the powerful role that fate and accident play in human history. Was it not an accident that brought about the emergence of Mohammed in the deserts of Hedjaz? Was it not an accident that gave Oliver Cromwell a weak son, Richard, who promptly lost the fruits of his father's revolution? A historian who, like Barbara Tuchman in her *The Guns of August*,[9] examines the causes of

[6] A. L. Rowse, *The Use of History* (New York: Macmillan Co., 1948), pp. 66–67.

[7] Morton White, *Foundations of Historical Knowledge* (New York: Harper & Row, 1965).

[8] Samuel E. Morison, *Vistas of History* (New York: Alfred A. Knopf, 1964), p. 23.

[9] Barbara Tuchman, *The Guns of August* (New York: Macmillan Co., 1962).

World War I, stands awed by the erratic nature of human beings who, placed by destiny in positions of great power, passively allowed themselves to be swept into an abyss by the tide of events.

It should be made clear, however, that to argue, as I have done, that history is not a social science does not mean that there are no fruitful avenues of cooperation between historians and social scientists. On the contrary, in recent years, many historians have used, with important benefits to historical scholarship, the insights, concepts, and modes of inquiry of the social sciences.

A variety of reasons and factors have contributed to the growing rapprochement and to the improving prospects for fruitful collaboration between history and the social sciences. The most important of these is the gradual recognition by leading social scientists that their respective disciplines are not so purely scientific as originally claimed, and the frequently expressed conviction by prominent historians that they need and value the use of social science concepts and modes of inquiry in their work. More and more historians have declared themselves ready to explore new ways of looking at man, the ultimate object of their study, in order to gain a better understanding of the nature of man and his behavior in the past. . . .

44

Foreign Language Teaching in 1975: How Will It Be Different?

Howard Lee Nostrand

"Foreign Language Teaching in 1975" is a helpful look to the immediate future in modern language teaching by a leader in the field. Nostrand does not rest content with the customary advocacy of the use of language laboratories and similar technology but penetrates more deeply in his analysis of the tasks to be accomplished by foreign language instruction if it is to be an effective part of the American curriculum. Reports in 1970 of the decline in foreign language teaching document further the importance of Nostrand's suggestions.

Howard Lee Nostrand is Professor of Romance Languages at the

Howard Lee Nostrand, "Foreign Language Teaching in 1975: How Will It Be Different?" *Audiovisual Instruction* (May, 1968), 447–449.

University of Washington in Seattle. He is well known for his help-ful and critical commentary on the role of language instruction in American schools.

Looking ahead is fun. But it is not an activity free from responsibility. It affects the future and it affects the present because long-range plans have a way of coming home to roost.

Even the way we structure our view of the future has a creative effect. Should we start by mapping the external situation and then fit in our itinerary? Or should we first formulate our purposes and then appraise the factual situation as assets and liabilities? I propose that we try to combine the advantages of the two procedures: first sketch out our purposes; then map out the landscape as objectively as we can, while we note at the same time which features are to be exploited and which are to be minimized or circumvented.

Will our basic purposes themselves change in a decade? In my view these purposes are to develop individuality and a good society. We want to build cross-cultural understanding and communication in such a way as to bring about a harmonious world order, enriched by diversity of cultures and com-posed of persons who can sustain and enjoy the cooperative effort essential for the creating of such a world order. These basic aims seem unlikely to change in the next decade, except that we shall raise our sights as new possibilities give new form to our aspirations and, in fact, increase our responsibility.

The factual landscape to be expected can be mapped out in five sectors: mechanization; the curriculum; the students; the surrounding society; and the teachers. As we try to visualize the conditions ahead, we shall do well to remember that, in the past, those who have viewed only with alarm or only with rosy hopes have proved to be lesser minds; the better minds have seen both sides of the ledger. Let me remind you, too, that I am no professional fortune teller: my fallible vision can do no more than prompt your critical reaction.

MECHANIZATION

Mechanization will be the area of greatest change; but this does not mean that technology will inevitably dictate. Contrary to the Marxist view, I am convinced that ideas, feelings, and aspirations can be causative forces.

Audiovisual models and instructions for language learning will be readily available in another decade. The 8mm sound projector will be common, and its film cartridges will be easily handled by persons or by machines. The learning laboratory's response to the learner will be determined by a com-puter and based upon how well he has performed in the preceding exercise. (The computerized response will not yet, however, be voice activated: the student will have to use his fingers to register his performance.) From the learner's standpoint, the language lab will be decentralized. He will dial a program from a public library, from a dormitory, or from home, and the program will be transmitted by phone, microwave, air-borne relay, or other medium, or perhaps by an accelerated "slow-scan" TV if the message is a visual one. The school library will be similarly decentralized and will be a retrieval center where information is stored by topic rather than simply in whole books.

But along with this decentralization for the user's convenience (and to save the expense of herding students together for individual activities), it will be an economy to centralize the program source. The same explanation of how to produce a sound, the same pattern drills, many of the same demonstrations of phrases in authentic social context can be used at various age levels from adult education to junior high school, or even in the primary grades. If the universities, junior colleges, and other schools of an urban or rural area jointly supported a central program source, they could afford to replace obsolete with new materials more rapidly, as the rate of improvement accelerates. Chester Electronic Laboratories in Connecticut already has a dial system that permits many listeners to eavesdrop on a single program without getting the busy signal. This system can be used for short exercises, a dozen or more playing simultaneously on a single continuous tape; longer tapes will be activated individually as they are called for. A shared source of audio materials can be initiated anytime, and the first intensive experiment will surely attract a subsidy to ease the difficult initial stage. Why wait?

The stubbornest problem will be to produce reliable and exciting instructional materials — for teaching the language skills, the analysis of language, the enjoyment of literature, and understanding of the foreign people's style of life — materials for the central sequence and materials to meet the special interest of the individual, in English or in the foreign language, reinforcing his motivation to learn the language. Where will the needed nuggets come from? Partly from teams of teachers who are given the time and who develop the ability to produce materials worth sharing through a national and international system of storage and retrieval. And partly from publishers: largely from them, in the case of the types of materials that can be sold at a good profit.

Publishing houses will tend to be controlled by large, diversified combines, which will not all be inevitably interested in the slow, research-based elaboration of language-teaching materials and methods, but which will have an inevitable interest in profitable production, in beating one another to the market, and, sometimes, in instilling a patriotic loyalty toward a conception of free enterprise that puts these latter values first. If power corrupts, there is reason to watch for renewed temptations to influence the ideology of the social studies, as well as the old temptation to spend more money on ingenious advertising than on an equally ingenious improvement of the product.

How can teachers exert their influence in favor of excellent materials and equipment? Individuals can talk with publishers and serve as consultants when invited (though here the competitive rivalry of free enterprise may interfere with the free exchange of ideas dear to the scholar). Individual teachers can also plead with school boards to stop buying low-fidelity equipment for the training of their children's language skills. But it will also be necessary for teachers to develop their professional organizations into effective means of hammering out and expressing a well-informed, forward-looking position on educational issues.

CURRICULUM

The curriculum will have changed a great deal in ten years. The classroom will no longer be its almost exclusive setting. Projects will take students out into community activities, to observe governmental processes, and to visit museums where remote activities are vividly simulated. Groups of students will be going off on long field trips to other regions and foreign countries, and foreign students will be paying long visits to us, with the assignment of taking home reports on our strange culture and peculiar subcultures.

Equally radical changes will be going on beneath the surface of the physical settings. The separate subjects of study will have yielded in part to cross-disciplinary issues and sequences, pursued under the guidance of inter-disciplinary teams of teachers, aides, and resource persons.

Many students will be bilingual and by senior high will be carrying on half their studies in their second language. The number of languages being learned in the United States will be much larger than today and so somewhat nearer the number of cultures with which the planet's white minority must deal in order to protect its interests and its freedom.

In each school a plurality of cultures will be represented — and respected — within the faculty and student body. No one value system will be the norm for all.

Long foreign language sequences will be an essential feature of the curriculum because we shall have to have not only government employees but businessmen, labor leaders, and members of all the professions who can communicate successfully with bearers of scores of different cultures. Every educated person will be needed to help build mutual understanding with at least one foreign people.

We shall not be free to waste the precious human resource of the childhood ability to speak a foreign language. And since many will need a different or an additional language in later life, we should teach the first foreign language in such a way as to produce an effective, self-confident language learner. FLES needs a head start in order to take its place in the required long sequences. The gratifying achievement of children in excellent FLES programs needs to be made the rule instead of the exception. Why wait?

STUDENTS

The students in 1975 will be harder to keep ahead of. Accustomed to cultural pluralism, many of them at home in a second language and culture, they will be impatient of the poorly prepared teacher. They will also, from junior high up, be more conscious of student power and more impatient with instruction that seems to them academic and irrelevant to their lives. They will be shortsighted and materialistic, yet also keen-minded, purposeful, and idealistic. We shall be even more dependent than now upon our ability to enlist their initiative, to meet them where they are, and to persuade them that they need the skills and understanding which we, at our best, can offer them. Why wait?

SURROUNDING SOCIETY

We must expect the surrounding society to be more impatient of academic education than ever: more materialistic, more anti-intellectual, more insistent that schooling be relevant to the specific competence the individual is to exercise in society. Yet we may also expect that by 1975 this trend will begin to reverse itself, with the approach of the "cybernetic revolution" that is predicted for the last quarter of this century.* As society meets its material needs with increasing opulence and decreasing effort, material wealth will be less prized and social prestige will attach rather to other achievements, such as the enjoyment of leisure and of all sorts of people; the flexibility to adapt to diverse conditions and changing exigencies; and the ability to visualize the moving targets of a swiftly evolving human situation.

Even before this revolutionary reversal, however, we can well hope that the American public will be more inclined than now to consider a foreign language useful. People will be more used to international business houses and professional meetings, foreign travel and study. They will therefore be more willing to support language teaching — provided the students prove effective in winning the cooperation and goodwill of the bearers of foreign cultures with whom they communicate. The pressure to teach efficiently will increase in the next decade, as it has in the decade behind us.

TEACHERS

We have looked at the main sectors of the factual surroundings we may expect in 1975. Now let us turn finally to the teachers ourselves. We will be more militant — against poor conditions for achieving excellence; against poor salaries; and against poor competence. We will be concerned with our effectiveness as a group and will wish we had begun in the 1960's to do several things: to have the personnel departments in our school districts require evidence of language competence for all new appointments; to resist the misassignment of unprepared persons to teach language classes; and, among our students, to encourage as prospective teachers those who have the intellect to meet the challenge of our broadening discipline, while suggesting other forms of service to those whose aptitude is too limited to mere lingual dexterity.

The demand for results, the need for efficiency, and the progress of mechanization will bring about a differentiation of roles among school personnel. There will be much less use for the erstwhile majority of 2 x 4 x 6 teachers

* See Glenn T. Seaborg, "Time, Leisure and the Computer: The Crisis of Modern Technology." *The Key Reporter* [Phi Beta Kappa] 32: 2–4; Spring 1967.

— those stuck between the two covers of a book, in the four walls of a classroom, and in the six periods of the old-fashioned school day. We will be forced upward or downward: either down among those who, very usefully, tend and service the machines, or up among those who excel in designing curricula, materials, and equipment, or in research bearing on language learning, or in evaluation, or in organizing an instructional team, or in inspiring a student to instruct himself for days at a stretch.

Certification of teachers will change. The beginning teacher will be recognized as being prepared only for limited contributions to the teaching program, and the differentiated responsibilities of career teachers will carry higher salaries as well as special prestige. An advanced level of certification will probably be added; and whether or not the special competences are formalized in this way, teacher performance will be more systematically evaluated than now, both by direct observation and by indirect evidence such as pupil achievement. Such analysis has its frightening aspects, and indeed the process can be cruelly subjective if it is operated by a paternalistic feudal hierarchy. To assure democracy and fairness, the practitioners of education — teachers and administrators together — must work out fair standards of evaluation and fair procedures for obtaining and utilizing the informed judgments of peers. For my part, I can see no way we can assure the humanity of teacher evaluation nor the proper influence of teachers upon teaching materials and equipment, unless we develop our subject-matter associations and our general professional organizations into instruments for formulating and expressing the policies of our profession at its best. This will take time, perhaps more time than we have.

Whether language teaching will be enjoyable and gratifying work in a decade from now or dehumanized and grimly efficient in a narrow-gauge educational function, misjudged as irrelevant to the urgent needs of the world, will depend a great deal on what we do meanwhile about the problems we have just reviewed. Why wait?

45

Cultural Change and the Curriculum: 1970–2000 A.D.

June Grant Shane and Harold G. Shane

*Once again we turn to the Shanes for a summary. In the follow-
ing article, they outline their tentative conclusions as to which
possible futures seem most likely to be realized, and the implications for the emerging curriculum of American schools. The views
of the authors are again based on solid fact and a hopeful assessment of mankind's prospects.*

One of the popular radio and comic strips which originated in the 1930's
was built around the adventures of a muscular character somewhat anach-
ronistically named Buck Rogers. Some of the wonders that his creator,
Dick Calkins, envisioned for Captain Rogers included: space ships and inter-
planetary travel; jumping belts; video telephones; electronic beams for medical
and defense purposes; and food in pill form. Mr. Calkins' prescience was not
limited to technological developments! He also forecast the mini-skirt and
women's high boot fashions of today when he created a wardrobe for Wilma
Deering, Buck's presumably platonic lady friend on various interstellar
voyages.

Interestingly, most of the changes that Calkins projected did not occur in
the twenty-fifth century but in the twentieth century — not in six hundred
years but in approximately thirty years. In other words, these developments
were a part of the experiences of many people living today; people whose experiences have carried them from the horse-and-buggy life of the early part
of the century to the electrical, nuclear energy and space travel world of the
seventies. How many of these people would have dreamed that most of the
fantasies depicted in the science fiction of the last hundred years would be
less amazing than the realities of 1970?

Our present century is viewed by Kenneth Boulding,[1] the economist, as
the middle period of a great transition in the history of the human race.
Within this period and within the memory of living people is a kind of di-

June Grant Shane and Harold G. Shane, "Cultural Change and the Curriculum:
1970–2000 A.D.," *Educational Technology* (April, 1970), 13–18. Reprinted by
permission.

[1] Kenneth Boulding. The Meaning of the Twentieth Century. In Ruth Nanda Anshen
(Ed.) *World Perspective*, Vol. 34, New York: Harper and Row, 1964.

viding point or watershed that separates the history of man into two parts. During the first part man moved from a "pre-civilized" to a "civilized" society. At present he is involved in a second great transition — one moving from a "civilized" to a "post-civilized"[2] society. Unfortunately, we seem to be both unknowing participants in an intermediate state of civilization and inadvertent midwives for the birth of a new era. For many of the participants in such midwifery, this is a strenuous, uncomfortable, and frequently disconcerting experience. According to Sir George Thompson,[3] the closest historical analogy, although an inadequate one, would be the permanent changes created by the invention of agriculture during the neolithic age. Even this explanation does not always help us to accommodate ourselves to the rapid acceleration in man's ability to make material progress and to his remarkable increasing powers over his environment.

THE IMPACT OF TOMORROW

The deranging influence of future shock. Alvin Toffler[4] has used the term *"future*-shock" to identify a condition which has begun to affect many persons in the U.S.; a condition that he predicts might be one of tomorrow's most important "psychological diseases." Toffler describes *"future*-shock" as a time-change phenomenon resulting from rapid socio-technical developments which have carried us from familiar yesterdays to unknown tomorrows. He describes it as "culture shock in one's own society"[5] and feels that its permeating quality is often more disorienting to people than is the culture shock which a traveler experiences in visiting countries where the customs and cues as to ways of living are radically different from his own. The impact of *future-*shock, however, is greater than *culture* shock because the visitor to a foreign country always can comfort himself with the thought that he may return to the familiar environs of his own land.[6]

This is not possible for the sufferer of *future*-shock. He cannot look homeward and feel secure knowing that he may once again function in easily recognizable situations with his old patterns of behavior. For him, the changes that have deranged his once-familiar environment are irrevocable. One cannot "return home" to yesterday.

We are now rapidly approaching the time depicted by George Orwell — the fateful year 1984. In fact, so near is this date that children enrolled in our elementary schools will be young adults and of voting age when Orwell's mystical date becomes a reality. Sixteen years thereafter we confront the beginning of the third millennium — the year 2000.

What will this new millennium be like? Will it be a chiliastic era — one of

---

[2] Boulding also suggests the use of "technological" or "developed" society if the word "post-civilization" seems objectionable.

[3] Sir George Thompson. *The Foreseeable Future.* Cambridge, London: The Syndics of the Cambridge University Press, 1960. Sir George is a British physicist and holder of the Nobel Laureate.

[4] Alvin Toffler. The Future as a Way of Life. *Horizons*, Summer, 1965, pp. 109–115.

[5] *Ibid.*, p. 109.

[6] Also cf. Harold G. Shane. Future-Shock and the Curriculum, *Phi Delta Kappan*, 49: 67–70. October, 1967.

"great happiness, perfect government, and freedom from imperfections in human existence"?[7] Or will it be one beginning in chaos and leading to a new dark age? What will the *degree* of change and the rate of change do to people? Surely, it will affect our conceptions of ourselves, our work, leisure, social living — indeed, every aspect of human endeavor.

THE CURRICULUM WORKER AND "INFORMATION OVERLOAD"

Among the many agents of educational change, the school curriculum specialist should be especially aware of developments that may affect man's future. As a professionally trained person, he is committed to facilitating the individual student's development of his potential. Because he carries this responsibility, there are many components to the curriculum planner's role. He must be concerned with (1) the integrity and dignity of the individual; (2) the dynamics of group behavior; (3) the learning process and qualities in the home and school environment that help mediate experience; (4) social trends that influence a student's present world and the world he will enter; and (5) the economic, political and technological developments that help shape people's life, their work and their leisure activities. All of these dimensions of the curriculum developer's responsibilities are appreciably influenced or tempered by our rapid movement from yesterday to tomorrow.

Curriculum development and coordination, for example, is complicated by the uneasiness of teachers and students who fear change. Such persons are not reassured by being told that change is inevitable. They resist change because they feel that the stability of the known is threatened by the insecurities of the unknown, and many of them simply are not sufficiently appraised of the importance of socio-technical developments in their lifetimes. Again, there are school workers and students who are unaware of what change demands. Both of these extremes can become severe problems.

At the same time, the curriculum developer's colleagues and their students can not entirely be blamed for their apprehensions or for their blind spots. The rapid changes have been too extensive for some people to assimilate. In the words of James R. Platt, "If the two billion years of life are represented by a 200 foot height . . . the 20,000 years of agriculture make a thick postage stamp . . . [and] the 400 years of science make the ink."[8] Because these changes are such recent ones, we are burdened with what may be called an "information overload." Indeed, one might say that almost without our understanding it, this overload is pressuring us into a very different view of life.

The nature of "information overload." Let us examine briefly some aspects of information overload. Television has exposed us to a broad spectrum of human transactions that have lost their familiar territorial limits of 50 — or even 15 — years ago. At the same time, large numbers of people all over the world have become aware of tangible goods and privileges that often are the

---

[7] The definition of millennium is taken from *Webster's Seventh New Collegiate Dictionary*. Springfield, Massachusetts: G. and C. Merriam Co., 1961, p. 538.
[8] James R. Platt. The Step to Man. *Science*, 149:613, August 6, 1965.

possessions of a minority of people.[9] This diffusion of knowledge with respect to the goods and privileges of the few represents a powerful source of discontent and a goading motivation for have-not members of the world's cultures — including that of the U.S. No longer can the individual wants and needs of the have-nots be ignored, nor can any one particular segment of any of the world's populations exist in isolation from the rest. A greater, more coordinated mankind seems all but inevitable as we move along in the "film of moisture on top of the ink on the postage stamp."[10]

This seems to imply that we must search with vision and compassion into ways in which communities of men — hopefully through improved education — may arrive at wise decisions. This will not be an easy goal to reach. As the world is learning, it is far less difficult to use the products of technology — the wonder drugs, paper clothing, computers, frozen foods, and the like — than to relinquish methods of thinking and ideas that have become obsolete in recent years. According to Irwin Bross,[11] this delay in the transmission of ideas is one of the factors which led our world civilizations to their present crises. Lawrence Frank, in a 1965 meeting, also emphasized the importance of ideas when he said, "My historical understanding indicates that ideas have been the most effective agent of change."[12]

Under the circumstances, one of the curriculum specialist's most important tasks becomes that of helping students have experiences that permit them to work with ideas — both in terms of understanding and of anticipating change. Perhaps nothing is more likely to stimulate the learner's thinking about man's personal involvement in planning tomorrow today than his participatory experimentation with ideas. As Bertrand de Jouvenel reminds us, "Obviously, we cannot affect the past, or that present moment which is now passing away; but only what is not yet; the future alone is sensitive to our actions."[13]

Generating the habit of forward looking encourages man to think explicitly about what he cannot avoid doing implicitly — conjecturing about the future.[14]

When startling and often irreversible changes occur rapidly, familiar psychological clues tend to be lost and people find themselves groping for ways in which they may function effectively in what seems to be a strange and incomprehensible world. It becomes difficult to comprehend how the people we know — those who have lived beside us for many years — were ever involved in shaping this disconcerting future. The frequent use of such expressions as: "What is the world coming to?" "Things were never like this in my time,"

[9] Daniel Bell. The Year 2000 — The Trajectory of an Idea. Toward the Year 2000: Work in Progress. *Daedalus*. V. 96, No. 3, Boston, Massachusetts: The American Academy of Arts and Science, 1967, p. 643.

[10] Platt, *op. cit.*, p. 613.

[11] Irwin D. Bross. *Design for Decision*, New York: The Free Press, 1965, The Macmillan Co., 1953, p. 3.

[12] *Daedalus, op. cit.*, p. 664.

[13] Bertrand de Jouvenel. Political Science and Prevision. *American Political Science Review*, 5:29, 1965.

[14] Statement by Bertrand de Jouvenel in a lecture delivered to RAND's Interdepartmental Seminar on November 30, 1964.

or "We never seemed to have so many problems!" attest to widespread reactions to time-change phenomena that occasionally beset even the most
stable and thoughtful among us.

As we generate a habit of looking forward, we should also stimulate man's
more effective use of one of his most tremendous abilities, one that decidedly
distinguishes him and sets him apart from other forms of life — his ability to
function as a decision-maker and shaper of his own life and future. The success of his journey into possible tomorrows is dependent both upon his use of
contemporary technological and sociological knowledge (or neglect of it) in
considering alternatives when planning future environmental designs. As we
learn how to mediate future possibilities, courses of actions actually can be
planned so that they do not lead to unalterable and disastrous consequences.
And this probably can be accomplished through more provocative, socially
relevant education.

The curriculum planner today needs to serve as a catalyst influencing
change as well as being helpful in the transmission of ideas. It is essential
that he encourage our youth to acquire the habit of anticipating tomorrow's
changes intelligently. This habit is difficult to imprint on the young since
the information with which they are loaded is approaching a circuit-breaking
point. Confusion is increased in many instances because we have looked
upon our present "concept map" of our environment as if it were an unchanging one, and therefore a valid map for use in the future. Actually, our
present knowledge depreciates rapidly, has very short validity, and must be
corrected by careful and continuing speculation about our role in an emergent
world.[15]

EDUCATIONAL CARTOGRAPHY FOR AN
UNFAMILIAR SOCIOEDUCATIONAL TERRAIN

Maps for educational futures. How does one draw a map for tomorrow?
Predictions, speculations and forecasts about the future have fascinated humans throughout the centuries as man searched for solutions to his problems.
At Delphi, for example, the garbled and cryptic phrases and sometimes incomprehensible sounds emanating from the priestess of Apollo were used to
sway public opinion with respect to politics, economics and religion in early
Greek times as the purported words of the sun god were interpreted to the
people by priests. During the sixteenth century, Nostradamus used verse as a
vehicle for expressing his cryptic prophecies. Although the prophecies were
vague and obscure and could be interpreted in many ways, even as late as the
1930's the old writings of Nostradamus were consulted. Feeling that he had
predicted the rise of Hitler, some people consulted his *Centuries* for future
gleanings.

Moving from oracles and prophecies, one learns that the idea of "reasoned
conjectures" was used as long ago as 1773 when J. L. Favier prepared a report
for Louis XV about foreseeable (i.e., probable) changes in the European

---

[15] *Ibid.,* p. 4.

system of power alliances. Favier's approach to studying possible developments has found a new currency among today's futurists.[16]

In our own recent past, pollsters like George Gallup and Elmo Roper used short-term forecasts in a pre-computerized era when attempting to assess public opinion. These forecasts, as did those of the Delphic oracle in ancient Greece, influenced American political and social thought and action.

Today, people seem to be either uneasy or intrigued by the advent of imaginative and usually scientifically oriented people who are employed to peer into the future where foresight blends with fantasy.[17] These scientific seers who might in the past have been considered either visionaries or crackpots are now recognized as able to perform a significant role in helping military, corporate and technological America move into the future with greater prescience and perhaps even to shape the possible future which lies before us. Indeed, as far back as the mid-1950's General Electric Company established a long-range planning corps to anticipate the potential shape of the future and its possible implications for the corporation.[18]

In addition to foundations and industry, government and scientific organizations both in the United States and in Europe were widely engaged in some form of future planning enterprises by 1970. Among participants in these groups are serious scholars who are carefully projecting trends (and their possible consequences) into the future so that we can learn to cope with and to benefit from technological advances and the need for innovations which they imply in the social, cultural, political, moral and spiritual dimensions of our lives. We will be able to look confidently into the future as computers *support* rather than *direct* our thinking. As this occurs we will have the opportunity of participating in one of the more important events in evolution. This is what Platt calls "the step to man." We have been *men*, he tells us. We can emerge into *man*.[19]

Some Educational Implications of Social Change

Both the field of curriculum planning and the work of the curriculum coordinator are going to be modified appreciably by elements in the discernible future that will create new opportunities, increase his responsibilities, and eventuate in important changes both in his role and in his preparation for service.

Until recently it was reasonable and proper to think of the past fading into the present and of the present flowing into the future. Now we find, in an unprecedented reverse of the tide, that the future has become so jammed with potential and variables that there is an *overspill from the future that is pouring into the present.* So rapid is change that half-formed developments

[16] Bertrand de Jouvenel. *The Art of Conjecture.* New York: Basic Books, Inc., 1967, p. 21.

[17] Tom Alexander. The Wild Birds Find a Corporate Roof. *Fortune*, August, 1964, p. 130.

[18] Brownlee Haydon. The Year 2000. Paper read at Wayne State University, March, 1967, p. 5 of typescript.

[19] Platt, *op. cit.*, p. 613.

are now mediating our present activities and plans to such an extent that even many highly literate Americans have yet to recognize them.

Let us now consider ten developments as envisioned by scholars in various disciplines that already are either theoretically feasible or in their early ascent stages and that seem to have a direct or oblique bearing on the curriculum change.

The education of very young children will be emphasized and priorities established for it. Not too long ago, anyone who suggested that intelligence might be other than fixed and unchangeable was frequently classified as a crackpot by his colleagues. Now, as new data are collected and organized, concepts and meanings as to the nature of the child and of man have changed. With increased insights into the modifiability of human development through experience, the early years of childhood are considered so critical that suggestions have been offered that education should be methodically planned by society to begin at about the one-year-old level.

To take advantage of these years when children learn so rapidly and effectively, proposals have varied from the use of "professional mothers" to a *kibbutzim* type of communal living arrangement.[20] These are suggestions for radically different patterns of family living since they deal with the years when children in our society usually have been most closely associated with their parents. Nevertheless, some writers contend and predict that changes of this nature will occur as the importance of early environmental influence continues to be stressed and as new ways are devised to stimulate the child's intellect. A few seers have gone so far as to argue that education of this nature is inevitable if a society with discord and discrimination eliminated is ever to be achieved.

Many questions regarding childhood in the future come to mind. Who helps plan the educational programs so that the numbers of failures in both human and educational enterprises are drastically reduced? What can be done now for young children to encourage the greater development and use of human potential and reduce the numbers needing remedial assistance during their pre-adolescent, adolescent and adult years?

Population trend estimates suggest that some 14 million persons will be enrolled in higher education in 25 to 30 years. Students presently studying in our colleges have increased from approximately 14 percent of our secondary school graduates in 1939 to 42 percent in 1966. Over two-thirds of the youth in our population are expected to complete a college education within the next 25 to 30 year period. Also, more and more persons are making claims against the world of higher education as employment continues its demands for high level technical and professional skills. It seems likely that our present institutions of higher learning will be significantly altered in the years ahead as people who have either been ignored by the educational system or who have neglected to take advantage of it knock on the schoolhouse door.[21]

---

[20] For a current view on the "kibbutzim kids," cf. Urie Bronfenbrenner, The Dream of the Kibbutz, *Saturday Review*, 52:72–73; 83–85, September 20, 1969.

[21] Cf. Alvin C. Eurich (Ed.) *Campus 1980*. New York: Delacorte Press, 1968.

Flexibility may prove to be the key to improved educational enterprises as resources are combined to lessen the gap between the "have" and "have not" schools. Certainly the curriculum planner will attempt to provide both for quality and equality in meeting the learner's educational, vocational and personal-social needs. Technological advances almost certainly will make it operationally and economically feasible for students and faculty to pursue both individual *and* coordinated group programs of study and research. Large educational compounds may emerge combining the resources of universities, museums, theaters, libraries, research institutes, hospital and other public and private institutions to create a highly varied responsive environment for education, health and leisure for people of all ages. Education — operating within the ivory tower with its formal lectures, class assignments and removal from many of the reality aspects of life — could disappear as the interrelatedness and interdependence of varied educational resources are recognized as being more important than any single organization operating separately.

Education will almost inevitably become continuous; some persons may prepare for a second or third career in their middle years. The expansion of knowledge, the increasing amount of leisure time, and the socially portentous technological changes that occur as a predominantly product society transforms into a primarily service society will require that people refresh and expand their knowledge, adapt, or replace their skills several times during their working careers, and constantly reformulate their conceptualization of education, work and leisure. Particularly, as technological advances alter concepts of "time-worthiness," personal fulfillment through *education* could be considered as essential to physical and spiritual welfare just as the *work ethic* has been stressed in the past. The curriculum developer is likely to find that helping to increase people's educational potential for moving from one occupation to another with ease and pleasurable anticipation can become as important to society as the less complex task of simply creating in the learner the ability to cope with new jobs.

In the discernible future the inhabitants of our large educational compounds probably will no longer be a predominantly selected group of adolescents and young adults. People of different ages will flow in and out of many different institutions at different periods in their lives. The idea of one university providing for most of an individual's continuing educational needs will diminish as new, cooperative and diversified inter-institutional relationships develop both here and in other countries. This seems wholesome since community concerns, educational concerns, national goals and interests, and international dimensions of trade and politics are more clearly understood by a more coordinated mankind.

Life spans will increase appreciably; old age will be postponed and eased as it begins to be treated more as a wasting disease than as an unavoidable fate at three-score and ten. Before long the chemistry of aging and knowledge of how to postpone it may be partially grasped, and man will need to give more thought as to what to do with his additional years of life. Determining who receives this added longevity has already raised ethical questions. Who, for example, will be among the first beneficiaries of the new machines and medicines devised to fight disease when at a given time not enough equipment and medications are available to meet all persons' needs?

As more effective ways of delaying death extend our life expectancy, they also place humans on the verge of a new way of life which promises to transform both our familiar institutions and our human interactions. The population explosion, for example, has already generated world concern over the problems of food and space. As human life is extended, radical changes also could occur in our social structure. In the past the number of young persons has always exceeded the number of old people. With the same number being born in a decade that die in a decade, major social transformations could occur 20 or more years hence if the number of persons within each age-stage is comparable to that of all other age groups.

Leisure, once a wistful dream for nearly all the world's peoples, can (beginning in the USA) become first a bore and then a problem — if not an actual danger. As man's life divides itself into one-third education, one-third productive activity, and one-third enjoyment of an interim of active retirement, the matter of making "worthy use of leisure time" may prove difficult.

Men may be at home or at least "around the house" for much longer periods of time. As more part-time jobs become available and as the workweek shortens, more women will be seeking opportunities for self-fulfillment away from the confines of the kitchen. They are likely to achieve them, too, since many home responsibilities will be eased or eliminated by new products. All the same, there remains the matter of determining who does what in planning and organizing for earning the family income, for home maintenance and child rearing. The decisions reached may well result in some novel reversals or changes with educational consequences in our present organization of home living and of male and female roles.

Some occupations and professions, as we know them, will vanish; others will continue to exist as new ones emerge. As affluence and leisure increase, it may also mean that some people literally will never engage in a paid form of work. What then happens to man, who, particularly in American society, has long used productive work as an actualizing factor in his life? As work becomes less important and less central an activity than it is now, what changes will govern the values which determine a man's contribution to society and the esteem in which we hold him? These developments pose interesting questions for both marriage and family relationships and suggest that the curriculum of the future may be designed to help people attain a balance between the pleasure of self-cultivation through leisure and the threat of tedium from too much surplus time.

Extensive supplementary schooling may be carried on at home through personalized self-instructional material. Schools, as a concomitant development, should have less formal class work and may become more like reference and social experience centers. Computer-based instruction already is offering the teaching profession an important although as yet largely unexploited array of tools for recognizing significant individual differences and helping to carry us more rapidly toward the goal of realizing the learning potential of children more fully. As computers become located in more and more educational enterprises, they also will move into our homes, transforming the family or recreation rooms into centers for private business, education, and recreation. It seems more than likely that computers also will assist us in meeting business problems, such as those required for managing a home and earning a living as well as offering appreciable intellectual and professional assistance. Rapid transmission of facsimile material will permit print-outs of library resources, as well as mail, newspapers and commercial materials — all tailored to individual specifications.

As it becomes possible to store millions of books within the confines of one small room, vast amounts of material become more rapidly and readily available. Our present library problems related to storage and circulation should diminish and our present library facilities may well become as anachronistic as the pyramids for storing the effects of the past. Three-dimensional television, 3-D photography and movies as well as other types of illustrations are likely to bring into every home the wealth of cultural experiences now enjoyed by only a limited number of people.

Furthermore, technology promises to provide men with the means of sharing in both past and present events and decisions to an extent that was not possible in previous generations. As this occurs, schools will become learning centers rather than mere repositories for past knowledge. In such centers people would no longer be passive recipients of information doled out by the teacher but will become active respondents in appraisals, discussions, interactions and transactions that have a bearing on learning.[22]

Nationwide personal information data banks are likely, their records beginning with one's birth certificate. Automation will permeate and expedite nearly all forms of record keeping. Privacy could well be threatened both by the increase in population and by diverse electronic-listening-viewing devices.

More and more automatic information processing devices become available for both extensive and intensive centralization of information. This clearly suggests that all kinds of information — both personal and business — both private and public — can be easily and rapidly stored and retrieved. As this takes place, massive quantities of information can be assembled speedily without a great deal of effort and without an individual even aware that data are being obtained. Educational data, medical histories, financial and adult records, credit assets and liabilities, traffic violations, recreational pursuits, vocational experiences, military records, personality profiles, and the like, were once housed in separate places. Now it is becoming possible to collect these bits and pieces of data and compile them to present a comprehensive picture of an individual's past personal history.

The danger of violating what is considered "personal privacy" has been noted, and warnings sounded lest additional pressures be placed upon people to contribute more and more personal information. As computers collect and collate information, record systems could become an alarming force for keeping men under Orwellian surveillance throughout their lifetimes. On the

---

[22] Even before 1970, experimentation in public education conducted *without a school plant* was underway. The community environment itself was the "school."

other hand, with wisdom, great good could come from information banks in speeding up business, in rapid diagnoses in case of illness, in identifications, and in educational practice. The question is, will society move soon enough so that traditional democratic principles are not jeopardized?

Personality will be modified appreciably by drugs. The improvement of learning and memory will be induced through chemical and electronic means. The transfer of experience may become possible. The possibilities of manipulating human behavior and modifying personality have moved from the realm of the possible to the realm of the probable not only through the use of drugs but through systematic stimulus control and neurosurgical intervention. In the near future experimental drugs are likely to be perfected so as to control perception, mood, fatigue, alertness, relaxation and fantasy as well as for more radical personality changes. As necessitated by personal problems, "artificial" relaxation therapy will be used to relieve tension when harmful levels are reached. For various medical reasons, human beings also might choose to hibernate for indeterminate periods of time, reviving at a time, say, when a cure has been found for a fatal disease or malignant condition.

Breakthroughs in the use of drugs to enhance the efficiency of learning have already achieved limited success along with chemical controls for some mental illness and certain aspects of senility. Current projections also include the possibilities of chemical and electronic means to raise the level of intelligence. It is also forecast that the brain can be electronically linked to computers to increase the application of the human intellect to problem solving and lead more or less directly to the improvement of human analytical ability. In light of past developments, these techniques should grow more efficient each year, promising to offer valuable help for normal learners, for the treatment of criminals, for the mentally retarded, and for the mentally ill. They also could threaten both individuals and society, since the effects of faulty human experimentation are sometimes irreversible.

Limited evidence, by 1970, also was available to suggest that knowledge and experiences might be transferred from one organism to another. Although successful with simple multicellular creatures and apparently with mice, the implications and uses of mental "molecule" transfers are not as yet clear where higher life forms are concerned.

Many individuals who are now well-nigh physically helpless will have their handicaps reduced or eliminated by human organ transplants, plastic or electronic implants, and improved therapy and surgery. Promising medical research and experimentation is contributing to our understanding of immunology which are almost certain to result in the transplanting of healthy organs to supplant those of the individual's that have been ravaged by disease or injured through accident. The 1967 pioneering heart transplant in South Africa is a recent major illustration of further achievements to be anticipated in the 1970's. Eventually, some organs undoubtedly will be replaced by mechanical substitutes. When this is accomplished, then we have the prospect of the advent of the *cyborg* — a coined term that comes from cybernetic and organic — or a human body that is a mixture of organic and inorganic parts.

Other predictions include the possibility of biochemically assisted growth of new organs and limbs. As these probabilities become realities, what will their effect be on man's perennial self-concept questions: "Who am I?" "Where am I going?" "What am I doing?" What will happen to man as his body changes — as he is part himself — part a stranger — or part a machine? How will our conceptions of ourselves be changed?

Genetic controls of birth defects and hereditary factors influencing the general physical nature of the child as well as prenatal selection of the sex of the unborn infant are likely in the next decades. Permanent and quite extensive "natural," prenatal or pre-conception changes can almost certainly be made (at the option of the parent) in his child's sex, coloration, height, weight, physique, hair growth, features and other biophysical attributes. We are only beginning to understand how our biological potentialities can be improved, varied and more fully utilized. While plant and animal studies have been carried on for a long time, the possibility of reshaping the human organism to insure a better start, rather than a focus on the "repair" aspects of a faulty product or unsatisfactory part at a later date, was not considered seriously. Recently, it was suggested that we are no further now from partial synthesis of human life than we were from the release of nuclear energy in 1920. Indeed, artificial life at the virus level was produced three years ago! Also in prospect is the control of hereditary defects by altering genes and modifying the genetic code.[23]

There is at least the theoretical prospect that man can escape damage from many diseases, avoid permanent incapacity from many accidents, and even alter the "biological housing" in which he exists. Man may become more sound in body and find himself raised above some of the more unkind vagaries of heredity — less the product of accident or change and more the product of careful, thoughtful human choice.

CONCLUSION

This preview of the world of 1975 to 1999 has presented some of the implications of the sudden "collision with tomorrow" which has taken place during the lifetime of most adults who came of age prior to the 1960's. Changes transpiring with great rapidity have thrown some of us out of phase with an era and also placed us on our mettle to face tomorrow with vision, with courage leavened with optimism, and with confidence in the future.

In curriculum development, which is a profession intimately linked to human development and its unbounded potentialities, there is particular reason to participate in this speculative process, to peer into the future, and to help turn possible problems into promising possibilities. This will require

[23] R. Michael Davidson. Man's Participating Evolution. *Current*, 105:4–10, March, 1969.

persistent thought and effort — but seldom in the history of man could such effort count for more. This *is* an era of superlatives — one unique in intellectual, technical and social potential. This *is* a time for men to participate in shaping a world of new promise. In the process we should remember that our knowledge determines the limits of our vision, and that the limits of our vision are the only boundaries of the world of the future that wise curriculum planning can help create.

Epilogue: The Year 2000:
Teacher Education

William Van Til

> *Part Three ends with an epilogue by the editor.* The Year 2000: Teacher Education *serves both as an overview of alternative futures for the curriculum of teacher education — a subject only obliquely touched on by other contributors — and as a summary of Part Three. The pamphlet may serve the latter function since speculation on future programs of teacher education necessarily involves preliminary consideration of problems encountered in studying the future and of possible patterns that may emerge in society and the schools.* The Year 2000: Teacher Education *originated as my presidential address to the National Society of College Teachers of Education in 1968.*

ON SPECULATING ON THE FUTURE

Some may say, "But the year 2000 is far away!" Is it, really? The year 2000 is as far in the future as the year 1936 is in the past. From 1968, the year 2000 is thirty-two years away; so is the year 1936.

Historians will point out parallels between 1936 after the initiation of Franklin D. Roosevelt's New Deal program and 1968 after the initiation

From William Van Til, *The Year 2000: Teacher Education* (Terre Haute, Indiana State University, 1968), 9–35. Copyright © 1968 by William Van Til. Reprinted by permission.

[1] Historians report that 1936 was the year of Roosevelt's second election during the era of the New Deal. The backbone of the Great Depression was being broken and such acts of social legislation as the establishment of the Social Security system and the Tennessee Valley Authority were already established historical facts. In Europe, Adolph Hitler, in power for three years, marched into the Rhineland and, in America, a struggle between isolationists and internationalists accelerated.

Historians will probably report that 1968 was the year of Lyndon B. Johnson's "comof Lyndon B. Johnson's Great Society program.[1] But they will also point out some major "system breaks," to use Kenneth E. Boulding's phrase,[2] meaning sudden changes in the characteristics of systems. Such discontinuities, sometimes termed "turning points" or "surprises," develop because of powerful social forces, unpredictable or only partially predictable in advance.

The Role of System Breaks. For the 1936–68 period, major system breaks included such events as World War II, 1939–1945; the first atomic bomb dropped on Japan, 1945; the outer space pioneering dating from the Soviet Union's Sputnik, 1957; and the United States participation in Asiatic land wars during the 1950's and 1960's.[3]

If we look for parallels and continuities between 1936 and 1968, we can find them. If we look for system breaks and discontinuities between 1936 and 1968 we can also find them.

What is the shape of things to come in the year 2000, thirty-two years away? Can we envision at all the tomorrow of 2000 from the viewpoint of 1968? Or will major system breaks with respect to war or technology or biology or international development so change the current scene that a contemporary Rip Van Winkle falling asleep in 1968 would, like Rip, wake to a totally unimaginable and incomprehensible environment in the year 2000?[4]

WORLD WAR OR FAMINE AS SYSTEM BREAKS. So, before venturing any extrapolations of data and trends, we will formulate and invoke Rip Van Winkle's law, "All bets are off if such major system breaks as world war or world famine occur." In a time when the grinning horror of a nuclear war marked by incalculable devastation or a population growth culminating

---

pletely irrevocable" decision not to seek or accept the nomination of his party after his term of office had expired. A war against poverty had been declared, with the outcome in doubt, and such acts of social legislation as Medicare and extended categorical federal aid to education were already established historical facts. In Asia, a war in Vietnam engaged American forces and drained our resources while the confrontation between whites and blacks in American cities escalated.

2 Kenneth E. Boulding, "Expecting the Unexpected: The Uncertain Future of Knowledge and Technology," *Prospective Changes in Society by 1980*, ed. Edgar L. Morphet and Charles O. Ryan (Denver: Designing Education for the Future, July, 1966), p. 203.

3 While prophets of 1936 might have predicted (and indeed did) the Second World War, no one could have predicted even from the vantage point of 1936 the exact alignments (the German-Russian non-aggression pact came in 1939) and certainly not the military development, extent, weaponry, or outcomes of the war. Few were the insiders in nuclear devastation. The science fiction writers had a monopoly on speculation on outer space conquest in 1936. Few students of the international scene in 1936 could have envisioned American men fighting in local wars on the Asian mainland following a victory in a major World War.

4 Rip, you may remember, fell asleep in the Kaatskill mountains "while the country was yet a province of Great Britain" and returned twenty years later to his village to hear his fellow residents talking about "rights of citizens — elections — members of congress — liberty — Bunker's Hill — heroes of seventy-six — and words which were a perfect babylonish jargon to the bewildered Van Winkle" and to hear "that there had been a revolutionary war — that the country had thrown off the yoke of old England — and that, instead of being a subject of his Majesty George the Third, he was now a free citizen of the United States." *Selected Writings of Washington Irving*, ed. Saxe Cummins (New York: Modern Library, 1945), pp. 14, 18.

in famine must be regarded as a nightmare possibility, Rip Van Winkle's law must more than ever be respected.

Technological Developments as System Breaks. But what about the role of technological developments in making the year 2000 unimaginable and incomprehensible from the viewpoint of 1968? How about the possibility of the wizardry and marvels of gimmicks and gadgets in a time of accelerating technology transforming the recognizability of the year 2000? Sociologist Daniel Bell, writing early in the *Daedalus* explorations, ventured a sober and unromantic assessment: "The simple point is that a complex society is not changed by a flick of the wrist. Considered from a viewpoint of gadgetry, the United States in the year 2000 will be more *like* the United States in the year 1967 than *different*. The basic framework of day-to-day life has been shaped in the last fifty years by the ways the automobile, the airplane, the telephone, and the television have brought people together and increased the networks and interactions among them. It is highly unlikely that in the next thirty-three years (if one takes the 2000 literally, not symbolically) the impending changes in technology will radically alter this framework."[5]

Sociologist Bell's judgment may be influenced by what another *Daedalus* contributor would term his nonscience background. In a *Daedalus* discussion, Ithiel Pool pointed out, "When I looked at the Rand Delphi predictions, I was struck by the difference between the predictions made by the science panel and those made by other panels. The nonscience panels essentially predicted that whatever was recently happening was going to continue, only a little more so."[6]

Today some scholars are speculating on system breaks which may grow out of technological developments. One possible system break relates to the encompassing social implications of the growth of computer technology. Economist Kenneth E. Boulding speculates, "The crucial problem here is whether the development of electronics, automation, cybernation, and the whole complex of control systems does not introduce as it were a new gear into the evolutionary process, the implications of which are as yet only barely apparent. The computer is an extension of the human mind in the way that a tool or even an automobile is an extension of the human body. The automobile left practically no human institution unchanged as a result of the increase in human mobility which it permitted. The impact of the computer is likely to be just as great, and indeed of the whole world electronic network which represents, as McLuhan has pointed out, an extension of the human nervous system and what is perhaps even more important, a linkage of our different nervous systems. It seems probable that all existing political and economic institutions will suffer some modifications as a result of this new technology; in what directions, however, it is hard to predict."[7]

William T. Knox of the Office of Science and Technology, Executive

---

[5] Daniel Bell, "The Year 2000 — The Trajectory of an Idea," *Daedalus* XCVI (Summer, 1967), 641–42.

[6] "Baselines for the Future," *Daedalus* XCVI, 659.

[7] Boulding, *Prospective* . . . 1980, p. 209.

Office of the President, predicts flatly and positively, *"The impact on U. S. society of this (computer systems) development will exceed the impact of the automobile."*[8, 9]

BIOLOGICAL DEVELOPMENTS AS SYSTEM BREAKS. Another possible "system break" grows out of developments in biology. Some observers believe that we are leaving a century in which physics was queen of the sciences and entering a new era. Robert Wood, an urbanist, says, "I think one shrewd point of departure would be to recognize that the physical sciences have had their day for a while, that there is an innovative turn to the life sciences, and that most of our problems will come from the new advances in genetics, pharmacology, artificial organs, and medicine."[10] Ernst Mayr, a biologist, comments in the *Daedalus* discussions that one of his colleagues regards our times as "the beginning of the century of biology."[11]

The biological transformation of man via genetics, DNA developments, chemicals, and drugs is on the threshold.[12]

INTERNATIONAL DEVELOPMENTS AS SYSTEM BREAKS. Still another foreseeable system break relates to the international scene. In the broadest terms, the problem is the extent to which the world will be nationally or globally oriented during the next thirty-two years.[13] In the narrower sense, the

[8] William T. Knox, "The New Look in Information Systems," *Prospective . . . 1980*, p. 223.

[9] "If the middle third of the twentieth century is known as the nuclear era, and if past times have been known as the age of steam, iron, power, or the automobile, then the next thirty-three years may well be known as the age of electronics, computers, automation, cybernation, data processing, or some related idea." Herman Kahn and Anthony J. Wiener, *The Year 2000: A Framework for Speculation on the Next Thirty-three Years* (New York: Macmillan Co., 1967), p. 86.

[10] "Baselines for the Future," *Daedalus* XCVI, 663.

[11] *Ibid.*

[12] The century of biology is both welcomed and deplored. Richard L. Shetler, as the President of General Learning Corporation, comments on "another era in which there may be some massive break-throughs by 1980 — the field of molecular biology, of imposing changes in and around the living cell, thus possibly changing the character and quality of life itself. All the overtones of 1984, of Orwell and Huxley, are there, of course. But there are other and more hopeful overtones, too — of conquering disease and ignorance, and of opening boundless new horizons to human experience. I hope we have the good sense and humanity to use such a tool wisely and not monstrously, if we are able to use it at all. But I have enough faith in our instincts to hope that we do not shrink from the adventure of using it." "Major Problems of Society in 1980," *Prospective . . . 1980*, p. 268.

On the other hand, Joseph Wood Krutch viewed man's possible use of biological developments with alarm. In his article, "What the Year 2000 Won't Be Like," humanist Krutch carried on his long-term feud with the determinists in which an earlier battle was his assault in *The Measure of Man* on B. F. Skinner's *Walden Two*. " 'Would you like to control the sex of your offspring? Would you like your son to be six feet tall? Seven feet? . . . We know of no intrinsic limitations to the lifespan. How long would you like to live?'

"How would *you* like to be able to determine this or that? To me, it seems that a more pertinent question would be: 'How would you like *someone else* to answer these questions for you?' And it most certainly would be *someone else!*" *Saturday Review*, January 20, 1968, p. 43.

[13] "Will the world separate out into two cultures, both within countries and between countries, in which a certain proportion of the people adapt through education to the

question is the extent to which the United States will follow the course of enhancing the immediate twentieth-century consumption of its citizenry as contrasted to the course of supporting the development of human and material resources abroad among underdeveloped peoples because of some combination of humanitarian and long-range survival considerations. If one extrapolated some current trends, the result would be ambivalent. Simultaneously, the United States is the long-range and altruistic nation of the Marshall Plan, the Agency for International Development, and the Peace Corps. It is also an immediate-consumption-oriented nation which reduces appropriations for foreign aid and which responds inadequately as the economic gap between the developed and underdeveloped lands grows wider and wider while the rich get richer and the poor get children. A world famine in the era of the population explosion might be the precipitator of a system break toward the global view. A system break might also be brought about by aggressive threats by coalitions of nations, newly industrialized and reaching for power.

THE EXPECTED AND THE UNEXPECTED. Thus, anyone who attempts to envisage the shape of things to come in 2000 for the sake of considering alternative futures in his own field of inquiry (in this case teacher education), and possibly helping to shape directions in his field of inquiry, must face a paradox. The paradox is that he must report as though assuming that there will occur no major system breaks or surprises. Yet, at the same time, his historical sense tells him that system breaks or surprises (and not necessarily those mentioned above) are likely to occur and may be unpredictable.[14] In such a dilemma, some would educate simply for surprises and forego all speculations, recognizing the wisdom of the early suggestion of Heraclitus that there is no permanent reality except the reality of change.

---

world of modern technology and hence enjoy its fruits, while another proportion fail to adapt and perhaps become not only relatively worse off but even absolutely so, in the sense that what they have had in the past of traditional culture collapses under the impact of the technical superculture and leaves them disorganized, delinquent, anemic, and poor?" Boulding, *Prospective* . . . 1980, pp. 209–10.

[14] Those who attempt to envisage the shapes of things to come must even take into account the possibility that they are now living through an actual system break as they speculate and write. For instance, we may now be living through a period of literal social revolution which may be moving toward a culmination in open warfare between whites and blacks and toward new patterns of social arrangements imposed by the victors, rather than simply living through a period of swift social change in relationships between Negroes and whites within established precedents. We may be living through a period of triumph of anarchy as world-wide youth revolt spreads, as alienation characterizes masses of mankind, as more and more of the young and old withdraw from the Establishment, rather than simply a period of youth dissent marked by temporary withdrawals which the established society can absorb.

Even between the first draft and the final editing of this pamphlet, President Johnson terminated the bombing of Hanoi and asked for negotiations in the war in Vietnam; simultaneously, President Johnson announced his decision to neither seek nor accept the nomination for presidency; Martin Luther King was assassinated and violence and destruction ensued in 125 communities; a general strike swept France; student protests with attendant violence developed at Columbia University; Robert F. Kennedy was assassinated at the close of the Democratic Primary in California; the problem of violence in America dominated political discussion. Swift and astounding social change? Definitely. An indication of major system breaks? Quite possibly.

Perhaps the only thing of which the prophet can be sure is that his predictions are bound to be wrong, in large or in small part, if not totally. He must recognize, with Boyd H. Bode, that the gods give no guarantees.

Yet, despite the inevitability of surprises in the pattern of change, men must try to see where they seem to be going. They must attempt to see what now seem to be reasonable possibilities, so that they can have some possible participation in influencing the future, in tempering trends with their values, in considering realistic alternatives, in short, in planning ahead. Educators who are committed to the improvement of the educational process and product must necessarily attempt to plan for educational change and participate in its direction and control as best they can. Abraham Lincoln said it well, "If we could first know where we are and whither we are tending, we could better judge what to do and how to do it." Not to attempt to look ahead is to be unintelligent. To look ahead without recognizing that surprises must be also anticipated is also to be unintelligent.

Consequently, the writer will attempt in this paper to follow the advice of Fred Charles Iklé, a *Daedalus* contributor; to infer from past observations to future ones, to use predictions which seem logically true, to depend on common sense, and to be aware of one's own inclinations to Utopianism.[15] Yet he will also recognize the role of the unexpected, as advised by Boulding.[16] He will regard such social changes as local or regional wars, extensive computer technology, extensive biological developments, and expanding international participation as likely to affect American life. But he will not regard these as system breaks. He will reserve that term for nuclear World War, the computer influential as the automobile, biological transformations, and sharply increased gap-reducing globalism; he will regard such sweeping developments as authentic system breaks, turning points, surprises.

So let us plunge into a description of the probable United States in the year 2000 (assuming current trends and substantial social changes, yet excluding system breaks) as the U.S. is envisaged by the scholar-prophets who are willing to speculate on possibilities or alternatives. Later, we will identify factors in this projection of the year 2000 which may influence education in 2000. Finally, we will attempt to describe the possible resultant nature of teacher education and the value choices as to alternative futures which may be before teacher education in the year 2000.

AMERICAN SOCIETY IN THE YEAR 2000

Some Projections The prophets assume that in the year 2000 the United States will still exist both as a nation and as a major world power. The states of the Union (by then possibly fifty-two in number, including the states

---

[15] "As said above, for the first step in 'guiding predictions' we have to infer from past observations to future ones, using theories and empirical laws from all branches of science as much as we can. Second, we should not overlook the usefulness of logically true predictions. Third, we also have to rely on common sense . . . . Fourth, the greater the role of this tacit reasoning, the more we must beware of the distorting effect of our emotions." "Can Social Predictions Be Evaluated?" *Daedalus* XCVI, 751.

[16] Boulding, *Prospective . . . 1980*, pp. 199–213.

of Puerto Rico and the Virgin Islands) will be more heavily populated than the United States of 1968.

Population Projections. The Bureau of Census machine in Washington, D.C., which tolls off the population, recorded 200 million Americans on November 20, 1967. In a recent projection by the Bureau of Census, the total population for the United States is calculated as 241 million in 1980.[17] Philip M. Hauser and Martin Taitel of the University of Chicago write, "The population of the United States . . . is being projected to exceed 300 million by the turn of the century."[18] They add, "The projections utilize conservative assumptions about the future. The critical one is the birth rate. If it should not decline during the sixties, and then remain at a lower level, the total population of the United States may well be over 250 million by 1980 and close to 350 million by the end of the century."[19,20]

Urbanism and Metropolitanism. Both the anticipated Americans of 2000 and the Americans already born will live in urban territory. "By 1980, between 75 and 80 percent of our population may live in urban territory, which would place almost as many persons in urban territory in 1980 as there are in the entire United States today."[21,22]

As for the year 2000, Harvey S. Perloff says, "At present about 140 million Americans, out of a total of 200 million, are classed as urban dwellers. By 2000 at least 280 million, out of a total population of about 340 million, are expected to be living in urban areas."[23]

Not only will the future America be urban, it will also be metropolitan. Americans will reside largely in what the Bureau of the Census now terms Standard Metropolitan Statistical Areas.[24,25]

[17] Philip M. Hauser and Martin Taitel, "Population Trends — Prologue to Educational Problems," Prospective . . . 1980, p. 25.

[18] Ibid., p. 24.

[19] Ibid., p. 54.

[20] Sensibly, they hedge their bet because of the great imponderable, fertility. No population analyst can ever forget the great miscalculation of the 1930's, based on the society of the Great Depression, when the experts predicted 165 million as the peak population of the United States to be reached about the year 2000. Hauser and Taitel say, "Experience is lacking with regard to reproductive behavior in an era of easy and effective birth-control, relative affluence and nuclear power as a factor in world politics." Ibid., p. 25. [Ed. Note: e.g., by 1970, some demographers projected 280 million by 2000.]

[21] Ibid., p. 41.

[22] William L. C. Wheaton, Professor of City Planning and Director, Institute of Urban and Regional Development, University of California, Berkeley, says, "In short, during the next fifteen years, we must build about as many cities as were created in the first 200 years of this nation's existence. The population of the United States is moving to cities, and primarily to metropolitan areas." "Urban and Metropolitan Development," Prospective . . . 1980, p. 139.

[23] "Modernizing Urban Development," Daedalus XCVI, 789.

[24] Hauser and Taitel, Prospective . . . 1980, p. 30.

[25] Standard Metropolitan Statistical Area (SMSA) is defined by Hauser and Taitel as "one or more central cities of 50,000 or more persons, the balance of the county or countries containing such a city or cities, and such contiguous counties as, by certain criteria, are 'essentially metropolitan in character and are socially and economically integrated with the central city.' " Ibid., p. 30.

Even for 1980, the predictions are for 70 percent of our population living in metro-

By 2000, some predict the agglomeration of many metropolitan areas into three megalopolises. Herman Kahn, formerly of Rand Corporation and now Director of Hudson Institute, and his colleague Anthony J. Wiener, report, "We have labeled these — only half-frivolously — "Boswash," "Chipitts," and "Sansan." Boswash identifies the megalopolis that will extend from Washington to Boston and contain almost one quarter of the American population (something under 80 million people). Chipitts, concentrated around the Great Lakes, may stretch from Chicago to Pittsburgh and north to Canada — thereby including Detroit, Toledo, Cleveland, Akron, Buffalo, and Rochester. This megalopolis seems likely to contain more than one eighth of the U.S. population (perhaps 40 million people or more). Sansan, a Pacific megalopolis that will presumably stretch from Santa Barbara (or even San Francisco) to San Diego, should contain more than one sixteenth of the population (perhaps 20 million people or more)."[26]

THE GROSS NATIONAL PRODUCT. The residents of the United States in the year 2000 are expected to have a substantially higher Gross National Product and GNP per capita.[27] Kahn and Wiener say, "The surprise-free United States economic scenario calls for a $1 trillion economy in 1975, 1.5 trillion in 1985, and about $3 trillion in year 2000. . . . The assumptions used in the projections for the 'Standard Society' yield a GNP for year 2000 (in terms of 1965 dollars) of $2.2 to $3.6 trillion; based upon a 1965 GNP of 681 billion, this range implies average annual rates of growth of GNP of 3.4 percent and 4.9 percent, respectively. Considering a year 2000 population of 318 million, per capita GNP would be slightly more than double the 1965 amount under the assumption of the low rate of productivity increase, and, under the high rate of increase, would be about 3.5 times the 1965 figure."[28]

TECHNOLOGICAL DEVELOPMENTS. In a United States which is more heavily populated, more densely urbanized, and wealthier, some recent social trends may be expected at least to continue and probably to accelerate. For instance, scientific knowledge and technological development are expected to expand further. As an illustration, nuclear power plants should be producing much of our power in 2000. The computer should be a remarkably influential force by the year 2000.[29,30]

---

politan areas. "By 1980, of some 170 million people in metropolitan areas, about 100 million are projected to be in suburbs, about 70 million in central cities." *Ibid.*, p. 37.

[26] "The Next Thirty-Three Years: A Framework for Speculation," *Daedalus* XCVI, 718–19.

[27] Joseph L. Fisher, President of Resources for the Future, says, "A two-thirds increase in GNP in the next fifteen years seems altogether reasonable; indeed if the rather higher rate of increase in the last several years continues, the 1980 GNP will be near the high estimate shown in the table rather than the medium." (His high estimate for 1980 in his table is 1,250 billions; medium estimate 1060 billions in 1960 dollars), "Natural Resource Trends and Their Implications," *Prospective . . . 1980*, p. 9.

[28] *The Year 2000 . . .* , pp. 167–68.

[29] "It is necessary to be skeptical of any sweeping but often meaningless or non-rigorous statements such as 'a computer is limited by the designer — it cannot create anything he does not put in,' or that 'a computer cannot be truly creative or original.' By the year 2000, computers are likely to match, simulate, or surpass some of man's most

The National Society and Creative Federalism. The nation may be expected to become increasingly "a national society," as Daniel Bell phrases it, characterized by more use of instrumentalities such as government, mass media, and modern transportation.[31] Yet this "national society" may not necessarily see governmental power concentrated in a highly centralized national government.[32] Some foresee a "creative federalism." Organizations may be expected to flourish, according to Grant McConnell, Professor of Political Science, University of Chicago, who quotes Tocqueville and judges that "it seems reasonably safe to predict that in the next few decades private and non-government associations will be important factors in our common social and political life."[33]

The Roles of Work and Leisure. In the economic realm, the trend in the American democracy which was also early reported by the French observer Alexis de Tocqueville, is anticipated to continue — what the few have today, the many will demand tomorrow.[34] So, despite probable continuing inequalities, goods and services will probably be diffused throughout the general population.

With the problem of production largely solved through the persistence of the historical American combination of facilities, geographic location, substantial resources base, and an innovating technology, the question of the work distribution among the population may become critical. Current trends indicate that the population may be increasingly characterized by what some term the masses and an elite or, if you prefer, the comman man and a leadership group. Many Americans may work about a thirty to thirty-two hour week.[35] The sabbatical, once the exclusive fringe benefit of professors, may be extended to labor, along with long vacations and opportunities for early

---

'human-like' intellectual abilities, including perhaps some of his aesthetic and creative capacities, in addition to having some new kinds of capabilities that human beings do not have." *Ibid.*, p. 89.

[30] There are some observers like Joseph Wood Krutch who says, "And although the man in the street still thinks of a brighter future only in terms of more, rather than less technology, there are at least a few who are beginning to ask if we are not becoming more dependent and vulnerable rather than more and more dependent and safe." "If You Don't Mind my Saying So . . ." *American Scholar* XXXII (Spring, 1966), 183–84.

[31] Bell, *Daedalus* XCVI, 643.

[32] Daniel J. Elazar, Political Scientist, Temple University, foresees for 1980 that
(1) All governments will continue to grow.
(2) Sharing will be equally important in the future and will even seem to increase. ("One of the characteristics of the Great Society Programs has been the increased emphasis on federal aid to anybody.")
(3) The states will have to act constantly and with greater vigor to maintain their traditional position as the keystones in the American governmental arch.
(4) Localities will have to struggle for policy — as distinct from administrative — control of the new programs.
"The American Partnership: The Next Half Generation," *Prospective . . . 1980*, pp. 111–15.

[33] "Non-Government Organizations in America," *Prospective . . . 1980*, pp. 123–24.

[34] Bell, *Daedalus* XCVI, 643.

[35] Kahn and Wiener, *The Year 2000 . . .* , p. 175.

retirement.[36] Other workers may do only nominal or occasional work, resting content with their relatively low level of societal provision for maintenance.[37] But a vital group of Americans should be needed to man the specialized key positions which they hold by virtue of varied types of intellectual mastery. These key men may be expected to overwork themselves because of a variety of drives, including prestige, status, differential income, and desire for accomplishment.

THE KNOWLEDGE EXPLOSION. The knowledge explosion may be anticipated to continue its convulsive leaps. But since time is not expansible and since human beings are limited in the amount they can retain, more and more emphasis will probably be placed on storage and retrieval facilities and on computers to reduce the intellectual version of manual labor. The mastery of knowledge sources may well become an imperative educational goal for the individual who aspires to leadership and social regard.[38]

GOALS AND DIRECTIONS. More questionable as to predictability are a nation's norms. Yet likely, if present trends are extrapolated, is a further shift in American orientation away from Max Weber's "Protestant ethic" of hard work, thrift, and spare living and toward leisure-oriented, free-spending and hedonistic living.[39]

It seems likely that the democratic way of life will continue to be the official ideology of the country and that the basic documents of democracy will probably continue to be venerated by the citizens and reinterpreted by the philosophers. Of the Jeffersonian trilogy, "life, liberty, and the pursuit of happiness," it seems quite possible that the latter may come into its own as never before. "Life" having been cushioned economically, and protected and extended medically, may increasingly be taken for granted.[40] "Liberty"

[36] "However, hours of work now average about 38½ per week, and by 1980 we anticipate something like a 36-hour work week. In addition, it may become common to have a sabbatical for labor; that is, a period in which a worker, after several years of work, may need retraining or additional training, travel, or to pursue some other activity of his choice." Gerhard Colm, "Prospective Economic Developments," *Prospective . . . 1980,* p. 92.

[37] "Let us assume, then, with expanded gross national product, greatly increased per capita income, the work week drastically reduced, retirement earlier (but active life-span longer), and vacations longer, that leisure time and recreation and the values surrounding these acquire a new emphasis. Some substantial percentage of the population is not working at all. There has been a great movement toward the welfare state, especially in the areas of medical care, housing, and subsidies for what previously would have been thought of as poor sectors of the population." Kahn and Wiener, *The Year 2000 . . .* , p. 194.

[38] Many such individuals will temporarily be placed in a relatively new occupation, that of graduate student, since, as Professor Joseph W. Gabarino tells us, "For a number of reasons, including the competition for good students and the early age of marriage in recent years, a growing proportion of our university students have been converted into a special type of 'employee'." "The Industrial Relations System," *Prospective . . . 1980,* p. 159.

[39] There Is a Basic, Long-Term, Multifold Trend Toward . . . Increasingly Sensate (empirical, this-worldly, secular, humanistic, pragmatic, utilitarian, contractual, epicurean, or hedonistic) cultures." Kahn and Wiener, *Daedalus* XCVI, 706.

[40] Indeed, debate may center on how long the old should be kept alive in the century of biology in which transplants of organs are taken for granted.

should still be a heated focus of struggle, particularly on the part of the sensitive who reject massive invasions of privacy by governmental fact banks and law enforcement agencies and who resist impersonal controls by extended bureaucracies. But "the pursuit of happiness" may well be the aspect of the official democratic ideology which will engage the energies of most Americans and which will perturb the reflective.

While hobbies proliferate, travel expands, and educational opportunities enlarge, the present trend of spectatoritis may also grow via sports, movies, concerts, wide screen TV, etc. Discussion may be rife among intellectuals as to how man and woman should best pursue happiness in a society of multiple options.

Utopia will not have arrived by 2000. Americans of the year 2000 may well have their particular social problems, even as Americans of 1968 now have theirs — Vietnam war, Negro-white relations, the persisting slums and ghettos, the urban jungle, alienated youth, etc. Some of the social problems we now face in 1968 were readily predictable by the forecasters; the contributors to the *Daedalus* discussions comment frequently on the prescience and wisdom of *Recent Social Trends,* a publication of the Hoover era, in foreseeing 1968 dilemmas.[41]

THE PERSISTENCE OF PROBLEMS.   Problems that lend themselves to technological solutions seem easier for Americans to cope with than problems which have largely social answers.[42] So one might anticipate that some problems now looming large for the last third of the twentieth century may well yield to the ingenuity of technology by the year of 2000. Illustrations that leap to mind are air and water pollution, with the attendant problem of waste disposal. But possibly more difficult for the year 2000 may be the struggle against social problems which eventually come home to roost. Such problems could include organized crime, environment, housing, governmental structures, and operation of voluntary associations.[43]

CRIME.   By organized crime, we mean the planned lawlessness of criminal syndicates rather than "crime in the streets," today's euphemism for Negro rioting and violence. Today's struggles against the Cosa Nostra are clearly ineffectual, though the Mafia-type operations of today may appear child's play compared with the procedures of future organizations making maximum use of technology, brain power, and apparent respectability. Tomorrow's struggle

---

[41] In retrospect, was it not also apparent that, with respect to Negro-white relations, our nation must sometime inherit the wind during the 20th century as a heritage of years of slavery and segregation for Negroes, while whites mouthed what Myrdal termed the American Creed?

[42] Bell writes in his introduction to *The Year 2000,* "The Connecticut Yankee at King Arthur's Court was able to introduce quickly all kinds of wonderful inventions from the nineteenth century, but he foundered when he sought to change the religion and the monarchy — a lesson in the comparative recalcitrance of technology and belief systems in social change." P. xxiii.

[43] Should we expect that by the year 2000, America will have resolved its major Negro-white problems through a major social drive on this obvious difficulty? How long, O Lord, how long? Or is the more realistic possibility to anticipate half-measures and the consequent persistence of the Negro-white confrontation into the twenty-first century?

against criminal syndicates which may operate systematically and precisely, will, in all probability, take place in a land rendered more vulnerable to organized crime by population density accompanied by individual invisibility, by a structure of living both more independent and more fragile, and by a climate of values in which striving for present gratifications is taken for granted.

ENVIRONMENT. Similarly, the year 2000 may be an era when Americans struggle for a better quality of the natural environment. As Joseph L. Fisher, President of Resources for the Future, suggests, "Conservation now and for the future will be at least as much involved in preserving the quality of the natural environment as it will be in maintaining a capacity to produce quantities of goods. As technology and management assure raw materials for the future, our attention will switch to the qualitative aspects of abating water and air pollution, preventing pesticide damage, and improving the design and use of both the rural and urban landscape."[44]

HOUSING. In relationship to the natural environment, housing may prove a continuous problem. Possibly, after many blighted areas in central cities are rebuilt with high-rise apartments, or cleared for urban recreation, the suburban rings may have become obsolescent and be candidates for reconstruction.[45] Or areas of metropolises may have become " 'slurbs' — a partially urbanized area in which the countryside has been effectively destroyed."[46,47]

GOVERNMENTAL STRUCTURES. Perhaps it will have taken the development of the megalopolises of Boswash, Chipitts, and Sansan predicted by Kahn and Wiener to drive home the absurdity and obsolescence of our governmental structures in metropolitan areas. We refer to the multiple local governments which proliferate in the suburbs which ring the metropolises in a nation of 56,508 local governments, not counting school districts.[48] Already the political scientists are agreed on the unreality of our local governmental structures. Authors predict, "With the continuation of extensive urbanization and metropolitanization during the next few decades *will come increased recognition that our 20th-century technological, economic and demographic units have governmental structures of 18- and 19th-century origin and design.*"[49,50] Per-

---

[44] *Prospective . . . 1980*, p. 14.

[45] Hauser and Taitel, *Prospective . . . 1980*, p. 37.

[46] Wheaton, *Prospective . . . 1980*, p. 145.

[47] William L. C. Wheaton points out that already "Our newer metropolitan areas are also beginning to suffer from obsolescence in neighborhood shopping centers. While they still contain tawdry and obsolete string shopping centers, vestiges of the streetcar era, they also contain small shopping centers which were quite modern in the 1930s, but have been rendered obsolete by the more advanced designs and merchandising skills of the 1950s and 60s." *Ibid.*, p. 148.

[48] Hauser and Taitel, *Prospective . . . 1980*, p. 42.

[49] *Ibid.*

[50] Wheaton, writing about aspects of urban and metropolitan government in which growth and change are necessary, says, "First among these is surely the establishment of metropolitan area governments or policies. Some of our older metropolitan areas have as many as a thousand local governments, the accumulation of a hundred years of political history and of slow growth both in urban population and in urban services.

haps the culmination of the drive for Negro rights will provide the crucial element in achieving consolidation in metropolitan areas and the breaking down of city-suburban isolation, rather than the continuance of the current 1968 pattern of central cities which are increasingly Negro and suburbs which are almost all white.[51] But possibly Black Power will result in black separatism, rather than racial integration, while white power preserves white separatism in a nation even more sharply divided.

ASSOCIATIONS. The role of voluntary associations and internal and external controls in such associations may be among the crucial problems of the year 2000. Grant McConnell points out that studies of private associations show that "they generally lack the constitutional restraints which we have learned to regard as essential in our public institutions of government."[52] He says that "their governing institutions and modes of operation often do not adequately reflect the diversity of interest and will among their members; it is also that sometimes they do not serve the principle of liberty well. We can expect this to be a continuing problem in our common life."[53,54]

SUMMARY ON SOCIETY. To this point we have reviewed four major "system breaks" or "surprises" which are, paradoxically, foreseeable and have forewarned of their possible havoc to extrapolation prophecies — the catastrophe of the occurrence of war or famine, the computer having become as influential as the automobile, the biological transformation of man, and the development of highly accelerated international support by the developed nations with substantial gap reduction between have and have-nots. We also have reviewed the data predictions of the scholar-prophets, hedged against "surprises" — expanded population, increased urban territory and metropolitan areas, higher Gross National Product and GNP per capita. We have reviewed trends predicted by the scholar-prophets — expansion of scientific knowledge and technological development, the national society marked by creative federalism and voluntary associations, diffusion of goods and services, less working time required of the common man and much expected of an intellectual leadership group, new communication tools to cope with the knowledge explosion, and a leisure-oriented pursuit of happiness. We have predicted the persistence of social problems, such as crime, environment, ob-

---

Under these circumstances of multiple governments, no effective local government is possible." *Prospective . . . 1980*, p. 143.

[51] Hauser and Taitel comment that today for the 24 Standard Metropolitan Statistical Areas which contain the 24 larger cities, the central city Negro population numbers 83% of all Negroes in those Standard Metropolitan Statistical Areas. Hauser and Taitel, *Prospective . . . 1980*, p. 45.

[52] McConnell, *Prospective . . . 1980*, p. 128.

[53] *Ibid.*, p. 129.

[54] McConnell also points out that "inside a small association, an individual can find community and a sense of relation with his fellow man and need not feel alone or helpless. . . . In this setting he is not alienated. Thus, he and his fellows are unlikely to engage in activities that might disrupt society and they can be brought into line when necessary." *Ibid.*, p. 126.

In terms of other social trends discussed earlier, this sounds like an important prescription for the year 2000.

solescence in housing, governmental structures, and roles of associations and members.

AMERICAN EDUCATION IN THE YEAR 2000

Breaks and Trends In the light of the above, what might education in the year 2000 be like? The question brings us again to the problem of "system breaks." In the event of major war, education becomes a zeal-for-our-side operation, a war support apparatus; in atomic catastrophe, what is left becomes a giant subsistence housing barracks. In the event of overwhelming impact of computer technology, the school becomes a clean factory in which workers quietly use machines. In the event of biological transformation, schools have a different population to educate. In the event of global emphasis, schools become oriented to vicarious and actual travel abroad and an American appropriation for education widely shared with the underdeveloped world. But if such system breaks do not occur, the following are likely developments in American education. (Whether these developments are desirable or undesirable is a completely different question on which the reader is invited to judge.)

THE EDUCATIONAL POPULATION. As to the population to be educated, elementary education should be quite manageable. By 1968 we have already achieved, in effect, elementary education for all of the children of all of the people. In the years to 2000, the numerical task for elementary schools will be only to absorb the population increase.[55]

For secondary education, by 1968 we had reduced the dropout rate with respect to high school graduation to less than one in three persons. We did this by almost doubling high school enrollment between 1950 and 1965 as secondary school enrollment rose from 6.7 million to 13 million. To absorb most of the youth population increase plus to hold many of the one-third who now drop out, "the high schools still have a few more years of rather rapid enrollment increases (about 13 percent between 1965 and 1970) before relief arrives in the form of smaller enrollment increases," as Hauser and Taitel point out.[56] Then to 2000 the increase will represent simply population increases plus completion of secondary education for those who formerly dropped out.

The greatest increase in enrollment percentages between 1968 and 2000 is expected to come on the college and university levels. Past increments include 61 percent in the decade of the 50's and 60 percent in the first half of the 1960's. A 61 percent increase is expected from 1965 to 1980.[57,58] The

[55] "During the sixties and seventies, the pressure on the grade schools will sharply decrease. Between 1965 and 1980, enrollment may increase by over 4 million or by only 12 percent. This is approximately an average of 1 percent per annum, an easily managed rate. The major problems, therefore, will not be those of rapidly achieving net increases in total quantities of facilities and personnel. Rather, emphasis will be upon the relocation, improvement and replacement of physical facilities, upon the improvement of personnel and upon the innovation and development of materials and techniques." Hauser and Taitel, *Prospective . . . 1980*, p. 52.

[56] *Ibid.*

[57] *Ibid.*, p. 53.

[58] According to Gerhard Colm, Chief Economist, National Planning Association, as to

period from 1980 to 2000 should be marked by still more growth in college and university attendance, though the volume is not easily predictable. In addition, adult education may expand markedly.[59]

As to urbanization and metropolitanism, the typical student of year 2000 will be among the 280 million of 340 million living in urban areas.[60] The very large majority will be living in metropolitan areas described by Hauser and Taitel.[61] Almost half may live in the Boswash, Chipitts and Sansan described by Kahn and Wiener.[62] So schools will be very largely located in urban settings, except for some universities consciously located by their founders on open land and temporarily away from the enveloping grasp of urbanism.[63]

SUPPORT FOR EDUCATION. The American student of the year 2000 will be living in a nation which, barring "surprises," can afford to support education out of its GNP.[64] For education will go on in a nation in which Kahn and Wiener suggest as their "Standard Society" projection, a low per capita GNP in 1965 dollars of $6,850 and a high per capita GNP of $11,550.[65]

Even more important, the student generation should be living in an era in the year 2000 in which education will probably be respected for its economic power. Even today, in 1968, leading economists stress the value of education in the economic development of the nation[66] while advertisers exhort potential dropouts to stay in school through familiarizing them with the relation between income and increased years of schooling.[67]

---

sheer numbers, the enrollment on the college level, from 1960 to 1980, will rise by more than 7 million human beings while enrollment on the elementary school level, from 1960 to 1980, will rise by just about the same number. more than 7 million. *Prospective . . . 1980*, p. 83.

[59] "Because men will live longer, the life cycle will become more and more of a problem as people do not pursue simply one career, but go through different career cycles . . . The problem of indecisiveness about what to educate for will increase. . . ." Bell, *Daedalus* XCVI, 667.

[60] Perloff, *Daedalus* XCVI, 789. [Ed. Note: In 1971, these figures appear too high.]

[61] Hauser and Taitel, *Prospective . . . 1980*, pp. 29–42.

[62] Kahn and Wiener, *Daedalus* XCVI, 718–19.

[63] "Institutionalized escapism may be imperative if the social order of the future continues to be subject to pathologies such as those so visible currently. The society of the future may be forced to introduce mechanisms for utilizing living time in nonfriction-producing settings." Luvern L. Cunningham, "Leadership and Control of Education," *Implications for Education of Prospective Changes in Society*, ed. Edgar L. Morphet and Charles O. Ryan (Denver: Designing Education for the Future, January, 1967), p. 186.

[64] Whether it *will* adequately support education is another question. By 2000 education will still have its problems but they should not be financial support problems — yet there will probably be financial crises throughout the later decades of the twentieth century which will be related to obsolete tax systems.

[65] *The Year 2000 . . .*, p. 168.

[66] As Kenneth E. Boulding says, "A great many studies have indicated that in terms of sheer rate of return on investment, investment in education brings a higher rate of return than that of any competitive industry." *Prospective . . . 1980*, p. 212.

[67] Nor is anyone particularly startled when Thomas A. Vanderslice of General Electric points out that "When a company, particularly a scientifically oriented company, contemplates moving into a community, quite often the decisive factor is not taxes, not the labor supply, and not the nearness to market. What really makes the difference is the quality of the school system. . . ." *Saturday Review*, January 13, 1968, p. 48.

By 2000, this continuing trend of respect for education may result in advanced education being taken for granted as the indispensable key to membership in an intellectual elite at the social controls. Indeed, as Michael Young predicts in *Rise of The Meritocracy, 1870–2034,* elitism based on education may be becoming so advanced as to provoke dissent from the masses by 2000.

The likelihood of the continuance of the explosion of knowledge trend should result in expanded use of computers and retrieval facilities at all educational levels, since man's cognitive apparatus is definitely finite rather than illimitably expansible, barring biological system breaks. How to accumulate relevant data will be regarded as far more significant than an outmoded stuffing of the memory.[68,69]

CURRICULUM DEVELOPMENT. In a national society characterized by creative federalism, curriculum making may be more and more the province of federations of professionals who develop concepts and create materials to implement their concepts. The parochialism of projects in the fifties and sixties which involved few others than specialists in a discipline may have been outgrown. It may be taken for granted in the development of projects and learning materials that specialists in the foundations — social, philosophical, and psychological — specialists in varied media, and curriculum specialists will be heavily utilized, in addition to liberal arts scholars in the disciplines. Rather than a single curriculum design for a field, such as PSSC physics, multiple designs may have been created, many by regional research and development laboratories which were first initiated in the 1960's.[70]

EDUCATIONAL ASSOCIATIONS AND EDUCATORS' ROLES. In the world of the year 2000, educational associations may be larger because of the increase of educators numerically and the necessity for the salary advancement, welfare provisions, and professional information which associations provide. Quite possibly, one major organization may bargain collectively and negotiate professionally for teachers.[71] Characteristic also may be both proliferation of

[68] "Computers will also presumably be used as teaching aids, with one computer giving simultaneous individual instruction to hundreds of students, each at his own console and topic, at any level from elementary to graduate school." Kahn and Wiener, *The Year 2000* . . . , p. 90.

[69] As Shetler says, "Just imagine the staggering possibilities of having all the world's great libraries, the accumulated knowledge of mankind, at your fingertips, of being able to select from them the information that is desired, and at the same time having a machine that can analyze, sift, integrate and calculate for us. There are machines that can, in a moment's time, go through successive calculations that would require hundreds of years in the slow motion calculating ability of our minds." *Prospective* . . . 1980, pp. 266–67.

[70] "I regard it as urgent that by 1980 the most resourceful administrative units such as cities, subdivisions of states, entire states, or clusters of states become aggressively engaged in curriculum development so that all schools will have a diversity of high-quality programs to choose from and we will not have drifted into nationwide curricular uniformity by default." Henry M. Brickell, "Local Organization and Administration of Education," *Implications* . . . , p. 231.

[71] My crystal ball tempts me to predict that the most remarkable and remarked-upon development as to educational organization will be the creation of the National Education

organizations to match new job titles in an increasingly specialized educational profession[72] and coordination through super-organizations or holding companies to relate the work of specialized groups to a larger focus.

By the year 2000, the roles of most teachers will have been heavily influenced by the existence of supporting personnel, the available technology, and the extension of specialization. Secretarial staff, teacher aides, instructors and assistant teachers may be the personal supporting staff of the coordinating teacher in the discharge of his responsibilities. A pool of technicians, evaluators, and researchers, available to the teacher, may also be drawn upon.[73] The coordinating teacher increasingly may be the master of the mix, as O. K. Moore has phrased it, drawing upon readily accessible libraries or banks of books, films, television programs, sound tapes, computer consoles, etc., and utilizing trips, individual guidance, independent study, guests, etc., for instructional purposes with the aid of his staff. Perhaps a third of the coordinating teacher's six-hour working day may be spent supervising student learning of content in the existent disciplines and interdisciplines. Another third may be spent with various staff members in coordinating and planning future learning experiences. The final third may represent his specialization in education; consequently, some teachers would be engaged in individual therapy; others in conducting analysis groups for discussion with students; others in preparing television presentations and tapes; others in association with specialists programming computers; others in developing evaluation techniques and tests, etc. These specializations would reflect the personalities and preferences of individual teachers, as well as their academic backgrounds.

Overall management of the individual school may be shared by an administration specialist and a curriculum specialist. Coordination of schools and other community enterprises, often physically clustered in an educational

---

Federation of Teachers, a coalition of the former National Education Association and the former American Federation of Teachers. NEFT, as it will inevitably be abbreviated, will grow out of a steady evolution of the National Education Association toward welfare concerns and the American Federation of Teachers toward professional concerns. After years of internecine warfare, rank and file movements in both organizations will result in amalgamation, despite the opposition of the managerial hierarchies and the swollen bureaucracies of the two organizations. Thus says the crystal ball — which possibly is cracked.

[72] "The present role of teacher will gradually evolve into a cluster of roles encompassing such discrete functions as team leader, formulator of detailed objectives, instructional sequence planner, script writer, presenter of information, evaluator of pupil responses, and designer of supplementary pupil experiences. The new administrative and supervisory specialties will include position titles such as Specialist in Outside Developments, Supervisor of Professional Training, Director of Equipment Acquisition and Maintenance, Cheif of Materials Production, Program Assessor, Coordinator of Temporary Personal Assignments, Professional Librarian, and Travel Officer. We can anticipate that an Assistant Superintendent for Development and Training will cap off the pyramid of such positions in the central office of the school system." Brickell, *Implications . . . ,* p. 227.

[73] "We can expect, even by 1980, an enormous expansion in sub-professional or para-professional full-time and part-time workers. Some will be attached to teachers as general aides, while others will serve as instructional machine operators, playground supervisors, information room clerks, data assistants, equipment maintenance technicians, travel aides, and so on." *Ibid.,* p. 227.

park, will be the responsibility of the superintendent, largely a political force in school and community, and his complex supporting staff. Some of the supporting staff may be worried about teachers who seem unable to utilize varied resources with ingenuity and who spend most of their teaching time standing before the class and talking at them.[74]

THE PURSUIT OF KNOWLEDGE AND LEISURE. For the students of the year 2000, both the pursuit of knowledge and the pursuit of leisure will be important. Their lives outside of schools will, as now, be divided variously between study and recreation but the settings will be different. More prosperous homes may be able to afford, in the year 2000, a home learning and information center. Such a center might include "video communication for both telephone and television (possibly including retrieval of taped material from libraries or other sources) and rapid transmission and reception of facsimiles (possibly including news, library materials, commercial announcements, instantaneous mail delivery, other printouts)."[75,76] The home center might mainly be used by young people but also by adults, much as a collection of books, or a telephone, or an encyclopedia in the home is used today by youth and also by parents.

We may see an absorption of recreational facilities into recreational parks, a process somewhat similar to the absorption of recreational facilities onto college campuses through student unions, gymnasiums, natatoriums, etc. Instead of returning to the neighborhood for recreation after school, the youth of 2000 may turn to centers for sports, arts, gossip, etc., which are embraced in the master plan for the youth environment. His excursions into the countryside may be made in part via the school camp, while his younger brother and sister may visit the farm maintained by the school system for educational purposes.[77]

SUMMARY ON EDUCATION. As to education in general in the year 2000, to this point we have commented on the possible influence of societal "system breaks" on education, on the probable especial increase in the college and university populations, on relations of education to increased urbanism, metropolitanism and per capita GNP, and on increasing emphasis on the importance of education. We have speculated on increased use of educational technology (especially computers), on future coordinated use of edu-

---

[74] "Very probably (I regret to assume) if one opens the door to a typical 1980 classroom and walks inside, the teacher will be standing up front talking." *Ibid.*, p. 216.

[75] Kahn and Wiener, *Daedalus* XCVI, 714.

[76] "The sum of all these uses suggest that the computer utility industry will become as fundamental as the power industry, and that the computer can be viewed as the most basic tool of the last third of the twentieth century. Individual computers (or at least consoles or other remote input devices) will become essential equipment for home, school, business, and profession, and the ability to use a computer skillfully and flexibly may become more widespread than the ability to play bridge or drive a car (and presumably much easier)." Kahn and Wiener, *The Year 2000 . . .* , p. 91.

[77] "It is much better to think in terms of the positive use of the countryside: for example, maintaining farms city children can visit for both recreational and educational purposes, or leasing open land for use by various groups in camping and in other related recreational activities." Perloff, *Daedalus* XCVI, p. 793.

cation personnel in projects, on development of associations, on changing teacher roles and on resources for students for learning and leisure.

Teacher Education in the Year 2000

We now turn to teacher education in the year 2000.[78] What might be some possible developments reflecting the social scene and related to the total education enterprise of the year 2000? What are some alternative future value choices?

Possible System Breaks in Education Again, as in our consideration of the social setting of the year 2000, a question immediately arises. How about major "system breaks" or "surprises"? The answer is much the same as that for education as a whole. But what of the possibility of minor system breaks in that smaller system called teacher education?

Teacher education may undergo its version of system breaks or surprises by 2000. Forces leading in the direction of system breaks include persistent sharp criticism of the efficacy of teacher education by students, teachers, and scholars; slow adaptation of teacher education to such fast-moving social forces as technology; general conservatism in teacher education; and admission of weaknesses by teacher educators themselves. Forces leading away from system breaks include the considerable autonomy of key social institutions in teacher education such as schools of education, teachers colleges, and state departments of education; the success of resistance to past "outside" proposals for change; and the lack of realistic alternatives to the present system.

If a system break appears in teacher education between 1968 and 2000, what form might it take? Among the possibilities are sharply reducing professional education preparation, and turning what remains of the teacher education effort over to the liberal arts scholars. Yet the need for some body of professional education content and the unwillingness of the liberal arts scholars to take over, as distinct from criticizing, have militated against broad acceptance of this type of system break.

Another possibility is teacher education taken over by teachers through their unions and organizations. Teachers then would be inducted into the profession through fellow teachers in on-the-job relationships. Yet, teachers are so involved in salary and welfare campaigns and in adaptations to new curricula and technology that presently they show no eagerness to assume the burden of preparing their successors.

Possibilities sometimes proposed include take-over of education by state departments of education. It seems likely that state department take-overs would result in either other versions of schools of education, though under differing auspices and perhaps located in state capitals, or apprenticeship systems of training, conducted by teachers stressing practice and supervised by college professors moved into state departments.

[78] At this point, footnotes and supporting data will be abandoned to dramatize that what follows is a beginning on speculation through material for dialogue, an attempt to open rather than close possibilities.

Another possible system break is teacher education in 2000 planned and conducted through an industry-government complex composed of the private corporations which will have developed technologies and a U.S. Office of Education operating as does a European or Asian Ministry of Education. Militating against this development are the Constitution of the United States, the historic American distribution of power among local, state, and national levels, and the prophecy of creative federalism.

The Continuing Program If such system breaks do not occur within teacher education, we will assume that teacher education will probably continue primarily under the aegis of colleges and universities in increasingly urban settings. It will probably include as program-influencing forces liberal arts college specialists in disciplines or interdisciplines and specialists in professional education, whether organized in departments, schools or colleges. The programs implemented by these college and university staff members may be influenced, but in changing ways, by such institutions as federal government, state departments of education, unions, and certification bodies. An additional influencing force may be the future teachers themselves, for the voices of students will probably be heard in the land. Both implementing and influencing agents will be heavily affected by the social setting of the year 2000 which we have sketched above and by the education taking place in this social setting.

MACHINES AND MEN IN TEACHER EDUCATION. Expanded population, expanded enrollments, and expanded teaching personnel combined with developing technology, the continuing knowledge explosion, and new social problems may result in a teacher education which, by the year 2000, differentiates between what can be learned through machines and what can be learned through the personal presence of liberal arts professors and teacher educators. Books will still be read in 2000 but, additionally, students individually and in groups will utilize film and television collections, computer-aided instruction, simulation, models, and various information and concept-oriented laboratories. The personal presence of teacher and liberal arts educators, no longer regularly required for lectures, may take the form of individual and group planning conferences, discussion leadership, research planning, field work leadership, and occasional major lectures on new insights not yet recorded by technology.

The first four years of higher education may stress general liberal education and specialization in a discipline or interdiscipline. These college years may be set in locales comparable to present day universities, though characterized by many more laboratories reflecting technological developments. But students may often be away from the campus, both for immersion in the field studies which may by then characterize instruction in the social sciences and humanities and for retreat to camp settings in the diminished countryside for absorption and contemplation of insights from field work and campus study carried on in urban and metropolitan areas.

A minimum of two intensive years beyond the general liberal education years may be devoted to study and practice of professional education as the minimum preparation for teaching. While centers of professional education, emphasizing laboratories for use of technology and for research, will probably persist on university campuses, a substantial proportion of the teacher education program may take place within public school settings. As educational parks develop in old and new cities, teacher education centers, university-related, may increasingly be included among the park facilities. Professional teacher educators may work within systems both as partners in the total educational enterprise and as teachers of teachers, pre-service and in-service. Those ghetto and other slum schools which persist may present a more formidable space problem for such programs, but rental of empty store fronts and other obsolescent space will probably provide headquarters for teacher educators and teachers-to-be at the scene of the action.

SEQUENCES OF PROFESSIONAL EDUCATION. In such public school settings, students in training may experience evolutionary sequences beginning with observation, going on to participation, including student teaching and culminating in internship. Each student, from his entrance into the two-year program, may have one continuing advisor throughout the entire program. Characteristics of the advisor may well include recent teaching experience on the level on which he now supervises beginning teaching, knowledge of professional education and subject content, and demonstrated skill in fostering self-actualizing personalities.

Observation may take place in a variety of settings; participation may be consciously planned to include both upper and lower income situations, largely urban and metropolitan, occasionally rural. Taking the cue from the development of field work in the social sciences, specialists in the foundation areas and the theory and practice areas may be concerned with both substantive content and field experiences in school and community. Instruction in the foundations areas and in theory and practice may be timed to coincide with observation and participation experiences. Some scholars in the foundation areas and in theory and practice may be engaged in research and study to be embodied in books and technology; other scholars may have as their role the interrelating of issues and ideas with the school and community experience being encountered by the future teacher.

All student teaching may be televised for frequent individual replay and study by the individual and also by the advisor and the individual, and for large and small group discussion by specialists in teacher education and teachers in training. For instance, the specialist in reading would include in his armory of materials television depiction of successful reading procedures as well as programs presenting problems posed for discussion.

Internship may be the transitional phase between preparation and independent teaching. As the focus of the final months of the program, internship may be accompanied by culminating seminars in which representatives of foundations, theory and practice, and the continuing counselor may participate, sometimes in the school and sometimes in the university research and laboratory settings.

More functional use of summer vacation periods by future teachers is a likely social development by 2000. The three summer vacations related to the two-year teacher education concentration may be divided among subsidized travel experiences abroad resembling more the Experiment in International Living than the traditional packaged Grand Tour, paid employment involving working with youth in summer school and community projects, and apprenticeship in research and development with educators who are carrying on studies or developing learning materials for the various technologies.

If a system break toward globalism, a highly accelerated American participation in foreign nations, should develop, the second year of the teaching preparation period for many young Americans may take place in underdeveloped countries, with, possibly, Puerto Rico and the Virgin Islands as staging areas and take-off points. Teaching, like diplomacy, may involve rotation in international assignments with occasional sabbatical-type returns to the United States for vacation, observation of American developments, and sharing of experiences.

ADVANCED STUDY OF EDUCATION. Bi-annual extended vacation periods, subsidized leaves of absence, and taken-for-granted sabbatical years for all teachers may often be given over by teachers to retooling and doctoral work. The return would often be from the public school scene of the action to the university or regional laboratories and centers of discussions. Some sabbatical experiences may result in career shifts, from, for instance, coordinator teaching roles to material development, computer programming, evaluation development, supervision, or curriculum development, accompanied by the attainment of the doctoral degree in a credentials society which requires this demonstration of specialization for a major career shift. Such periods may also provide opportunities for the expanding number of paraprofessionals, assistant teachers, retreads from other occupations including housewifery, to be educated to become coordinating teachers.

But we should not forget that in a leisure-oriented society in which teachers are well organized in the interest of salary and welfare, many teachers may not aspire beyond their original posts and the ascending salary steps won by their negotiators. Vacations and sabbaticals may be used by many for leisure and renewal. Consequently, if teachers are to keep up with fast-developing educational technology and practice, in-service education as a part of the basic teacher working day would be essential. Here teacher education based in school systems, local and metropolitan, or operating from regional centers, would play a crucial role.

Thus teacher educators of the year 2000 may be involved in conducting two-year pre-service training programs in school and university settings; helping paraprofessionals to professional status via institutes, workshops, etc.; educating specialists at the doctoral level in university settings; and participating as partners with school systems in in-service education of the permanent teaching staff.

Possible Splits in Teacher Education One may predict with fair safety that in the year 2000 there will still be splits among educators over teacher education. It is probable that the liberal arts-professional education schism may persist. Yet it may be less virulent than during the 1950's when open warfare prevailed. Perhaps we may have reached, by the year 2000, a type of 38th parallel in the struggle, with a stalemate resulting in four collegiate years allotted to liberal arts and subject specialization and two years allotted to professional education.

It is also probable that the philosophers will not have become completely reconciled. We may still be hearing, under whatever titles, the cases for essentialism, reconstruction, progressivism, realism, idealism, etc. But the discussion may be increasingly ecumenical and oriented to dialogue rather than acrimonious.

The Technologists and the Social Emphasizers. Possibly such historic splits may be muted by a new split which may now be on the horizon — the split between the scientific research wing of teacher educators, here termed the technologists, and the humanistic philosophical wing of teacher educators, here termed the social emphasizers. The two wings are likely to perceive education differently and to stress differing values.

The technologists may stress the compression and synthesis of exploding knowledge into a variety of technologies for learning. The social emphasizers may stress examination of the human dilemmas of mankind through the posing and testing of alternatives.

The technologists may foster research, based largely on physical science models, which can be translated into quantitative terms and embodied in storage and retrieval technology. The social emphasizers may foster research, based largely on social science models, which can be synthesized and made available to decision-making bodies ranging from the electorate to institutionalized in-groups.

The technologists may point to past educational breakthroughs in technical competencies based on scientific research and development, and involving innovation, evaluation, feedback, and diffusion. They may see man's technological quests as mankind's best bet. The social emphasizers may point to past gains in control over social difficulties through use of problem-solving in the educational process and to catastrophes which continue to threaten human survival. They may urge that the world can afford technological failure while social failure would be fatal.

The technologists may look forward to increased experimentation into affecting human potential through controlled conditioning, drugs and chemicals, and influences on intellectual acuteness. The social emphasizers may view with distinct reserve the extension of experimentation on modifying human potential, citing the dignity of human personality, unsuccessful genetic experimentation toward a new breed, and reminding the public of the horrors of the Hitler regime.

The technologists may be preoccupied with closely defined, value-free laboratory studies of education-related techniques intended to foster production and efficiency. The social emphasizers may be preoccupied with the quality of life, work, and leisure, the possible ways for man to pursue happiness, and attendant value-oriented consideration of alternatives through schools.

The technologists may argue for acceptance of a split between elite and masses by pointing out the accelerating concentration of knowledge for decision-making in elites and uncertainty about decisions on the part of the common man under the severely restricted condition of information in the communication system, upon which the masses depend. The social emphasizers may claim that such acknowledgment merely defines the urgent problem to be faced by mankind: finding ways of making the knowledge of the elite accessible to the masses so that the common man may use intelligence in problem-solving and the leaders may be humanely oriented in their endeavors.

The technologists may be impressed by the order and efficiency of the new technology which is increasingly characteristic of school and society. The social emphasizers may be impressed by the planlessness and even chaos related to persistence of crime, poor land use, obsolete housing, ineffective government structures, competing interest groups, and other problems currently unpredictable.

The technologists may be pleased by the logic and clarity of the content developed in many subjects by projects which continually update knowledge. The social emphasizers may be troubled by the turbulence within man and disorder in society.

The technologists may develop and support teacher-proof materials. The social emphasizers may develop and support creativity in teaching and autonomous self-actualizing teachers.

The technologists may be charged with stressing things and ignoring people. The social emphasizers may be charged with stressing people and ignoring things.

Occasional versatile teacher educators may have the educational background and personality structure to harmoniously reconcile both the technologist and the social emphasis viewpoints. But the majority may lean to one or the other persuasion and may combat their opponents academically. They may even be heard speaking disparagingly of them at parties at which both old and new forms of libations and stimulants are served.

There is only one way in which to close the venture into the year 2000 represented by this paper. It is to predict, with appropriate uncertainty, that before the year 2000 is reached, one or more major and minor system breaks, whether anticipated or not even dimly envisaged, will take place. These developments will have a profound influence on the future of mankind, including the activity termed teacher education. One insignificant pigmy outcome of such developments will be that the venture into the future represented by this paper on tomorrow's teacher education will largely be of historical interest to whoever might come upon it in the year 2000.

Index

Absolutism, supervisory personnel, 46–49
  teachers', 112
Academic curriculum, boredom inspired
  by, 64
Academic disciplines, new interest in, 10
Academic education, criticism of, 2
Academic freedom, 94
Academic subjects, lack of interest in, 75
Academic withdrawal, need for, 77
Acceptance, manipulation of, 6
Accrediting agencies, curriculum change,
  204
Achievement, false, recognition of, 18, 24
  need for, 117
  parental criticism of, 51
  performance and, 73, 96
  propaganda in, 85
  rewarding of, 27, 96
Achievement motivation, 121
Achievement Motivation Development Proj-
  ect (Harvard), 117, 120
Adaptation, of content, 66
Adaptive education, 281–284
Administration, apathy of, 51
  authority of, endangering, 43
  future of, 372
Administrators, stupidity among, 329
Adolescence, education and, 75
Adult culture, rejection of, 148–149
Affective dimension, 109–113
Affective education, 8, 109–113, 113–122
Affective Education Research Project, 113
Affluence, and radicalism, 94
  unimportance of, 63
African culture, teaching of, 52–53
African studies, Harvard, 166
  need for, 161
Afro-American studies, Harvard, 166
  need for, 161
Alexander, Tom, 260
Allport, Gordon, 111
Alschuler, Alfred, 117, 120
Altbach, Philip G., 158
Alternative schools, 181–184
Anderson, N. S., 282
Anti-war sentiment, 149
Apathy, 27
  acceptance of, 30–31
  of administration, 51
Apprenticeship, support for, 76
Area committees, 173

Aristotle, 74
Arms race, educating for, 87–89
Art, intellectual challenge of, 31, 42, 44
  neglect of, 124, 141–147
Assignment, doing/not doing, 25
Associations, of the future, 368
Atkinson, Richard C., 273
Atlanta University, black studies, 167
Attendance, motivating, 93
Attitude, positive, need for, 109
Audiovisual models, foreign language teach-
  ing, 341
Authoritarianism, teachers', 24, 112
  threat of, 226
Authoritative leadership, 262
Authority, parental, 238
  resistance to, 74
Authors, children, writing for, 59
  contemporary, teaching of, 203

Background, pupils', relating to, 40–49
Bacon, Sir Francis, 84
Balance of terror, 87–89
"Ballad of the Landlord," 40, 45–47
Barondes, Stan, 182
Barr, Donald, 178
Barton, William H., 195
Begle, E. G., 322
Behavior, feelings and, 119
  modifying, 233
  television affects, 252
Bell, Daniel, 260, 262, 358
Bell, Max S., 223, 224, 320–329
Benjamin, Harold, 2
Bestor, Arthur E., 2
Binet, A., 278
Biochemistry, 184
Biological developments, system breaks, 359
Biological Sciences Curriculum, 141, 142
Birmingham, John, 7, 101–106
Birth defects, control of, 355
Bissell, Harold, 118
Black community, curriculum adaptation,
  104
Black culture, 5
Black history course, 100–101
Black person, African culture, 52
  crisis-oriented nature, 159
  cultural identity, 163
  curriculum, 5, 29–39
  dissent by, 3

Black person, African culture (*cont.*)
  education of, 5
    Boston, 5, 29–39, 40–49
    New York, 49–53, 53–61, 73, 75
    Philadelphia, 8, 113–122
    West Coast, 23–29
  ghetto education, 4, 23–29
  higher education, problem, 125
  history of, 5
    avoided, 40–41
    teaching, 41
  leaders, motivational force of, 40
  political power, 158
  political traumatization, 150
  revolution by, 227
  school environment, 96–99
Black Power, 156, 368
Black studies, 156–168
  definition, 164–165
  issues in, 162–163
  legitimacy of, 157
  objectives, 167
  oversimplification, 156
  problems of, 162–163, 167–168
  rationale, 165–166
  scholarship and, 162–168
Bloom, Benjamin, 179
Bobbitt, Franklin, 301
Bode, Boyd H., 9, 10, 11, 12, 17, 70, 361
Bolvin, J. O., 279
Books, black children's consumption, 52–53
  consistency in editions needed, 29
  outdated, 40
  reform in, 321
  written for children, 59
Boredom, academic curriculum, 64
  classroom, 31, 94
Borton, Terry, 113–122
Boston, black education, 5, 29–39, 40–49
Boulding, Kenneth, 219, 344, 358, 361
Brainerd, R. C., 282
Brameld, Theodore, 124, 125, 129–133
Brian, D., 272
Bross, Irwin, 347
Brown, George, 118, 119
Brubacher, J. S., 278
Bruner, Jerome S., 3, 54, 69, 132, 332–334
Budget, money supply, 195, 197–198
Burk, Frederick, 70, 278
Burke, Edmund, 53, 228
Burton, William H., 2
Butts, E. Freeman, 2

Calhoun, J. B., 244
Cambridge Report, 325
Career Prediction Test Battery, 312
Carmichael, Stokely, 156
Carnegie Corporation, 67
Carnegie Study of the Education of Educators, 67
Carver, George Washington, 40

Change, absorption of, 243
  agents of, 127, 201–210
  experiencing, 243
  status of, 201–202
Charters, W. W., Sr., 301
Child-centered curriculum, 62, 177–179
Childhood, contemporary, 226
  future for, 227
Chomsky, Noam, 137
Citizenship, success and, 230
  virtues of, 87
City, as educational environment, 76
Civilization, and education, 83
Civil rights, controversy over, 45
Civil War, history of, slanted, 41
Clark, Grenville, 154
Class discussion, intellectual challenge, 31, 34
Class stratification, rigidity of, 74
Cleaver, Eldridge, 104
Closeness, future of, 244
Cobb, R., 146
Coercion, avoidance of, 75
  of education, 22
Cofigurative culture, 235
Coleman, James, 78, 115
Coleman Report, 273
College admission, fanatical stress, 95
College board exams, preparing for, 73
Communication, in education, 190
Communism, understanding of, need for, 99
Compassionate critics, 4
Compensatory education, 123, 215
Competition, relaxation of, 56
Compulsion, lack of, 56
Compulsory education, criticism of, 7
  critique of, 90
  dissension in, 6–7
  reasons for, 81–85
Compulsory mis-education, 6
Computer(s), impersonality, 192
  influence of, future, 368
  instruction by, 222, 270–276
  use of, 231
Computer-aided instruction, 282–283, 288–296
  predictable, 300
  problems, 301
  skill drudgery, 303
  systems approach, 303
Computer techniques, 292
Computer technology, 270–276
  professional practice, 298–305
Conant, James B., 16, 67, 75
Concepts, teaching of, 36
  verbalizing, 38
Conceptual sciences, 142
Conformity, manipulation to accept, 6
  emphasis on, 98
Conservatism, in media, 223, 288–298

Content, adaptation of, 66
  boredom inspired by, 64
  changing, 64
  curriculum continuum, 217
  deviation in, 65
  relation to learner, 63
  relevance of, 62
Context, annexing, 257
Continuing curriculum, 211–218
Continuity, in education, 211–218
Continuum concept, 215–218
Control, exercising, 24
Cooley, W. W., 279
Core curriculum, 135
Counter-culture, 7, 79–92
Counts, George, 9, 10, 11, 12, 17
Cremin, Lawrence A., 2, 10, 13
Crime, projected, 366
Critics, types of, defined, 4
Crosby, Muriel, 127, 201–210
Cross-cutting approach, 129–133
Cultural change, curriculum and, 334–356
Cultural interests, 185
Culturally disadvantaged, black student, 160
  curriculum for, 65, 175–180
  curriculum change, 123
  curriculum innovations, 126
  special education for, 126
Cultural traditions, 236
Culture, African, 52–53
  contemporary, confusing, 212
  development of, 240
  education and, 83, 185
  moral nature, 88
  rejection of, 148–149
  science, interaction with, 310
  students', ignoring of, 104
  types of, 235
Culture-centric curriculum change concept, 257
Culture shock, 345
  future shock and, 249–250
Curriculum, absurdity in, 20
  agreement on, 20
  anti-integrational, 133
  approach to, 124, 129–133
  attention, lack of, 294
  black community, irrelevance of, 104
  broadness in, need for, 128
  child-centered, 62, 177–179
  continuing, 211–218
  creating, 72
  cultural change, 344–356
  culturally disadvantaged, 65, 175–180
  development of, 293, 346
  experience and, 62
  failure and, 109
  foreign language, 341
  for the future, 219–224
  future aspects, 306–379
  future-planning, 258–269

future planning approach, 265
future shock, 249–258
human objectives, 114
individualized, 271
instructional technology, 190–194
invisible, 8, 107–109
lifetime, 255
love in, 140
meaningful, making of, 108
modifying, 72
for the 1970's, 123–128
outmoded, 99
outside of classroom, 124, 132
person-to-person contact, 294
phantom, 252
primary school, coherence of, 57
problem-centered, 140
problems, in the 1970's, 125
pro-structural, 133
reexamination of, 290
reform of, 6, 66–72, 104, 110, 125, 290, 291, 295
relevance of, 62–66, 148–152
secondary school, changes, 203
social order and, 2
status quo, criticisms of, 1
structured innovations, 126
students' voices in selection, 100, 105
Curriculum centers, 115
Curriculum change, agents of, 200–210
  culture-centric concept, 257
  forces affecting, 195–200
  interrelationship of forces, 200
  methods of, 200–210
  priorities in, 169–174
  responsibility for, 209–210
Curriculum content, mathematical, year 1991, 324
Curriculum continuum, content of, 217
  new directions, 213–215
Curriculum development, of future, 371
  separationist/isolationist forms, 125
Curriculum organization, forms of, 125, 129–133
Curriculum Reform Movement, 290, 291, 295
Curriculum worker, information overload, 346
Cybernetics, 252
Cyborg unit, phasing in, 256

Darling, Ding, 146
Deficiencies, meeting, 180
Degradation, of people, 112–113
Democratic values, 12
Dennison, George, 2, 5, 53–61, 177
Deprivation, of intelligence, 28
  problem of, 25
Designing Education for the Future (project), 220
Deviant student, support for, 133

Deviation, of content, 65
Dewey, John, 6, 9, 10, 11, 12, 15, 17, 54, 70, 74, 136, 138, 149, 299, 303, 335
Dialogue systems, 273
Dictionary, intellectual challenge, 30
Didactic code, of teaching, 172
Diploma equivalency, 179
Direct approach, 27
Directions, projected, 365
Discipline, formal, lack of, 56
    relaxing, 50
Disciplines proposal, 3, 124, 134–140
Disillusionment, student, 96–99
Disinterested student, 18
Dissatisfaction, extent of, 1
Dissenting forces, curriculum change, 208
Doll, Robert C., 127, 195–200
Double promotion, 215
Driver education, 207
Drop Out Center (Teachers'), 182
Dropout problem, elimination of, 215
    in the 1970's, 123
    schools contribute to, 44
Drugs, usage of, increasing, 354
Dual progress plan, 15
DuBois, W. E. B., 160
Dubos, René, 186, 188

Earth Science Curriculum, 141, 142
East Harlem, education in, 5, 29–39
Ecology, 193–194
Education, advanced study, 377
    affective dimension, 109–113
    changes, insignificance of, 29
    child-dictated, banality, 71
    choice in, need for, 73–78
    communications in, 190
    continuing experience, 232
    continuing process, 351
    continuity in, 211–218
    contrary to nature, 79–92
    control problem, 160
    defined, 79
    dissatisfaction with, 126, 181–184
    ecological balance, 194
    emotion related to, 8, 113–122
    environment, living in, 98–99
    experience and, 74
    future of, 215–218, 224, 229, 357–379
        mapping out, 348
    general, inadequate, 123
    intellectual development, 68
    levels of, traditional emphasis, 254
    money wasted on, 76
    needs and, 74, 90
    new directions, 214–215
    nonsense in, 20
    obsolescence, 230
    primary school and, 57
        problem of, 81
    pupils' problems, 59
    purpose in, 67
    relevance, 62–66
    selectivity in, 82
    standardization in, 274–275
    status quo, 158
    students' feelings and, 119
    support for, 1970's, 123, 370
    system breaks, 374
    of very young, 350
    vocabulary of, 138
    in year 2000, 369–374
Educational associations, of future, 371
Educational cartography, 348
Educational Development Corporation, 115
Educational goals, U.S./Soviet, 2–3
Educational objectives, 114
Educational population, 369
Educational system, status quo, 94
Educational technology, 223, 298–305
Educational television, 14, 299
Efficiency, of future-planning expert, 267
Egerton, John, 287
Elam, Stanley, 277
Elementary school level, in mini-schools, 53–61, 73, 75
Elementary schools, choice in, need, 73
Emory University, black studies, 167
Emotions, students', 119
Engler, David, 126, 190–194
Enjoyment, of curriculum, 108
Enrichment experiences, need for, 30
Environment, deteriorating, 123
    educating for, 98–99
    educational, 76
    in future, 367
    foreign languages, 342
    learning and, 246
    particular, demands of, 159
    relationships to, 6, 53–61
    school, controlling, 56
Equilibrium theories, 145
Essential education, deciding on, 19
Establishment, The, reaction to, 94
    slavishness to, 46–49
Experience, curriculum and, 62
    education and, 74
    lack of, 65
    learning as, 58, 59
Experimentalism, philosophy of, 13
Extrinsic subject matter, 11

Faculty, and future education, 217
Failure, actual fear of, 17–23
    in curriculum goals, 109
    elimination of, 215
    reasons for, 4, 17–23
    rejection of, 58
    responsibility for, 202–204

social manifestations, 192
Falk, Richard, 153
Family, origin of, teaching, 37
Famine, as system break, 357
Fawcett, Harold, 135
Featherstone, Joseph, 54
Federal government, curriculum change, 205
  financial aid by, 197–198
Federalism, year 2000, 364
Feelings, students', integrating, 119
Financial aid, governmental, 197–198
First Street School, 53–61, 73, 75
Fisk University, curriculum, 164
Flexner, Abraham, 70
Foreign language(s), 224, 338–343
  curriculum, 341
  environment, 342
  instruction in, 137
  students, 341–342
  teachers, 342
  teaching of, future of, 338–341
    mechanization, 339–341
Forster, William E., 84
Foshay, Arthur W., 15, 124, 125, 134–141
Franchise industry, curriculum change, 205
Frank, Lawrence K., 262, 347
Frazier, T. E., 14
Freedom, defining, 54
  in education, 14
Friedenberg, Edgar, 89
Frost, Robert, 43
Frymier, Jack R., 8, 109–113
Functional literacy, 76
Future-planning, 258–269
  approach to, 265
  caveats for, 268
  experts, selecting, 267
  ORPHIC procedures, 265
Future shock, and curriculum, 249–258
  coping with, 252–257
  deranging influence, 345
  educational sources, 250–252
Futurism, development of, 222, 249–258, 258–269
  escapism and, 220

Gallup, George, 349
Game playing, emphasis on, 120
Gardner, John, 69, 320
Garrison, William Lloyd, 41, 42
General education development test, 179
Generalities, analysis and interpretation, 25
Generation gap, 106, 234–241
  education's contribution to, 76
Ghetto, life in, 93–96
Ghetto schools, 4, 23–29, 95
Glaser, R., 279
Glasser, William, 181
Goals, identifying, 74

projected, 365
Goodlad, John L., 221, 229–234
Goodman, Paul, 6, 7, 54, 73–78, 89, 115, 149
Goslin, Willard, 2
Government, curriculum change, 205
  financial aid by, 197–198
Governmental structures, future, 367
Gordon, T. J., 260, 262
Grades, high marks, obsession with, 96
Grants, financial, 198
Greene, Mary F., 54
Gross national product, effect of, 227
  projected, 363
Guilt problems, coercive education and, 23

Haber, Harvey, 181
Hamilton, Charles V., 125, 156–161
Handicaps, physical, reduced, 354
Harmon, Willis, 120
Harrison, A., 264
Harvard Project Physics, 136
Hatred, teaching of, 109
Hauser, Philip M., 243, 362, 369, 370
Havighurst, Robert J., 126, 175–180
Healy, T. S., 287
Helmer, Olaf, 259, 260, 262, 263
Henry, Jules, 89
Hentoff, Nat, 5, 49–53, 54
Hereditary factors, control of, 355
Herndon, James, 4, 23–29, 54, 89, 181
Heterogeneity, impressing, 286–287
Hicks, Hanne Lane, 8, 107–109
Higher education, future enrollment, 350
High school, radicalism in, 7, 93–101
  underground press, 7, 101–108
History, black people, role of, 157
History books, slanting of, 41
Holmes, Oliver Wendell, 185
Holt, John, 2, 4, 17–23, 54, 58, 89, 115, 177, 178, 181
Housing, in future, 367
Hughes, Langston, 40, 45, 47
Human affairs, 125
Humanism, 127, 190–194
  failure of, 191
  and instructional technology, 185–194
Humanist approach, 185–189
Humanities, 127, 185–189
Human nature, character of, 130
  problems of, 222, 242–247
Human objectives, 114
Human person, programs appealing to, 171
Human rights, controversy over, 45
Human Training Development Institute, 118
Hunt, Maurice P., 125, 148–155
Hurd, Paul D., 310
Hutchins, Robert, 154
Huxley, Aldous, 219, 233, 289

Hypocrisy, in education, 96

Ignorance, parental, effect of, 45
Iklé, Fred Charles, 361
Imagination, lack of, 29–39
  need for, 108, 254
  supervisors', 46–49
Incentive, rewards and, 27
Incidental education, 81
Incompetence, academic, 115
Independent study, advanced students, 104
Individual differences, 287
Individualization, concepts of, 280
Individualized drill, 272
Individualized instruction, 127, 213, 222, 277–278
Individually prescribed instruction, 270
Industrialization, end to, 89–92
Industrial prosperity, education and, 84
Industrial society, 86–87
Industry, curriculum change, 205
  labor force, 247
Information overload, 346
Innovations, 208
  curriculum, 126, 169–171
  and curriculum change, 206
  in instruction, 135
  unfamiliar techniques, 251
Inquiry, concepts of, 142
Institutional change, 295–296
Institutionalized religion, 248
Instruction, appraisal of, 284
  computer aided, 282–283, 288–296, 301–303
  evaluation of, 284
  functions of, 135
  human to human, 230
  individualized, 278–281
  individualized/personalized, 127
  individually prescribed, 279
  innovations in, 135
  meaningful, 64
  pacing of, 280
  past achievement and, 280
  revolution in, 277–288
Instructional aids, of the future, 232
Instructional media, 280
Instructional technology, 190–194
  humanism and, 185–194
Integration, artificial/irrelevant, 18
Intellectual ability, challenging, 29–39
Intellectual curiosity, satisfaction of, 23
  smothering of, 18, 21
Intellectual development, education as, 68
Intellectual growth, capacity for, 18
Intellectually gifted children's classes, 50
Intellectual power, and future-power expert, 267
Intellectuals, growth and development, 68
Intelligence, deprivation of, 28

Interdisciplinary curriculum building, 126, 175–180
Interest, creating, 105
  destroying, 18
International developments, as system breaks, 359
Internship, 291
Interpersonal living, religion and, 248
Interpersonal relationships, 242–249
  learning in, 245–247
Intimacy, future of, 244
Invisible curriculum, 8, 107–109
Irrelevance, recognizing, 63

Jamal, N. K., 93, 96–99
James, William, 188
Jerman, M., 272
Jim Crowism, 45
Johnson, Gerald, 294
Jouvenal, Bertrand de, 261, 347

Kahn, Herman, 186, 188, 220, 227, 264, 363, 367, 370
Kandel, I. L., 290
Keller, Charles R., 15
Kennan, Richard Barnes, 2
Kierkegaard, Søren, 289
Kilpatrick, William Heard, 9, 10, 11, 17
Klein, Bob, 105–106
Klopfer, Leopold E., 223, 224, 306–319
Knowledge, curriculum change, 195, 198–199
  future, demands of, 21
    pursuit of, 373
  integration of, 123
  integration/relevance, 139
  mastery of, 169
  updating and reconstructing, 15
  unessential, teaching of, 21
Knowledge explosion, 365
Knowledge machine, 288–298
Knox, William T., 358
Kohl, Herbert, 3, 5, 29–39, 54, 177, 178, 181
Kopkind, Alexander, 260
Kozol, Jonathan, 2, 5, 40–48, 54, 89, 115, 181
Kropotkin, Prince, 78
Krug, Mark M., 223, 224, 330–338
Krutch, Joseph Wood, 126, 185–189

Labor force, 247
Language study, intellectual challenge, 35
Language laboratories, 298
Leadership, and direction, 262
  teachers', 233
Learning, capacity for, 18
  defined, 55, 58
  environment and, 246
  future of, 229–234

interpersonal relationships, 245–247
  invisible curriculum, 108
Learning desire, smothering of, 21
Leisure, future, 373
  year 2000, 364
Leonard, George, 121, 181, 288, 289, 292
Lerner, Max, 147
Libarle, Marc, 7, 93–101
Liberal arts college, 78
Liberal education, nature and content, 68
Libertarian values, 55
Liberalism, American, 151
Liberal-reformist tradition, rejection, 150
Liberty, curtailment of, 29
Library, automated, 232
  intellectual challenge, 39
  source material from, 48
License, technology and, 143–144
Life, respect for, teaching, 110
Life spans, increasing, 351
Lifetime curriculum, 255
Lindvall, C. M., 279
Lipset, Seymour Martin, 158
Listening, reading problem and, 59
Living, preparation for, 246
  teaching of, 109–113
Love, and culture, 240
  teaching of, 111
Love sentiment, contemporary, 149
Low-ability groups, 28
Lucas, George, 146

Man, biological transformation, 368
  nature and, 144–145
Man-machine interaction, 221, 230
Marks, eliminating, 215
Marqusee, Michael, 93, 94–96
Massé, Pierre, 261
Mass media, banality of, 68
Masters Program (Puerto Rico), 179
Mathematics, 10, 223, 320–329
  computer technology, 271
  future of, 320–329
  reform in, 320
Mayer, Martin, 15, 67
McCarthyism, education and, 2
McClelland, David, 116–117
McConnell, Grant, 364
McLuhan, Marshall, 146, 252, 288, 289, 290, 292, 358
McMurrin, Sterling, 10
Mead, Margaret, 221, 234–241
Meals, Donald W., 301
Meaning, need for, 116
Megalopolises, projected, 363
Melby, Ernest, 2
Mendlovitz, Saul, 153
Merton, Thomas, 87
Metcalf, Lawrence E., 125, 148–155

Methods, 127, 195–200
  competency in, 76
  for the disadvantaged, 176–177
  human objectives and, 114
  placating student, 96
  skills and, 25
Metropolitanism, projections, 362, 370
Michael, Donald N., 221
Mini-school, 5, 53–61, 73, 75
Minority groups, educating, 124
Misbehavior, reasons for, 26
Mississippi Freedom Schools, 53
Mood, for classroom work, 26
Mitzel, Harold E., 222, 272–288
Moore, O. K., 372
Moral nature, of culture, 88
Motivation, need for, 121
  of a student, 18
Multidisciplinary problems, 124–125
Music, intellectual challenge, 31, 44
Music appreciation/rock music, 104
Mythology, intellectual challenge, 35

n-Ach, 117
Names, derivation of, challenge, 37
National Association of Independent Schools, 183
National Defense Education Act, 3, 10
National Defense Education Act Institutes, 72
National Endowment for the Humanities, 167
Nationalism, education and, 84–85, 87–89
National problems, teaching of, 99
National society, year 2000, 364
National Training Laboratory, 118
Natural resources, allocation of, 328
Needs, curriculum change and, 195, 199–200
  education and, 90
  meeting of, 74
  self-image, meeting, 180
Negro. *See* Black
Neill, A. S., 6, 55, 75, 178
Newberg, Norman, 115
Newmann, Fred, 292
New Schools Exchange, 181, 182, 183
Newspapers, high school underground, 101–106
New York City, education, unimaginative, 29–30
  mini-schools. *See* First Street School
Nonverbal experience, 119
Nostrand, Howard Lee, 224, 338–343

Oettinger, A. G., 280
Oliver, Donald, 292
Oppenheimer, Robert, 198
Organization, future mandates for, 255

Organizational changes, 215
ORPHIC techniques, 258
  future planning and, 265
Orthodoxy, 82
Orwell, George, 210, 289, 345
Outcome values, 262

Palomares, Uvalo, 118
Parents, and administrators, 56
  authority of, 238
  and pupils' achievement, 51
  school discipline, 50
Parkhurst, H. H., 70, 278
Parkway Schools (Philadelphia), 126, 182
Pask, G., 278
Peculiarities, concentration on, 236
Performance, achievement and, 73, 96
  evaluating, 199
Perloff, Harvey S., 362
Personal information data banks, 353
Personalization, 171
Personality, modified by drugs, 354
Personalized instruction, 127, 213
Personal privacy, violation of, 353
PERT, 261, 262
Pessimism, enlightened, 145
Peterson, Peter, 292
Phantom curriculum, 252
Philadelphia, education in, 8, 113–122
  Parkway program, 126, 182
Physical dominance, law of, 32
Physical education, 294
Physical Science Study Committee (PSSC)
  physics project, 10, 136
Piaget, Jean, 54
Platt, James R., 346
Poetry, intellectual challenge, 43, 44
Policy changes, in future program, 216
Population explosion, problem of, 242
Population projections, 362
Post-figurative culture, 235
Potter, Carl, 183
Poverty, effect of, 123
Power, curriculum change and, 195, 196–
    197
  rebellion against, 239
Practices, in educational program, 216
Prefigurative culture, 235
Preparatory academy, academic subjects, 75
  choice, need for, 73
Prevoyance, 260
Primary school, coherent curriculum, 57
Printed words, speech and, 59
Problems, of the individual, 170
  persistence of, 366
  personal, of youth, 154–155
Problem solving, 136
Process values, 262
Professional education, sequences in, 376
Professionalism, in teaching, 172
Professional people, need for, 307–308

Program Evaluation and Review Technique,
    261, 262
Programmed learning, 13, 178, 231
Progressive education, academic education
    and, 2
  obsolescence of, 2, 6, 66–72
Progressive Education Association, 11, 13,
    135
Progressivism, 68
Project method, 11–14
Promotion, abolishment of, 215
Propaganda, education and, 85–87
Prospective Scientists stream, 311
  high school in, 315–317
Protestant ethic, 365
Public education, universality of, 2
Public opinion, assessing, 349
Public schools, failure of, 68
  mindlessness of, 69
  organizing, 68
Puerto Rico, educational survey, 62–63, 64
  Masters Program, 179
Pupils, respect for, lack of, 44
  underrating of, standard of, 43

Racial antagonism, 3
Racial difference, 63
  teacher-pupil, 26
Racism, among faculty, 99–101
Radicalism, among affluent, 94
  of students, 101–106
Radical students, high school, 7, 93–101
Rath, G. J., 282
Reading, intellectual challenge, 30
  relevance and, 62
Reading ability, relevance of, 63
Reading Improvement Teachers, 51
Reading level, 49–50, 52
Reading problem, 59, 60
Reading readiness, 42
Reality, in children's books, 59
  ignoring of, 45
  introduction of, 64
  relating to, in classroom, 44
Record keeping, mechanical, 353
Reform, curriculum, 6, 66–72, 104, 110,
    125, 290, 291, 295
Regimentation, of individuals, 74
Relationships, pupil-teacher, 38
Relevance, of curriculum, 6, 62–66
  humanism and, 189
  search for, 124
Religion, interpersonal living and, 248
  rejection of, 149
Remedial work, 215
Report cards, not favored, 56, 215
Research, and education, 78
Research scientists, need for, 307
Respect, need for, of student, 108
Responsibility, of humanist, 188–189
Restlessness, classroom, overcoming, 31

Revolution, student, 123, 234–241
Rickover, Hyman G., 2
Rights/responsibilities, students', 105
Robinson, Donald W., 126, 181–184
Rogers, Carl R., 118, 221, 242–249
Rogers, Vergil, 2
Romano, David, 93–94
Roper, Elmo, 349
Roszak, Theodore, 7, 79–92, 140
Rote learning, 38–39
Rote memory, 104
Routines, conventional, 57
Rowen, Henry S., 261
Rugg, Harold, 70
Ryan, O., 54

Sabbatical leave, 326, 364
Sanitation, lack of, 5, 49–53
  standard of, 56–57
Sarton, George, 309
Saylor, Galen, 207
Schaefer, Robert J., 71, 72
Scholarship, and black studies, 162–168
School, functions, evolving, 289
  new models, 291–292
School buildings, adequacy of, 42
School establishment, circumventing, 297
School Mathematics Study Group, 322, 326
School program, organization of, 9–11
School work, 169–184
Schwab, Joseph, 134
Science, and culture, interaction, 310
  defined, 142–145
  progress in, 185
Science curriculum, 124, 141–147
  conceptual sciences, 142
  elementary, year 1991, 315
Science education, 223, 306–319
  future of, 306–319
  goals, 309
  1991 pattern, 310
Scientific Literary stream, 311
  high school in, 317–319
Secondary level, preparatory academies, 73
Segregated schools, teaching problem in, 41
Self-awareness, development of, 214
Self-examination, 69
Self-image needs, meeting, 180
Self-realization centers, 255
Self-renewal, 69
Seligson, Tom, 7, 93–101
Sex education, 82, 202
Shane, Harold G., 128, 211–218, 222, 224,
  249–258, 258–269, 344–356
Shane, June Grant, 222, 224, 258–269,
  344–356
Shapiro, Elliott, 5, 49–53
Shelley, Percy Bysshe, 91
Silberman, Charles, 6, 66–72
Skaife, Robert A., 2
Skills, mastery of, 169

teaching, 25, 26
Skinner, B. F., 14, 279
Slums, in the 1970's, 123
Smith, Lillian, 67
Snow, C. P., 228
Snow, Susan, 93, 99–101, 143
Social change, educational implications,
  349–355
  future of, 224, 344–356
  pace of, 202
Social concerns, 154–155
Social conditions, curriculum and, 44
Social emphasis and, 378
Social issues, 225–229
Social movement, curriculum and, 150
Social order, curriculum and, 2
Social reconstruction, 129
Social sciences, 223, 330–338
Social studies, neglect of, 124, 141–147
  future and, 330–338
Social studies program, functions of, 136
Society, in year 2000, 361
Sohn, Louis, 154
Solo, Leonard, 182
Soviet Union, challenge by, 202
  educational advances by, 2–3
  U.S. rivalry, 251
Spanish-speaking students, 28
Special education, 215
Specialization, future of, 372
Speech, and printed words, 59
Sports events, intellectual challenge, 32
Staab, Fred, 183
Standardization, 274–275
Stark, John R., 300
State government, curriculum change, 207
  financial aid by, 197–198
Stoddard, George, 15
Stone, Marshall, 323, 325
Structure, concepts of. 142
Student power, 104
Student unrest, 286
Students for Democratic Action, 102, 103
Stupidity, 17, 329
  encouragement of, 19
Subject disciplines, 6
Subject matter, interrelationship, 14
Success, and citizenship, 230
Superiority, need for, 50
Supervisors, arbitrariness, 46–49
  hackneyed approach by, 43
Suppes, Patrick, 222, 270–276
Supplementary schooling, increase in, 351
Survival, question of, 243
Symbols, unnecessary use of, 19
System, The, attitudes toward, 150
Systems approach, 296–297
  problems in, 301
System breaks, 228, 374
  role of, 357
Szilard, Leo, 289

Taitel, Martin, 362, 369, 370
Talking typewriter, 303
Tanner, R. Thomas, 124, 141–147
Teacher Drop-Out Center, 182, 183
Teacher education, continuing program, 375
  machines in, future of, 375
  splits in, 377
  in year 2000, 356–379
Teacher-pupil ratio, 54
Teachers, foreign language, 342
  mathematics, status of, 322
  narrowness of, 233
  passivity, 51
  power of, growth, 65
  role of, and responsibility, 304
    future, 371
Teaching, competencies in, 146
  future of, 229–234
  professional practice, 298–305
Teaching machines, 13, 230
Teaching skills, developing, 200
Team teaching, 132
Technical know-how, 76
Technological changes, 184
Technological development, systems break, 358
  projects, 363
Technological revolution, 270–305
Technology, and the future, 222
  license and, 143–144
  mankind and, 143
  social emphasis, 378
Television, banality of, 68
  behavior and, 252
  education and, 230
TEMPO, forecasting by, 261
Tests, in disfavor, 56
Thinking, individual, circumscribed, 95
  intuitive/involved, 151
Thompson, Sir George, 345
Thought pattern, students', 150
Tolstoy, Leo, 6, 7, 55, 80, 82, 84, 90
Travel, education through, 124, 132
Trend census, 266
Tyler, R. W., 280

Underground movement, students', 101–106
Underground press, high school, 7, 101–106
Understanding, definition of, 137
Unessential knowledge, teaching of, 21
United Nations, controversial, 45
Universities, academic withdrawal, 77
  campus politics, 161
  curriculum change, 204
  defined, 77
  research at, 78
University level, choice at, need for, 73
Urban crowding, 243

Urbanism, projections, 362
  year 2000, 370
Utopia(s), projected, 366
  preferred, 153–154
  relevance of, 151–153
Utopian thought, 219

Values, post-figurative, 238
Van Campen, Joseph, 274
Van Til, William, 9–17, 62–66, 195, 221, 225–229, 298–305, 357–379
Verbal communication, 38
Vietnam war, 3, 155, 226
Violence, 110
  need for, 151
  school, 55
  in the 1970's, 123
Vocabulary, children's special, 36
  of general education, 138
Vocabulary building, intellectual challenge, 36
Vocational education, 206, 290–291
Voluntary work, opportunity for, 105

War, threat of, 237
Washburne, Carleton W., 70, 213n, 339
Ways, Max, 260
Weapons race, educating for, 87–89
Weber, Max, 365
Wells, H. G., 219, 260
Western Behavioral Sciences Institute, 118
Whitehead, Alfred North, 15, 70
White House Conference on Education (1965), 71
Wiener, Anthony J., 186, 188, 220, 227, 264, 363, 367, 370
Wiles, Kimball, 220
Wilhelms, Fred T., 126, 169–174
Wilson, Elizabeth C., 223, 288–298
Wilson, H. A., 273
Winnetka Plan, 213n
Word history, intellectual challenge, 34
Wordsworth, William, 45
Work, in year 2000, 364
Work-oriented system, improvement of, 139
Work plan, consistency in, 25
Working class, 94
World community, 236
World government, utopian, 154
World war, as system break, 357
World War II, effect of, 237
Wright, Stephen J., 125, 162–168

Yeats, William Butler, 43
Young, Michael, 371
Youth, dissatisfaction of, 234–241

Zacharias, Gerrold, 71, 136